The publisher gratefully acknowledges the generous support of the Sue Tsao Endowment Fund in Chinese Studies of the University of California Press Foundation.

Colonial Project, National Game

ASIA PACIFIC MODERN

Takashi Fujitani, Series Editor

1. *Erotic Grotesque Nonsense: The Mass Culture of Japanese Modern Times,* by Miriam Silverberg

2. *Visuality and Identity: Sinophone Articulations across the Pacific,* by Shu-mei Shih

3. *The Politics of Gender in Colonial Korea: Education, Labor, and Health, 1910-1945,* by Theodore Jun Yoo

4. *Frontier Constitutions: Christianity and Colonial Empire in the Nineteenth Century,* by John D. Blanco

5. *Tropics of Savagery: The Culture of Japanese Empire in Comparative Frame,* by Robert Thomas Tierney

6. *Colonial Project, National Game: A History of Baseball in Taiwan,* by Andrew D. Morris

Colonial Project, National Game

A History of Baseball in Taiwan

———

Andrew D. Morris

UNIVERSITY OF CALIFORNIA PRESS

Berkeley   Los Angeles   London

University of California Press, one of the most distinguished university presses in the United States, enriches lives around the world by advancing scholarship in the humanities, social sciences, and natural sciences. Its activities are supported by the UC Press Foundation and by philanthropic contributions from individuals and institutions. For more information, visit www.ucpress.edu.

University of California Press
Berkeley and Los Angeles, California

University of California Press, Ltd.
London, England

Library of Congress Cataloging-in-Publication Data

Morris, Andrew D.
    Colonial project, national game : a history of baseball in Taiwan / Andrew D. Morris.
        p.   cm.
    Includes bibliographical references and index.
    ISBN 978-0-520-26279-9 (cloth : alk. paper)
    1. Baseball—Taiwan—History.   2. Baseball players—Taiwan—History.
I. Title.
    GV863.795.A1M67   2010
    796.357095124'9—dc22   2010012580

Manufactured in the United States of America

20   19   18   17   16   15   14   13   12   11
10   9   8   7   6   5   4   3   2   1

This book is printed on Cascades Enviro 100, a 100% post consumer waste, recycled, de-inked fiber. FSC recycled certified and processed chlorine free. It is acid free, Ecologo certified, and manufactured by BioGas energy.

For my left-handed Aaron

CONTENTS

Acknowledgments   *ix*
Map of Taiwan   *xii*

    Introduction   *1*

1. Baseball in Japanese Taiwan, 1895–1920s   *7*

2. Making Racial Harmony in Taiwan Baseball, 1931–1945   *30*

3. Early Nationalist Rule, 1945–1967: "There's no Mandarin in baseball"   *54*

4. Team of Taiwan, Long Live the Republic of China: Youth Baseball
    in Taiwan, 1968–1969   *79*

5. "Chinese" Baseball and Its Discontents, 1970s–1980s   *104*

6. *Homu-Ran Batta:* Professional Baseball in Taiwan, 1990–Present   *125*

    Conclusion: Baseball's Second Century in Taiwan   *149*

Appendix: Taiwanese Professional Baseball Teams and National
    Origin of Foreign Players   *167*
Notes   *171*
Glossary of Chinese, Japanese, and Taiwanese Terms and Names   *225*
Selected Bibliography   *235*
Index   *259*

Photographs follow page 78

ACKNOWLEDGMENTS

There are, as always, a humbling number of people to thank for the assistance, kindness, and wisdom they have offered me during the course of this project. In Taiwan, I was fortunate to spend two summers at the wonderful Academia Sinica: one in the Institute of Modern History and one in the Institute of Taiwan History's new digs at the far western end of the legendary complex in Nangang. Directors Chen Yung-fa and Hsu Hsueh-chi were generous in allowing me to conduct research and take part in seminars at their institutes. Professor Chen Yi-shen (and his family) and Professor Yu Chien-ming showed their true and generous friendship again and again in making my time there very enjoyable. Staff at the National Central Library, including the beautiful new Taiwan Branch in Zhonghe, were also of much assistance. Ms. Reiko Yamane at the Japanese Baseball Hall of Fame and Museum in Tokyo was also very helpful and made my short visit there a fruitful one.

My good friends Xie Shiyuan and Liu Chin-ping, true scholars and gentlemen, provided me with valuable materials and important perspectives that have driven this project. Professor Hsu I-hsiung, of National Taiwan Normal University (NTNU), remains very gracious and helpful as well. I am proud to count Dr. Peng Ming-min among my acquaintances; he and Wu Hui-lan have been as kind and giving as they are inspirational. Cai Wuzhang of the Kanō Alumni Association was profoundly generous with his time and resources; this proud school could probably have no finer representative of the Kanō spirit than Mr. Cai. I am grateful to the famed coach Jian Yongchang for taking me into his home, presenting me with copies of his many publications, and sharing his memories of eight decades of Taiwanese baseball. Lin Mei-Chun has been very generous with her knowledge of Japanese-era sport in Taiwan. Several former players in Taiwan—in particular, Xie Changheng, Lin Huawei,

Tony Metoyer, Will Flynt, and George Hinshaw—were giving of their time in helping me to better understand the game there. And Gregory Harper was generous in sharing with me the memory of his brother Milt, who left his beloved family, teammates, and friends far too soon.

There is a long list of friends and colleagues who helped me think about this work in profitable ways: Wu Wenxing, Wu Mi-cha, Liu Hong-yuh, Lee Jane-Shing, Paul Katz, Alice Chu, Stéphane Corcuff, Wei-Der Shu, Mark Harrison, Tak Fujitani, Shumei Shih, Jeff Wasserstrom, Roald Maliangkay, Thomas Gold, Joseph Allen, William Kelly, Paul Festa, Robert Weller, Michael Herzfeld, Hsien-hao Liao, Barak Kushner, Bi-yu Chang, Marc Moskowitz, David Jordan, Scott Simon, Nancy Guy, Mark Dyreson, Suzanne Cahill, Robert Edelman, Joseph Esherick, Paul Pickowicz, Jeffrey Wilson, Sam Yamashita, my undergraduate mentor Arthur Rosenbaum, John McKinstry, and several of my colleagues and students at Cal Poly. I was also lucky to have four fine student researchers at different moments of this project—Yue Ming Mei and Li-Chia Ong at Colgate University, and Jamie McCulley and Yumi Shiraishi at Cal Poly.

I met Professor Tsai Jen-hsiung in 1995. His generosity, sharp questions, and endless connections changed my life and, indeed, the field of sport history in East Asia. He passed away at far too young an age in 2009 as I was finishing revisions to this work. It saddens me greatly that he was not able to see this project reach completion. However, it is good to know that the colleges and universities of Taiwan are home to dozens of Professor Tsai's students, who can continue to spread his passion for historical inquiry.

A Fulbright Research Award in 2007 was valuable in the completion of this project, as was the help of Dr. Wu Jing-jyi and his staff at the Fulbright Taiwan Foundation for Scholarly Exchange. Generous support from the Cal Poly College of Liberal Arts and History Department was also very much appreciated; someday historians will marvel at the criminal lack of support that these institutions receive from the taxpayers of my strange home state. Many thanks are also due Janice Stone in the Kennedy Library at Cal Poly, who is a researcher's dream come true. I owe my editor Reed Malcolm at the University of California Press many thanks for his enthusiastic support of this project. His colleagues there, including Kalicia Pivirotto, Jacqueline Volin, and Christopher Pitts have made this a very enjoyable endeavor.

I would also like to thank my and my wife's extended families for their years of support and encouragement. Finally, I suppose I should thank my two kind but flawed landlords in 1991 and 1992 who rented rooms to me on Jin-De North Road in Taizhong. I lived just blocks from the municipal baseball stadium that provided me with the original impetus that this history would be worth pondering.

In 2004 I took my then four-year-old daughter Shaina to a Uni-President Lions professional baseball game in Taizhong. Although she only lasted for about two innings in the heat and noise, she told me that with the pounding of the fan-club drummers in the next section she could "feel her heart beating." Is it too melodramatic to say that Shaina, my son Aaron, and my wife Ricky are the ones who allow me to feel my heart beating every day I am with them? I owe them every thanks and gratitude for all the happiness and fulfillment with which they have blessed me.

Taiwan

Introduction

In March 2009, Taiwan's national baseball team faced its bitter rival, the Chinese national team, in the Asia Round of the World Baseball Classic at the Tokyo Dome. Baseball, an integral part of Taiwanese culture for more than a century, is still relatively unpopular and unknown in the People's Republic of China (PRC). But that did not stop the PRC team, managed by American Terry Collins, from defeating Taiwan (the Republic of China, or ROC) by a decisive score of 4–1, the second straight Chinese upset of Taiwan.

Coach Ye Zhixian made a public apology to the people of Taiwan upon his team's return home, but that was hardly sufficient, considering the tremendous national humiliation the loss to China represented. Reporters and television commentators commiserated that "the national game's honor is no more" and that "baseball in this country is dead!" Others pondered, "Where has Taiwan baseball's dignity gone?" "Can baseball be saved?" One miserable fan wrote, "Taiwan has nothing left anymore. We might as well disband the Taiwanese team and let China be our national team. They're going to unify us anyways." Another newspaper editorialist asked simply, "What is there now that Taiwan could still beat China at?"[1]

This event, and the palpable anguish that surrounded it in Taiwan, summoned several trends and relationships from the complicated twentieth century, which saw baseball become the all-but-official national game of the island. A Meiji-era import to Japan, baseball was quickly, strategically, and thoroughly distributed throughout the growing empire. For a short time, baseball was the exclusive province of Japanese bankers, engineers, other colonists and their sons, but before long the game became part of the national culture propagated by the Japanese government, media, corporations, educational apparatus, and military. Baseball was the sport of the

Japanese empire, and during Japan's colonization of Taiwan it became an expression of the Japanese spirit that all in Taiwan would be expected to learn and live.

The ROC's takeover of Taiwan following World War II had implications for this Japanese game, but its usefulness in training and exhibiting skills of teamwork and discipline appealed to the Chinese regime, which had already sponsored modern sports for two decades on the mainland. Before long, in ROC-ruled Taiwan, baseball became part of the national culture propagated by the *Chinese* government, media, corporations, educational apparatus, and military, now almost seamlessly becoming an expression of the Chinese spirit that all in Taiwan would be expected to learn and live. The 2000 election of Chen Shui-bian, the first president of the ROC in Taiwan who was not a member of the Chinese Nationalist Party (KMT, Guomindang), signified for many the completion of a democratic Taiwanese recovery of their island after four centuries of Dutch, Spanish, Manchu, Japanese, and Chinese colonial rule. And just one week after this election, Chen explicitly identified baseball as part of the national culture propagated by the *Taiwanese* government,[2] an expression of the Taiwanese spirit that all on this "Beautiful Island" would finally be free to learn and live.

The preoccupation with baseball as a Taiwanese "national game" is somewhat precious, given its organic connections to Japanese and American cultures and its late adoption by the Chinese Nationalist one-party state. But it is an understandable preoccupation nonetheless. Baseball has served for almost a century as a useful device and meaningful artifact of Taiwanese society and culture even though, in the end, its significance is much more about *global* processes of colonialism, imperialism, the cold war, and capitalism than about limited notions of a Taiwanese nation. The game in Taiwan today is still experienced as a reminder of the profound influence of Japanese and American culture, and indeed, of transnational capitalism on Taiwan. But "global game" has little resonance to the Taiwanese populist politician (not least because baseball trails soccer and basketball as truly global games); only an ideology of baseball as a Taiwanese "national game" seems a useful answer to the blustery nationalism that often emanates from the PRC, some ninety miles away. The fear and isolation that China's rise has created in early twenty-first-century Taiwan have led people there to celebrate fervently and enthusiastically their uniqueness, linguistic and otherwise, vis-à-vis the "Chinese mainland," often via once-Japanese cultural artifacts like baseball.

It is striking that baseball, an element of the decidedly exploitative half-century of Japanese rule on the island, can now be experienced so thoroughly as simply "Taiwanese." Indeed, the game introduced by the Japanese colonial regime has never thoroughly shed its Japanese heritage. From the name of the game—many still use the Taiwanese name "*ia-kiu*" (from the Japanese *yakyū*) as opposed to the Mandarin "*bangqiu*"—to the Taiwanese-Japanese-English playground calls of "*sutoraiku*" (strike) and "*a-u-to*" (out), baseball's Japanese "origins" are still an important part of Taiwanese heritage, both historically and ideologically.

The conditions just outlined make the history of Taiwanese baseball unique in the sporting world. Some models of colonial sport, such as that portrayed in the film *Trobriand Cricket,* in which natives on that New Guinea island transform cricket into a magical, mocking send-up of the colonial game,[3] are clearly not useful in analyzing this history in Taiwan. The colonial era of Japanese rule hardly provided the space for second-class imperial subjects in Taiwan to alter greatly the basic ideologies attached to the game, or to create a Taiwanese equivalent of Ireland's "Gaelic games" meant to stand alone from and opposed to British culture. Since World War II, the global relevance of modern sporting ideology has made it impractical or even impossible to imagine wholesale transformations of this universalized model.[4]

Other models of colonial culture and sport are more helpful. Bernard Cohn's description of "investigative modalities" present in all modern forms of colonialism is useful in understanding how the Japanese sought to "classify, categorize, and bound" the social and cultural world of Taiwan in order to better control and exploit it.[5] As chapter 1 will show, the desire of the Japanese to get their hands on the natural resources of Taiwan's "savage lands"—the mountains of the island's central and eastern regions—was directly entwined with their exhaustive research there, and ultimately with their plan to civilize the regions' Austronesian Aborigine inhabitants through baseball. Leo Ching's work, especially his groundbreaking 2001 book *Becoming "Japanese,"*[6] is of the highest importance on this topic. His explanations of the intersections of colonial culture and the official Japanese rhetoric of assimilation and imperial subject-making have inspired much of my work, although I do propose in chapter 2 ways that baseball works even better than colonial-era drama or film to illustrate how Taiwan's colonization was experienced by Taiwanese and Japanese subjects alike.

The Japanese project to create an island of imperial subjects should also be framed in terms of Homi Bhabha's notions of "colonial mimicry," which Bhabha describes as "the desire for a reformed, recognizable Other, *as a subject of difference that is almost the same, but not quite. . . .* In order to be effective, mimicry must continually produce its slippage, its excess, its difference."[7] Baseball became a crucial site for the production of civilized Taiwanese subjects at the same time that the excellence of the Taiwanese in the game was used to call attention to the Japanese colonial regime's success in transforming a once-savage and backward populace. The history of the game of cricket provides a useful backdrop here as well. C. L. R. James documented early and famously how in the British West Indies, the inspired performances of standout black cricketers won West Indians a respect from the colonizing population that was hard to achieve otherwise.[8] As in cricket, the baseball triumph of two generations of Taiwanese baseball players and teams did much to convince Japanese people of the worthiness of their cosubjects from this far-off island, even if distinctions were maintained between those who had been born with a Japanese spirit and those who merely had mastered it through study and practice.

Following James, the British imperial model of sportsmanship and the construction of a standard athletic masculinity, as described by Patrick McDevitt,[9] provide one of the best models of baseball's colonial functions in Taiwan. However, the British pattern fails to account for one special facet of Japanese colonialism, especially in Taiwan. While a British ideal of sport, progress, and masculinity was applied to their colonial subjects, sports could also be used to expose a moral—if not biological—gap between them and their lessers. Japanese characterizations—still justified by many today—of their more righteous and race-appropriate brand of "Asia for the Asians" colonialism are surely odious for their historical obscuration. Still, by the 1920s these ideologies of Japanese colonial rule meant by definition that baseball could *not* be used to define or prove such important racial or moral distinctions between Japanese and Taiwanese. Indeed, it was often the case that the opposite was true; in chapter 2 I discuss the history of Taiwan's famed "triracial" Kanō baseball team, admired in Japan for their ability to inspire the public with the hope that the achievements of a "new untouched race" of Taiwanese Aborigines could revive a cynical and jaded modern Japan.[10]

Taiwan's experiences after its transfer to Nationalist Chinese rule in 1945 make this history even more unique. Most historians studying Chinese Taiwan in the decades that followed—with the distinct exception of George Kerr and his landmark *Formosa Betrayed*—concentrated on the cold war diplomatic and military ties between the ROC government and the United States. Recently, however, more historians have tried to understand the social and cultural implications of this experience, which was much less the "Retrocession" of KMT ideology—a long-heralded and historically just "return" of Taiwan to Chinese rule—than a contingent and hurried big-power transfer of a small peripheral island from one fading empire to another.

Steven Phillips's book *Between Assimilation and Independence* provides an excellent study of this truly liminal and unpredictable moment in Taiwan's history.[11] The KMT's understanding of these events as a victorious takeover of an island of six million shameless and degraded "collaborators" did not just represent an ideology. It had a real impact on the life chances of Taiwanese people, who had become quite used to the modern ways of the Japanese empire.

The topic of baseball in Taiwan has been studied most recently by Junwei Yu, a professor of recreation and sport management in Taiwan. His 2007 book *Playing In Isolation* offers the first book-length English-language history of the topic.[12] Yu attempts to cover the entire twentieth century, although the work is not truly comprehensive; the book's main contribution comes with Yu's attention to the history of the Little League Baseball program that brought so much attention and scrutiny to

Taiwan in the 1970s and 1980s. Yu is a true muckraker, and his connections within Taiwan's baseball world are valuable. His explanation of the historical basis behind several youth baseball scandals is useful in helping us to understand the pressures on Taiwan's baseball-playing youth to bring glory and prestige to the reeling, near-pariah state of the Chiang-era Republic of China in Taiwan. However, this work pays much less attention to the crucial and lasting influences of Japanese colonial rule on the game and on Taiwanese society as a whole. The work's greatest flaw is revealed in its title—Yu takes the relationship between baseball and the diplomatic isolation that the ROC suffered in the 1970s and '80s to stand for the entire century. In fact, my work shows that the modern history of Taiwan and its national game are actually defined by the precise *opposite* of "isolation." The history of this island is one of a fascinating, complex, and conscious *engagement* with the powerful peoples and technologies that have defined Taiwan so, a true embeddedness in the flows of culture that have transformed totally Taiwanese life again and again in the last 110 years.

In order to best address this history, I use throughout this book ideas of "glocalization"—a recent scholarly term used to describe the local implementation of globalized forms, or, in the words of Roland Robertson, "the simultaneity—the co-presence—of both universalizing and particularizing tendencies" that appear so often in, and complicate our understanding of, these forms.[13] This dual nature of globalization often escapes analyses that can tend to focus on one-sided models of cultural contact, like the famed notion of "Cocacolonization," which describes a simple imprint of American ways on vulnerable Others.[14] It does not roll off the tongue, but I have found this fittingly playful formulation of "glocalization" to be very appropriate in describing modern Taiwanese culture and its formation at the hands of the complex historical legacies just described. And this is without even mentioning the remarkable and striking quality of contemporary Taiwanese culture's self-conscious, ideological combination of the global and the local, the cosmopolitan and the provincial, the international and the Taiwanese—the game of baseball is a perfect example of all of this.

A local television commercial for Kentucky Fried Chicken that aired to great public pleasure in the summer of 2004 can actually help explain this "playful" tension and hybridity. The advertisement featured a Taiwanese tour guide haplessly attempting to impress a group of PRC Chinese tourists with the sights of the island. After Sun Moon Lake and Jade Mountain fail to stir these boastful and condescending mainlanders, the resourceful tour guide decides to feed them "Taiwanese" Kentucky Fried Chicken—strips of meat that are even spicier than Sichuan's famed cuisine. Finally the guide wins respect for the island, confirmed when the loudest mouth of the bunch (a dead ringer for former president Jiang Zemin) proclaims in caricatured PRC Mandarin, "Now we must not look down on Taiwan." When the innovative recipes of Chicken Capital U.S.A. can so easily serve the purposes of breakthrough "state-to-state" diplomacy between Taiwan and China, we know that there is more at work than simple descriptions of Cocacolonization or McWorld. At the same time, it is one principle of this work as well that this hybridity not obscure the often violent historical context of modern colonialism and imperialism that brought these peoples and ideas together in the first place.

The chapters that follow trace globalized forces like colonialism and imperialism and their effects on the peoples of Taiwan by examining the game that has introduced and represented so many of these ideologies and transformations. Chapters 1 and 2 cover the period of Japanese colonial rule when baseball was introduced to the valuable new colony of Taiwan. Baseball not only served as a mode of assimilation for Han ethnic Chinese and Austronesian Aborigine subjects of the emperor, but also represented on the field itself the open space that Taiwan promised for the inculcation of modern, civilized Japanese ways of living and dying. Chapter 3 addresses the history of this Japanese national game in Taiwan under the new Chinese KMT regime that took over Taiwan after Japan's defeat in World War II. We can learn much about the significance of baseball in Taiwan by understanding how the KMT, while trying desperately to erase traces of Japan's half-century of governance and cultural domination, was forced to allow this Japanese game of baseball to remain as such a tangible expression of Taiwanese pride and endeavor.

Chapters 4 and 5 examine the Little League regime that became the focus of Taiwanese baseball culture, as well as the bane of American youth baseball stars and their parents, from 1968 until the late 1980s. As Chiang-ruled, martial-law Taiwan became more isolated with the world's growing acceptance of the PRC, the twelve-year-old Taiwanese baseball stars that played every August in Williamsport, Pennsylvania, were somehow understood to be the finest expression of Chinese culture, dignity, and national glory (not to mention the future Taiwanese "retaking" of the mainland about which the KMT still fantasized).

As these brilliant players grew up, they revived and reinforced decades-old national and postcolonial hierarchies when they went to play professionally in Japan under Japanese names and often as Japanese naturalized citizens. In chapter 6, I look at the response in Taiwan to these events and the resulting development of Taiwan's own professional baseball leagues that were explicitly designed to advance and express a "glocalized" agenda for Taiwan, a marriage of the native and the foreign, the local and the international. By 1999 and 2000, this tension between the global and the Taiwanese became even more complicated when Taiwan's finest players began signing with American major league teams, increasing the island's visibility abroad but weakening its own baseball structure. Finally, in my concluding chapter, I attempt to center this whole century of Taiwan's modern history on the Austronesian Aborigine peoples, the diverse population who despite their small numbers offer through their often bitter experiences the most revealing histories of this fascinating and complex island.

1

Baseball in Japanese Taiwan, 1895–1920s

[Formosa] has served the purpose of educating us in the art of colonization.
INAZO NITOBÉ, *THE JAPANESE NATION*, 1912

Japan's southern island of lush betel nut,
Island of high mountains, now our island,
A beautiful young island,
TTK, TTK, Rah—T—Rah—T—Rah—K.
ANTHEM OF THE TAIWAN SPORTS ASSOCIATION
(*TAIWAN TAIIKU KYŌKAI*), 1933

In December 1998, *Asahi Shimbun* CEO Nagayama Yoshitaka made a short visit to southern Taiwan. He told his hosts that he had only one purpose for making this trip: to fulfill the lifelong wish that his friend, the famed and recently deceased author Shiba Ryōtarō, had never realized—to run a lap around the bases at the Jiayi Institute of Technology.[1] Shiba late in life became known as an influential Taiwanophile, but his nostalgic view of a Japanese Taiwan, centered on its baseball culture,[2] is perfectly common some six decades after the end of the colonial empire. The mimetic qualities of Nitobe Inazō's quotation in the epigraph are also telling, and his and Shiba's views provide appropriate bookends to a twentieth century of close, complicated ties between Taiwan and Japan.[3]

Japan's career in Taiwan and its own vibrant baseball culture sprang from the same historical moment in 1895. This was the year that Meiji Japan, after defeating the Qing dynasty, seized its first colony—the malarial, bandit-and-opium-ridden island of Taiwan. This was also the year that Chūma Kanoe, a recently graduated star student-athlete at Tokyo's elite No. 1 High School, who later would publish Japan's first book of baseball research, coined a new Japanese name for the popular sport of *bēsubōru*. This new name, *yakyū*[4]—literally, "ball game in the open"—reflected perfectly the Meiji colonialist ambitions that were so often voiced in the language of expanse and open space. The pastoral imagination already built into

American baseball, after spreading to Japan in the 1870s and 1880s,[5] was refracted into an important element of the Meiji colonialist vision of different East Asian nations' territories as so much open, wild, available space.

John Noyes has written on this idea of "colonial space," explaining that the "colonial landscape is not found by the colonizer as a neutral and empty space, no matter how often he assures us that this is so. This is one of the most persistent myths of colonization."[6] Indeed, the "open" game of baseball surged in popularity in Japan at the exact moment of the Meiji empire's emergence as a world power and concomitant grab for colonial territories throughout East Asia. The familiar and often-propagated stereotype of baseball in Japan is that the game was an inspired but overdisciplined mimicry of a more authentic American baseball culture.[7] However, it is easy to see how this cultural form's resonance was more likely its perfect fit within Japan's new "colonial narrative"—which, according to Thomas Nolden, displays the spatial practice of colonialism (for instance, conquest and settlement) by representing the space of colonized land according to concepts of modern knowledge.[8] In this and the next chapter I will attempt to treat *yakyū* in Taiwan from within this understanding of its importance to the half-century of Japanese colonial rule, emphasizing the complicated, layered, and contradictory subject-positions constructed by and for those players and spectators participating in the national game.

DOWN TO THE COLONY

At the end of 1895, just months after taking the frontier island of Taiwan from a partially relieved Qing dynasty, Japan integrated it (along with most of Okinawa) into its new Western Standard time zone *(seibu hyōjunji)*.[9] Taiwan would now be integrated into, if still left an hour behind, the modern Meiji order in many ways. There was still much dirty work to do in addressing societal "evils" never mastered by the Qing. In justifying the often violent measures taken against brigands and Taiwan's Austronesian Aborigines, even the famed educator Nitobe admitted that the Japanese had to serve as a "cruel master," and London's admiring *Spectator* still had to predict that much of Japan's work in Taiwan "might mean something unpleasantly like extermination."[10] Besides these institutional prerogatives, the cause of civilization and "colonial success," which could only be gained through "justice seasoned with mercy,"[11] also depended on cultural forms that would reproduce these new colonial ties and hierarchies in everyday life.

Modern sport was well established by this moment as one crucial way of showing a people's fitness for inclusion in the new world order.[12] Yu Chien-ming has discussed how, even from the earliest years of Japanese rule, colonial planners felt responsible for making use of "globalized notions of physical education to transform Taiwanese bodies."[13] In Taiwan, sport would become part of Japan's "civilizing process" as colonists strove to exhibit the qualities that made Japan so superior to the backward culture of the vanquished Chinese. Chief Civil Administrator Gotō Shimpei was well known for his support of physical culture as state policy; in 1903 the *Taiwan Nichinichi Shimpō* reprinted older comments of his on the relationship between men's and women's fitness and national economic strength.[14] This policy could take the form of activities designed for Taiwanese subjects, like physical education in schools for boys and girls, or movements against the "low customs" *(rōshū)* of women's foot binding or men's Manchu-style queue ("pigtail") hairstyles. Or it could be illustrated through aggressive physical forms such as judō, kendō, sumo, or even equestrian events, which were explicitly restricted to Japanese participation at this time of armed resistance toward the new regime.[15] A 1933 book published by the Taiwan Sports Association reflected on the activities of this earlier era that served as such visible colonial "elements of control" *(tōseiteki no mono)*[16]—hinting clearly at physical culture's important position in the relations and hierarchies of colonialism.

Sport's very presence in Taiwan, then, had implications in terms of both global culture and local reception. In recent decades, Sony cofounder Akio Morita coined the phrase *global localization,* which one observer has described as "brand strategy at one side of the spectrum and customer expectations the other."[17] Likewise, an online dictionary (no printed ones have bothered) defines *glocalization* as "the creation of products or services intended for the global market, but customized to suit the local culture."[18] While my interest is hardly so mercenary, it is important to see how the term has come to apply more broadly to cultural trends of hybridizing across local and global meanings and settings. For example, in his study of Tokyo Disneyland, Aviad Raz uses the term *glocalization* to describe the tension between global cultural production and local acquisition and "the more colorful and playful themes characterizing the (usually ingenious) local practices of consumption."[19]

It is fitting with regard to my study that much of the discussion of "glocalization" originates in Japan. The native term that Roland Robertson associates with this discourse is *dochakuka,* which has historically been used to describe the act of adjusting to regional markets. The complicated cultural position of baseball during Japan's colonial occupation of Taiwan well represents this tension between imperialist and globalizing forces and the "expectations" and demands of a Taiwanese population. The colonial project opened up a space for hybrid identity among those Taiwanese who took part in Japanese social and cultural rituals while also negotiating meanings of status and opportunity within their own society.

The topic of baseball presents unique problems with any analysis of global-local linkages at this time. Baseball—so typically of the Meiji period in Japan—arrived in Taiwan as the national sport *(kokugi),* but with a history in Japan of only two decades. Thus, the very fact of Japan's introduction of the game to Taiwan indicates that any treatment of the game must account for this double-layer of imperialism and colonialism wound tightly within Japanese baseball. The heated debates among Meiji politicians over which colonial model Taiwan should follow—the

French example of assimilation and integrated empire, or the British pattern of a separate legal system for each colony—remind us of the careful planning that went into the cultural politics of colonialism. Indeed, every cultural and educational import was judged carefully by how it would contribute to the proper functioning of what Gotō called this "colonial laboratory."

During the first two decades of baseball's career in Taiwan, the game was maintained as a purely Japanese realm. *Yakyū* was imported to the colony around 1897,[20] at which time it was the pastime of colonial bureaucrats, bankers, and their sons in Taihoku (Taipei). In 1906, the first organized games were held between teams from the Taiwan Colonial Government High School, the National Language *(Kokugo)* School Teacher Education Department, and the Taihoku Night School Association. It is appropriate that those who would teach Japan's "national language" to colonial subjects were also involved with cultivating Japan's "national game" in Taiwan, as *kokugo* was understood by many as a tool to unite Asia and provide for "linguistic assimilation of subjugated people into the Japanese nation."[21]

These competitions in baseball—another activity soon imagined to integrate the empire—soon spread around the island. In the south, sugar corporations became the center of baseball culture. Taiwan's status as a potential "sugar bowl" was one reason for Meiji Japan's interest in the island at a time when the newly modernizing empire was importing three-quarters of their increasing sugar consumption. The fertile coastal plains in the Tainan area were the first lands planted by corporate-imperialist entities like the Colonial Government and Mitsui Sugar.[22] These large southern plantations became the equivalent of company towns, with dormitories, Japanese-style homes, schools for Japanese children, and, of course, the baseball fields that hosted this crucial element of the colonial enterprise. (Importantly, the labor needs of these sugar enterprises meant that there were many Han Taiwanese[23] laborers on hand who absorbed baseball culture in this setting.)[24] By the mid-1910s there were teams all over Taiwan representing businesses, occupational and medical schools, military units, railroad and postal offices, bureaucratic and legal agencies, engineering firms, banks, newspapers, private clubs, and merchant associations. In 1915, northern and southern baseball associations were established in Taihoku and Tainan in order to further organize and routinize this colonial institution.[25]

A 1915 Japanese collection of photos from Taiwan evokes the ways the game fit in with other elements of colonial prerogative and achievement. A sample sequence of eight photos from this English-subtitled album went: "Phajus grandifolius Lour," "The Installation of the God at Kagi Shrine," "The Head Office, Taiwan Gendarmerie Station," "The Base-Ball Matches by Vigorous Youths of South Formosa," "Formosan Customs No. 14: Formosan Mending Formosan Shoes," "Park at Chōsōkei," "The Athletic Meeting of the Japanese and Formosan School Children throughout Akō Prefecture," and "Railway Car Station of Hokumon."[26] The Japanese were in Taiwan not only to get access to the island's natural resources and to construct empire, but also to study, to interrogate, to monitor, to understand, to define, and then to reshape Taiwan culture and society in the image of their modern Japanese home islands.

These baseball teams and competitions served the same functions—of class, racial, gender, and political status—as cricket clubs did in the British Empire. Stakes were high, though, and the "thunderously renowned" and recently graduated Waseda University pitcher Iseda Gō's propitious arrival at the colonial Business Property Bureau *(Shokusan kyoku)* in 1914 began a new era of recruiting ringers from the home islands into the Taiwan baseball scene. Many of Iseda's friends and teammates followed, as industrialists, fire chiefs, sugar CEOs, and colonial officials invested much money to attract Japanese star players to play in Taiwan.[27]

On 18 June 1915, a baseball game held in Taihoku captured much of the significance of the sport in Japan's successful colony. Two all-star teams, featuring the best players of the Prefectural Government, Railroad Bureau, Civil Engineers, Finance Bureau, and Business Property Bureau squads, met in the Twentieth Anniversary of [Colonial] Rule Commemorative Game.[28] This celebration (marking the anniversary of the peaceful assumption of rule in the capital of Taihoku) mimicked early Taishō-era notions of unity and was the perfect way to demonstrate the fair, sporting, and enlightened Japanese commitment to their colony.

Similar to the model developed in Japan proper at this time, these teams—and many others representing government agencies and private corporations—competed throughout Taiwan in tournaments sponsored by government agencies and newspaper companies.[29] The ties between media outlets and baseball in Japan are well documented (see, for example, the Yomiuri and Asahi corporations); William Kelly has described this adaptation of the schoolboy and amateur game as a form of "edu-tainment" designed to commodify the "spiritualism" preached in high school baseball for years.[30] The colonial government's explicit involvement is also noteworthy; the curriculum of local branches of Tokyo's Colonial Development University (formerly the Taiwan Society) included baseball practice as an important skill for future colonial bureaucrats as early as 1907.[31] This pattern resembles greatly the uses of cricket in the British Empire, whose "Oxbridge-educated civil servants . . . spread both the play and the philosophy of cricket in the belief that it created a cross-cultural bond amongst members of an artificial political entity," and "separated the rulers from indigenous society."[32] Or, to paraphrase another scholar of cricket, baseball was brought to Taiwan largely "as a criticism of native lifestyles."[33]

At this same moment, links to Japan proper and the growing Japanese understanding of Taiwan as a genuine part of their nation became formalized by the "extension of the homeland" *(naichi enchō)* policy beginning in 1918. More and more Japanese were educated, officially registered, and even buried in Taiwan. It can be said that the realm of baseball in many ways anticipated this strengthening of colonial-metropolitan ties; starting in 1917, the colonial government in Taiwan began hosting visiting university teams from schools like Waseda University (which, along with Keiō University, represents the oldest baseball tradition in Japan). During the summer of 1917, Waseda swept eight games in Manchuria and Korea, and that winter set off on a "southern expedition" (*nansei*, a term with military connotations) to their present and future colonies, Taiwan and the Philippines.[34] *Sport and Interest* carried several articles about the visit a month in advance. In January the magazine published lengthy articles about each game; Waseda won seven of eight against Taihoku and Taiwan all-star teams (which consisted only of Japanese players). The games were played before several thousand fans in the colonial seat of Taihoku and the growing port city of Takao (Gaoxiong), as a new and more intense "baseball fever" gripped Taiwan. This issue of *SI* also included a large photograph of the scoreboard after the one game when the Taiwan All-Stars were able to defeat Waseda.[35] The private Hōsei University (another one of the famed "Tokyo Big Six" baseball programs) visited Taihoku and the smaller southwestern city Kagi (Jiayi) the following year, winning eight of nine games against Ensui (Yanshui) Harbor Sugar and an all-star team from the capital.[36]

These famed teams were followed by American naval and minor league teams, who usually fared quite well against the Taihoku competition. For example, in January 1921 the Herb Hunter All-Americans, a barnstorming club consisting of marginal major leaguers and Pacific Coast League players, blasted the All-Taiwan team, 26–0. *Taiwan Nichinichi Shimpō* headline writers were generous with their similes the next day, describing the contest as: "Merciless game: [Like] a sumo match between a child and an adult, Like the difference between an arrow and a cannon."[37] Games against teams of American sailors aboard visiting warships, however, were usually more competitive, and were advertised as reference to Japan's status as a first-rate colonial power.[38]

Baseball spectatorship was also rapidly becoming an important element of Japanese civilization in the otherwise "wild" colonial setting of Taiwan. A 1917 yearbook from Tainan No. 1 High School in the south showed a large crowd of people, dressed in business, military, agricultural, and leisure attire, surrounding the field at a Southern Baseball Tournament game between Taiwan Sugar and Ensui Sugar, the two preeminent southern baseball powers.[39] Japanese baseball etiquette was formalized enough that in 1917 the magazine *Sport and Interest* could complain about "those immoral and unmannered Taiwanese people (many hundreds of them) who brought their chairs and stood on top of them to watch [over the screen set up for just this reason] the game inside the park."[40] That this game, between the Waseda University and Colonial Military squads, was of so much interest to the colonized, if not yet fully civilized, Taiwanese was already taken for granted. Two decades of colonial occupation had brought many Taiwanese, especially in Taihoku, well into the Japanese cultural milieu. Why, then, were Taiwanese people still not allowed to play the game with the Japanese?

Historians in Taiwan have identified two men named Lin and Li on the 1919

Taihoku Medical School roster as the first Taiwanese baseball players to join an organized team.[41] For two decades before this, the game remained, at least publicly, a Japanese realm. There were surely exceptions, as young Taiwanese men—perhaps the children of elites or people living near the large southern sugar plantations that served as local centers of baseball culture—picked up the Japanese game in settings and moments unrecorded by history. Legend also has it that in the early 1910s, Taiwan Governor-General Sakuma Samata encouraged the development of the sport among Taiwanese youth. As he explained it, this was his humble way of repaying the local deity Mazu, who in 1906 had appeared to his ailing wife in a dream and miraculously cured her.[42]

Colonial rule also brought physical benefits to the general population. Japanese surveys conducted all over Taiwan showed a growth in height among those born after 1895, especially among men and in the north;[43] indeed, colonists congratulated themselves on turning Taiwan from a "sick zone" into a "healthy land."[44] But despite the improved physical condition of the colonized Taiwanese, a 1915 issue of *Taiwan Sports World* referred to the contemporary ban on native participation in baseball.[45] The reason for this is probably best explained as an intense fear that the Japanese could be bested by their colonial subjects—a prospect that was near impossible in any other realm of life in Taiwan, given the strict discriminatory laws in effect for the first two decades of colonial rule. Wu Zhuoliu's classic novel *Orphan of Asia* immortalized the sanctimonious and hypocritical Japanese elites and officials who would, on one hand, call for "harmony" and "Japanese-Taiwanese unity," but on the other, carry out clearly discriminatory policies against Taiwanese underlings. The book's protagonist Hu Taiming represents the Taiwanese subject striving for equality, who is bothered by both Japanese hypocrisy and Taiwanese resentment—a position that it would be easy to imagine shared by the earliest Taiwanese baseball players who joined in this national game.[46]

George Orwell, in his classic 1936 essay "Shooting an Elephant," claimed from personal experience that in the colonial setting, "every white man's life in the East, was one long struggle not to be laughed at." In racialist language that betrayed the fundamental contradictions of colonial rule, Orwell wrote: "When a nimble Burman tripped me up on the football field and the referee (another Burman) looked the other way, the crowd yelled with hideous laughter. This happened more than once. In the end the sneering yellow faces of young men that met me everywhere, the insults hooted after me when I was at a safe distance, got badly on my nerves." Just years removed from the difficult ten-year process of quelling bandit and rebel gangs throughout Taiwan, it is clear why the Japanese would want to avoid any opportunity for their own colonial subjects to sneer and hoot at them in this way. As Orwell explained the true foundation of the colonial mentality, "If anything went wrong . . . it was quite probable that some of [the natives] would laugh. That would never do."[47]

Other justifications for this ban in Taiwan have been cited. Historian Suzuki

Akira has bizarrely claimed that the 1913 advent of the Far Eastern Championship Games, which regularly pitted Japanese against Chinese baseball teams, made it strategically self-defeating for the Japanese to allow the Taiwanese to learn the game and transmit it to their long-lost mainland cousins.[48] More typical was the citation of scared and confused Taiwanese who could not have understood the value of the Japanese game anyway. In 1916, Muramatsu Ichizō, a bureaucrat who was in Taiwan for almost all of Japan's half-century occupation, recalled happily how turn-of-the-century "ignorant islanders" shunned baseball and sport in general, were afraid of baseball bats, and "would watch with closed minds and look on the [baseball] heroism of we Japanese as strange."[49] The same year, a writer using the name "Forever-Young Student" kicked off the publication Sport and Interest with an article on the "golden age" of Taiwan baseball. In the heady early colonial 1900s, he remembered, young Japanese "in a flash, with no hesitation, would put on their light white clothing, head out past the Southern Gate and put all their energy into practicing their baseball skills, these youthful sounds drawing strange looks from the natives. . . . [Now] the sound of the ball hitting the mitt gives Japanese (naichijin) untold nostalgia and thrill."[50] And in 1933, historian Takemura Toyotoshi discussed the islanders' former total ignorance about any modern sports.[51]

Western missionaries and imperialists in China and Korea have passed down similar stories—usually involving local elites who, upon seeing fit Westerners exerting themselves in the game of tennis, ask why they do not instead have their servants run around for them—that are so similar that they can only be apocryphal.[52] Yet they do point to what seems like a universal colonial treatment of these liminal physical cultures; for all their talk of civilization, the colonists seem genuinely threatened by "natives" playing "their" game. In 1896, just one year into Japan's occupation of Taiwan, baseball became a national phenomenon when Tokyo's elite No. 1 High School (Ichikō) team bested a team of Americans from the Yokohama Country Athletic Club. Ichikō players, the first Japanese ever to enter the Americans' field, were greeted with howls and taunts that temporarily unnerved them before they destroyed the YCAC Yankees, 29–4.[53] Likewise, British colonial cricketers in India originally sneered at the Parsi bourgeoisie who dared to take part in the imperial ritual.[54]

In other words, if there was an exclusive Japanese monopoly on modern sporting exertion and competition during the early colonial era, one could profitably analyze the discourse through which the Japanese explained this particular superiority. The question becomes even more interesting, however, when we see that such a monopoly seems not to have existed at all. Julean Arnold, in his 1908 report on Taiwan for the U.S. Bureau of Education, wrote:

> One of the most hopeful features in the education of the Chinese native lies in the interest which he manifests in athletic games. The public school yard, during the fifteen minutes' recess at the end of each hour, presents as animated a scene as does that of any western school. The Chinese child loves play and takes a keen delight in all games.

Already interclass and interschool athletic meets have been held, and not only do the pupils delight in them, but the parents exhibit a surprising amount of pleasure at seeing their children participate in these sports.

And about the new schools for the native Taiwanese students, he pointed out: "Tennis courts, athletic fields and gymnastic apparatus are provided. Owing to the interest taken by the native students in athletics, their physical condition is being much improved. Athletic and bicycle meets between the different schools are held each year and prove to be of great benefit."[55] Assuming that Arnold's careful observations were not totally falsified, we are left to conclude that this longstanding Taiwanese opposition to modern physical culture was merely colonial legend, a series of memories and tales crafted to naturalize the otherwise immoral business of colonialism.

The history of colonial and postcolonial Taiwan becomes more complicated when we realize that Taiwanese observers for decades have also made use of this bogus colonial discourse of what weak and fearful natives their forebears and peers supposedly were. Su Zhengsheng, a standout player in the late 1920s, has described how other Taiwanese before his time did not dare to get near hard baseballs, and how even those who did would first pray for safety at the City God Temple.[56] Historian Gao Zhengyuan has written on Taiwanese who, fearful of the swinging wooden bats involved, would get nowhere near the game they derided as "firewood-ball" (chaiqiu).[57] These self-Orientalizing intellectual moves that internalize the myth of the "lazy native"[58] and that condemn traditional Chinese culture using the colonists' own terms—and the specific modernizing and colonial-apologist positions implicated here—say more about 1990s identity politics than they do about the colony of the 1920s. Of more immediate interest to us here is the historical moment when Taiwanese participation in the Japanese culture of baseball became politically correct, useful, and unavoidable.

WASHED AND IMPERIALIZED

It is a question . . . what are the effects upon a people living under a strange sovereignty after the first, second, or third generation, or what moral changes take place in a people by a change of national language, &c.
GOTŌ SHIMPEI, "THE ADMINISTRATION OF FORMOSA (TAIWAN)," 1910

Contact with Japanese people has always triggered in us mixed feelings of inferiority and awe.
SUN TA-CHUAN, VICE CHAIRMAN OF THE COUNCIL OF ABORIGINAL AFFAIRS, 1999

Although World War I left fifteen million dead in Europe, this was a war in which Japan fared quite well. Oligarch Inoue Kaoru proclaimed that the horrors of this war actually masked its "divine aid . . . for the development of the destiny of Japan," as Japanese leaders used the resulting geopolitical vacuum in Asia to solidify their claims to dominance.[59] After more than two decades of careful colonial rule, the Japanese understood Taiwan to be a genuine part of their nation, the "extension of the homeland" mentioned earlier. Also emboldened at this moment were many Taiwanese elites in Tokyo and Taihoku, like the Enlightenment Society (Keihatsukai), New People's Society (Shinminkai), Taiwanese Cultural Association (Taiwan bunka kyōkai), and the organizers of the journal *Taiwan Youth (Taiwan seinen)*. Not knowing that U.S. President Woodrow Wilson never meant to extend his lofty principles of self-determination to Asians, they began voicing demands for "local autonomy" *(chihō jichi)*.[60] Even conservative Japanese leaders once opposed to these notions came to see this "reformist" movement calling for equality under the emperor as infinitely preferable to more radical forms of anticolonialism led by socialist and independence-minded organizations.[61]

This near-consensus led to new modes of colonial rule. By 1919, the colonial regime had provided many drastic improvements—in fields such as public health, agriculture, transportation, communications, and banking and currency—in their twenty-four years in Taiwan. However, as second-class imperial subjects, only 1.51 percent of the Taiwanese population of 3.54 million had been acculturated in Japanese schools.[62] After all, as Nitobe, the first chair of Colonial Studies at Tokyo University, said of his natives, "their bodies had to be nourished before their minds."[63] However, in 1922, the government boasted of its "unprecedented reforms," issuing an Education Ordinance that officially repudiated the former "matter of discrimination between home islanders, natives, and savages,"[64] even if students were still largely segregated into three different tracks of education.

The new language of *dōka* (assimilation)—defined by Leo Ching as "the rhetoric of the Japanese Empire for pacifying the liberal tendencies in colonial Taiwan and differentiating itself from [violent] Western colonialism"[65]—was quickly reflected in cultural policies and discourse, including modern sport. In his classic memoir of colonized Taiwan, novelist Wu Zhuoliu wrote about an interscholastic sports meet in rural Shinchiku (Xinzhu) Prefecture in 1920.[66] At the 1921 Fifth Far Eastern Games in Shanghai, the Japanese team included four "Taiwan athletes," of whom two were Han-ethnic Taiwanese and two were ethnic Japanese.[67] In November 1922, Shimomura Hiroshi, CEO of the newspaper *Asahi Shimbun,* visited Taiwan and recommended that the colony begin sending a representative to the national high school baseball tournament that the paper sponsored at Kōshien every summer.[68] (The year before, Pusan Commercial High School of Korea and Dalian Commercial High School of Manchuria had taken part.) The fact that modern sport developed most quickly in Japan's other colony, Korea, at the same time[69] suggests that imperial officials took seriously the notion of assimilating their colonized populations through sport.

Paul Katz has argued that these postwar educational reforms were part of the official long-term response to the Ta-pa-ni Incident of 1915, a violent anticolonial uprising in the mountains of south central Taiwan led by bands of Han and Aborigine Taiwanese and costing more than one thousand lives.[70] While there is a gap of several years between the asserted cause and effect, the new policies of "racial coeducation" are consistent with a postwar reckoning of the costs of colonial discrimination. Not only could young Taiwanese subjects now join their Japanese peers in rituals of emperor worship,[71] they were also encouraged to develop their physiques by receiving three hours of *taisō* physical education instruction per week.[72] Under this logic of the "extension of the homeland" and "assimilation," commentators now were writing that "sports should be encouraged more. More baseball and tennis teams should be established, allowing homelanders [Japanese] and islanders to join together in groups, being active together in the sunlight and outdoors."[73] The notion of Taiwanese young people playing Japan's "national game"—a new experiment in glocalization—now seemed to make colonial sense.

In 1925, just two years after the West Indies cricket tour of England, immortalized by C. L. R. James in *Beyond a Boundary*,[74] Japan hosted a similar visit by a baseball team from far-off Karenkō (Hualian) on the east coast of Taiwan. In 1921, a Han Taiwanese resident of Karenkō named Lin Guixing had formed a Takasago Baseball Team of Amis Aborigine boys. Two years later, the team changed their name to the Nōkō Baseball Team (named for a nearby mountain, and literally meaning "High-Ability") when they all enrolled in the Karenkō Agricultural Study Institute. Some of these players were also embraced by local Japanese teams; one Amis youth (named in Japanese "Sauma") achieved local fame by pitching a sixteen-inning complete game for the Karenkō Railroad team in June 1923.

After showing great progress in just three years, the team was invited to play a series of games all around Taiwan and then on the Japanese "mainland" itself. The team was sponsored by construction magnate Umeno Seitarō, whose firms had built the harbor and nearby highways,[75] and Karenkō subprefecture magistrate Eguchi Ryōzaburō. Eguchi had much riding on the success of this team, having boasted in 1923 that the "raw savages" in his subprefecture had been "washed and imperialized . . . [a product of] correcting their customs and violent blood and letting them understand the true spirit of sport," and that their exposure to the Japanese national game had "deepened their transformation by education."[76]

Taiwan's Austronesian Aborigines, who in 1925 made up 2.1 percent of the island's population,[77] had experienced intensely the previous three decades of Japanese colonial rule. As early as 1874, the photographer John Thomson, familiar with Taiwan's Aborigines, had declared their support crucial to the sake of a prospective Japanese occupation of Taiwan.[78] Indeed, the Japanese took over Taiwan eager to avoid conflicts with the occupants of the important and rich mountain areas, whose population had already been antagonized with Qing dynasty modernization programs in the late nineteenth century.

The new regime's "savage governance" *(riban jigyō)* began with the effort to construct what Bernard Cohn calls "investigative modalities" present in all modern forms of colonialism.[79] The new regime gathered much knowledge about the Aboriginal residents of Taiwan—in Paul Barclay's words, "troublesome subjects who were nonetheless ethnologically interesting"[80]—using linguistic and anthropological data to classify them into several different tribes, and even presenting the results of this research at the Paris Exhibition of 1900.[81] The ethnographic data collected over fifteen years on these original peoples of Taiwan was transformed into "usable forms" with the 1910 "Five-Year Plan for Work in Governing the Savages."

By now, the regime was actively using the military to "open" up these "savage lands" *(banchi),* in order to disarm this population and to gain access to the rich camphor and marble resources there.[82] This phase of "savage governance" took several forms. Colonial authorities led many tours of Japan proper for Aborigine leaders in order to demonstrate the home islands' "metropolitan grandeur" and the superior logic of the colonial regime.[83] However, when officials felt that these Aborigine populations were too "obstinate and bigoted" in rejecting policies intended to promote "civilization,"[84] brutal campaigns of "subjugation" were employed, including the first air raids in Asian history, carried out on unruly mountain villages in 1913 and 1914.[85] As Nitobe Inazō put it plainly, "Primitive peoples are motivated by awe."[86] Nitobe happened to be the son-in-law of Joseph Elkinton, a Quaker missionary expert in the field of "civilizing" American Indians. Together with Gotō Shimpei, the island's chief civil administrator, he would use the American policies of "civilizing," policing, and destroying Native Americans as a model for their own Aboriginal policies in Taiwan.[87] Travel writer T. Philip Terry used baldly racist terms to express his admiration for the military's role in this project: "Compared to the benighted islanders they seem like beings from another and brighter world—as in truth they are. As a rule they are as restless as a bug-professor in July—mapping the country, classifying the plants, climbing unexplored mtns., . . . and pushing their drag-nets closer and closer about the murderous savage tribes."[88]

Often, Aborigines were referred to as belonging to one of three generalized categories: "cooked" (i.e., by the bright civilization of the Japanese, *juku*), "transformed" *(ka),* and "raw" *(sei).* This added an additional level of ethnocentric detail to the categories Qing officials had used in Taiwan.[89] At other times, this body of knowledge was used to describe Aboriginal peoples as a single "Takasago" race. "Takasago" was a complicated term that referred both to the Aborigines' mountainous home regions and also to pine tree spirits in Japanese mythology; it constituted at once moves to assert both an Aborigine marginality *and* organic "East Asian" ethnic ties between Japan and the islanders.[90] The Takasago Baseball Team's prominent use of this term is thus very significant. It is as if Coach Lin agreed to subsume his own Han ethnicity within a larger Aborigine-centered claim to Taiwan's important cultural position within the Japanese Empire. These Amis youth were neither the first nor the last to tie this term to baseball prowess, however. In even more complex instances, an all-Japanese team founded in 1909 took the name "Takasago," a presumptuous marker of true cultural imperialism and the urban imagination of "going native" in wild Taiwan.[91] Two decades later, Han Taiwanese teams in the southern city of Takao, alienated from the educational and bureaucratic networks that typically sustained the baseball enterprise, formed their own Takasago Baseball League in 1931, seemingly as a sarcastic rebuttal of imperial rhetoric of inclusion.[92]

Lin Guixing, the original coach of the famed Takasago/Nōkō squad, had been one of the first Taiwanese players to join an official baseball team. Pitching in 1919 for the Karenkō Business School team no doubt made him familiar with the possibilities and contradictions within this tricky realm of assimilation. After graduation, he went to work and play baseball for the Japan Rising Sun Company, which was owned by the baseball-mad construction magnate Umeno, mentioned earlier. Then, after organizing his own "Takasago" squad of Amis Aborigine boys, Lin was able to set up games against local Japanese company teams. This team soon became Nōkō, a truly assimilationist move that had the team name now metonymizing the mountainous terrain that so many Aborigines called home. This is when the Japanese patrons Umeno and Magistrate Eguchi took over, hiring a Coach Yano from Tokyo baseball power Keiō University and sponsoring a team tour around Taiwan.[93] Even though the east coast of Taiwan did not have any elite schools (as in the north) or sugar corporations (as in the south), which served as logical homes to colonial baseball fever, this official attention in Karenkō was possible because of the extraordinary concentration of Japanese in what was an otherwise lightly populated region. In 1929, the liberal economic historian Yanaihara Tadao called the eastern coast "home island-ized," as native Japanese subjects made up 17 percent of the population there, compared with 4.6 percent in Taiwan as a whole—the result of two decades of policies encouraging Japanese to immigrate to eastern Taiwan.[94]

"Savage governance" in the 1910s had been bloody, the regime putting down over 150 Aborigine uprisings by 1920.[95] The more enlightened postwar form of colonial rule would utilize the written word and other elements of Japanese civilization. The colonial presence in a formerly "savage" region led to the continuance of Cohn's "investigative modalities"—here the definition of a body of ethnographic and geographic information about the particular region of eastern Taiwan. The launch of the *Eastern Taiwan Research Series,* published by the Taihoku-based Eastern Taiwan Research Association in 1923, is indicative of this pattern. The first article of the series, a long report on Karenkō Prefecture, included more than six pages on the "savage Team Nōkō" *(banjin chiimu Nōkōdan),* the typical appellation for this squad. The author first observed that the players' physiques were "masculine and built like stone forts," but then made the observation that the "savage Team Nōkō is a creation of Eastern Taiwan, after all, a Taiwanese entity and not a Japanese entity, and this is no exaggeration."[96]

Much of the piece was devoted to an interview with Team Nōkō's official sponsor, Magistrate Eguchi, who spoke grandly of the promise of the once "raw savage"
(seiban) Amis Aborigines transformed by this contact with "imperial" culture and
"civilization." Now, the future would bring savages traveling by airplane or even becoming scientists and politicians.[97] Japanese colonialism was never supposed to stop
at the British goal in India, famously voiced by Thomas Macaulay in 1835, of merely
"[doing] our best to form a class who may be interpreters between us and the millions whom we govern." Baseball was one way of making *all* of Taiwan's population
Japanese "in taste, in opinions, in morals, and in intellect."[98]

Familiar notions of racial hierarchy ran deep, as did the fundamental contradictions of colonialist discourse: Eguchi described the "savages'" baseball skills as
both innate *(sententeki)* and as conditioned by primitive hunting customs and
childhood games of throwing rocks at birds. He praised their cleverness in using
"savage language" to discuss strategy on the field, confusing any Japanese opponents, even though they were fluent in the Japanese terminology and language of
baseball. Yet this savage consciousness was not always a benefit. Eguchi had to admit that "as for the functioning of their brains, there are some insufficiencies. When
a game starts to become complicated or confusing, the team starts to act chaoti-
cally. They are not yet totally refined in [the practice of] teamwork *(chiimuwūku)*."
Despite these problems, which he ironically attributed to their "humble thinking
and psychology of having been controlled [by others]," he was still confident that
Team Nōkō's performance would serve as "savage propaganda" *(banjin senden)*.
Their inspiring performance would no doubt help to convince the people of Japan
that Taiwan was no longer an "uncivilized" *(hibunmei)* part of the empire,[99] at the
same time that it reassured Japanese imperial subjects of the power of their modern culture to comfort and guide a still-dependent people as they entered the modern world.[100]

These thoughts also allow us to see how the program of *dōka* assimilation worked
differently for Han and Aborigines, a question rarely asked by historians. For more
than three decades, until the bloody Musha Incident of 1930 (described in the next
chapter), Japanese colonizers consistently used a similar language of "savagery" in
order to create an Aboriginal foil to their efforts of civilization in Taiwan. Making
the Austronesian population into "savages"—for example, the 1910s invention of
the discourse of atavistic Aborigine "headhunting"[101]—would allow the regime to
civilize, imperialize, teach, and wash clean this population, providing the ultimate
"savage propaganda" for the benevolence and progressiveness of Japanese colonialism. As Leo Ching has explained, "This constellation of images of deficiency,
nakedness, and infantilism . . . [justified] Japanese intervention. . . . The presence
of the heathen Other is instrumental in colonialism's perpetual need for self-affir-
mation through demonstrations of moral superiority."[102] At the same time, however, we see that the ambiguities of this relationship go beyond Ching's formula-

tion here; the Japanese/civilized realm of baseball was special, as it allowed these savages to excel using only their "native" and "primitive" gifts. Taiwan baseball thus exposed the essential contradictions of colonialism, at the very same time that it strengthened and invigorated it.

The complicated discourse of "savage Team Nōkō," then, was crucial to the functioning of colonial rule throughout all of Taiwan, not just the isolated harbor town of Karenkō. Their renown was such that in 1924, the visiting Japanese Daimai team paid a visit to the east coast to play the famed ex-savages (and beat them 22–4).[103] That fall, Team Nōkō made a publicized trip over the mountains to play up and down the west coast of Taiwan, taking along with them (as their cheering squad, and to provide more "savage propaganda") sixty Aborigine classmates celebrating their graduation from the Karenkō Agricultural Study Institute. Nōkō won five of ten games on their tour, three of their losses coming against superior competition in the colonial capital of Taihoku.[104] This spectacle of colonial success was a popular one; some seven thousand fans watched Nōkō play Taihoku Commercial High School on a Wednesday,[105] and five thousand watched them play the Taishō semi-pro team, visiting from the home islands, two days later.[106] Statistics compiled by the *Taiwan Nichinichi Shimpō* indicate that Nōkō played an exciting but messy brand of baseball—in their three games in the capital Nōkō players stole fourteen bases but also committed twenty errors—that the reporter thought was best explained by these Aborigines' unique combination of naïve and innocent character mixed with preternatural courage and strength.[107]

The culturalist ideology of *dōka*—here of transforming the savages by guiding their raw ritual physicality into the modern form of team sports—was more important, however. The players were listed on rosters with *katakana* versions of their Aborigine names (like catcher Komodo or third baseman Kisa), exoticizing them in an exciting and accessible way.[108] After games, fans crowded the players to shake their hands, and prominent colonial personages publicly invited them to meals. Aramaki Ichitada, the Japanese head of the Tainan Baseball Association, could only cry "two trails of hot tears" upon watching this performance, and a branch chairman of the Bank of Formosa publicly proclaimed that these Amis Aborigines and the Japanese were of the same blood after all.[109] The *Nichinichi Shimpō* stated that these subjects were "not an alien race, but in fact lovable fellow subjects. They had become cruel and violent savages because of their geographic isolation and the slower development of their culture, but after receiving superior education and guidance, they were now kind brothers."[110]

This celebration continued the following summer when Team Nōkō's colonial and corporate well-wishers, including the *Taiwan Nichinichi Shimpō*, paid for them to embark on a trip to Japan proper. Fifteen players, ranging in age from seventeen to twenty-two, were accompanied by Magistrate Eguchi and a small retinue of colonial hands eager to show off their walking demonstration of the magic of *dōka* pol-

icy. Before leaving Taiwan, though, the group stopped in Taihoku to meet their bene-
factors in the governor-general's administration and show them firsthand the products of the "islandwide savage education enterprise."[111] Several players were invited
to speak on "the savage life" at a public Savage Lecture Address held at the Railroad
Hotel and prepare this "perfect Taiwan propaganda" for the home islands audience.
After an opening address by a representative from the *Osaka Asahi Shimbun,* Nōkō
third baseman Kisa spoke on "Our Life" and delivered a harmonica solo. He then
yielded the podium to second baseman Rōsawai, who gave a speech on "Our Emo-
tions and Tears" and sang solo another "savage song," and star pitcher-catcher Komodo, who spoke on "Our [Type of] Baseball."[112] It is in perfect keeping with the
model of glocalization that we see, simultaneously, such a sincere sense of accomplishment on the part of the colonial government, and what seems to have been a
long-awaited chance for these Amis Aborigines to show their supposed masters their
true talents, modern dreams and honest feelings about the colonial experience.

After seven days at sea, the Nōkō squad arrived in Tokyo. They were immediately whisked off to visit the offices of three national newspapers, the Tokyo city
government, Crown Prince Hirohito's palace, and the Meiji Shrine.[113] The *Taiwan
Nichinichi Shimpō* commented proudly that when the players appeared in Tokyo in
their gray school uniforms, the Japanese home islanders' "eyes came out of their
heads" in shock at their civilized and disciplined bearing.[114] Visits to shrines, universities, and museums continued throughout the visit as—much like the tours
offered to Aboriginal leaders described by Leo Ching—these Aborigine athletes
became the "subjects of seeing," at the same time they were exposed to all the "tech-
nological and discursive arrangements of colonial power."[115] It was no coincidence
that an article on Nōkō's visit in the Tokyo journal *Baseball World* was coauthored
by an official from the Taiwan Colonial Police Headquarters.[116]

When the games finally began, Nōkō took the initiative, running up a score of
28–0 against their first opponents, the weak Toshimaku Normal School team, in
just four innings. Once the baseball authorities realized that Nōkō was "just like
any [good] Japanese school team," they sent their best teams, starting with Waseda
High School, against the visitors.[117] Days later, a massive crowd of twenty thousand
Nagoya fans came out to watch their Aichi No. 1 High School squad play Nōkō.[118]
In their travels that took them all the way to Hiroshima, the "savage children"
(bandō) won four of their nine games, losing four and tying one, and again won
wide praise for their "serious attitude and scientific strategies."[119]

Bert Scruggs, citing Homi Bhabha's notions of "colonial mimicry" (cited here in
the introduction), has written simply that "the colonizers want the colonized to re-
semble them but still remain different."[120] This model explains the intersecting Japanese characterizations of the Japanese-but-savage (or was it savage-but-Japanese?)
Team Nōkō. Hans Gumbrecht has described white longing and fantasies of "authenticity" with regard to 1920s African-American and jazz culture, and how whites

needed to find in jazz "an uncanny strength for which they ha[d] no appropriate words." Taiwan's Aborigines, similarly to many Japanese, served as "a new untouched race . . . [that could bring a] shimmering stream of fertility"[121] to an exhausted empire. Colonialism and the dream of a Japanese-dominated Asia could only be sustained by this dynamic (but not contradictory) tension.

Having set up these codes of "Japanese" and "savage," however, it was not long before these collapsed, this instability leaving space for hope for the empire. Kinoshita Makoto, Minister of Home Affairs in Taiwan, submitted a piece to the *Taiwan Nichinichi Shimpō* that he hoped summed up the feelings of his countrymen in the home islands, anticipating the coming day when these former savages could become useful and healthy members of Japanese society.[122] This same newspaper published an article at the conclusion of the trip proclaiming the breathtaking usefulness of Nōkō's visit to Japan (and their sponsorship of it), citing the Kanagawa No. 1 High School principal's declaration that Taiwan's Aborigines no longer would be treated with contempt and scorn in Japan. Anyone who had come into contact with these young men understood that they were lovable and similar to ethnic Japanese, a far cry from the "evil and slavish" stereotype they had suffered from for centuries. The "beautiful sympathy" this mission had garnered was enough to do away with the conservative theories that denied Aborigine talents and usefulness to the empire.[123]

By definition, records of savage Team Nōkō and their trip overwhelmingly bear the weight of these colonial dreams, desires, and fears. There are very few traces that would allow us to analyze exactly how these young Aborigine men understood their participation in the Japanese national game of baseball. One hint can be found in the many photographs published of the team in newspapers like *Nichinichi Shimpō*, which show the players seemingly very comfortable in the "NOKO" uniforms that marked them as civilized imperial subjects. Another can be found in the decision by four of Nōkō's star players—the young Amis Aborigine men known in Japanese as Inada Teruo, Itō Jirō, Itō Masao, and Nishimura Kazō, all seventeen or eighteen years of age—to stay on in Japan and play for Heian High School in Kyoto. They led Heian to the famed Kōshien High School Baseball Tournament in 1927 and 1928, and the first three of these players went on to play and study at Hōsei University.[124] These Aborigine men are remembered as pioneers among the many Taiwanese players who went on to pursue fruitful collegiate and professional baseball careers in the "home islands" of Japan. They also demonstrate the ability of "assimilating" Taiwanese subjects who made the best of their rare opportunities to study in Japan proper. In 1925, there were only 275 Taiwanese high school students studying in Japan, and these four were very possibly the only Taiwanese Aborigines to be able to ascend in this way toward a truly "Japanese" status within the empire.[125]

Several scholars in Taiwan have employed sociologist Erving Goffman's work to describe Aborigines' historical identities and their lives under Japanese colonialism vis-à-vis the constant Japanese slander of the Aborigines as "savages" unable to act in other than the most corporeal and instinctual of ways.[126] Here, once again, an examination of baseball helps prove clearly that Aborigine participation in Japanese rituals of state, modernity, and masculinity by no means implies acceptance of these stereotypes. Instead, we are reminded that both Aborigine and Han Taiwanese were able to overcome, contravene, and ultimately make a mockery of these stereotypes and the tokenistic "assimilationist" perspective—and often with the assistance of liberal Japanese colonial agents—by making important and significant use of baseball, one of the only avenues toward success for members of nonelite socioeconomic classes.

This is also an important reminder about how utterly *historical* (and obviously *not* inherent or racial) the Aborigine presence in Taiwanese baseball has been over the last eighty-plus years. We will see throughout the rest of this book how, for the rest of the twentieth century and beyond, Japanese and Chinese imaginations of Taiwan's Austronesian Aborigine populations consisted largely of notions of their inherent genetic physicality. The many successes of Aboriginal baseball players in Taiwan became an important part of this ethnic mythology—very much like white fantasies of African Americans' "natural" abilities in basketball and track and field—as, in both cases, racial essentialism has proved a more comforting analytical tool than socioeconomic investigation and understandings of class, sport, and violence.

While the Han Taiwanese—aside from a few notorious bands of turn-of-the-century bandits—were seen by the colonial regime as easily recivilized and integrated into a Japanese-led Asia, the Aborigine population posed a much more practical and truly existential challenge to Japanese colonialism. Commentators and fans in Taiwan today still marvel at what they imagine to be uniquely "Aborigine" skills and determination that have made so many of these young men into baseball stars.[127] Yet it is precisely the Japanese attention to and interrogation of Taiwanese Aborigines, their goals and fantasies of "civilizing" them, and their nightmares of failing, that gave rise to the concept of savage Team Nōkō and the subsequent project to channel "genetic" Aborigine rage and fierceness onto the expansive fields of the game of baseball.

NOT JAPANESE AND NOT CHINESE EITHER:
1920s HAN TAIWANESE BASEBALL

Baseball in Japanese Taiwan was a cultural institution that could be manipulated for personal advantage by colonial subjects and elite colonial administrators alike. These contestations over baseball more than eighty years ago, while different from contemporary models of glocalization driven by multinational capitalism, can still be explained with Aviad Raz's model of the tension between global cultural production and local acquisition.[128] Indeed, few interactions could have been more tense than the Japanese campaign to "civilize" Taiwan's Austronesian populations via official colonial policies of "impartiality and equal favor" *(isshi dōjin)*. Their supposed physicality and aggression, the possibility of their conquest by the Japanese, and the equal possibility of their atavistic return to "headhunting" and utter savagery, made them central to the ideology of colonialism. Baseball—a sign of commitment to modern notions of disciplined speed and violence, sportsmanlike quests for victory, "fair" divisions of superior and inferior, and the capacity for individual initiative and subordination to the group required of the modern subject-citizen—was by the 1920s an important field of negotiation for colonizer and colonized alike in Japanese Taiwan.

By the mid-1920s, colonial efforts to assimilate the Taiwanese—while maintaining the difference crucial to the colonial enterprise—seemed to be paying off. In 1924, American travel writer Harry Franck observed of Japanese and Taiwanese schoolchildren that "at times it is difficult to tell the two races of pupils apart at a glance; but the self-sufficient air of the one and the disorganized, straggling temperament of the others, who seldom march in formation even to or from school, are alone indicative."[129] Franck seemed to comprehend the point of Taiwan's then (mostly) separate-but-equal education system. Ethnic Japanese students and a few elite Japanese-speaking Taiwanese could attend primary schools *(shōgakkō)*, while the great majority of Taiwanese students attended public elementary schools *(kō-gakkō)*;[130] 1923 seems to be the year when baseball teams from these still-segregated schools began playing each other regularly.

In May 1923, the *Tainan New Times* announced a youth baseball tournament featuring five local teams, two of which were mostly Japanese teams (one Han player each) from primary schools, and three all-Taiwanese public school squads. While the children were fulfilling their new *dōka*-assimilated destinies as equal Japanese subjects, the parents and fans in attendance at such contests, both "home islanders and natives" who had their doubts about the nature of this equality, evidently were giving voice to troubling ethnic-specific passions "in the heat of competition." The newspaper—pretending that Japanese and Taiwanese bias against the other constituted equally serious moral violations—declared that this discrimination *(ku-betsu)* caused ill feelings and that the crowd's responsibility was merely to give moral support to the children.[131] Here we see very clearly the contradiction of Japanese colonialism, that, in Ming-cheng Lo's words, "emphasized the similarities between the colonizers and colonized without collapsing their hierarchical distinctions."[132]

Taiwanese participation in baseball, the art and symbol of the colonizing metropolis, reflects an important aspect of the experience of almost any colonized people. Edward Said has discussed the "collaborative" aspect of the life of colonized intellectuals, whose long-term strategies for liberation depended on being able to "learn the ways of the [colonizer], translate his works, pick up his habits."[133] In Taiwan, baseball in particular was one way in which the colonized population sought to negotiate their relationship with the colonizing power, on terms that the Japanese could not but accept.[134]

While the national game could serve as a valuable site for Taiwanese children to learn the ways of Japanese civilization, the playing field also gave Taiwanese natives the rare chance to compete "fairly." Since ethnic Japanese enjoyed a clear advantage in a Taiwan where the norms were now those of Japanese language, education, and culture, it was usually hard to be more Japanese than the Japanese. Baseball was different, and thus fits the models of glocalization defined earlier, where there always exist great tensions between global cultural production and local acquisition. One familiar example is C. L. R. James's discussions of West Indies cricket, where by the early 1900s the inspired performances of standout black cricketers had forced white populations to give West Indians a respect they would not have granted otherwise.[135]

In 1925, the Chinese-language newspaper *Taiwan Minbao* featured an editorial that exhibited how important modern notions of assimilation, equality, and sport had become. Addressing the continued inequity of access to the best schools in Taihoku, the paper cited (in English) the concept of "Fair Play," defining it in Chinese as "fair and just competition" (*gongming zhengda de jingzheng*). The piece went on pointedly, if not sarcastically, to assert that "the ancients would not have known about Fair Play but would have called it *bushidō* [the Japanese way of the warrior] . . . [unfortunately] people today have not improved on the ways of the ancients."[136] This indigenous usage of Japanese-introduced modern bourgeois concepts to critique the colonial regime hints that any examination of physical culture during this era of *dōka* assimilation, then, must address the complicated patterns that the glocalization model reveals about—once again in Morita's words—Taiwanese "customer expectations" with regard to the empire's "brand strategy."

The Taiwanese sociologist Chang Li-ke has cited similar moments of confrontation or critiques of colonialism as sure evidence of "resistance" (*dikang*) in Taiwan's baseball history, posing this against other patterns of "emulation/imitation" (*fangtong*).[137] Paul Dimeo has described the rise of Bengali soccer at this same historical moment as "acceptance of the British moral system."[138] However, a perspective informed by glocalization asks us to look past these anachronistic extremes—of both an authentic Taiwanese defiance often celebrated in cheap nationalism and the inauthentic passivity cited by critiques of a too-obedient Taiwanese subjectivity. Understanding the significance of baseball in colonial Taiwan lies in seeing how this "resistance" and identification with the Japanese colonizer actually operated at the same time, within the same people, and at the same moments. Many memories of that period are problematic and have been warped by the weight of eight decades of much more judgmental conclusions about Taiwan's history. Here, Stuart Hall's thoughts on postcolonial scholarship are useful; he reflected in 1996 that this work has obliged "us to re-read the very binary form in which the colonial encounter has for so long itself been represented. It obliges us to re-read the binaries as forms of transculturation, of cultural translation, destined to trouble the here/there cultural binaries for ever."[139] Our goal here is to explore how colonial baseball created a true transculturation, a convergence of "Taiwanese" and "Japanese" that defies the simple binary.

We can find such a satisfying level of psychological complexity in the words and memories of Mr. Jian Yongchang, a legendary coach who grew up under Japanese rule. From 2001 to 2003, Jian self-published his autobiography in six volumes, the language of each alternating between Japanese and Chinese. Wartime recollections, for example, are included in the sixth volume, titled *Hito no isshō: Taiwanjin no monogatari,* while his memories of the Chinese Nationalists' takeover of Taiwan and subsequent brutality that turned Taiwan into "hell" are recounted in the fourth volume, *Ren de yisheng: Taiwanren de xiao gushi.*[140] When I interviewed Jian in 2004, I asked him to talk about his attraction to baseball as a child in 1920s Shinchiku Prefecture; he explained that he liked the game because Taiwanese children were told that they "were not Japanese, and were not Chinese either."[141]

This way of discussing baseball and colonized youngsters' senses of identity does not gibe well with the elite position, voiced by the renowned Taiwanese doctor-critic-politician Jiang Weishui, that Taiwanese could play the role of "a medium to promote good will between Japan and China."[142] Nor does it share the drama of novelist Wu Zhuoliu's discussion of the "emptiness [and] dull self-hatred" felt by young men at the time.[143] Indeed, it is much closer to the writings of Ye Shengji, a Taiwanese student in Japan whose diary Barry Fong has analyzed. Ye wrote very frankly about his "two hometowns" in discussing the ambivalence of his "internally split double life" and his identity as a colonial subject.[144]

Coach Jian's writings clearly show how baseball was a corporeal way to create such purposefully ambivalent identity for two generations of young people in Taiwan. Young Taiwanese understood perfectly the purpose of *dōka,* which was to turn them into almost-equal imperial subjects. Jian's self-presentation in print or in person is not easily categorized or explained (on prominent display in his Taipei sitting room is a picture of himself posing with Chiang Kai-shek in 1969), and thus his explanations are much more convincing than simple, melodramatic memories of resistance or emulation. His memories suggest the active and fluid process of creating identity—in this case, the calculus of how exactly he and others like him would enter into the dominant Japanese colonial culture: *How* Japanese would one be? What *kind* of Japanese subject would one be? A *dōka*-style Japanese? A Taiwanese Japanese? And what exactly would that be? It is useful here to consider philosopher Martha Nussbaum's description of "the bankrupt route of defining authenticity as rebellion";[145] the Japanese colonial regime wanted the Taiwanese to play baseball too badly for this activity to simply be considered "resistance."

Jian's first exposure to baseball in 1920s Shinchiku was watching Japanese land surveyors play "catch-ball" *(kyatchi bōru)* during breaks. There was no baseball "*chi-imu*" (team) at Takei (Daxi) Public Elementary School, so students like Jian also had to content themselves with playing *kyatchi bōru*. However, when a local tournament was organized, Jian's teacher Mishima Yukibumi put together a team so that the Taiwanese boys could compete with the all-Japanese primary school in town. (Jian's school team was victorious; a photo of his squad is featured in another of his self-published books.)[146] The case of Coach Mishima, with whom Jian kept in touch well into the 1970s, also complicates our view of colonialism. In class, Mishima would readily praise the wisdom and insight of the late Chinese revolutionary Sun Yat-sen, making him a favorite of students like Jian. (The school principal, however, warned Mishima about this "problem" with his thinking, and would stand outside the classroom pretending to prune the bushes while monitoring this problematic agent of colonial rule.)[147] The sixth volume of Jian's memoirs devote seven pages to reprinting a 1972 letter from Mishima to his former student, as well as a photo of Jian's children posing stiffly with Mishima in their home long after the end of colonial rule.[148] Once again, the logic of *dōka* is stood on its head. And yet, at the same time it is made more genuine, as we consider the unique workings of assimilation, the humane bonds of family and school, and the fun and multiple meanings of baseball in small-town Taiwan.

At the beginning of this chapter, we cited Aviad Raz's use of the term glocalization to describe "the more colorful and playful themes characterizing the (usually ingenious) local practices of consumption." These playful memories are often what come out in oral histories of the Taiwanese "consumption" of baseball and their use of it to produce their own identities as colonial subjects. Xiao Changgun, who would later coach some of Taiwan's finest players in the elementary and high schools of Gaoxiong, grew up playing baseball in the port city then called Takao. The mostly Japanese primary schools and all-Taiwanese public schools played two baseball seasons, spring and autumn, in the 1920s. The realities of colonial Taiwan were such that, on average, Taiwanese children started school later than their Japanese counterparts. In a 2000 interview, Xiao joked about the clear advantage that this gave the public school teams, and about how "the Japanese were not too happy to lose" to the Taiwanese. At the same time, in terms that explicitly question the *dōka* ideology of assimilation in which Xiao was taking part, he laments that Taiwanese children like himself could never quite trust their baseball coaches, who all were Japanese, to coach them in the correct ways.[149]

Writers at the Chinese-language newspaper *Taiwan Minbao* also engaged in a fair share of playful commentary about the attitudes of the Japanese in Taiwan. In August 1929, five teams—four from Japanese primary schools and one from a public elementary school in Takao—met in Taihoku to play a two-day islandwide youth baseball tournament before three to four thousand fans. "But who would have thought," asked the paper, "that in this Taiwan where the home islanders *(neidiren)* have absolutely every advantage in every possible situation, that out of these five teams Takao No. 1 Public School would win the final victory?" The result was given away by the subtitle of the article: "Home islanders in attendance show their disapproval, jeering and heatedly cursing, turning the stadium into a chaotic mess."[150] Perhaps the only advantage for Taiwanese in the colonial education system was that their primary school students were older (up to age fourteen or fifteen) and thus their baseball teams were potentially better. This proved intolerable for many Japanese colonials who only saw an important hierarchy threatened.

Although many of the players were perhaps too young and too "assimilated" to see it as such, Taiwanese intellectuals at this important newspaper—who condemned the Japanese fans' "shameless, unbearable, and cruel words"—saw baseball as an opportunity to reject publicly the inequalities of colonialism.[151] Indeed, modern sport—with its inherent measures of comparison, superiority, and strength—seemed to be an effective discourse in which to twist the knife. In 1929 the same *Taiwan Minbao* commented on the excellence of Filipino swimmers visiting Taiwan. Noting that Taiwan had no good swimmers, the paper pondered the "white rule" of the Philippines that evidently fostered "a happy and carefree attitude, a relaxed and easy body and mind, making others truly envy them."[152] This "envy" for the subjects of white colonialism suggests that romantic notions of anticolonial "resistance" probably do not provide the best explanations for the passions of 1920s Taiwanese for dignity and equality as imperial subjects. Yet it does hint at the consciousness that the strength and fitness learned through modern sport could still be deployed by Taiwanese in playful, or even not-so-playful, ways.

2

Making Racial Harmony in
Taiwan Baseball, 1931–1945

Taiwanese people today will also become loyal and brave Japanese nationals in the future.

LATE 1920S–1930S TEXTBOOKS, CITED BY EIJI OGUMA

By 1930, after thirty-five years of colonial rule, Taiwan had been transformed into a relatively stable, peaceful, and prosperous Japanese colony. With a population that was still 95 percent rural, Taiwan had become a reliable "sugar bowl" and "rice basket," providing foodstuffs and light industrial products for Japan's home islands. In the cities, thousands of college-educated Taiwanese, as one scholar described, had "entered the ranks of Japanese [intellectuals], becoming almost indistinguishable from them."[1] And an official government publication had boasted in 1929, "Today one may travel alone and unarmed without the slightest danger of molestation at the hands of savages or bandits—except in certain small sections of the mountain fastnesses where the head-hunters have not as yet been entirely tamed."[2]

Indeed, the government felt comfortable enough with its progress in civilizing and modernizing the island to schedule an "Islandwide High School Baseball Tournament to Commemorate Three Hundred Years of Culture" (Bunka sanbyaku nen kinen zentō chūtō gakkō yakyū taikai) on the Tainan No. 1 High School grounds.[3] Lasting from 26 to 28 October 1930, this tournament pitted nine of Taiwan's finest teams against each other in a clumsily conceived effort to celebrate the longstanding institution of global, not just Japanese, colonialism. According to this chronology, "culture" had arrived in Taiwan in 1630, eight years into the Dutch occupation of southwestern Taiwan,[4] where the population consisted of some seventy thousand plains Aborigines and one thousand Chinese sojourners and traders, apparently cultureless to the last.[5] The ahistorical point, clearly, was to credit and naturalize the global system by which Japan and their Western contemporaries had achieved such wealth and power.

This narrative of colonialist success was shattered, however, the very day after the self-congratulatory tournament was convened. The date of 27 October 1930 was also chosen for the annual interscholastic sports meet in Musha (Wushe in Chinese), a model village deep in the mountains of central Taiwan. As the national flag was raised and the national anthem played, some three hundred Seediq Atayal Aborigine braves, seeking revenge for continued humiliations and violence at the hands of Japanese police, crashed onto the grounds and began stabbing and shooting the Japanese home islanders in attendance. Some 134 Japanese were massacred in what came to be known as the Musha Incident, before the military brutally quelled the rebellion with aerial attacks and poison gas.

Leo Ching has documented very skillfully how this violent uprising "deeply shook, [and] momentarily destabilized, Japanese rule" and how Japanese cultural producers reacted by creating stories and films in subsequent years that reordered the relationship between colonizer and "savage." An example was the song and film "The Bell of Sayon," about an Aboriginal maiden who dies helping her Japanese teacher (and local police officer) carry his luggage down a steep mountain pass. Like the British mythologization of Pocahontas, this discourse was meant to transform "the aborigines from an unruly population to patriotic subjects in the post-Musha era."[6] While Ching's reading of these cultural productions is astute, the time lag between Musha and these works—for example, the film *Sayon* was released thirteen years later, in 1943—complicates notions of directly causal connection. The realm of baseball, by this time crucial to notions of modernity and nationalism in Japan, was a cultural space in which both colonizer and subject much more immediately addressed the implications of the bloodshed of October 1930.

ENACTING THE IMPERIAL WISH OF EQUALITY: KANŌ BASEBALL IN THE POST-MUSHA ERA

An "event" [serving as a turning point in historical narrative] would then be whatever threatens the structures of existing everyday-worlds without being accessible for formulation and interpretation within them.
HANS ULRICH GUMBRECHT, IN 1926: LIVING AT THE EDGE OF TIME, 1997

In August 1931, Japan's hallowed Kōshien National High School Baseball Tournament, held at Nishinomiya near Osaka, provided a gratifying sign of the resolution of the Musha disaster just ten months earlier. There, a team from southern Taiwan's Tainan District Kagi Agriculture and Forestry Institute (Tainan shūritsu Kagi nōrin gakkō, abbreviated Kanō) captured the imaginations of a Japanese public still recovering from the shock of the violent rejection of Japanese colonialism.[7]

What made the Kanō team special at this historical moment was its triethnic composition; in 1931 its starting nine was made up of four Taiwan Aborigines, two Han Taiwanese, and three Japanese players. This 1931 Kanō squad won the Taiwan championship and became the first team ever to qualify for Kōshien with Taiwanese (Aborigine or Han) players on its roster. This Kanō team also became a powerful symbol of how Japanese colonialism was *supposed* to be working—producing colonial subjects who could work together in performing the cultural rituals of the Japanese state. Newspaper reporters fawned on these Taiwanese "barefoot spirits" and their "lion-like spirit of bravery and struggle" that marked them as the newly (if just barely) civilized product of a successful colonial model.[8] Reports like these allow us to see the obsession that many Japanese had with the savage manhood associated with the Taiwanese "wild." The same ferocity and bravery that could be employed in massacring Japanese colonials could also come in handy, if channeled correctly, on the baseball field, as Taiwanese subjects (and especially the Aborigine players) were imagined as being both ultraprimitive *and* ultramodern. This vitality was imagined as being able to revive the sagging spirits of the jaded modern empire.

In the perfect ending to this moral fable of colonialism and the spread of civilization to Taiwan, Kanō made it to the championship game before finally losing to the powerful team from Chūkyō Business School, 4–0. The exploits of this "harmonious triethnic" team *(san minzoku no kyōchō)* remain the source of much nostalgia and postcolonial ideology eight decades later; unpacking this narrative and its surrounding mythology offers much insight into the lasting impact of the Japanese rule of Taiwan.

The school known as Kanō was founded in 1919 as the intersection of two important colonial trends. One was the colonial regime's efforts to finally irrigate, develop, and exploit the fertile Jiayi-Tainan plains. After five years of careful land surveys, the school was founded in order to train a modern workforce for this important enterprise (and also for the eventual colonization of Southeast Asia).[9] The composition of this student body—mostly Han Taiwanese, but also including several ethnic Japanese and a small number of Aborigine students—is also a reflection of the post-Wilsonian language of *dōka* assimilation discussed in the previous chapter. It is also important to understand how transformative this early exposure to colonial Japanese civilization was understood to be: in 1922, after twenty-five years of operating several "savage" elementary schools exclusively for Taiwan's Aborigine children, this special status was eliminated and the schools were folded under the broader heading of the public elementary school *(kōgakkō)*.[10] And according to the official census of Taiwan, by 1925 the Japanese regime was counting Aborigines who had "ceased to be savages but were sufficiently 'tamed' to be designated as 'Taiwanese.'"[11]

As we have seen in chapter 1, the game of baseball was one of the transformative and assimilative forces in colonial Taiwan. After baseball flourished in southern Taiwan for a decade, an algebra teacher named Andō Shinya organized a Kanō school team in 1928 (see figure 1), its starters numbering four Japanese, three Aborigines and two Han Taiwanese youth. Kanō's status as a less-than-elite vocational school is directly reflected in the fact that this team already exhibited the famed and unique "triethnic" composition that would be fetishized in later years. High schools of any social prestige had few Taiwanese and no Aborigine students (very few of the latter ever continued on past middle school); the Kanō story could only have occurred at a marginal school and city such as this. (For example, in 1929, of the three thousand students who applied for admission in Taiwan's six vocational schools, just six of them were Aborigines, and just two of these were admitted.)[12]

This marginality was consistently evident to Kanō baseball players in other ways too; unlike Japanese-majority high schools, Kanō never had a baseball field of their own, and the team had to practice every day at the municipal field downtown.[13] This field was built in 1917, toward the top of a hill overlooking the city of Kagi (Jiayi), and significantly, right next to the city's Shintō shrine.[14] Both structures survive today, although in altered forms. The baseball stadium was replaced by a state-of-the-art park in 1997. While most other Shintō shrines in Taiwan were demolished by the Chinese Nationalist government in 1945, this Jiayi shrine somehow survived as a martyr's shrine until being transformed into the city's Historical Materials Museum by the proindependence Democratic Progressive Party (DPP) mayor in 1998. But a walk on this beautiful hillside, where the all-Japanese Kagi High School was also built in 1924, can teach us much about geography and hierarchy, and again Kanō's marginality under Japanese rule.

Kanō alumni often remember this marginality in provocative ways. Liu Jinyao, a native of Douliu in central Taiwan, studied at Kanō in the late 1920s and early 1930s. In 1993, Liu remembered that once after a Kanō baseball game—a victory over crosstown rival Kagi High—Japanese students from the losing side wanted to "start some trouble" with the majority Taiwanese Kanō crowd. Liu proudly related how he and his mates, under the direction of their dormitory residential advisor, united that night to fight their foes for "justice." Along the same masculinist lines, he was just as proud in describing how Kanō athletic meets were much more exciting *(renao)* for all of the local girls who, while avoiding the Kagi High meets, crowded the stands to cheer on their beaus from Kanō.[15] It is possible to see the gendered mechanisms that Taiwanese students used in hammering out a sense of unique identity from within colonial occupation. Former star player Hong Taishan recently recounted at age eighty-three his own memory of the significance of Kanō baseball to Taiwanese identity. During the early 1930s, Hong was a student at Shirakawa Public School for Taiwanese children, but he remembered that even as a youngster he understood clearly the rivalry between Kanō and Kagi High as one between "Taiwanese" and "Japanese."[16] Again, the Kanō experience was one understood as one of marginality—albeit often an attractive and authentic marginality; the tension between playing with *and* against "the Japanese" could often be resolved only by recourse to transcendent modern tropes of masculinity.

However, during the Kanō baseball team's early years (and perhaps to the dismay of the local beauties), they played very poorly. At the important Islandwide High School Baseball Tournament in 1928, Kanō lost 13–0 to Taichū Commercial School as the team managed just three hits and committed seven errors. As face-conscious administrators in Taiwan had done for a decade and a half, Principal Higuchi Takashi looked to the ranks of Waseda University graduates and located a more accomplished coach: Kondō Hyōtarō, who had toured the United States with his high school team and who happened to be working as an accountant at nearby Kagi Commercial School.[17]

Kondō recruited athletes from the school's tennis and track and field teams in order to bring the baseball team up to the high local standards. "*Tenisu*" was another important modern cultural form useful in assimilating Taiwanese youth. In 1924, the same city of Kagi had hosted an islandwide tennis tourney, in which more than two hundred players competed for the right to represent Taiwan at the nationals in the home islands of Japan.[18] Two years later, in an important sign of assimilation and imperial grace, the brother of one of these champions was among six men and four women selected to play in a Meiji Shrine Tennis Invitational held at the sacred grounds in Tokyo.[19] However, the elite and bounded game of tennis never developed into a powerful ideology for empire and assimilation like the "wild," more popular team sport of baseball.

For several decades, an extensive mythology has surrounded Coach Kondō—particularly his Spartan attitude toward training and his proto-Branch Rickey blindness to ethnic difference in the name of baseball excellence. (An official biography by Taiwan's National Council on Physical Fitness and Sports has praised recently his philosophy of "nondiscrimination by nationality or ethnicity" *[bu fen guoji, bu fen zuqun]*, anachronistic terms and categories that never would have occurred to Japanese in colonial Taiwan.)[20] If this interpretation of Aborigine participation in Kanō baseball seems forced and teleological, it is not to say that there were not real implications for the lives of these players, who again constituted most of the Aborigine population exposed to this level of education.

Tuo Hongshan was the oldest of ten children in an Amis Aborigine family living in the far mountains of Taitō Prefecture, when he left to attend Kanō and join its first baseball team in 1928. In a 2001 interview, Tuo remembered that first Kanō team as consisting of nine Aborigines, three Japanese, and two Taiwanese players. Historical records indicate that there were actually only three Aborigine players out of twelve young men on that team[21]—but the distortion in his memory says much about how accepted and important these Aborigine players felt at the school. It was at Kanō that Tuo took a Japanese name, Mayama Uichi, and then received the opportunity to study in Japan after graduation. He turned it down and went home to serve as the principal of a local elementary school, before retiring to become a Christian missionary in his middle age. This type of mobility, needless to say, was impossible to imagine for almost any other member of Taiwan's mountain Aborigine tribes, and thus must become an important part of understanding the legacy of Kanō baseball.[22] Again, although celebrations of the team's unique "triethnic" composition suggest the politically motivated "multiculturalism" discourse employed by ethnic Taiwanese since the 1990s (and critiqued by Allen Chun[23] and Edward Vickers[24]), it is true that baseball allowed Taiwanese youth to excel on a rarely equal "playing field."

Another part of the Coach Kondō mythology, as many former players have testified in oral histories and memoirs—in terms that tell us much about postcolonial Taiwan—is Kondō's "Japanese" integrity, fairness, and spirit of sacrifice. His teams practiced every day, except when it rained, when they would retreat to classrooms to review rules and strategy. Players were not allowed to degrade their strength or eyesight by watching movies, and were taught to treat baseball as a battle and not a game. Kondō employed only the "highest principles of leadership" and held himself to high standards as well; once when sick with malaria over vacation, he insisted on attending practice on a stretcher. Decades later, Sasada Toshio, a Japanese native of Taiwan who played under Kondō, remembered a poem that the coach wrote and would often have the players recite:

> The ball is the soul.
> If the ball is not correct then the soul is not proper.
> If the soul is proper the ball will be correct.[25]

Su Zhengsheng, the former starting center fielder for Kanō, was later recognized in Taiwan as a "brilliant and battle-tested elder of our country's baseball." In 1997, Su described the Kanō baseball atmosphere as one of "impartiality and equal favor" *(isshi dōjin),* also the official Shōwa era description of "fair" treatment of colonized populations. Interestingly, Su cites as proof of this attitude an incident when an Aborigine player missed a "take" sign, swung, and hit a triple, only to be excoriated so thoroughly by Coach Kondō that he quit the team.[26] Another quite ambivalent endorsement of Kondō comes from former star slugger Hong Taishan. Hong was interviewed (in Japanese) in 1995 by Nishiwaki Yoshitomo, a policeman from Hyogo Prefecture who has published two giant volumes on his obsession, baseball in Japanese-ruled Taiwan. Describing Coach Kondō's "Spartan style . . . [that would] knock today's players down in one day," Hong characterized Kondō as an *"oni kantoku,"* or "devil/wizard-manager."[27] In another interview in 2003, Hong elaborated on his coach's Spartan methods. He described to scholar Xie Shiyuan the system of age hierarchy *(xuezhangzhi)* that governed the team. On a player's first day with the team, he would be beaten and boxed on the ears. After that, there would be all sorts of chores and beatings for the younger players, although Hong proudly pointed out that this violence "was not about Japanese or Taiwanese," but just age hierarchy. In the same interview, Hong stretches our ability to share his admiration for his coach, who would scream at Taiwanese or Aborigine players who made mistakes on the field, (respectively) "Go back to China *(Shina)!*" and "Go back to the mountains!"[28] "Fairness" is an unlikely euphemistic discourse in which to remember this kind of harsh experience, but it reminds us how near violence always was to even the enjoyable realms of colonial culture.

After two years of such treatment under Coach Kondō, the team from Kagi Agriculture and Forestry Institute somehow reached a pinnacle of excellence in 1931, with a starting nine made up of four Aborigines, three ethnic Japanese, and two Han Taiwanese players (see figure 2). (It is important to note that the three Japanese were the seventh through ninth hitters in the lineup, and also that four of the five backup players were Japanese,[29] in much the same way that NBA benchwarmers until quite recently were overwhelmingly white.) In July of that year, they captured the Ninth Islandwide High School Baseball Tournament championship despite, as Kanō center fielder Su Zhengsheng remembered in 1997, the Japanese umpires' unceasing efforts to throw the game to the all-Japanese squad from Taihoku Commercial School. Su's memories of this moment revealed even more complexity when he told how, after winning the game after eleven trying innings, the entire team broke down sobbing loudly: "Our Kanō team traditions were actually just like those of the Japanese teams. If you have ever seen Kōshien [championship] games on television, you will see that after every game the losing team will cry, some even sobbing loudly with their noses running. But we Kanō players would never cry after losing; we would only cry after winning."[30]

Just like the Japanese, but different. In the citation of Bhabha and Scruggs in the introduction and chapter 1, I described this ideological formulation as an act of the colonizing agent, meant both to elucidate and fog the twisted logic of colonialist assimilation. Here, however, as with Jian Yongchang's project of creating an identity from within the constraints of "not Japanese, and not Chinese either" (see chapter 1), we see that this strategy also was an important element of the Taiwanese experience of colonialism. And again, we see the ways in which Taiwanese marginality was defined largely through tropes of masculinity in ways that intersected nicely with the colonial discourse of "wild" Taiwan.

By 1931, high school baseball in Taiwan had become every bit the popular obsession it was in the home islands. The Asahi-published *Baseball Bulletin (Yakyū sokuhō)* was sold at twenty-two bookstores and newsstands in the capital, and fifty more in nine different cities across Taiwan.[31] Before 1931, the Islandwide High School Baseball Tournament, the biggest baseball event in Taiwan, had been dominated by ethnic Japanese. According to Officer Nishiwaki's painfully gathered records, in eight previous tournaments dating back to 1923, thirty-eight of the forty-six teams participating consisted only of Japanese players. Of the 536 total players, just twenty-eight (5.2 percent) were Taiwanese. (Fourteen of these had been on an all-Taiwanese squad from Taichū No. 1 High in 1930, and ten had been on three previous Kanō squads. Four teams from Tainan No. 1 High, Taihoku Commercial, and Taihoku Vocational had started one Taiwanese player each.)[32] Some fifteen thousand fans were in attendance when Kanō prevailed over the biases of the Japanese umpires and won their fourth straight game to capture the Taiwan championship, fulfilling every Japanese boy's dream of qualifying for the Kōshien national tournament.

The next day, Kagi's mayor and public servants, Kanō principal Shimauchi Tsuneaki and the student body, and thousands of baseball fans greeted the champions at the train station and accompanied them to a victory celebration at the Kagi city center. Despite all the rivalries implicated in these contests, this pride was not simply southern or ethnically Taiwanese. Before leaving for Japan proper, the Kanō team was hosted over several days in the capital by Taihoku No. 1 High School. Several other all-Japanese school teams also sent their star players to take part in three "sendoff contests" (sōbetsu shiai) to help prepare Kanō for the stiff competition they would soon be facing at Kōshien. The thousands of fans who bought tickets—twenty sen each, or ten sen for students—would also be satisfied knowing that the proceeds would pay for Kanō's trip to Japan.[33]

Again, a historical perspective reminds us that at this moment in 1931 there was much at stake. The entire logic for empire and colonial rule was what inspired the Japanese residents of Taiwan to see, experience, purchase, and cheer for this commonality with Taiwanese subjects (both Han and Aborigine), even if things were actually more complicated than this. The episodes and details recounted in this chapter, reported in the Taiwan Nichinichi Shimpō, still allow us to see a "Taiwanese" identity and unity that—despite certain postwar memories to the contrary—very much included ethnic Japanese residents of the colony. While this is not simply to judge as successful the colonial policies of dōka assimilation, it is important to see how Japan's "national game" of baseball was an important way for all imperial subjects to unite in amity as well as in competition. All of these different types of subjects—Han, Aborigine, and home islander—would have had very different interests in this amity, of course. And we should not forget Hui-yu Caroline Ts'ai's observation that notions and policies of "assimilation" often merely served "to perpetuate the relative dominance of the Japanese and often ended up by suppressing alternative ideologies or ways of life of the subordinates."[34] For the ethnic Japanese residents of Taiwan, though, the specter of the Musha massacre meant that this promise of assimilation was extremely politicized and self-conscious; for the sake of their survival in Taiwan, this long-advertised camaraderie and equality under the watchful imperial gaze now had to be made real.[35]

The Kanō team arrived for the 1931 Kōshien tournament as one of twenty-two district representatives, which also included Keijō (Seoul) Commercial High and Dairen Commercial High from Japan's other colonial holdings in Korea and Manchuria. The ideological sensitivity of these two teams' presence at the tournament was minimized by the fact that these were all-Japanese teams, safe reminders of the colonial presence in otherwise tumultuous parts of the empire. The Kanō team, however, started four walking reminders—an Aborigine left fielder, short-stop, catcher, and third baseman—of the bloody Musha rebellion and its bloodier suppression. Some 631 teams throughout the empire had competed to reach Kōshien, but of the twenty-two who made it, the presence of Kanō was the most significant. That same year, Taiwan governor-general Ōta Masahiro had written in his *Outline of Policies for Savage Governance (Rihan seisaku taikō)* that: "Although there have been some changes in the savage governing policy, its ultimate goal has always been to enact the imperial wish of equality and to honor them with impe-rialization [i.e., Japanization]. This has always been the consistent and fundamen-tal spirit."[36] Soon after the Musha violence, Ōta, viewed as an expert in dealing with uncooperative colonial populations, came to Taiwan directly from the post of di-rector of the Kwantung Leased Territory in China's northeast. If he protested too much in the declaration just cited, we can at least see how high the stakes were in the colonial project in Taiwan.

It is difficult to relate to an American audience the Japanese enthusiasm for the yearly Kōshien high school baseball tournament, perhaps best described as a cross between the Super Bowl, NCAA "March Madness," and *American Idol* in its cen-trality to Japanese popular culture. On average, more than one hundred baseball fans applied for each of the stadium's seventy thousand seats for the tournament.[37] At the opening ceremonies, this general excitement intersected with Kanō's special status when their team was the last to enter the field, receiving the loudest ovation of all.[38] Exoticizing plugs by the *Asahi Shimbun* for Kanō's "fierce offensive" attack and their ability to "fly [around the bases] like swift horses" had aroused a burning curiosity in the team as well.[39]

In the games themselves, Kanō continued to thrill the public—"shocking the entire Japanese nation,"[40] as a Japanese historian put it two years later—by sweep-ing their first three games by the combined score of 32–9. This qualified Kanō to play Chūkyō Business School in the championship game, which was hyped not only on the front page of the *Taiwan Nichinichi Shimpō*, but also in the *Tōkyō Asahi Shim-bun* as well,[41] who on page three also featured articles referring gratuitously to "Kagi's terrifying ferocity" *(osoru beki Kagi no mōki)* and describing them as the "fiercely vigorous and brave Kagi Agriculture and Forestry" *(mōyū Kagi Nōrin).*[42] The power of the Japanese apprehension about the Aborigines—and their chances of ever truly civilizing them—made for an exciting metonymy where the four Aborigine play-ers on the team could stand for a whole team, a whole school, a whole wild Taiwan. As in white fantasies of African-American jazz culture in the 1920s, the Japanese public seemed to be hooked on the notion of the Taiwanese Aborigine as "ultra-primitive and ultramodern"—a force who could bring tension and excitement to a "tame" and jaded modern Japan.[43]

Back home, festive crowds gathered in and outside stores that sold radios in or-der to listen to the broadcasts.[44] But on the field itself, the young men from Chūkyō were less awed by the Kanō hype. A photo in *Baseball World* from before this game shows Chūkyō leadoff hitter and left fielder Ōshika shaking hands with Kanō starting pitcher Wu Mingjie (ethnically Han Taiwanese) almost scornfully. Ōshika looks at the camera with obvious distaste while Wu, a good four inches taller but clearly the subordinate, looks at his opponent with doe-eyed discomfort.[45] Wu, exhausted from starting his fourth game in just seven days, was not able to overcome this intimidation. Once the game began, he lacked his usually brilliant control and walked eight batters. Kanō batters also were overmatched by the Chūkyō pitcher known as "The Big Wheel" *(daisharin)*. Yoshida Masao shut them out 4–0, winning what would be his first of three consecutive national championship games from 1931 to 1933.[46]

This second-place Kanō finish was perhaps the perfect ending for Japan's baseball world. Historian Suzuki Akira has described how, in rooting for these exotic and exciting new subjects of the emperor, Japanese fans found a convenient way to exhibit solidarity with the subjects of their far-flung empire.[47] The flowering ideology of a Japanese-led "harmony among the races" throughout Asia made the successful cooperation and integration of this Aborigine-Han-Japanese combination much more exciting. The triracial team "proved," in an extremely visible fashion, the colonial myth of "assimilation"—that both Han and Aborigine Taiwanese were willing and able to take part alongside Japanese in the cultural rituals of the Japanese state.

Sportswriter Tobita Suishū was known as the "father of school baseball" in Japan for his legendary leadership of the Waseda University team two decades earlier. He became the first of many commentators to rhapsodize on the almost-tragic Kanō story, the next day praising their "pugnacious spirit and ability to ignore the fact that the other teams were so much more experienced in battle." Paying attention to and reifying the important "triracial" trope, Tobita wrote dreamily: "When the sun sets on the Kōshien diamond, and all the young warriors who took part in the tournament have gone home, pictures of the Kagi Agriculture and Forestry Institute players battling on the field—like [Aborigine outfielder] Hirano's baserunning, [Han outfielder] Su's strong arms, and [Japanese second baseman] Kawahara's solid defense—float one by one across the seas of my mind."

Tobita was a moralistic baseball writer in the mode of America's Grantland Rice, known for his lengthy discourses on "the unselfish way *(mushidō)* of baseball" and "soulful baseball" *(tamashii no yakyū)*.[48] Especially given his status in the history of the game in Japan, his spirited endorsement on the front page of the *Asahi Shimbun* made Kanō a vibrant and crucial element of post-Musha baseball and imperial ideology. Likewise, the great playwright and film magnate Kikuchi Kan immediately declared himself utterly fascinated and emotionally captured by Kanō's performance: "Seeing the homelanders [Japanese], islanders [Taiwanese], and Takasago [Aborigines]—of different races, but working together in harmony as they battled toward the same goal—was something that moved me to tears."[49] Japanese media elites were quick in staking claim to what they defined as a moral victory for colonialism as well as for Kanō.

Colonial hierarchies were quickly reinforced when four of Kanō's star players were approached by different schools and asked to stay on and play baseball in Japan. The Amis Aborigine third baseman Tuo Hongshan, as mentioned earlier, was the only one to turn down this offer.[50] But Taiwanese star pitcher Wu Mingjie and center fielder Su Zhengsheng, as well as the Puyuma Aborigine shortstop Uematsu Koichi (originally named Akawats, and later known in Chinese as Chen Gengyuan), all took these offers. Su and Uematsu played and studied at the Yokohama College of Commerce before returning to Taiwan, while Wu played at the storied Waseda University before playing for several semipro teams and moving on to a business career in Japan, where he lived for half a century before dying in 1983. Once again, then, the mobility earned by these Taiwanese and Aborigine players has to be understood within the hegemonic colonial implications of baseball's career in Taiwan.

A useful comparison to the Kanō mania of 1931 can be seen in the annual Intercity Baseball Tournament (Toshi taikō yakyū taikai), sponsored by the *Tōkyō Nichinichi Shimbun,* predecessor of the Mainichi Newspaper Company. The competition, established in 1927, was played at the Meiji Jingu Stadium, on the sacred grounds of the Shintō shrine dedicated to the souls of the Meiji Emperor and his empress. In 1931, just days before Kanō made their debut at the Kōshien championships, the Intercity Tournament featured fifteen teams from throughout the empire, including the colonial outposts Dairen, Seoul, and Taihoku. The Taiwanese capital was represented by a team from the Taihoku Transportation Department, who reached the semifinals before falling to the eventual champions from Tokyo.[51] This team, however, consisted solely of ethnic Japanese residents of Taihoku, a fact that made this team totally uninteresting to the Japanese public. The Intercity Tournament was (and remains today) a major event in Japan's baseball culture, but there is no evidence that the Tokyo public cared a whit about this home islander (and nonsavage) team from Taiwan. Taihoku Transportation's dominant victories over Seoul's Ryūyama (Yongsan) Railroad Team and the All-Osakans held no social or colonial significance for the public. These games had no resonance with larger issues or crises as did the Kanō triumphs. Where the latter performances fit perfectly within, and even helped to write by themselves, a happy and fulfilling ending to the colonial crisis of the time, the Taihoku Transportation appearances were just baseball games.

In 1931, if the half-savage Kanō team had beat the poster boys from Aichi in central Japan, it may have been too much for even the most enthusiastic colonizer to accept. But a hard-fought loss in the championship game—one that allowed the Taiwanese to exhibit all the properly Japanese values of sacrifice and teamwork, to be (in Scruggs's words, see chapter 1) "virtual Japanese"[52] while not defeating the *real* Japanese—was the perfect ending for this first post-Musha national tournament. It is for this reason that this 1931 Kanō team is still a popular nostalgic symbol in today's Japan. The Kanō legend lives on because just months after the horrible massacre at Musha, this team of "assimilated" Han, Aboriginal, and Japanese players were able to use the modern opportunities provided by the Japanese state to transform themselves into imperial subjects. Of course, the irony is that the six Taiwanese players on the starting roster probably also saw their victories as a statement of Taiwanese (Han or Aborigine, "not Chinese and not Japanese") will and skill that could no longer be dismissed by the Japanese colonizing power. But the fact that this Kanō triumph could be understood in such very different ways is merely proof of the important and liminal position that baseball held in colonial Taiwan.

Another comparison to the British colonial history of cricket is useful here. Just two years after this Kanō moment, in 1933, the West Indies cricket team toured England under the captaincy of a white Cambridge graduate. The West Indian stay there was marked both by publicly voiced suspicion of their "black" bad manners and of their colonial timidity. Then, in a rhetorical move of great hypocrisy, English reporters criticized the West Indians for their unsportsmanlike use of "bodyline" bowling—throwing at the batsmen in order to neutralize their batting skills—a tactic that the English side themselves had perfected just months earlier in defeating Australia.[53] One does not have to buy into the vain discourse of Japan's superior brand of colonialism—which focused on the natural "racial" affinities between them and their Asian colonial populations—in order to see that their Taiwanese cosubjects filled a very different ideological purpose. Again, the crisis of 1931 meant that Japanese could not afford to mock the Taiwanese; instead, the collective anxiety about the fate of the empire required the constant celebration of unity played out so skillfully at the 1931 Kōshien tournament.

The Kanō moment of self-conscious, and even desperate, public participation in the official colonial discourse of *dōka* (assimilation) also allows us to reconsider recent historiography on Japanese Taiwan. Leo Ching's explication of this ideology— the mission to assimilate into Japanese subject-citizenship these formerly benighted Taiwanese—is the most elegant. He concludes that "the possibility of *dōka* lies precisely in its impossibility, in its continuous *deferment* of its materialization." That is to say, while even liberals of the time remarked convincingly on the artificiality of trying to transplant some Japanese "essence" in others, this goal of proving the unique Japanese ability of colonizing Taiwan (and indeed all of Asia) was too tempting to abandon. Therefore, as Ching describes, the ideology of *dōka* is best understood as a "problematic of the colonizer," where every failure of assimilation was experienced as a failure of the Japanese regime.[54] The exploits of the 1931 Kanō team, performed within the important frame of the "national game" of baseball, allow us to see these Japanese fears about their empire at a moment when the bloody Musha uprising had left the public feeling quite vulnerable.[55] Baseball made for a uniquely safe zone for the contemplation of competition, racial rivalries, and the fate of Japan's empire. The recognition of the second-place young men from far-off Kagi is as fine an illustration as there is of the pure relief that this time, assimilation had succeeded.

Between the years 1931 and 1936, Kanō would send five teams to the Kōshien high school championships in Japan, but none had the cultural impact of the iconic 1931 team. The 1935 team, led by Amis Aborigine pitcher Higashi Kumon (later known in Chinese as Lan Deming) came the closest to matching their success. Higashi's arrival at Kanō is usually explained in one of two ways. The simplest is that he was recruited to the school to follow in the footsteps of his older brother Higashi Kazuichi (or Lan Dehe), the starting catcher for the 1931 team. The costly cross-island trip and tuition were funded by a scholarship from the Taitō prefectural government, once again proving the thoroughness of these eastern regions' commitment to making their name via the Japanese national game of baseball. More romantic and nostalgic writers, Japanese and Chinese alike, however, prefer to emphasize the more novelistic and colonial-idealized elements of his life: His preternatural "submarine" (literally *andāsurō*, "underthrow") pitching motion was honed as a child throwing rocks at birds trying to steal his fisherman father's catch. He was then picked up by the local sugar company team, only to have his unique abilities discovered by a local Japanese innkeeper, who personally escorted him across the island to prosper at the baseball powerhouse that was Kanō.[56]

Higashi/Lan's story is also usually told in a tragic mode, for several reasons. He was the team's best player and starting pitcher—dubbed *Kaiwan* (literally "fantastic arm," but more typically "remarkable ability") by the Japanese media—when Kanō reached the Kōshien quarterfinals in 1935.[57] But somehow this legendary player doomed his team by botching a steal of home in the ninth inning and then balking in the winning run in the tenth inning.[58] The next day, famed writer Tobita immortalized Higashi in the *Asahi Shimbun* by lamenting the pitcher's balk as a "tragic ending [at which] we the audience could only sigh." He sought "to comfort the Kanō team" by reminding them that "the will of Heaven" was at work, and concluded that "only pitcher Higashi's spirit of struggle can be blamed, and the crowd who loved the entire team's mastery cried tears of sympathy [for them]."[59] The trope of tragedy in Higashi's life is developed further by pointing out that the Tokyo Giants, so impressed with his showing at Kōshien, twice sent representatives to Taiwan to ask him to join their team in 1936. Perhaps since this was the first year of Japanese professional baseball, Higashi did not understand the chance for fame and fortune he was passing up; instead, he went home to work for his home Taitō Prefecture out of gratitude for their earlier support.[60]

Forty years later, historian Suzuki Akira interviewed Higashi (now Lan) for his ruminations on Aborigine history, *Dedicated to the Takasago People*. The seventh chapter was titled, "The glory of Kōshien, the present reality of pitcher Higashi." Suzuki emphasized the tragic gap between Higashi's nationwide fame as a young

Aborigine pitcher under the Japanese and Lan's present reality in Chinese Nationalist-ruled Taiwan, where he worked as a poor janitor at a Taipei elementary school for a monthly salary equivalent to ¥25,000 (US$85). Lan's new wife tells Suzuki that long before she married the former star, she always admired him: "Even though he was Amis [Aborigine], he was the most handsome man in Taiwan." But still, the story is a tragic one: after thirty degrading years in KMT-ruled Taiwan, Lan reflects pitifully (but perhaps satisfyingly for Suzuki's purposes) on all he had as a colonial subject: "Shit, I used to be Japanese."[61]

It is in such ways that the history of Japanese Taiwan can be told in the clearly ahistorical mode of "tragedy." Hans Gumbrecht, in his brilliant work *In 1926*, claims that a discourse of tragedy expresses "nothing but an elementary unwillingness to discuss guilt or responsibility at all."[62] This begs the question, then, of why both Taiwanese and Japanese authors over the last several decades insist on this ideologically loaded type of voice. Revisionist work like that of right-wing cartoonist Kobayashi Yoshinori—namely, his use of images of Taiwanese gratitude for the fifty-year colonial era in order to posit nationalist critiques of a weak Japan today—is well-known.[63] This discourse becomes more problematic when we see contemporary Taiwanese authors celebrating a similar nostalgic discourse.

In 1997 the alumni magazine for National Chiayi University, Kanō's current incarnation, published its first issue, packed with articles about its proud baseball tradition. The head of the school's alumni association penned one piece, joyfully relating how Japanese newspapers and television programs today still hold up the Kanō teams as "an example for the younger generation of how to withstand bitterness and endure hard work."[64] One such television broadcast was made in 1996 by both TV Tokyo and Mainichi Broadcasting System, who visited the secluded mountain home of Tuo Hongshan, the former Kanō star who left baseball and education to become a Christian missionary. A photograph from the broadcast shows the eighty-eight-year-old Tuo and his eighty-four-year-old former teammate Su Zhengsheng hamming it up for the benefit of their visitors, posing in batting stances with umbrellas on a dirt path in front of Tuo's home.[65] In the end, these mutually constitutive Taiwanese and Japanese discourses—of "tragedy" in Japan's rule of Taiwan, and of pride in the former colonial masters' condescension toward the island—eventually tell us as much about "nativist" or "anti-Chinese" politics in Taiwan today as they do about these standout 1930s Kanō baseball teams. Yet any reckoning of the Japanese era must account for these colonial ideologies that still strongly inform the Taiwanese postcolonial.

In 2002, Taiwan's National Council on Physical Fitness and Sports produced a documentary on Kanō and Japanese-era baseball in general. "Legend and Glory" opened with a vivid example of how the postcolonial can redefine notions of both "Taiwanese" and "Japanese." Su Zhengsheng, eighty-nine years of age and fit in his spotless Kanō uniform, sang the official team anthem for a school function in 2001.

Arms swinging rhythmically as they did seventy years earlier, Su sang with vigor about the pride and diligence learned at his alma mater. The last two lines saw him substitute Chinese pronunciations of two Japanese compound words. But if this hinted at some ethnic Chinese pride creeping into his memories of the colonial period, this notion was quickly erased when he skipped ahead to the coda. Where players once shouted "Kanō, Kanō, *pure pure pure* [play, play, play]," Su belted out "*Dahe, Dahe,* play, play, play." And *Dahe?* Merely the Chinese pronunciation of the Japanese *Yamato*—the racialized term used in World War II to express the notion of a pure and militaristic Japanese people.[66]

Su had been a successful Japanese subject—and the memory of this status clearly was dear to him—but this departure from the colonial script also shows reflection on this loss, his own loss, and the loss of this now-despised Yamato mission. Japan's "imperialism of sameness," to use Ts'ai's term,[67] as mighty an ideological construct as it had once been, could only ever be transient, could only ever have produced mixed legacies of shame and nostalgia for the power it had promised. Su's performance and the haunting hybridity of which he sang in 2001 takes us directly to the heart of the Taiwanese postcolonial. Indeed, it is hard to imagine a more compellingly conflicted performance of the Taiwanese experience under Japanese colonialism, or one that captures more poignantly the rich and complex nature of baseball's role in this history.

BASEBALL AND TAIWAN IN THE JAPANESE EMPIRE

Besides the exploits of these famed teams, however, there was much happening in baseball in 1930s Taiwan that allows us to understand more fully the dimensions of Taiwanese-Japanese identity and aspirations. Indeed, some of these expressions were even formulated as an explicit rejection of the colonial regime's assimilationist fetish. As mentioned in chapter 1, Han-ethnic Taiwanese teams in the southern city of Takao (Gaoxiong) established their own Takasago Baseball League in 1931. These players, who did not enjoy access to the schools and corporations that sponsored official baseball teams, likely were sustained by this sarcastic and symbolic rejection of imperial rhetoric of inclusion.[68]

For the most part, however, baseball maintained a virtually hegemonic grasp on Taiwanese imaginations of modern identity and culture. There was no analogue in colonial Taiwan to Ireland's culture of "Gaelic games," sports valued largely for their difference from British games, and codified in the late nineteenth century as specifically Irish by the anticolonial Gaelic Athletic Association.[69] An institution like "Gaelic games," meant to set Irish men apart from British and colonial modes of masculinity,[70] would not have made sense in Taiwan. Japanese rule was so thoroughly associated with modernity, efficiency, and progress that only a Japanese game, like baseball, could function in narrating a uniquely Han or Aborigine manhood under Japanese rule. There likewise was no Taiwanese counterpart to the mainland Chinese cult of *guoshu*, or "national [martial] arts," formulated during the Nanjing Decade (1927–1937) as a uniquely Chinese sport, uniquely qualified to strengthen Chinese bodies and minds against imperialist enemies.[71]

We must remember, however, that the Taiwanese did not share this Irish or mainland Chinese obsession with *embodying* the nation and race in defiance of a powerful enemy. The most important popular movements in interwar Taiwan were not about independence, but about achieving fuller inclusion as Japanese subject-citizens. These most active elites under Japanese rule were truly Fanon's "partisans of . . . the new order."[72] Likewise, the extent of a "Taiwanese consciousness" during this period consisted mostly of the choice to see oneself as a Taiwanese subject of the Japanese Empire.[73] (As Tay-sheng Wang has explained, this is due also to the fact that the colonial government used the threat of Emergency Ordinance No. 24 of 1898, the "Bandit Punishment Law," to "terror[ize]" any who would rebel directly against Japanese rule.)[74] The Chinese and Irish-style insistence on difference through masculine physical exertion simply would have had no place in colonial Taiwan.

Tracing these marks of the colonial inscribed on 1930s Taiwanese baseball illustrates the totalizing nature of this cultural realm. Peng Ming-min would later trade his baseball mitt for the pen, enduring much sacrifice as he led the struggle for Taiwanese self-determination and independence during the Chinese Nationalist era. But as a boy in 1930s Takao, young Peng was the typical Taiwanese schoolboy obsessed with baseball. In a conversation with me in 1999, Peng fondly remembered huddling around the radio with his brother to listen to colonial broadcasts of the Japanese high school championships at Kōshien every spring. In his memoir *A Taste of Freedom,* Peng recalled: "By this time I was an ardent baseball fan. When Babe Ruth visited Japan I boldly wrote a letter to him and in return received his autograph, which became my treasure. . . . [I] reserved my greatest enthusiasm for baseball. Our school masters took baseball very seriously, treating it almost as if it were a military training program. Although I was a poor batter, I was an excellent fielder, and played on our team when it won a citywide championship. Needless to say, my Babe Ruth autograph gave me great prestige among my classmates."[75] Peng later lost this valuable souvenir in the wreckage of Tokyo in 1945,[76] but his enthusiasm was typical for millions of young colonial subjects like him.

One of the key sites for integration of the empire through baseball was the Intercity Baseball Tournament played at the Meiji Jingu Stadium, as mentioned in the previous section. The first tournament was held in 1927 with twelve competing teams, including a squad from Seoul and the eventual champion Mantetsu Railroad Black Lions from Dairen, a port leased from the Chinese government. In 1930, the year before Taiwan sent a team to Kōshien, a team from the Transportation Department in Taihoku represented the colony at the Intercity Tournament. In a vivid illustration of how baseball enabled often seamless movement across colonial geography and served notions of imperial integration, the Taihoku team featured a star Japanese pitcher who had played for the Seoul team in this tournament just the year before.[77]

Other Japanese social elites, if not suited to this level of empire-wide competition, still made important use of baseball to lay claim to their status as agents of the colonial mission. Takemura Toyotoshi, in his 1933 *History of Sports in Taiwan,* lists several contemporary leagues constituted on the basis of modern or colonial occupations: a Taihoku Printers Baseball League with eight teams, a Finance Men Baseball League, a Central Taiwan Railroad Workers League, and an Islandwide Postal Workers League. Most telling in the associations between elite status and a modern identity was the Free Men *(jiyūjin)* Baseball League, founded in 1932 and featuring teams like the Doctors, Reporters, Defense Lawyers, Pharmacists, and Dentists.[78]

In October and November of 1935, the colonial regime put on a spectacular Taiwan Exposition Commemorating Forty Years of [Japanese] Rule *(Shisei yonju shunen kinen Taiwan hakurankai)* at Taihoku. The exposition featured exhibits on everything colonial and modern, from disease prevention, flight, forest reclamation, and the Taiwan pineapple, sugar, and camphor industries to Korean customs and a radio-controlled animatronic Momotaro the Peach Boy. After years of demonstration of Aborigine excellence in baseball, the racial hierarchy that governed this "assimilated" colony was exhibited in the popular Gallery of Savage Peoples *(banzoku sankōkan),* featuring 6,450 Aborigines in various states of "savage" undress and daily life.[79]

The exposition would not have been complete without an athletic meet, featuring a Taiwan-Korea-Manchukuo Baseball Challenge Tournament.[80] The Manchurian puppet state was represented by a team from Dairen, the seaport city that was a main focus of Japanese sporting efforts.[81] The *Taiwan Nichinichi Shimpō* reported excitedly about the visit, describing in lengthy articles that the Dairen team had recently played the famed Tokyo Giants in Fukuoka, and that the squad would be arriving in Taiwan aboard the *Hōraimaru* accompanied by famous legal, meteorological, and natural gas experts also coming to join the exposition.[82] Besides the round-robin tourney at the exposition, these (all-Japanese) squads from Korea and Manchuria also toured Taiwan, making this display of the achievements of imperialism available to baseball fans all over the island. Thus, baseball was also imagined as one of many crucial technologies for the maintenance of an assimilated, competitive, and fit empire.

The notion of integration is also illustrated by the Hōsei University baseball team's visits to Taiwan in the early 1930s. Hōsei University, one of the Tokyo Six Universities and a traditional baseball power, was known for its beautiful wooded campus that adjoined the Yasukuni Shrine, the primary national shrine for Japan's war dead. In 1931, the publishers of the *Taiwan Nichinichi Shimpō* invited this prestigious squad to play several school, bureaucratic, and all-star teams throughout Taiwan.

Perfecting this symbolic (and profitable) unity of the metropole and the colony was the fact that the Hōsei team included Amis Aborigine brothers Itō Jirō and Itō Masao—two of the four members of eastern Taiwan's "savage Team Nōkō" who stayed on in Japan after their famed 1925 visit. Now, it was not just the Taichū all-stars, the Railroad Bureau, and the famed Kanō school teams getting to go head-to-head against the proud representative of the Japanese imperial game, but a popular experience that seemed to confirm the many layers of Taiwan's true integration into the empire.[83]

The most solemn use of baseball to invoke the imperial cause was the series of islandwide amateur and interscholastic baseball tournaments held as official dedications to the Kenkō Shintō Shrine (Kenkō jinja) between 1933 to 1942. The Japanese regime built over two hundred shrines in Taiwan, all dedicated to different deities, emperors, princes, and war dead. The Kenkō Shrine, a beautiful, lush, sprawling complex, was completed in 1928, the first shrine dedicated expressly to the 16,805 Japanese souls martyred in the conquest of Taiwan some three decades earlier.[84] Colonial memories of conquest and fantasies of "equal treatment under the emperor" clearly were incongruous; popular baseball and rugby tournaments (the latter actually held there first, during the year of the shrine's completion)[85] were an effective method in obscuring the tensions inherent in such a religio-militaristic presence.

The land occupied by the Kenkō Shrine, filled as it was by majestic structures, solemn pathways, torii gates, lush gardens, lakes, and bridges, however, allowed no physical space for such a compensatory sporting maneuver. The games themselves were held at Maruyama Field, built near the grounds of the Taiwan Shrine (Taiwan jinja), the highest ranking Shintō shrine in Taiwan, built in 1923 for Crown Prince Hirohito's visit to Taiwan. This sacred site had been dedicated in 1901 to Prince Kitashirakawa Yoshihisa (who died of dysentery and malaria during the 1895 invasion), the three deities of cultivation, and Amaterasu the sun goddess—although American naval officer and scholar George Kerr described it as more "a political symbol of imperial Japanese rule . . . constructed at grievous cost to the Formosan people, a 'conqueror's shrine.' "[86]

Thus, the many baseball tournaments held at the shrine between 1933 and 1942 provide a chance to see the liminal intersection between these very different but equally effective modes of colonial cultural rule. Baseball and rugby teams from the Takao All-Stars to famed school powers like Kanō and Taihoku Commercial School[87] took part in these yearly sacred sporting tournaments that exposed the contradictions in the wartime program of "imperialization" (or kōminka, literally, "imperial-subjectification"). How would culture—be it a conquering state religion or a game brought to Meiji Japan by American PE teachers—enable Taiwanese people to become true subjects of the Japanese Empire? Was it clear to all that in a time of total war, as was the case by 1937, a program of assimilation would not be enough to guarantee that the ethnic Chinese majority would support the "right" side? Could the intervention of the souls of Prince Kitashirakawa and the other 16,804 soldiers-made-deities residing in the Kenkō Shrine provide for a safer imperial bet?

KŌMINKA, TOTAL WAR
AND THE IMPERIAL GAME

Initiating justice through victory,
Raising my head to don the righteous crown of laurel,
I wait to stand up and take my spear
And save the degraded and muddied world.

TAINAN FIRST HIGH SCHOOL BASEBALL TEAM ANTHEM, 1934

During the 1920s and 1930s, an official system of "local autonomy" ensured more low-level official control by Japanese colonists and Taiwanese elites. In 1935, local elections were held, with suffrage extended to the 3.3 percent of the population (Japanese or Taiwanese) who had paid taxes of five yen or higher and who could write the name of their favorite candidate.[88]

These expanded rights for Taiwanese as Japanese subjects would soon be accompanied by additional responsibilities as well, with the beginning of Japan's total war against China in 1937. The colonial regime undertook the forcible de-Sinicization of Taiwan's ethnic Chinese majority, to be replaced by pure imperial Japanese culture in the intense movement to create imperial subjects (*kōminka undō*). In order to mobilize true Japanese sentiments during wartime, for example, the use of the national language was pushed even harder. Chinese-language sections of newspapers were eliminated, the Taiwanese dialect was forbidden on public buses, and the government even unveiled a public campaign to "sweep away non-Japanese speakers."[89]

Any "un-Japanese" cultural institution could be suppressed during the *kōminka* movement—Taiwanese Buddhist temples were transformed into official Shintō shrines and traditional puppet theater was banned, as was the wearing of traditional Chinese clothing in public.[90] In Leo Ching's words, *kōminka* "constituted a colonial *objectification* by forcefully turning a project into practice, by rendering the ideal into the material." Now the onus of this transformation would be on Taiwanese subjects themselves: "Becoming Japanese became the sole responsibility of the colonized."[91]

An example of this new colonial reality can be seen in the way that the *kōminka* campaign intersected with the 1936 founding of the professional Japanese Baseball League. A common wartime slogan referred to the power of Japan's populace as "one hundred million balls of fire," even though the population of Japan proper was only seventy million; the presence of another flaming thirty million depended on Taiwanese and Korean self-transformation into true imperial subjects.[92] The professional baseball league provided an important opportunity for this conversion at the precise moment that war called for visible examples of Taiwanese imperial subjects.

The greatest of these balls of fire was Wu Bo, a contributor to the great Kanō school baseball tradition described earlier. An athletic wunderkind as a youngster, Wu was recruited by Olympic gold-medal track star Nanbu Chuhei to attend Japan's famous Waseda University. Wu decided to stay at home in Kagi, attending Kanō and starring on their 1935 and 1936 championship teams. After graduating, he signed with the proud Tokyo Giants baseball team in 1937, just as this new imperial program of *kōminka* was inaugurated. Wu, known in Japan as Go Ha (the Sino-Japanese reading of Wu Bo), played for the Giants for seven years, acquiring the esteemed nickname "the Human Locomotive" *(ningen kikansha)* for his rare speed and power. In 1943 Wu took the Japanese name Go Shōsei, keeping the same surname, pronounced Go in Japanese, but notably (despite the nationalistic pressures of wartime) resisting the native Japanese *kun* reading of Kure.

Go led the Japanese Baseball League in runs, hits, and batting average and was named league MVP that year. However, after that season he left the Giants, never playing another game for them. One author has offered an explanation for his unlikely departure that suggests the limits of *kōminka*. The late Gao Zhengyuan wrote in 1994 that when the Giants traveled to Manchukuo after the 1943 season to rally Japanese troops stationed there, Go refused to go with the team, giving the Japanese baseball community an unacceptably impolite reminder of his ethnic Chinese identity.[93] However, I have not been able to corroborate this story, and several facts make it unlikely. In 1940 the Giants, along with the other eight teams in the JBL, played a seventy-two-game Manchuria Summer League schedule as they toured the huge puppet state.[94] Go started in the Giants outfield on that wartime tour, making it hard to understand why a similar tour three years later would be so objectionable. Go was also known for leading player blood drives for Japanese troops during the war,[95] and after leaving the Giants in 1943 he took an even more proper Japanese name (Ishii Masayuki) for the remainder of the wartime period. I have located no other explanation of Go's split with the Giants,[96] although Gao's account raises vivid historical possibilities as to the role of Taiwanese players in the crisis of late–World War II Japan. Whatever the reasons for his leaving, it seems not to have been scarring for either Go or the Japanese baseball community. After leaving the Giants in 1943, he went on to play for thirteen more years with the Hanshin Tigers and Mainichi Orions, and stayed in Japan for the rest of his life after his career was over. In 1995 he became the first Taiwanese player inducted (as a Giant, incidentally) to the Japanese Baseball Hall of Fame.[97]

Wu Xinheng, another Kanō product, played in Japan under the names Go Shintei (again, the Sino-Japanese reading of his original name) and the *kōminka*-inspired and more "truly" Japanese name Hagiwara Hiroshi. Wu played nine years for the Yamato Baseball Club and the Tokyo/Yomiuri Giants, playing in three all-star games along the way.[98] There were Taiwan Aborigine standouts in the Japanese leagues as well, reminding the Japanese baseball public that Aborigines had been a part of this national culture now for more than a decade. Itō Jirō (Luo Daohou) of the famed "Savage Team Nōkō" played for the Tokyo Senators from 1936 to 1939. Okamura Toshiaki (Ye Tiansong), another Amis star, played for the Nankai franchise from 1939 to 1949.

In general, corporeal methods of training—not just changing names and speaking Japanese—seem to have become an important part of the kōminka movement. Hui-yu Caroline Ts'ai, in her work on wartime mobilization, has described the role of militaristic physical training, labeled "drilling to become imperial subjects" (kōmin rensei).[99] And records from the governor-general's office from 1941 to 1943 show explicit government encouragement of sumo wrestling among Taiwan's Aborigine population for the purposes of inspiring a more authentic understanding of the Japanese essence.[100] However, even though baseball was not envisioned as a game that could directly offer martial instruction, baseball clearly retained a powerful resonance with the notion of the uniquely Japanese essence and spirit that one could only but learn from the game.

Despite the incredible ravages and pressures of wartime, much seemed to stay the same within the Taiwan baseball community. Teams representing Taiwan cities (and now including some Taiwanese players) joined the aforementioned Intercity Baseball Tournament, which was held through 1942.[101] Semipro teams stayed active for most of the war; in 1943 the Monopoly Bureau won a bidding war for the nineteen-year-old Kanō graduate Hong Taishan, having to guarantee a salary of sixty-eight yen per month, as well as a prized tobacco and alcohol sales license for his family, to acquire his talents.[102] And the various shrine tournaments, including a High School Baseball Tournament Dedicated to the Taiwanese Martyrs' Shrine (Gokoku jinja hōnō chūtō gakkō yakyū taikai), continued through 1942.[103]

Baseball took on new modes of nationalistic and practical use as well. In 1940, as part of the empire-wide celebration of the two thousand and six hundredth anniversary of the mythical founding of Japan, the central city of Taichū (Taizhong) hosted an eight-team Islandwide High School Baseball Tournament to Commemorate Two Thousand and Six Hundred Years of the [Japanese] Era (Kigen nisen roppyaku nen hōshuku zentō chūtō gakkō yakyū taikai).[104] This type of ideological background would have added even more solemnity and gravity to the national game. As the war went on, baseball became more instrumental to the nationalistic cause. By 1943, the only mention of baseball in the media (even though it had survived at the popular level) had to do with games played to provide entertainment and condolences for wounded military personnel (imon yakyū taikai). Reports came in throughout that year telling of baseball teams playing such "sympathy calls" to

"white-robed warriors" *(hakui no yūshi)* recuperating in military hospitals from Taihoku to Tainan to Heitō (Pingdong) in the southwest.[105]

But affairs in the baseball community, like the plight of the empire in general,
were growing grimmer. In 1943, Maruyama Field, the premier field in Taihoku, was
turned into a triage center for the military.[106] Tainan's municipal baseball field was
turned into a potato field.[107] And the next year, as the *Taiwan Nichinichi Shimpō*'s
last ever article about baseball mentioned, the city of Heitō had to plow under their
field in hopes of recuperating the estimated thirty-one thousand kilograms of grain
the land could produce.[108] As wartime conditions became more and more desperate, the residents of Taiwan would have to shoulder the burdens of war and colonialism without the assimilating, nationalizing, and socializing game of baseball.

THE LEGACY OF "EQUAL TREATMENT"

Orphan of Asia, Wu Zhuoliu's classic novel of colonial identity and alienation, ends
with the protagonist Hu Taiming going mad, screaming at others (but clearly im-
plicating himself):

> Fool!
> You say you're a compatriot,
> But you're just a hound,
> Imperial errand-boy,
> Exemplary youth,
> Exemplary arbitrator,
> Praiseworthy teacher,
> Hah!
> Fool![109]

The sorry end of Japan's occupation of Taiwan, marked as it was by the physical,
mental, and social degradations of war, brought out a much more self-critical narrative of life under Japanese colonialism than ever before. While promising equality, the *kōminka* movement could now be seen as a "vicious" policy bringing the
"annihilation of cultural differences."[110] Shocked at the extremes to which their colonial protectors would exploit the Taiwanese people and land, many residents of the
island looked forward to the arrival of the victorious Chinese Nationalists. But as
we will see in following chapters, baseball was a unique realm where Taiwanese
people could hold on to and speak openly about the more positive contributions
made during the fifty years of Japanese rule.

Though the sport functioned for the first twenty-five years of colonial rule as a
marker of Japanese exclusivity and superiority, baseball during the 1920s and '30s
became an important point of mediation with ideas of modernity and of Japanese
subjecthood. Taiwan did not just produce an elite class of standout baseball players. The sport became popular at all levels, making baseball the dominant sport in

the colony as it was in the home islands of Japan. Baseball allowed the colonized Taiwanese, as Said has written of "native intellectuals" in other settings, to work within the constraints of the system in order to "liberate their energies from the oppressing cultural matrix that produced them."[111]

Indeed, this physical realm of baseball was one fraught with many tensions and contradictions; participation in Japan's "national game" allowed Taiwanese people to prove and live their acculturation into the colonial order at the very moment that their baseball successes worked to subvert it.[112] Baseball was a liminal realm, where the Japanese exclusion of Taiwanese teams or players would have given the lie to Japan's entire colonial enterprise. Taiwanese subjects, both Chinese and Aborigine, could use Japanese-taught baseball skills and customs to appeal for equal treatment within the national framework. And in the case of Taiwan's Austronesian Aborigine population, the centrality of "savage governance" to colonial ideology—and of baseball in addressing these colonial desires and fears—makes it clear just how crucial these peoples (despite their small numbers in terms of population) really were to the history of baseball in Japanese Taiwan. Without their presence in the resource-rich mountain areas, it is entirely possible to imagine a Taiwan where baseball was merely a *game*, like rugby or tennis.

Finally, the contemporary nostalgic and ideological power of the Kanō legacy of "triracial cooperation" *(sanzu gonghe)* is worthy of comment. Today, Kanō serves unanimously as the face of Japanese-era baseball in Taiwan, but this "triracial" arrangement was very atypical during this time. The great majority of school baseball teams in that period were from either all-Japanese primary schools or all-Taiwanese public elementary schools, while high school teams of a dozen or more youth may have included one Taiwanese player. None of the prestigious high schools fielding competitive teams could ever have had so many Taiwanese and Aborigine players. Ultimately, this memory of pan–East Asian cross-racial cooperation ends up obscuring much more violence and inequality than it illuminates in specific instances like this, where imperialist ideology could be directly strengthened by isolated cases of equal access. Thus, this troubling fact in turn suggests that much of the history of Taiwan's "national game" is remembered largely in terms colored by Taiwan's half-century of oppressive Nationalist Chinese rule and a resulting nostalgia for the "good old days" as a Japanese colony.

This gratitude for the Japanese legacy of "equal treatment" under the emperor has been revived and employed in both Taiwan and Japan, after 1945 and up until the present day, albeit under very different political conditions. But it is worth ending this chapter with one story of genuine bonds forged through the national game in Japanese Taiwan. In 2006, an eighty-two-year-old Japanese man named Konno Tadao decided to act on his longtime love for the 1941–42 Kanō baseball squad. He wrote to the Tokyo Broadcasting System, asking if they could help locate his old hero, the Taiwanese slugger Hong Taishan. Konno was born in Taiwan and attended Taihoku Industrial School, itself a baseball power, but had always admired the more storied (and ideologically significant) Kanō teams. Some sixty-four years after watching Hong play, Konno was able to meet his idol when TBS flew the eighty-two-year-old Hong to Japan for what Taiwan's *Liberty Times* called a "tearful reunion."[113] Now, Konno meeting his old idol was no more of a "reunion" that it would be for me to meet Henry Aaron or Jim Rice. But the hierarchies that this language betrays—as does the idea that an elderly baseball fan could have a childhood hero delivered to him almost on demand—remind us of the power that these decades-old affections of Taiwanese baseball retain still.

3

Early Nationalist Rule, 1945–1967

"There's no Mandarin in baseball"

Why is it that Japanese is a bad thing? It is because it has been armoured. But once the armour is removed and it reverts to its original state, then Japanese is not bad at all. In this disarmed condition, it can serve the positive function of cultural transmission because many cultural works of the world have been translated into Japanese. . . . A culture expressed in Japanese is not necessarily a Japanese culture.

WU ZHUOLIU, "AN OPINION ON THE ABOLITION OF JAPANESE," 1946

Baseball in Taiwan actually dates to 1948.

FREE CHINA REVIEW, 1992

In late 1945, the Chinese Nationalist Party (Guomindang or KMT) took the reins of Taiwan's government. In order to achieve a true Chinese "Retrocession" (*Guangfu,* literally, "Glorious Return"),[1] the Nationalists set about stripping Taiwanese culture of its Japanese legacies while simultaneously restoring an essential and timeless "Chineseness," which the Taiwanese people presumably had been longing for for half a century. That these "Chinese traditions" were in fact quite recent Nationalist inventions—which by definition could not have been part of a Taiwanese consciousness before 1945—hardly seemed to matter.

Few arriving in Taiwan as part of the Nationalist diaspora understood how difficult this transformation was going to be. In his self-published autobiography, Taiwan's famed baseball coach Jian Yongchang included a photo of fifty-five students with their still-beloved Japanese teachers taken on 28 October 1945, two and a half months after Japan's surrender in World War II.[2] The Taiwanese, who were still grateful to and fond of their Japanese teachers, peers, and neighbors, could not have understood the weight of the Nationalist grudge against the vanquished Japanese enemy. Policies of "de-Taiwanization" were enforced, officially degrading any distinctively Taiwanese customs. Hsu Chung Mao has written on official programs of decolonization *(qu zhiminhua)*, such as the mass changing of street and geographical names, the conversion of all public civic meeting halls *(kōkaidō)* to Sun Yat-sen halls *(Zhongshantang)*, and the outlawing of Japanese *geta* sandals and Japanese speech in schools.[3]

These policies were designed not only to cut the colonial links to Japan, but also to nip in the bud any heretical links between a culturally distinctive and politically separate Taiwan.[4] They were even applied to the baseball realm; the Japanese stigma that the game carried in the late 1940s was so potent that many Guomindang-fearing school administrators were not willing to accept the presence of a baseball team on their campuses.[5]

The glocalized relationship, negotiated in complicated dialectical patterns over decades, between Japan's modern "national sport" and the Japanese imperial subjects of Taiwan, was incomprehensible to the official one-dimensional Nationalizing discourse. After arriving in Taiwan, the KMT and other recent mainland immigrants associated with the party seldom failed to describe themselves as "victors" over the Japanese, and by easy extension, over the Taiwanese. The Taiwanese people, in contrast, were portrayed as shameless collaborators, a "degraded people" lacking the heroic instincts of their mainland cousins[6]—indeed, simply "children" compared to the more worldly population of the ROC proper.[7] One mainstream ROC media report on Taiwanese athletes described them as confused and disoriented by the "slave life" they had led for the past half a century.[8] In 1945, the party's Taiwan Investigation Committee could only recommend that "after the takeover the cultural policy should be focused on promoting national consciousness and eradicating the slave mentality."[9]

Taiwanese intellectuals tried to fight this characterization, hoping to critique the new Chinese government for creating such silly hierarchies in the newly reunified Republic of China, and even to get proper credit for having learned about capitalist democracy under the Japanese![10] However, these were not terms that were going to win the argument. The Nationalist perspective, drawn from a combination of victorious swagger and a historical understanding of Chinese culture as a fundamentally assimilative force,[11] could not grasp that, as Martin Sökefeld has explained, "systems of colonization inscribe their marks so deeply . . . that they cannot simply be eradicated by the political act of declaring independence."[12]

During the first year of transition, the official newspaper *Taiwan New Life Times*, which had inherited the offices and printers of the Japanese *Nichinichi Shimpō*, included one Japanese page in their four-page daily for the convenience of their readership. But it must have seemed strange, if not infuriating, to have to explain the usefulness of sports to the future of the Chinese nation-race *in Japanese*, as did an article in April 1946.[13] After one year, the Nationalist government announced a ban on Japanese-language periodicals.[14] Although this effectively killed off the potential of an entire generation who had been schooled in Japanese, the government also began to confiscate items like records, publications, and flags in order to aid their mission of "eradicating" Japanese influence.[15] While the transition year indicates that the Nationalist regime took time to consider the effects of such a ban, the general state of popular discontent in Taiwan by the end of 1946 made it an easy decision to erase these trouble-making colonial remnants.

At the same time, however, state agents involved in Retrocession efforts also seemed to realize what a valuable exception baseball could be to the rule of destroying the defeated Japanese culture. For the past two decades, the Nationalist state had promoted physical culture in their attempts to nurture a strong and healthy Chinese populace and state on the mainland, indeed calling it the key to building a modern national consciousness, "throwing off once and for all the danger of [national] extinction."[16] Official endorsement of baseball soon became one method of officially "Sinicizing" a powerful and popular cultural realm that still represented a Pandora's box of colonial thinking and customs.

Some Nationalist sporting events seemed to pointedly not include baseball. In the first two days of October 1946, the newspaper *Minbao* advertised two southern athletic meets (in Tainan County and Gangshan Township, the latter of which held their meet "in front of the old Shintō Shrine *[shenshe]*"), neither of which featured a baseball competition.[17] And yet, many Taiwanese people worked to integrate baseball into Nationalist forms with seeming ease. Su Zhengsheng, the 1930s Kanō star cited so often in the previous chapter, quickly worked toward this goal, organizing a Three People's Principles Youth Corps Baseball Tournament soon after the Nationalists' arrival.[18]

Baseball was included at the First Taiwan Provincial Games, held in October 1946 at National Taiwan University. Twenty counties, cities, colleges, and government organizations sent baseball teams to this high-profile competition, eventually won by the Penghu County squad led by ex-Kanō slugger Hong Taishan. Generalissimo Chiang Kai-shek and his wife Song Meiling, visiting Taiwan for the first anniversary of Retrocession, attended the games personally.[19] The government clearly felt that it was crucial to put on such a meet, which was the first provincial competition to be held in all of the Republic of China since the outbreak of the war with Japan in 1937. There was much at stake; the *Minbao* stated: "The goal of the meet is to make the compatriots of all of Taiwan understand the importance of national/racial *(minzu)*[20] health—and not for the purpose of producing athletes for specific competitive events, which is the same and just as meaningless as circus performances."[21] To this end, the well-funded Provincial Police Command (Jingbei silingbu) spent the equivalent of two million Taiwan dollars (US$9,000) in gold to put on the meet.[22] (The literal-minded commander in charge of the meet wrote, thirty-three years later [!], that the ROC government would have to make sure that they had a proper budget for a similarly unifying athletic meet when they finally retook the mainland.)[23]

Chiang's official speech at the games started out on a note of joy. He described his happiness that Taiwan was returning to a state of freedom and equality in the Chinese motherland after fifty-one years [sic] under the iron heel of Japanese imperialism. But as he continued, Chiang's address took on a harder edge. He reminded the Taiwanese people that they were now masters of the nation—a privilege that came with responsibilities that had to be understood in order to strengthen a "Three People's Principles" nation and restore the classic virtues of the Chinese people.[24] But, as the newspapers had to report just six days later, a "vicious" fight on the soccer field between two unnamed teams showed the violence in Taiwanese society that ROC sports were still powerless to bring under control. When one player repeatedly kicked another player in the groin, both teams began fighting, only to be joined by members of the crowd. The melee only ended when soldiers began firing their guns into the air. To such a spectacle, judged by the *Minbao* to be a great "stain" on ROC sports culture, the newspaper could only remind people of the new order in Nationalist Taiwan—the need for absolute obedience, correct behavior, and the fact that the referee had absolute power.[25]

BASEBALL IN THE SHADOW OF 28 FEBRUARY

In general, the sense that baseball could be appropriate and useful to the Nationalist rule of Taiwan was growing. The Taipei city government had planned the first Mayor's Cup Baseball Tournament to take place in March 1947,[26] but at the last moment had to postpone this event. On the evening of 27 February 1947, several Guomindang agents beat up a forty-year-old widow for selling black market cigarettes. When word spread of the incident, pent-up Taiwanese anger at the Nationalist regime erupted in forms ranging from organized protests to premeditated violence against random mainland officials and soldiers. Protesters removed the characters for "China" from official and commercial signs, displayed Japanese-language banners that stated "Down With Military Tyranny," and chanted slogans in the Taiwanese language like "The Taiwanese want revenge now!" "Beat the mainlanders!" "Kill the pigs!" "Let Taiwan rule itself!" and "Let's have a new democracy!" Over the next four days, through 4 March, violence erupted throughout all of Taiwan's cities as the retribution for one original act of violence grew into a full-fledged urban uprising against Guomindang rule.[27] Over the next several months, the Nationalists systematically arrested and executed thousands of Taiwanese elites—professors, doctors, lawyers, professionals, college and even high school students—that they imagined to pose a threat to the regime. These killings, now known as the February 28 Massacre, began the era of "white terror" *(baise kongbu)* that lasted for decades under Nationalist rule.

It is telling that the baseball world was not able to escape this horror. Chen Gengyuan was a Puyuma Aborigine who had excelled for Kanō's "triracial squad" in the early 1930s under the Japanese name Uematsu Kōichi, and who then had the opportunity to study in Yokohama. As of 1946, by which time Taiwan's "triracial" balance had undergone a momentous shift, he was the new baseball coach at his alma mater, now renamed Taiwan Provincial Jiayi Agriculture Vocational School (Taiwan shengli Jiayi nongye zhiye xuexiao). When the violence of 28 February began, Chen was forced to flee Jiayi for his Taidong hometown in the remote southeastern coast, where he remained for the rest of his life. His team remained proud of this now-criminal Japanese heritage, however, retaining proudly the team logo "KANO" on their uniforms at tournaments all that autumn.[28] Lin Guixing, coach of the great Amis Aborigine Nōkō teams of the 1920s, was not as lucky as Chen. Lin was killed on 1 August 1947, during the violent and sustained cleansing of a generation of native Taiwanese leaders.[29]

A baseball tournament was held in Taiwan in August 1947, even as the wave of political murder continued. The Fudan University and Shanghai Pandas teams came across the straits to play against teams from Taipei, Taizhong, Taiwan Power, Taiwan Sugar, and Taiwan Coal, as if all was well in the Republic that bloody summer.[30] The Taiwan Coal team's trip to Shanghai that fall was another sign of how this Japanese game could be used to express Taiwan's position as an integral part of the Chinese motherland.[31]

However, baseball proved harder to Sinicize or nationalize than the Guomindang may have expected. The official name of the game changed virtually overnight, from *yakyū* to the more precise and nonideological Mandarin *bangqiu* ("bat-ball"). People actually playing the game would have been little affected by this, however; the Japanese name lives on as *ia-kiu* among many Taiwanese speakers even today. The on-field terminology of the game was unchanged, consisting of a jumble of English-Japanese-Taiwanese terms like *pitcha, kyatcha, homuran, sutoraiku,* and *a-u-to* (out) that hopelessly betrayed baseball's glocalized history. When I interviewed Coach Jian Yongchang in the summer of 2004, I asked him about Taipei baseball in the early ROC period, the pressures to speak Mandarin throughout society, and whether the large banks that sponsored baseball teams attempted to enforce any sort of language policy on the field. Mr. Jian looked at me blankly and explained, as if to a child, "There's no Mandarin in baseball" *(Bangqiu meiyou guoyu).*[32]

In 1949, a Taiwan Province Baseball Association (Taiwan sheng bangqiu xiehui) was formed, chaired by future ROC vice president Xie Dongmin, organizing annual provincial baseball tournaments at all levels of play.[33] Xie was a native Taiwanese who had lived in mainland China for twenty years, studying, working in journalism, and eventually becoming a major figure in wartime propaganda and political work.[34] Men like Xie—known to Taiwanese as "half-mountain people" *(banshanren,* for their loyalties to the mainland regime)—appeared inherently more reliable to the Guomindang in handling the dangerous realm of baseball, despite the fact that their extended tenure in China would mean profound unfamiliarity with the game.

Another similar personage was Zhang Wojun, a native Taiwanese scholar who was a major literary figure in Beijing/Beiping from the 1920s to the 1940s, and who was put in charge of the popular baseball team sponsored by Taiwan Cooperative Bank (Hezuo jinku) in the late 1940s. Zhang was very familiar with much of Japanese culture; he had lived under Japanese occupation in Beiping for eight years and had also translated from Japanese dozens of books and articles on poetry, leftist and realist literature, demography and sociology, and Marxism. Many Chinese who remained in enemy-held areas for this long came under suspicion for having been collaborators with the hated Japanese. But even with this stigma, and despite the fact that he had absorbed nothing about the game of baseball, Zhang's "half-mountain" status still qualified him to manage this potentially subversive game.[35] In this way, baseball fits in with other realms of government where KMT-loyal Taiwanese received explicit favoritism, to the increasing anger of the literate and professional Taiwanese population.[36]

An important point about these Nationalist efforts to promote baseball during the immediate postwar period is that Taiwan was clearly the only region of the Republic of China with any sustained baseball tradition. When the Taiwan Province Baseball Team won the championship at China's Seventh National Games in Shanghai in 1948, there were only three other teams entered—the national Police and Air Force teams, both of which were stacked with Taiwanese players, and the Philippines "Overseas Chinese" team.[37] In other words, the new ROC government of Taiwan could hardly promote baseball as a Chinese custom. Their work to hijack the game's unique popularity in Taiwan for their own uses still had to be in explicitly Taiwanese terms.[38] The game of basketball soon became fashionable in Taiwan, promoted by the sizable mainlander population (*waishengren*, literally "provincial outsiders")[39] concentrated in the north. But baseball remained an arena where Taiwanese people could successfully, and without any fear of reprisal, challenge the Guomindang's policies of "de-Taiwanization" and claims to represent a true Chinese culture that Taiwanese needed for their own good.

THE "FREE CHINA CHINESE" AND
BASEBALL DURING THE COLD WAR

The vagaries of decolonization, Retrocession, and the white terror do not provide the full extent of this history. The Taiwanese people now had to contend with the reality of an invigorated American cold war imperialism that sought to dictate affairs in Taiwan and throughout Asia as a whole. Taiwan's baseball history offers a look at this process as well. In 1951, the first ever All-Taiwan baseball team was organized for a series of games versus Filipino teams in Manila. The Manila sporting public fell in love with the Free China Taiwan Baseball Team (Ziyou Zhongguo Taiwan bangqiudui), as they were officially known, especially the astounding home run hitting of ex-Kanō star Hong Taishan. But the young team from Taiwan made an even deeper impression when they "volunteered" to give blood to American soldiers recuperating in Manila hospitals from casualties sustained in the Korean War.[40] This episode, though anecdotal, provides a profound metaphor to describe life in small Asian nations during the depths of the cold war. In the end, the greatest triumphs that could be won were in activities (like baseball) defined and approved by the United States, in locales dependent on and exposed to American beneficence and greed, and in ways that figuratively sucked life from these locales as they were integrated into America's new postwar empire.

Another Taiwan squad, accompanied by more than one hundred physical education "experts," politicians, and businessmen eager to take advantage of the trip to strengthen contacts with overseas Chinese in Southeast Asia, visited the Philippines in April and May of 1953. This time—again in a pattern that fit perfectly within the cold war anticommunist framework of American empire—they played five games against local teams, two games against U.S. Navy teams stationed in Subic Bay, and one against a Japanese semipro team in Manila.[41] In 1955 the same squad visited South Korea, but with one big difference. Now, avoiding the possibility that anyone could interpret the existence of a "Taiwan" baseball team as a separation between Taiwan and the Republic of China, the team was known ineloquently as the "Free China Chinese Baseball Team" (Ziyou Zhongguo Zhonghua bangqiudui).[42] The obvious connections between Japan's former baseball-crazed colonies were officially ignored (if that could be possible) in a 1954 effort to organize an Asian Baseball League with the Philippines, South Korea, Japan, and Taiwan as members.[43] But one report in Taiwan's *United Daily News* made it clear how new the ROC still was to baseball when it published the score of one game between Free China and the South Korean Army as: "First inning: 2 to 3, second inning, 0 to 0. Third inning, 1 to 1, fourth and fifth innings, 0 to 0. Sixth inning, 0 to 1, seventh, eighth and ninth innings all 0 to 0."[44]

This cold war usefulness of baseball does not mean that the Nationalist government was actually investing much money in the game at home. Far more favored by KMT coffers were the games of basketball and soccer, both of which had been named co-"national pastimes" *(guomin youxi)* of the Republic of China back in 1936.[45] Baseball, on the other hand, as one Taiwan independence advocate put it in 1969, "always had to eat the cold rice, because the Chinese [mainlanders of the KMT regime] do not understand it."[46] Several anecdotes from players and coaches from the late 1940s and early 1950s testify to this lack of support for baseball in newly Chinese Taiwan. Huang Renhui, star of the ROC Navy baseball team in the 1950s, remembered stopping over in Japan on one of these trips to Korea and having to "beg for food" because of the meager provisions granted by the government.[47] Huang also remembered the Taipei New Park field being so bad that one second baseman chose to turn around and let ground balls hit his back when fielding in order to be sure of keeping them in play.[48] This situation was not helped much by the fact that the American military had taken over Taiwan's best baseball field, the complex at Yuanshan Field (formerly Maruyama Field and the Taiwan Shintō Shrine), as an administration center.[49]

Clearly, Taiwan's landscape—in terms of politics, the economy, society, and culture—was totally changed by the postwar presence of the American military. By 1949, the often brutal nature of Guomindang rule in Taiwan and the acceptance of a Communist victory in China had convinced the Truman administration to give up on Chiang's "ChiNats," to swear off publicly aiding Chiang, and to allow the island to be "liberated" by the Communists. But when North Korean forces invaded South Korea in June 1950, launching the first hot war of the cold war era, the importance of keeping Taiwan, this potential "unsinkable aircraft carrier," out of Communist Chinese hands became crucial. A worldwide struggle against Soviet and Chinese communism could not allow the surrender of any possible anti-Communist allies, no matter how brutal or unpopular. The U.S. military command was ordered to defend Taiwan as a base of operations against China, renewing the ROC's status as a loyal client state and giving tacit American approval to the harsh regime for more than two decades to come.[50]

As billions of American taxpayers' dollars flowed into Taiwan during the 1950s—the minority not earmarked for the military funneled into communications, transportation, and agricultural and industrial development—the United States saw its presence in Taiwan as a transformative one. This included support of the "American" game of baseball. In September 1952, American baseball authorities showed their approval of the Taiwanese playing what they assumed to be "their" game, donating a championship trophy for the annual Provincial Baseball Tournament.[51] In May 1953, officials planned to observe the second anniversary of the U.S. Military Assistance Advisory Group's (MAAG) presence in Taiwan with a tournament between nine Taiwanese and American military and government teams, played free of charge for crowds in Taipei's New Park.[52] In 1955, the American presence at a twelve-team baseball tournament sponsored by Hua Nan Bank (Huanan yinhang) was also made clear. A ninety-second newsreel showed the tournament opening with a female drill team (referred to as the "Girls' Cheerleading Team" [nüzi lala-dui]) marching around the basepaths, followed by doves flying out of a massive baseball, six feet in diameter and marked with the Hua Nan logo. But the games could only begin after Commander Smith from MAAG gave a speech and threw out the first pitch.[53] Taiwanese players learned to use this imposed and imagined American baseball influence to their advantage; Huang Renhui remembered that when playing against teams from the American Seventh Fleet stationed in Taiwan, he and his teammates would purposely lose so that the Americans would be in such a good mood that they would give their superior equipment to their valiant but lesser Taiwanese rivals.[54]

Lin Huawei, who achieved fame playing on 1970s youth teams, in Japan in the 1980s, and then coaching Taiwan's national team in the 1990s, remembers the American presence in his hometown's baseball community during the 1960s. He told me that one of his fondest and most transformative childhood baseball memories was drinking his first Coca-Cola at a game sponsored by American troops at the field across the street from his Tainan home.[55] Historian Xie Shiyuan devotes much attention to the phenomenon that this fizzy commodity played in the southern baseball communities of Tainan and Gaoxiong. The prospect of acquiring a few cans of Coke to enjoy with teammates or family members brought out many Taiwanese players' best acting instincts; the Americans were generous with their sugar water only after victories, so these games too saw many purposeful losses on the part of Taiwanese Coke lovers. (The games were also popular among the general public for the opportunities they presented to buy cigarettes and alcohol from enterprising GIs.)[56]

The mention of Coca-Cola obviously raises our analytical antennae; today, only McDonald's and Starbucks are cited as a more dead giveaway of the soulless ravages of American cultural imperialism. Yet it is important to not let the power of this cliché distract us from the complex formations of postcolonial baseball in the 1960s. The particular history of the city of Tainan is a case in point: the same field that Lin lived near is notable for having been hit hard by American bombers in the final weeks of World War II. (It was in their flight line as they approached the main Japanese airfield in Tainan.) More importantly, the massive Japanese influence on baseball in southern Taiwan problematizes efforts to talk about baseball as merely a "potent symbol of the West" for Taiwanese people. But young Lin's first nip of Coke and his memories of it should not be ignored; some sites of Taiwanese baseball in the 1950s and 1960s *did* include, on top of half a century of Japanese colonial and postcolonial inscriptions, a cold war imprint of the industrial military complex, its corporate extensions, and the desire for American commodities that enabled the spread of American empire.

And if the Americans in Taiwan felt proud that they were spreading "their" game to Taiwan,[57] this ahistorical understanding would not have been opposed by the Nationalist government: what better way to help erase the Japanese traces from the game of baseball? In November 1953, the *United Daily News* published an 1,800-word piece on the history of baseball. It was only after four long paragraphs on the development of baseball in America that baseball's seemingly irrelevant roots in Japanese Taiwan were mentioned. The author characterized colonial-era baseball as an elite game that was not part of the average Taiwanese subject's life, as opposed to the period of Nationalist rule, when teams could finally "spring forth like bamboo shoots after a spring rain."[58] This incredible reimagining of Taiwan's recent history—even if it meant privileging the American role—gives a sense of how thoroughly "Sinicized" Nationalist Taiwan would have to be.

When I interviewed Jian Yongchang in August 2004, he proudly presented me with a copy of his 1960 translation of Al Campanis's renowned *The Dodgers' Way to Play Baseball,* originally published in 1954 as an early attempt to promote a Brooklyn Dodger "brand" and sensibility. Half a century later, Jian was proud of his laborious 360-page undertaking, which also included a translation of the official rules of baseball[59] as an important effort to standardize anew this complicated game. It would be tempting to assume that this was another act by a thoroughly culturally imperialized agent, except for three things—first, Jian's complicated identity as a loyal Japanese subject and dedicated enemy of the Chinese Nationalists; second, the fact that Jian's own title for the work, *Zenyang da bangqiu* (How to play baseball), mentions neither the Dodgers or America; and third (and most revealing), the fact that Jian translated the work from the *Japanese* translation of Campanis! Jian revealed to me that undertaking this translation was how he finally got around to learning how to write in Chinese after fifteen years of Nationalist rule in Taiwan;[60] it is hard to imagine a more potent critique of the postwar American–KMT hegemony than this. Jian even remembered with disgust a specific gripe that the KMT had with his translation—their insistence that he not use *benleida* as a direct translation for the Japanese *honruida* (home run), but that he change the phrase to a more properly Chinese (or at least not Japanese) *quanleida.* Again, it is important to contextualize the "evidence" of American influence in Taiwanese baseball in order to understand how deep and on how many levels the Japanese currents ran.

The Nationalist government's attempts to mark baseball as a "Free Chinese" pastime—even in 1979 an official government film still insisted that baseball had little following in Taiwan until the KMT takeover of 1945[61]—never seemed to resonate. Meanwhile, after four decades of official sponsorship in the mainland, the ROC "national pastime" of basketball was promoted more thoroughly and wholeheartedly. Sun Liren, named in 1950 the Commander in Chief of the ROC Army, had even led the Chinese national basketball team to a gold medal at the Fifth Far Eastern Games in Shanghai in 1921.[62] The two best books on basketball in Taiwan also testify to the game's almost totalizing mainlander character during this time. Revealingly, the 1999 book *The Tunnel of Time,* by the well-known player and coach Liu Junqing, who was born in Shandong Province in 1945 and moved to Taiwan as a young child, does not even mention the Japanese era.[63] Historian Chia-Mou Chen has discussed the ways in which basketball, both more "Chinese" and "American," and not burdened by baseball's colonial heritage, was simply a more useful and manipulable symbol in the KMT's efforts to "fight communism" through sport.[64] On the other hand, however, one of the most haunting literary representations of 1960s

Taiwan, Chen Yingzhen's short story "First Assignment," leaves the game of basketball as a very different kind of signifier. Published in 1966, two years before Chen
went to prison for subversive activity, the story employs the bounce of a basketball
to stand for the ultimate hollowness and banality of mainlanders' lives in Taiwan
as the game becomes a bond between two lonely middle-aged mainlander men. One
alternates between mourning his late son and reliving memories of playing in a national soccer tournament in Shanghai; the other man will soon kill himself. They
come to understand during their game that the "Chinese" qualities and experiences
that draw them together have come to be obsolete in 1960s Taiwan.[65]

Another literary representation of Taiwanese sport—this time baseball—eluci-
dates the subethnic tensions that existed between Han Taiwanese and mainlander
populations in the 1960s. Author Ku Ling (aka Wang Yuren), who was born in Taiwan to a Manchu family, remembered life in the provisional housing complexes
(*juancun*) constructed for Nationalist military personnel and their families who
came to Taiwan. His story "Thinking of My Brothers in the Military Projects" (1985)
uses baseball as a pivot to remember both the innocence of the 1960s and also the
class and subethnic hostilities that the native Taiwanese kids would take out on their
"mainlander" peers like Wang. Even if they played baseball together late into the
evenings, there seem to have been too many threatening confrontations for the game
to have remained anything more than one more artifact of the difference between
Taiwanese and "mainlander" children.[66]

The Nationalist regime failed to appropriate effectively the game of baseball for
its own purposes. Indeed, the most lasting imprint the government made on the game
during their first two decades in Taiwan was the insertion of their methods of "white
terror" into the baseball world. One famed coach was killed and another was driven
into exile by the paroxysms of 1947, but this was not the end of political violence in
Taiwan; recent research has revealed that Chiang's government executed 1,017
people during the 1950s for political offenses.[67] And countless are those whose lives
were simply ruined by Chiang's secret police acting in the name of anticommunism.
In 1952, Xie Yufa, a native of Miaoli in northern Taiwan, was dedicating his life to
his two passions: playing center field for the Chinese Petroleum Corporation
(Zhongguo shiyou) baseball team and participating in a liberal study society. Someone must have traduced Xie, for one night while he and his teammates celebrated a
victory at a banquet, the affair was crashed by agents of the secret police. Xie moved
too quickly for them and was able to escape. However, arrested in his place were three
of his teammates, including team captain Chen Yanchuan, who, for their nonin-
volvement in Xie's left-leaning studies, earned stays of six to twelve years in prison.
As a matter of course, Chen's photography shop was shut down, his wife endured
years of surveillance and intimidation at work, and his brother was kicked out of
National Taiwan University.[68] And the Nationalists wondered why many Taiwanese
had begun to remember fondly the colonial regime that preceded them.

CHINESE NATIONALIST BASEBALL
AND JAPANESE IDENTITY

*[This visit to Taiwan by the Waseda University team] marks the first time that
our nation's baseball team has hosted a foreign team.*

TAIWAN PROVINCE BASEBALL ASSOCIATION SECRETARY-GENERAL
XIE GUOCHENG, 1953

In December 1953, the famed Waseda University baseball team arrived in Taipei
for a ten-game Sino-Japanese Goodwill and Friendship Baseball Tournament
(Zhong-Ri qinshan youyi bangqiu bisai). The Waseda team had visited Taiwan
thirty-six years earlier as fellow Japanese subjects, in 1917, but now they came as
representatives of another (and recently defeated) nation. That first day of the visit,
Manager Tonooka Mojūrō was gracious in a speech at the Hua Nan Commercial
Bank, expressing his honor at leading Japan's first sports team to visit Free China.[69]

There was no need to mention—and indeed Tonooka professed that he had
brought his team to Taiwan "only to learn"—that Taiwan's baseball tradition was a
product of Japanese rule and had nothing to do with China. But this subtext came
through loud and clear. Taipei alumni of Waseda joined the team in a banquet during their first evening in Taiwan,[70] and alumni a bit farther south, in Taoyuan,
Xinzhu, and Miaoli met until late in the evening on 24 December planning their
alma mater's visit to Xinzhu the next day.[71] This clear enthusiasm for the former
colonial metropole rankled others. The author of the *United Daily News* "In Black
and White" column had had enough of Waseda on their first day in Taiwan, writing with a palpable statist and mainlander authority:

> We heard that when Japan's Waseda University baseball team arrived in Taiwan the
> day before yesterday, there were people—and not a few—at the Songshan Airport
> knocking over the furniture in an effort to welcome them. We don't oppose elderly
> fans, who love baseball for baseball's sake and who want to welcome a famous team
> from a neighboring ally. But when people of influence in local society and govern-
> ment officials become "Waseda alumni" and welcome them with flattery and cere-
> mony, one can't help but frown upon this a bit.
>
> One should be amiable, of course. But in certain types of citizen diplomacy, if one
> forgets one's place in society and despite one's age becomes a fan in welcoming a for-
> eign guest, you start to lose your sense of self. Most will have a pretty bad impression
> of you.[72]

"We" and "you" were not terribly vague categories in 1953 Taiwan. It is easy to see
how much these reunions of Taiwanese and Japanese friends—defying virtually all
claims of Chinese Nationalist legitimacy and Retrocession—truly disturbed those
who identified with the Chinese state.

The Waseda team won nine of ten games played in five cities up and down Taiwan's west coast, losing only the seventh game to an All-Taiwan team. Even in this

defeat, the Japanese influence on Taiwanese baseball was clear; the Taiwan team, managed by former Kanō star Su Zhengsheng, scored their two runs on the strength of four sacrifice bunts, perhaps the most "Japanese" of all strategies.[73] But things got even messier on the last day of the tour, when the Waseda and All-Taiwan squads played a "mixed" game in Taipei, where twenty-one former fellow Japanese "balls of fire" took the field in a show of unity. On 6 January 1954, a "red" team consisting of six Taiwanese and four Japanese players faced off against a "white" team of seven Japanese and four Taiwanese for one last contest,[74] no doubt creating a homosocial environment that, fortified by nostalgia for the recent Japanese ideology of equality and assimilation, was even more threatening than usual. Premier Chen Cheng saw the Waseda team off on January 8, hoping perhaps to cut Nationalist losses while he still could before events became even more strange. In a speech given for their departure, he told the Japanese visitors that he hoped they now "understood Free China better."[75] Chen, a brave and decent veteran of two decades of Nationalist anti-Japanese and anti-Communist warfare, may have had no idea exactly how well Manager Tonooka and his men understood Taiwan.

Baseball in Taiwan, the Nationalist media's and government officials' efforts aside, would remain a Japanese-influenced realm of culture for decades, even to the present. The regime had managed, via the political murders of 1947 and years of "white terror," to reduce the influence of Japanese-educated doctors, teachers, intellectuals, and professionals. But the baseball fields of Taiwan were still full of men (and a few women) who not only had grown up under Japanese rule, but also still identified strongly with the Japanese cultural heritage they had learned through the game of *yakyū*.

Many were the big-name players and coaches in the early Retrocession period, such as Hong Taishan, who had made their names as Japanese baseball stars. The First Taiwan Provincial Games, mentioned earlier as an important exhibition of sport's role in re-Sinicizing and nationalizing Taiwan, was dominated by the legacy of Japanese-era baseball, especially Kanō. All sixteen members of the Jiayi City team were Kanō alumni or current players, all of the tournament officials were Kanō graduates, and nine players on the Taidong County team had played in Japan's national Kōshien tournament before 1945.[76]

Many of the strongest teams established during the early Nationalist period were sponsored by banks; the most prominent league was the Taipei Bankers Association (Taibei shi yinhang gonghui), itself a model of corporate sponsorship that harkened to the Japanese era. Chroniclers like Yu Junwei and Zeng Wencheng have described this period of Taiwanese baseball—dominated by the six-team bank league[77]—as "the golden era of baseball,"[78] or in an equally nostalgizing and commodifying fashion, the era of "eating a lot and watching baseball" *(chia-pa khoaⁿ ia-kiu)*.[79] However, I am less concerned here with these judgments about baseball's "popularity" or "authenticity" than I am with the fascinating ways in which they were composed of a combination of Japanese and KMT "Chinese" influence. Stuart Hall has explored this postcolonial moment thus: "What 'post-colonial' certainly is not is one of those periodisations based on epochal 'stages', when everything is reversed at the same moment, all the old relations disappear for ever and entirely new ones come to replace them. . . . [The postcolonial moment] is characterized by the persistence of many of the effects of colonization, but at the same time their displacement from the coloniser/colonised axis to their internalization within the decolonized society itself. . . . 'The colonial' is not dead, since it lives on in its 'after-effects.'"[80] Baseball—because of its ability at times to transcend Nationalist anti-Japanese ideology—was one site where the colonial lived on most vividly, now in a way very internalized by those who played and enjoyed the game in the late 1940s and 1950s.

Taiwan Cooperative Bank housed an important team established in 1948 by four baseball-playing "employees" including Zhang Xingxian. Zhang's story is a fascinating one; perhaps the finest athlete in Japanese Taiwan, he competed in the 1932 and 1936 Olympic Games for Japan as Chō Seiken. Several writers later worked to "salvage" the name of "Taiwan's first Olympian" from the ranks of presumably traitorous collaborationist athletes. For example, an author in 1996 who called him one of the first two "Chinese" Olympians was proud to report that Zhang never took a formally Japanese name.[81] But only 7 percent of Taiwanese people ever took Japanese names, so this fact establishes little. What we do know is that Zhang spoke frankly to power, publishing an article in the March 1951 issue of the liberal *Spectacle Miscellanea* that was critical of the Taiwan sports program six years into Chinese Nationalist rule.[82]

Taiwan Cooperative's first coach was Li Shiji, a graduate of Kanō who studied and played baseball for four years at the Yokohama College of Commerce before returning to his hometown of Tainan to serve in local government.[83] These men saw this work as continuing the culture and way of life that they had learned for decades as Japanese subjects. Indeed, four decades later, team member Jian Yongchang remembered Taiwan Cooperative and the popular (six-team) Bank League as being "just like" the Tokyo Big Six University League for its centrality to Taipei culture,[84] and the Taiwan Cooperative–Hua Nan Bank games being just as exciting as the epic Waseda-Keiō collegiate rivalry in Japan.[85] However, even in 1999, a chronicler of the renowned Gaoxiong-based Taiwan Electric (Taiwan dianli gongsi) team took exception to the popular notion that Taiwan Cooperative had stronger ties to Japan, explaining all of Taiwan Electric's Japanese connections, especially to Meiji University.[86]

At the same time, however, the existence of these bank teams and their concentration in Taipei owed much to the Nationalist reconcentration of power in the northern capital. Jian may have deadpanned with me in an interview that "There's no Mandarin in baseball," but there was Nationalist and corporate influence in how the game was organized. Taiwan Cooperative was just one of the teams that recruited heavily in southern Taiwan, scouting high school games in order to find players (from Tainan especially) to "work" at the bank. These young men would earn high salaries and standard bank employee benefits, while their most important tasks, of course, were simply practicing and playing baseball after a short stint in the office each day. These ringers seemed often to experience the mainlander banking world of Taipei via distinct tokenism; Jian was the only native Taiwanese of the twenty-five employees in his division. These Taiwanese players were the only bank employees publicly targeted by the "National Language Promotion Movement" *(guoyu tuixing yundong)* of the time, the only ones whose indulgence in alcohol was judged to be a subethnic pathology (as opposed to an unavoidable after-work responsibility), and also the only employees whose performance reviews had nothing to do with actual work performance (they were judged simply by their contributions on the baseball field).[87]

Postwar Japan, as anthropologist William Kelly has explained, became oriented around Tokyo as a single center, with Osaka as a distinct second city, as opposed to the prewar "bipolar" urban order.[88] These baseball formations in Taiwan also show us how its own postwar development mirrored Japan's, where the important port of Takao—once a crucial link in Japan's powerful and vivid ideology of the "southern advance" into Southeast Asia[89]—was now as Gaoxiong demoted to a distant runner-up to Taipei's centrality in Chinese Taiwan. Fang Shuiquan, who later became a legendary semipro and youth coach in Taiwan, was one of these young men recruited to the north, leaving Tainan's Sankandian Sugar Factory team at age twenty-one to join the Cooperative Bank squad. But the Japanese influence mattered here too; this factory, where Fang's father worked during the Japanese era, was also the place where Fang had come into contact with baseball as a youngster.[90]

This mixture of Japanese cultural and Nationalist structural influence was typical at the semipro level, the elite stage for Taiwan's baseball players long before they would send stars to the Japanese pro leagues in the 1980s and found their own in 1990. Hong Taishan, the famous slugging star, was—like the players just mentioned—recruited away from Taiwan Electric in Gaoxiong to play for Chang Hwa Bank's Taipei squad.[91] Taiwan Coal (Taiwan shitan), quickly reorganized under the Nationalists in 1945, established a baseball team that same year, loaded with players from Kanō in the south.[92]

Subjectivities under Japanese rule could vary greatly for this generation of postwar baseball stars in Taiwan. Zeng Ji'en, one of Taiwan's most celebrated managers, brought a different form of Japanese baseball experience to the postwar game. At age nineteen, Zeng left his southern home, a Hakka village in Heitō (Pingdong) where he learned to play baseball with rocks, pomelos, and longan fruit, for Hiroshima. There he trained to be an air mechanic for the Imperial Navy,[93] as one of the 8,419 "Taiwan boy laborers" *(Taiwan shōnenkō)* sent to Japan during this time. Chen

Runbo, who later was a star shortstop for Taiwan Electric, the Navy, and Cooperative Bank, was also drafted as part of a similar wave of "volunteers" in 1943.[94]

Huiyu Caroline Ts'ai has studied these labor drafts and their ultimate effects on postwar history, concluding that "the colonial subjectivity [the colonial regime] had shaped was ironically turned into a cultural and political critique against the new regime—in the name of colonial modernity."[95] This ends up being a fine explanation of Zeng's account of his Japanese life and its implications for his Nationalist Chinese career. After working as a navy air mechanic in the Philippines, Zeng returned to Taiwan, where he eventually undertook similar work for the ROC Air Force after 1945. He soon established, captained, and coached a baseball team at the Air Force No. 3 Factory in Taizhong, making use of the baseball equipment left behind a year before by the defeated Japanese air crews. He soon became known as a brilliant pitcher and manager for the Air Force No. 3 Factory team, winning a Presidential Second-Class Special Skills Award in 1958. But Zeng always insisted that he had picked up his distinctive "militarized management style" from his experience in the Japanese Imperial Navy,[96] a clear "cultural and political critique against the new regime," in Ts'ai's words. Even the defeated Japanese military authority structure could be utilized in a patent critique of the Nationalist regime.

Those who had played *yakyū* as Japanese often, like Jian, used this colonial standard in evaluating the game in Nationalist Taiwan. Hong Taishan, years later, still compared Taiwanese players to the standard set by the Japanese.[97] Huang Renhui recalled that in the 1950s, his and his teammates' fondest wish was to have a Japanese-made glove or bat, instead of the substandard products available in Taiwan.[98] Wu Xiangmu, a future junior high and professional coaching legend, started playing baseball in 1948 in his Tainan elementary school, but even then already worshipped the players like Hong Taishan who had played for the greatest Japanese teams.[99] And the players who were past their prime—like pitcher Lan Deming, the former Higashi Kumon who starred for Kanō in the mid-1930s—also remembered the colonial era as a golden age. Lan, already twenty-nine when the Nationalists took Taiwan, tried his best to hang on, playing on various teams like Taiwan Coal until he was forty-six.[100] But this paled to the luck of "real" Japanese like his former catcher at Kanō, Imakurusu Sunao, who (to Lan's incredible pain and envy) went on to play for the professional Seibu Lions.[101]

This postcolonial subjectivity took its strongest forms when actual Japanese baseball players and teams visited Taiwan in order to share experiences through the game of (depending on whom one asked) *bangqiu*, as "free" capitalist and anticommunist nations, or *yakyū*, as fellow former "equal" subjects of the Japanese Empire. We know who preferred each of these imaginings. At the end of 1955, the ROC government began to announce a New Year's Day "China"-Japan-Korea baseball tourney in Taipei—clearly the most cold war–oriented way of scheduling such an event.[102] But when the Korean team could not make it to Taiwan, the meaning of the entire enterprise shifted when this became instead a thirteen-game tour of the island for Japan's Meiji University baseball team. The visit began innocently enough in Taipei, with Meiji defeating Taiwan Cooperative Bank and the All-Taiwan team before crowds of ten thousand and twenty thousand,[103] and the visit seemed to be set up in the safest, most "Chinese" way possible. Two Japanese dignitaries were also in Taiwan at that moment, the ambassador to Taiwan, who toured the properly "Chinese" historical sites of southern Taiwan, and the president of Meiji University, Dr. Kojima Akira, who spoke on the ROC government's noble preservation of Chinese culture in Taiwan.[104] On the Meiji team's last day in Taiwan, they had the honor of meeting President Chiang Kai-shek to "talk about sports."[105] Even the Meiji team's game in Jiayi—home to the Kanō squad that won so much renown in 1930s Japan—was played in the Sun Yat-sen Baseball Stadium.[106]

But in general, the flavor of the visit was different in the much less de-Japanized south. In Pingdong, the team toured sugar factories and a "savage village"[107]—structural, cultural, and ideological artifacts, of course, of the half century of colonial rule that had ended just ten years before. All of these Meiji players would have remembered very clearly when Taiwan had been part of the empire, when Japanese ate Taiwan's sugar and created colonial forms of knowledge about its "savage" Aborigine population. It could only have been a postcolonial nostalgic thrill for all the players involved when Meiji took on the All-Pingdong and All-Taiwan squads at the Taiwan Sugar Main Factory in Pingdong.

There would be many of these visits by Japanese teams in the 1950s and early 1960s; Waseda University made newsworthy visits to Taiwan again in 1957, 1963, and 1964. Their 1957 arrival was the immediate impetus for the construction of the Taipei Municipal Stadium on Nanjing East Road, where it stood for forty-three years.[108] Their 1963 visit was even more spectacular, as they exported for the first time their storied rivalry with Keiō University. At least twice the *United Daily News* insulted the intelligence of its Taiwanese readers, going out of its way to explain the significance of this rivalry by comparing it to competitions like the Oxford-Cambridge crew contest or the Harvard-Yale football game.[109] Such annotation was perhaps helpful to mainlander readers unfamiliar with the Japanese game of baseball. But any Taiwanese observer would have understood the historical and nostalgic significance of the "Waseda-Keiō War" *(Sōkeisen)*, and especially of having the games played in Taiwan for the first time. This historic contest, always big news in Taiwan since its inauguration in 1903, now would give many Taiwanese the chance, in some ways, to relive the Japanese era—on Nationalist Chinese soil.

The first game in Taipei was hosted by Xie Dongmin, the Nationalists' trusted Taiwanese politician who had led the official baseball bureaucracy since 1949. But the show was stolen by the many Taiwanese Waseda and Keiō alumni, who were a visible part of this event, sponsoring banquets, forming massive cheering sections, and even gaining mention in the official *United Daily News* so typically predisposed against pro-Japan nostalgia.[110] In all, Waseda and Keiō played six games up and down Taiwan, including games before unprecedented (and since unmatched) crowds of twenty-five thousand and forty thousand fans in Taizhong and Tainan, respectively.[111]

Another exciting development during this visit were the challenges issued by Taiwan's Navy and Land Bank (the latter a direct descendant of the colonial-era *Kangyō ginkō*) baseball teams against Waseda and Keiō when the teams returned to Taipei. The Navy team had reason to be confident against the Japanese standouts; in Gaoxiong some fifteen months earlier, they had scored a stirring victory against a team from Kumagaya City that previously had won the world semipro championship.[112] One can also imagine the plain excitement of Taiwanese players, trained almost unanimously by coaches who remembered and reified the colonial era, now having the chance to take on these legendary squads. Four Taiwan-Japan games were played, with the Navy and Land Bank teams eventually losing to each visiting side. The games were competitive though, even if the stands were only half full for these contests, which obviously were inferior and less meaningful than Waseda versus Keiō.[113] Official media like the *United Daily News* may have tried to downplay the visit, giving the games second billing beneath events like the Korean Agricultural Bank basketball team's visit to Taiwan,[114] but, again, there was little mistaking the exciting, subversive, and no doubt cathartic experience that this series of Japanese university baseball games represented to so many Taiwanese people who remembered the colonial era or grew up under those who could not forget it.

Finally, one more series of visits from Japan caught the fancy of Taiwan's baseball fans during the 1950s and early 1960s. Several Japanese women's baseball teams toured the island on the invitation of Taiwanese corporate sponsors eager to tap into the postcolonial and novelty values that these teams seemed to represent. In 1957, Hua Nan Bank invited the Tokyo Women's Baseball Club to take part in their second annual Big Golden Statue invitational, the premier tournament of the era, and importantly, to play against both women's teams and men's teams, like the Hua Nan Old Boys.[115] The next spring, the Sankyō Pharmaceutical Corporation women's baseball team toured northern Taiwan, playing the All-Taipei and All-Taiwan women's squads as well as the Kainan Vocational School boys' team.[116] American historian Susan Cahn has described the American attitude in the 1920s toward women's sports as a "carnivalesque fascination . . . [with this] total inversion of established gender relations."[117] This likely explains the allure of these tours, although it would have been complicated further by recent memories of Japanese colonial rule. Were these teams more threatening because they were made up of women? Or less threatening because they represented a "softer" side of the Japanese than Taiwan had experienced? Or was this vagueness and liminality actually the point?

In 1959, the Salonpas women's baseball team, representing the Hisamitsu Pharmaceutical Company, visited Taiwan to play an eleven-game schedule against men's teams up and down the island over two weeks. After several Salonpas victories, the

Nationalist media was eager to report on the visitors' only loss in Taiwan, proclaiming that the Japanese women had been "cruelly defeated at the hands of Kainan [Vocational School]."[118] Salonpas's overall insult to Taiwanese masculinity was addressed just a month later, though, when the *United Daily News* announced a real coup. Salonpas team captain Tazawa Sanae had fallen in love with Chen Chaoyi, a baseball-playing employee of the Bank of Taiwan from one of Salonpas's vanquished foes in southern Taiwan. This fit perfectly the stock story, cited by Cahn, of the woman athlete who after excelling in competition, finally "drops her 'mask' and becomes her true feminine self, illustrated by . . . the search for male love."[119] With this timely twist, it became less important that Tazawa's Salonpas team had defeated these men than the fact that one of them was able to win her heart, thus striking a rare blow for Nationalist and Taiwanese masculinity.[120]

Again, though, not everyone in the Nationalist media was impressed by the specter of Japanese women's baseball in Taiwan. The *United Daily News* featured a mocking column in 1958 after the Sankyō team was honored in Xinzhu with a "firecracker welcome," with the author testifying that the city's residents thought it was all "much ado about nothing." He continued: "It's been ten-plus years since Retrocession, but the popular psychology of Japan-worship and Japan-flattery has not been eliminated by our independent sovereignty. Compared with the Korean attitude that speaking Japanese is a shameful thought, it is hard not to say that [Taiwanese people's] bones are just too soft. Just because a ballclub comes to visit, the sponsor does not have to feel so flattered like it was some great unexpected favor."[121]

The enthusiasm with which so many Taiwanese chose to remember their connections to Japan—especially when shown a mere women's baseball team—had this writer forgetting to pretend that there was no such thing as a subethnic rivalry between proper anti-Japanese mainlanders and the slavish colonized Taiwanese.

OH SADAHARU/WANG CHEN-CHU
AND CHINESENESS IN 1960s TAIWAN

> *Let's be nationalistic* (minzu zhuyi) *for a second: in the world of sports, which Chinese person has ever reached heights from which one would be scared to look down? Of course there is only one answer: Wang Chen-Chu (a.k.a. Oh Sadaharu).*
>
> ZHANG BEILEI, 1998

Perhaps the most memorable, influential, and complicated Japanese connection forged at this time was through the persona of Oh Sadaharu, the great Yomiuri Giants slugger. The finest player in Japanese baseball history, Oh was a unique figure, beloved in Taiwan by both "locals" and "mainlanders," baseball fans and plain old nationalists.[122]

Many sources incorrectly refer to Oh as a Taiwanese national;[123] this is not the case. Oh, who actually romanizes his own name as "C. C. Wang" or "Chen-Chu Wang," was born in Japan to a Chinese father, Wang Shifu, who had emigrated from Zhejiang Province as a young man, and a Japanese mother, Tōzumi Tomi, a native of Toyama Prefecture. Oh to this day has never taken Japanese citizenship, and still carries a passport of the Republic of China. Of course, although the ROC ruled China when his father left for Japan, by the 1960s they presided only over Taiwan.

As Oh ascended to superstardom with the Yomiuri Giants, he became, in the eyes of the Chinese Nationalist Party, an overseas Chinese idol who had triumphed over Japanese discrimination, and in the eyes of many Taiwanese people, a former fellow subject of the Japanese Empire who had triumphed over his Chinese heritage. The writer cited in the epigraph, who referred to *minzu zhuyi*, the formulation of a racial nationalism used in both Chinese and Japanese, inadvertently explained part of the complexity of Taiwan's love affair with Oh/Wang.

In April 1964, during Oh's sixth season with the Giants, Taiwan's *United Daily News* celebrated Japanese youth's seemingly unanimous affection for "Wang-Chang" *[sic]*. In case this fact seemed troubling, the reporter was quick to praise Oh's Chinese virtues and to cite actress Awashima Chikage, who said that Oh was "not just a Japanese Chinese but a world Chinese." (And also, for the benefit of certain readers, to explain what a home run was.)[124] Taiwan's newspapers carried more news about Oh that year, reporting his new single-season home run record that September and also adding, more importantly, that he hoped within two or three years to marry a "female Chinese compatriot."[125]

In 1965, the ROC government directly reached out to Oh by awarding him the annual Outstanding Overseas Chinese Youth Award.[126] At the end of that year, the twenty-five year old made a celebrated and successful "return to his motherland" (*fan zuguo*) when he visited Taiwan for the first time. As the KMT media put it, this was in order to "give tribute to the great President Chiang [Kai-shek]."[127] The excitement and tension of Oh/Wang's eight days in Taiwan are shown best in the official newsreel, compiled and released by the ROC Government Information Office, which posits a unique Nationalist Chineseness shared by Oh and his hosts in Taiwan.

After the newly crowned MVP of Japanese baseball arrived in Taipei on 4 December, the vice president of the Japan-based Wang Chen-Chu Overseas Chinese Fan Club and leader of the star's entourage in Taiwan, Liu Tianlu, made a dramatic and palpably defensive announcement to the press. Lest anyone doubt his client's singular devotion to his fellow exiles in Taiwan, Lu told how Oh, a "good and aware youth who loved his country [i.e., the ROC on Taiwan]," had heroically and "resolutely refused the [CCP] commie bandits' shameless seduction" and invitations to visit the mainland.[128] As his reward, the patriotic Oh was taken the next day to the Sun Yat-sen Museum to look at antique Chinese relics, and to Taipei County to lay a wreath for the late ROC premier and vice president Chen Cheng. His hitting demonstration at Taipei Municipal Stadium delayed, Oh was taken instead to the offices of the ROC Baseball Association to present an autographed bat to association head Xie Dongmin. This proved an uncomfortable event when Xie (the Taiwanese politician chosen for his years spent in the mainland with the Nationalists) showed his utter unfamiliarity with the bat, which he clearly had no idea how to hold. Xie's pathetic attempt at a swing—screened throughout Taiwan on the official newsreel—visibly embarrassed his celebrated guest, who no doubt at that moment was feeling much more Oh than Wang.

He spent 6 December learning about the ROC's many Air Force martyrs, seeing the scenery, visiting the presidential palace and the foreign ministry,[129] and addressing published reports that he was in Taiwan to find a girlfriend and that he had struck up a relationship with movie star Zhang Meiyao.[130] The handsome Oh clearly had no problem in this department; the official newsreel showed him flirting capably with stewardesses aboard the fast train to Taizhong two days later. But it was surely exhausting for Oh, despite his constant public insistences that he merely hoped someday to meet an educated woman who would show love and respect to his parents and assist him in his career,[131] to have to answer such personal questions.

On 7 December, Oh put on a hitting demonstration in his street clothes at the Taipei Municipal Stadium before twenty thousand fans, providing narration and tips on his unique "scarecrow" stance and home run swing in Japanese. After taking in a game between the ROC Air Force and Tenth Credit Union teams, Oh then left to meet Chiang Ching-kuo, son of President Chiang and head of Taiwan's secret police and the militaristic China Youth Anti-Communist National Salvation Corps (Zhongguo qingnian fangong jiuguotuan). Oh spoke through an interpreter at this meeting before receiving a medal from Chiang. These honors were not easily won, however; Oh's hosts in Taiwan were ruthless in their scheduling. On 9 December, for example, Oh spent a day in and around Taizhong, the self-described "City of Culture," observing the proceedings at the Provincial Assembly and being guided through the Chinese garden outside, visiting the Provincial Government inland at Zhongxing, taking in lectures on Taiwan's geology and models of its modern infrastructure, and finally putting on another hitting demonstration at the Taizhong Municipal Stadium (after speaking to the crowd, "so packed as to be watertight," through an interpreter this time). It could have been worse, however; after Oh left, newspapers told of the hurt feelings among leaders of the Ningbo Natives' Association who, on the basis of their hailing from the same part of China as Oh's father, felt owed a banquet with the star.[132]

This preoccupation with Oh says much about official attitudes toward baseball in Taiwan besides the singular case of photogenic half-Chinese bachelors from Japan. Oh's visit to Taiwan totally overshadowed the ROC's participation in the Sixth Asian Baseball Championships in Manila taking place the same week. On 4 December, when Oh's itinerary in Taiwan merited a 1,194-word story in the government's *United Daily News,* the opening of Asia's biggest biennial competition won just eighty-two words in the same paper.[133] And even with a win over eventual champions Japan, the national team had to share billing with news of the return of the ROC cycling team from their competition in Manila, receiving (in column space) much less than half of the piece on Oh's ex-girlfriend two days earlier.[134] In all, the first fifteen days of December saw the *United Daily News* publish thirty-five articles on Oh's eight days in Taiwan and nine very short articles on the ten-day Asian Championships, a fair measure of how officially unimportant this still-Japanese game was unless it could directly reify mythologies of Chineseness in Nationalist Taiwan.

It is hard to know exactly how Oh's visit helped his understanding of his Chinese identity. Perhaps self-conscious at the difficulty with which he could play the role of Wang, though, Oh did tell President Chiang himself two days later that he would be sure to work on his Mandarin Chinese before his next return to Taiwan.[135] His insistence on keeping ROC citizenship—as opposed to Japanese or PRC citizenship, both of which were offered to Oh many times, and the latter of which his father eventually accepted[136]—for the last four decades does indicate the loyalty and regard he came to feel for the people and government of Taiwan.

Oh returned to Taiwan twice more in the 1960s, once a year later for his honeymoon with wife Koyae Kyoko, who, the newspapers were ecstatic to report, actually took ROC citizenship under the Sinicized name Wang Gongzi.[137] Good sports, and perhaps revealing of Oh's wish to become more Wang, the couple took time out of their busy schedule at the beautiful Sun Moon Lake to appear at the baseball game between Taiwan Cooperative Bank and Japan Oil, and to visit President Chiang and his wife Song Meiling at their Blue Jade Mansion mountain villa (built by the Japanese in 1916).[138] Reporters got a piece of Oh again when he got stuck in the airport, delayed from the Honolulu segment of their honeymoon after he left his passport with his Japanese-Chinese guide. Politely, he told of his affection for Taiwan's food and friendly spirit, and promised (again) that he would soon get around to studying Chinese with his wife.[139]

Just a bit more than a year later, Oh's third trip was even more momentous for the baseball world when his Yomiuri Giants team carried out their spring training in Taizhong. Eager to impress their world-famous guests, who were three championships into their "V9" decade of dominance, the provincial government quickly shelled out NT$520,000 to renovate the Taizhong Municipal Stadium for the training session.[140] Six young standout players from the Provincial Physical Education College, whose campus backs up against the stadium, were allowed to train with these gods, who they actually found "affable, genial, and easy to approach."[141] An 8mm film that baseball player and artist Chen Yanchuan made of Oh and teammate Nagashima Shigeo circulated for years in pre-TV baseball circles in Miaoli.[142]

For the last four decades, Oh has continued to play an important role in the development of baseball in Taiwan, offering moral and technical support and helping standout players hook up with Japanese teams. A 1989 biopic of Oh, produced by the state's Central Motion Pictures Company, attempted to finally set down a strong case for the slugger to be understood as a Chinese hero who triumphed over the blatant discrimination that he, his father, and brother suffered in Japan. "Honor Thy Father"—the title an obvious reference to a uniquely Chinese value of filial piety— features one developed Japanese character, his personal batting coach Arakawa Hiroshi, who works continuously with Ōh and even learns to make a fine plate of Chinese noodles in the process. But the rest of the "Japanese" cast exist simply as a faceless backdrop of haters, worshipping fans, or haters turned worshipping fans.[143] The Nationalist judgment, made here just at the historical moment that the party's "Chinese" character was being finally exposed as illegitimate, is clear: Oh's place in history is as a wise and humble hero of the Chinese race.

This identity has been challenged in recent years by explicitly (if not gratuitously) "Taiwanese" politicians fond of Oh's Japanese heritage, and then again by National- ist loyalists invested in Oh as a "Chinese" hero. This has placed Oh in the middle of Taiwan's recent explicit repoliticization of baseball, as he has been the conspicuous guest of pandering politicians across the spectrum since 1999. In 2001, then Presi- dent Chen Shui-bian awarded Oh with a Third-Class Presidential Order of the Bril- liant Star and named him ROC Ambassador without Portfolio.[144] Not to be outdone, Taipei's KMT mayor Ma Ying-jeou (who is now ROC president) threw out the first pitch at a home game for the Oh-managed Fukuoka Hawks.[145] His party also teamed up with the explicitly prounification People First Party (Qinmindang) in hosting Oh's Hawks in Taiwan in 2003, and made news for not inviting then President Chen to sit in the VIP seats.[146] Oh's legacy perhaps will never be resolved neatly, but his pres- ence as one of the most famous Japanese and Chinese people of the late twentieth century has inspired Taiwanese people of almost all backgrounds and ideologies.

In this chapter I have investigated the rich variety of meanings behind the theory and practice of baseball in postwar Taiwan. The Chinese Nationalist Party, after tak- ing control of Taiwan in 1945, attempted to transform, Sinicize, and decolonize the game that had served as an important icon of Japanese Taiwan. It was common to see mentions of baseball games held to commemorate orthodox "Chinese" events, like the 1953 celebrations honoring the eighty-seventh anniversary of Sun Yat-sen's birth in the far southern town of Pingdong.[147] However, more fraught with mean- ing were the moments when official KMT nationalism and anticommunism ran squarely into the legacy of colonialism, as when Taiwan's "Free China" baseball team visited Seoul in 1955. They met President Syngman Rhee, who declared publicly that these squads represented "the two most determined, glorious, and advanced anticommunist countries, working together in friendship and solidarity to do bat- tle against their shared enemy."[148] Few historical figures' legacies date more squarely to the cold war 1950s than Rhee. But any observer could only have reflected on the baseball heritage shared by the Taiwanese (who call the game *ia-kiu*) and the Koreans (who call it *yagoo*) and their shared histories as colonies of Japan (who brought them both the game *yakyū*).

Baseball, then, is also central to the story of Taiwan's rapid and traumatic transition, from wartime to decolonization, and then on to a new oppression delivered in the rhetoric of Retrocession to Chinese rule. Said's model predicts decolonized intellectuals' work for the "rediscovery and repatriation of what had been suppressed in the natives' past by the processes of imperialism."[149] However, in Taiwan after 28 February 1947, the notion of a Taiwanese "rediscovery" of their Chinese heritage was unthinkable. By this moment, original support for Chinese rule of Taiwan had been dashed violently and unmercifully by the actions of tens of thousands of carpetbagging KMT troops, bureaucrats, and hangers-on. Relieved and enthusiastic searching for a "Chinese" Taiwan, among Taiwanese, quickly gave way to a yearning for cultural artifacts from the good old colonial days. Baseball was one of these artifacts, and this complicated picture of a Taiwan stuck between a Japanese rock and a Guomindang hard place explains much of baseball's continued popularity after the Japanese were long gone from Taiwan.

This official KMT patronage meant that baseball could serve as a "safe" realm for Taiwanese consciousness. However, the awkwardness of baseball's Japanese heritage made it unfit for any major role in the popular culture of this oppressive one-party era. Thus, the game exhibited little presence among the official cultural or educational apparatus of the Nationalist government. But the game did survive in different realms of recreation and memory. This includes the friendships that many Taiwanese had with Japanese people, or Taiwanese affection for Japanese culture. Baseball contacts with Japanese teams were revived very quickly, with the Waseda University and Meiji University teams coming to Taiwan in the early and mid-1950s. It also included the continuing Taiwanese enthusiasm for Japanese professional and high school baseball—with newspaper reports and magazines sent to Taiwanese fans by their teachers, neighbors, and friends who had returned to Japan. Baseball was thus one of the few areas of Retrocession-era society and culture where the Japanese influence still could be relived safely and exuberantly.

One perfect example of the KMT's attempt to displace baseball can be seen in Joseph Allen's masterful study of Taipei Park, built by the Japanese in around 1906, and now called February 28 Peace Park. The Japanese park included a baseball diamond in the eastern section that served as a center for Taiwanese baseball for many decades into the 1960s. That part of the park, however, was transformed dramatically and significantly by the removal of the baseball diamond and its substitution with a formal pond-pavilion complex built in the "northern palace" style recognized as officially "Chinese" in the 1960s and 1970s.[150]

Another final example of this official redefinition of baseball came with the ROC

Baseball Association's triumphant announcement in February 1962 that the "lords" of American baseball, the New York Yankees, would be coming to "Free China" that fall to celebrate the ROC's National Day on 10 October.[151] This represented a bold gambit to define Taiwanese baseball within an American frame—in place, of course, of the Japanese imprint that still defined this realm. Baseball had to be co-opted, and the cold war anticommunist understandings now had to trump nostalgic and postcolonial ones.

This excitement at "Mickey Mentle" and his teammates toasting Chiang Kai-shek and his Chinese Republic was dashed two months later, however, when the Yankees disclosed that they would ask Taiwan authorities to pay the club US$30,000 for the trouble of the visit.[152] Xie Guocheng, in embarrassment, stalled by saying he would try to "come to an understanding" with the Yankees, although the *United Daily News* openly mocked his attempt to bargain with the American "lords." (The Baseball Association's haste to announce this visit for as early as National Day is also evident in the fact that the Yankees were still occupied by Game 5 of the World Series when that date came.) Taiwan authorities instead turned their attentions to the Detroit Tigers, who hopefully would be cheaper since they had finished second to the Yankees the year before.[153] Finally, it turned out that neither team would make the trip to Taiwan, and face was saved only by burying this news as the fifth item in a May article on the tournament to select the volleyball team representing Taiwan at the Asian Games.[154]

This nonevent captured the Nationalists' dilemma with regard to the cold war and the postcolonial—how exactly to make use of postwar American hegemony to erase the many powerful memories and keenly recalled precedents of Japanese Taiwan. For all their manipulation of Taiwan for their own purposes, though, the Americans never really could do this for the KMT.[155] Reconstructed memories of Japan's "harsh but fair" rule of Taiwan lived on in whispers and loaded gestures (like participation in baseball) until they could be voiced again, more than four decades later, in the 1990s. But events unrelated to any of the KMT's doing—namely the dramatic 1968 triumph by a team of Bunun Aborigine youth over a Japanese Little League power—would provide the space, finally, for the ruling party to redefine the game that compelled so many in Taiwan.

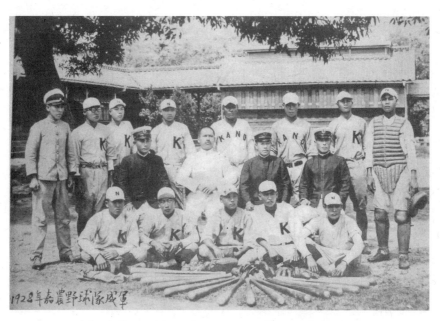

1928年嘉農野球隊成軍

FIGURE 1. Kanō baseball team, 1928. Photo courtesy of Cai Wuzhang.

FIGURE 2. Kanō players from left: Chen Gengyuan (Uematsu Kōichi), Wu Mingjie, and Lan Dehe (Higashi Kazuichi), 1931. Chen and Lan were Aborigines from Taitō (Taidong), in southeastern Taiwan. Photo courtesy of Cai Wuzhang.

FIGURE 3. Kanō players from left: Yang Yuanxiong and Okuda Hajime, Kodama Gen and Sonobe Hisashi, 1936. Photos courtesy of Cai Wuzhang.

FIGURE 4. Kanō team, Islandwide High School Baseball Tournament, Taihoku (Taipei), July 1936. Photo courtesy of Cai Wuzhang.

FIGURE 5. "Little Baseball Hero" (Bangqiu xiao yinghao), comic serial published in *Prince* magazine, 1970.

FIGURE 6. Tainan Giants, the 1973 Little League world champions, who swept their three Williamsport opponents by a total score of 57–0 with three no-hitters.

FIGURE 7. Amis Aborigine pitcher Guo Yuanzhi (Kaku Genji) and family, 1999.

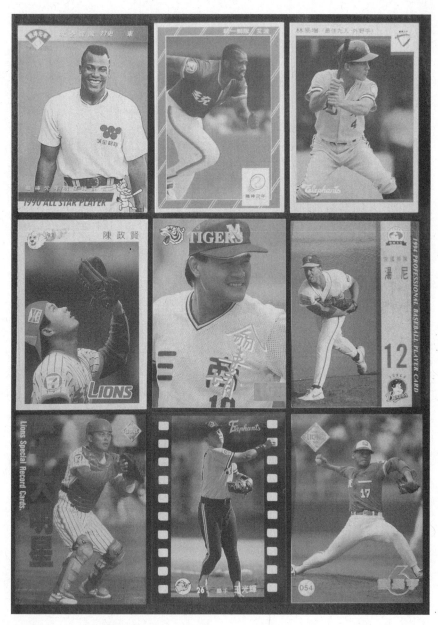

FIGURE 8: CPBL player cards, 1990–1993.

FIGURE 9. "The Uni-President Lions invite you to watch pro baseball and drink a Big Gulp," 1991 advertisement. The players shown include Tony Metoyer (top row, far left), Zeng Zhizhen ("The Ninja Catcher," top, third from left), Milt Harper (top, third from right), and Xie Changheng (top, far right).

FIGURE 10. "OK, you rogue, I won't steal anymore!" The African-American "major league stolen base king" is foiled by the Taiwanese shortstop's plate of "stinky tofu." Cartoon from Ao You-xiang, *Pro Baseball Rhapsody* (1994), 42.

FIGURE 11. Monument at the entrance of the National Jiayi University (formerly Kanō) campus, unveiled in 2001. Inscribed "Kanō, Champions of All Under Heaven" *(Tianxia Jianong),* the monument is a massive replica of the plaque (the original of which went missing at the end of World War II) that the school received for their stirring second-place finish at the Japanese national high school baseball championship tournament of 1931.

FIGURE 12. New York Yankees star Chien-ming Wang pitching hamburgers, Taipei, 2007. Photo courtesy of Brian Greene.

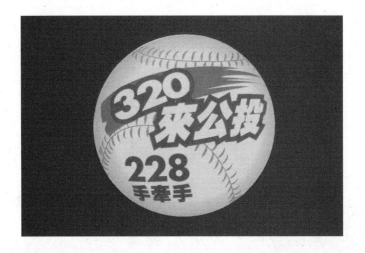

FIGURE 13. *(Top)* DPP campaign button for 20 March 2004 referendum on relations with the PRC, also mentioning the 28 February "Hands across Taiwan" (a five-hundred-kilometer human chain) staged to promote the Taiwanese spirit.

FIGURE 14. *(Bottom)* An NT$500 bill issued in 2000, which replaced the old bill with Chiang Kai-shek's portrait. Pictured are Puyuma Aborigine boys from Taidong County, here celebrating their team's Pacific Cup championship.

FIGURE 15. Campaign sign for DPP Zhanghua County legislative candidate Chiu Chuang-chin, Huatan, 2007. His jersey reads, "Legislative Yuan."

4

Team of Taiwan, Long Live the Republic of China

Youth Baseball in Taiwan, 1968–1969

Yu Hung-kai participates in the World Little League Championship in the United States with the Taichung Golden Dragons. The team wins the world little league championship and Yu is honored with the nickname of the "Rich General."

"ABORIGINAL MILESTONES, 1951 A.D.–1998 A.D.," 1998

Taiwan (Formosa) is neither free nor China. . . . Taiwanese love baseball, but not Chinese mainlanders in Taiwan.

HANDBILL DISTRIBUTED IN WILLIAMSPORT, PENNSYLVANIA, BY UNITED FORMOSANS IN AMERICA FOR INDEPENDENCE, 1969

Taiwan's first great postwar Olympic athlete was C. K. Yang (Yang Chuanguang), who won a silver medal in the decathlon at the Rome Olympics in 1960. To this day, his epic battle there with close friend and UCLA track and field teammate Rafer Johnson is known as one of the most touching and memorable moments in Olympic history. Yang, known around the world as the "Asian Iron Man," set the world decathlon record in 1963. That same year he was even named by the American magazine *Sports Illustrated* to be the "World's Best Athlete."[1] ROC Olympic Committee chief Hao Gengsheng called Yang "the model of the 'modern Chinese man,'"[2] although the situation was more complex than this. Yang was an Amis Aborigine from Taidong County in eastern Taiwan, and his triumph spotlighted the position of Taiwan's Austronesian Aboriginal population again after a decade and a half of Nationalist rule.

Chroniclers of Taiwanese baseball history have made much of the fact that Chen Gengyuan, the 1930s Kanō baseball star who had to flee the Nationalists' February 1947 massacres in Jiayi for his east coast hometown, coached a young C. K. Yang at the Taidong Agricultural School in the late 1940s.[3] Whether or not this actually speaks to an organic Kanō or Aborigine essence at the soul of Taiwanese sport, it does remind us of how Taiwan's modern rulers have viewed the Aborigines as an inherently physical foil, or even a complement, to Japanese or Chinese "civilization." The Nationalist regime made much of their patently condescending and paternalistic policies to "make the mountains like the plains" *(shandi pingdihua)*—a poorly conceived approach proceeding from the modern Chinese "assimilationist" assumption that Taiwan's complexity could be solved by merely ideologically leveling it.

Official popular culture, as Darryl Sterk has found, used gendered tropes of a maiden-like Aborigine frontier to create a canon of Chinese "rescue fantasies" in the threatening terrain of Taiwan's mountains.[4] But a striking 1972 article published by a Hong Kong scholar in the *Journal of Negro Education* told a sad story of vast inequity between Taiwan's mountains and the plains, and of a self-destructive fatalism that had taken root among Aborigines after almost three decades of Nationalist rule.[5] Trying to "make the mountains like the plains" seems to have exhausted the regime, leading them to conclude—in their own propaganda on "Administrative Improvement in Mountainous Regions of Taiwan"—that, when it came down to it, "The causes of poverty of the aboriginal people are in the people themselves, and include: laziness, superstition, alcoholism, lack of economic concepts, conservatism, stubbornness, and lack of desire for advancement, etc."[6]

This notion of the Austronesian Aborigines' unique physical gift—and curse—again became salient to the realm of sport in 1967. Taiwan's China National Amateur Athletic Federation (Zhonghua quanguo tiyu xiejinhui) decided that success in the next year's Olympic Games at Mexico City would depend on better use of their mountain compatriots' *(shanbao)* natural talents, especially in track and field and boxing. The federation formed a Mountain Areas Development Association (Shandi jianshe xiehui), and scheduled a Mountain Areas Athletic Meet for 12 November (Sun Yat-sen's birthday) in Pingdong.[7]

The language used by authorities in describing the logic for such a meet was fascinating and obvious. One standard phrase used was that these efforts would serve to "excavate" *(fajue)* athletic talent hidden among Taiwan's 190,000 "mountain compatriots."[8] Another key metaphor was the discussion of eastern Taiwan as a "precious deposit of track and field talent" *(tianjing yundong rencai de baozang)* that had to be further exploited so that this region could "produce athletes in abundance" *(shengchan yundongyuan).*[9] The Nationalist trope of "excavating" valuable and concealed "resources" recalls nothing so much as the precise reason for Japan's colonial interest in Taiwan, ignited a century before by their dreams of the camphor and marble that surrounded the natives. And to speak of Aboriginal talents as "concealed"—for a people as long-exploited as Taiwan's first peoples—ignored totally and gratuitously the ways that they were so forcibly marginalized and dispossessed over the last three centuries.

The limits of this new Nationalist benevolence became clear in November, when it was announced that—despite all of the Olympic-grade ore to be mined out of Taiwan's eastern half—the CNAAF had decided not to fund the Mountain Areas Athletic Meet after all. That the reasons for this decision were mutually contradictory—first, most of the physically fit Aborigines were in the military and would not be able to participate, and second, after a decade and a half of the official Nationalist policy to "make the mountains like the plains" the conditions enjoyed by mountain Aborigine youth were actually not that bad anyway—did not seem to matter. The *United Daily News* article on this decision still maintained that a policy of "excavation" had to be followed,[10] although the government did not ever invest in holding such a meet until 1988.[11] But just months after this decision to again formally neglect the "mountain areas," the Taiwan sports world happened upon a "precious deposit" of baseball talent that would change history.

MAPLE LEAF LEGEND: HONGYE, 1968

Aborigines also have their own things to be proud of.
THE EDUCATOR MONTHLY, 1995

It is one of life's grisly ironies that what is a catastrophe for most of mankind, invariably works to the advantage of a few who live on the fringes of the human community. On the other hand, it is a grisly irony to live on the fringes of the human community.
PHILIP ROTH, *THE GREAT AMERICAN NOVEL*, 1973

In May 1968, Taipei hosted the twentieth Province-wide Students' Cup, an annual tournament held to determine the Taiwan boys' baseball champion. The winner that year was Maple Leaf (Hongye) Elementary School, a team made up of Bunun Aborigine youth representing their tiny Taidong County school of just one hundred students. Their triumphs, as explained below, were the impetus for the development of Taiwan's legendary Little League Baseball program. This group of young Aborigine boys also became almost instantly an iconic symbol of (depending on whom one asks) a uniquely ROC or Taiwanese capitalist spirit for their ability to overcome incredible obstacles (specifically those placed in the way of Taiwan's Aborigines by the ROC government or the Taiwanese people).[12]

In 1963, Lin Zhupeng was a new principal, trying to think of a way to keep the children of the tiny and impoverished Maple Leaf Village in school. He noticed the popularity of a local baseball tournament, and thought it might capture the interests of his students as well.[13] Lin had no real budget for such an enterprise, but the students did not mind at all the simple facilities and equipment he could offer. Their training methods—like practicing hitting by swinging a stick into a tire nailed to a tree (and playing barefoot, of course)—would become iconic representations of Taiwan's triumphant "economic miracle" and a national leap to prosperity and success during the 1970s.[14] But at the time they reflected only the real poverty of the village. In a 2000 public television broadcast, Lin reflected on other difficulties he faced organizing this team. The first time he took his team to the neighboring Beinan Township for a game, several of the boys returned with diarrhea. Parents were hysterical, figuring a curse had been placed on the boys by witches of Beinan, an area historically at war with Maple Leaf. Lin, a modern educated man through and through, explained to them (and to his TV interviewer thirty-five years later) that it was simply a result of all the noshing the rambunctious boys had done on the bus.[15]

Lin also would find solutions for the team's general poverty as well. The first mention of Maple Leaf—village, school, or team—in the *United Daily News* came with a 1965 piece titled "Small, small hunger, Big, big warmth and friendship" on the benevolent efforts to fund the team's trip to the seventeenth annual Students' Cup. Kind car owners, policemen, and restaurateurs contributed time, money, food, and living space in order to allow Maple Leaf to get all the way to Taipei, where they finished fourth overall (out of thirty teams), and back home again.[16] The point of articles like this was obviously not to point out the grinding poverty in which most of Taiwan's Aborigine children lived, but to give proper credit to the bourgeoisie— including the owner of the Mainland Restaurant in Yilan City—who were starting to make things happen in 1960s Taiwan.

After winning this islandwide tournament in 1966 and finishing in second place in 1967, Maple Leaf was featured in another *United Daily News* article in 1968. Unfortunately this piece also attested to Maple Leaf's lack of funds; the team was in arrears after travelling to a tournament in Tainan and likely would not be able to make it to Taipei for the Students' Cup that May.[17] This time the team's beneficiaries were better known, and included three former political prisoners released from Taiwan's feared Green Island prison. One, Cai Kunlin, had done ten years for participating in the wrong kind of study society, and was now publishing the children's magazine *Prince (Wangzi)*.[18] Cai's background and political instincts made him perhaps the first figure in Taiwan to grasp the subversive value of backing a team and a cause that mocked the KMT regime's rhetoric of helping their "mountain compatriots." After learning about the team's predicament in a news article, Cai contacted Maple Leaf principal Hu Xueli, who guaranteed that his team would win the championship if *Prince* magazine could get them to Taipei and feed them two meals a day.[19] This Maple Leaf investment—namely, these two meals and the use of the magazine's automobile for team transport and their office floors for accommodations[20]—became a profitable one for publisher Cai, who would put out the first book on the Maple Leaf story in 1968.[21] But the political statement that this represented was also very significant.

Once in Taipei, the boys of Maple Leaf won the Students' Cup. Five thousand fans braved the rain to see Maple Leaf defeat the powerful Chuiyang Elementary School team (from Jiayi) on a dramatic game-ending home run.[22] But this great triumph was just the beginning. Three months later, the ROC Baseball Association hosted a team from Wakayama, Japan, home of that year's Little League World Series champions. (The United Daily News made it clear that the visitors from Wakayama were not the same ones who had just won the world championship,[23] but this distinction has been forgotten by a majority of Taiwanese baseball fans. It did not help that an article on the same page of that day's United Daily News proclaimed the Japanese team arriving in Taipei to be "last year's world Little League champions."[24])

Wakayama's first game was a 1–0 defeat of Chuiyang, the national runners-up from Jiayi.[25] But over the next four days, the Maple Leaf boys defeated Wakayama three times (including one game where they made up the basis of a national all-star team). The third of these victories has been lost to history, most likely because of the chaotic atmosphere at the event itself. Excited to attend "the most exciting game in Xinzhu in twenty years," some thirty thousand baseball-mad fans crowded into the tiny facilities at Building-China High School meant to accommodate only five thousand bodies. The beginning of the game was delayed by forty minutes so that police and Boy Scouts could gain control of the situation. But when Gu Jincai led off the bottom of the first inning with a home run, hysterical Taiwanese fans standing along the first- and third-baselines poured onto the field in celebration. The game was delayed several times by such interruptions, a fact unbecoming to KMT notions of control and discipline, and apparently for this reason is rarely cited.[26]

The first two victories, achieved at Taipei Municipal Stadium, however, are legendary. The twenty thousand fans who managed to get tickets for each of these historic games were joined by an islandwide television audience treated to more than thirteen hours of Taiwan Television broadcasts on the first game alone.[27] The first game, a 7–0 Maple Leaf blowout in which no Wakayama player even got so far as second base, not only energized Taiwanese society in an unprecedented way, but also allowed for the first time a visible, explicit playing-out of the success of the capitalist ideology in Taiwan.

Newspaper descriptions of the amazing scene in Taipei touched on the predictable, like the civilizing presence of enthusiastic women and girls who "were not afraid of the brilliant heat, holding their umbrellas and cheering." The United Daily News described how during the middle of one inning, "someone from some magazine" ran onto the field, accompanied by several youth wearing advertisement sandwich boards, and gave out red envelopes filled with money to several Maple Leaf players. The paper scolded the publisher for using such forward advertising methods "in front of the foreign players,"[28] but somehow missed the fact that cash and wealth constituted the way in which so many people in Taiwan seemed to experience this event. The same article explained how ecstatic fans ran onto the field, throwing ten-, fifty-, and one hundred-yuan (US$0.40, $1.25, and $2.50) bills into the air. In 2000, Maple Leaf catcher Jiang Honghui, in halting and accented Mandarin, recalled how after his sixth-inning grand slam home run he was "running around the bases and looking at all that money."

The material comforts of success in the big city color much of how these former players remember their youthful fame. Another one of Jiang's dearest memories of his playing career was how well he and his mates ate in Taipei: "Up in the mountains we didn't eat well, just sweet potatoes and pumpkin." But in the city, hosted by well-meaning businessmen, the sky was the limit; his friend "Jiang Wanxing could eat eleven bowls of rice!"[29]

The day after this first victory the team was hosted by Chiang Ching-kuo, the president's son and leader of the China Youth Anti-Communist National Salvation Corps, who promised that someday he would travel to Taidong and visit the children there. The pledge made by provincial chairman Huang Jie, a gift of NT$100,000 (US$2,500) to the team out of Ministry of Education funds, was more impressive. (In the spirit of good sportsmanship, the Ministry of Education also announced a gift of NT$2,000 [US$50] to the Chuiyang team that had lost to Wakayama.) The United Daily News announced proudly that they had raised NT$8,800 (US$220) to be distributed to the team, in amounts ranging from NT$100 to NT$1,000 (US$25) depending on each player's contributions to the win.[30] The next day, the team met Chiang again, and TV stars and Taipei city councilmen also injected themselves into the Maple Leaf story by making small public gifts to the children to commemorate their "exceptional spirit of struggling through difficulty."[31] In another detail that is often overlooked, the second Taipei victory over Wakayama was technically achieved by an ROC all-star team. However, since seven of the nine starting players (including catcher Jiang Honghui, who hit another grand slam) were from Maple Leaf,[32] this win has been remembered as theirs alone. The next round of public charity was for Maple Leaf alone as well, like a NT$1 million (US$25,000) gift from Qingchuan Private Commercial School in Taipei.[33]

Almost instantly, these Bunun Aborigine boys from Maple Leaf came to serve as a metaphor for the economic successes that Taiwan's middle classes were starting to enjoy. Committed to succeeding in Taiwan where they had failed in China, the Nationalist regime now relied on and managed a well-educated (and well-disciplined) workforce, a stable monetary system, strong power and transport infrastructures left behind by the Japanese, and the planning of skilled analysts to create a booming export economy by the late 1960s.[34] Indeed, in the two-plus decades after World War II, among Asian countries only Japan had achieved a more equal income distribution and higher rates of income growth than Taiwan.[35] And again, that these baseball victories had been achieved by children who were surely among the very poorest in all of Taiwan actually allowed for the discussion of even more dimensions of Nationalist capitalist success on Taiwan.

There were a few critiques of Taiwan's Maple Leaf fever. The day after Maple Leaf's first victory, United Daily News columnist He Fan (Xia Chengying), a KMT stalwart from Beijing, pointed out (for once) that baseball was not a Chinese sport and that the hubbub surrounding Maple Leaf went against the amateur ideals of youth sport.[36] Much more common, though, were sentiments like those in the "In Black and White" column of that same day's *UDN*, which celebrated "Maple Leaf's victory [as] not a 'miracle,' but the result of strict training and great struggle. . . . Without much funding [they succeeded] with the local authorities' fervent advocacy and the team members' painstaking preparation. They lacked the most elementary equipment, using sticks for bats and rocks for baseballs, but practiced without end, and progressed without end to reach the superior level they have achieved today. May the spirit and success of the Maple Leaf team excite and inspire everyone!"[37] Thus, even these young Bunun Aborigines' staggering poverty became totally subsumed within national narratives of success under Chiang Kai-shek's KMT.

It is a truism to see a "new era of baseball" beginning in 1968 with these momentous and visible wins. Another important change that resulted was the government's realization of just how much nationalistic sentiment could come from a children's game that had received virtually no support from the Chinese Nationalist regime in Taiwan. August 1968 was the moment when people began to see baseball as having explicit and genuine identifications with the ROC regime, instead of the overwhelming Japanese colonial associations that the game bore for the first two decades of Nationalist rule. But although much of the stir over Maple Leaf can be attributed to a burgeoning Taiwanese nationalism, especially in the face of a decade of Maoist failures on the mainland, this is hardly sufficient explanation. Taiwanese men's baseball teams had defeated powerful Japanese teams before (as noted in chapter 3) to much less hullabaloo, and at moments during the 1950s and 1960s when an anti-Japanese nationalism would have made more immediate sense.

The Maple Leaf team's economic background made all the difference. These boys' proven ability to rise from grinding poverty to astounding success—when guided in the right way by benevolent overseers—seemed to reflect the new possibilities in a capitalist, industrializing Taiwan. This team fit the capitalist ideology that teaches us to rely on oneself and one's supervisors in order to succeed against any obstacle. The children's poverty, utter lack of urban sophistication, and wild nature made their success (and against the Japanese, of all people) even more compelling and actually logical. For decades a particular phrase—"unrestrained and carefree" *(bu shou jushu, ziyou zizai)*[38]—has been used again and again to describe these boys and to explain their success. This element of the children's imagined collective character, and the notion of "restraint" as a shackle on capitalist creativity, speaks to the totalizing nature with which the capitalist ideology had come to define this fast-moving new world of late-'60s Taiwan. And their accomplishments confirmed for Taiwanese people one more element of the capitalist myth—that, in the end, success or defeat really only has to do with one's own capabilities, desire, and ability to soldier on, even if it means leaving one's loving and beautiful (but destitute) family

and hometown behind. That this understanding of the Maple Leaf team as a symbol of Taiwan's hard-earned "miracle" has remained constant despite political changes
and democratization tells us much about the power of this ideology introduced by
the ruling KMT.

These victories against the youngsters from Japan were not just triumphs of a
Chinese nationalism, but in fact very public narratives of how rising standards of
living (funded to a healthy degree by four billion dollars from American taxpayers over the period 1951 to 1965)[39] would have been achieved anyway once the
masses had been prodded along with the right mixture of official benevolence and
"advocacy." The team's repeated meetings with the Generalissimo's son Chiang
Ching-kuo melded well with this understanding; one September issue of the weekly
Newsdom featured on its cover a photo of a Maple Leaf player bowing to a mag-
nanimous-looking Chiang.[40]

MAPLE LEAF INTO NATION
AND HISTORY, 1968–PRESENT

Official memories of the Maple Leaf victories have followed this triumphalist-
capitalist line for four decades now. Pop singer Zhang Guanlu had a hit single in
1979 with the song "Maple Leaf Hometown" ("Hongye guxiang") that went in part:

> Hometown, hometown, I'm leaving this beautiful hometown,
> Parting, parting, after we part we must find each other again.
> Meeting again will be so sweet, we must work our hardest,
> Working toward the goal of success and victory.
> Going to build a new hope, we will be together forever.[41]

A syrupy account of Taiwan's "economic miracle" and the social dislocation that
came with capitalist development, to be sure. But it notably portrayed success, victory, and hope as things that could only be found *away* from an impoverished drain
like Maple Leaf.

In 1988, after two decades of planning, the boys' story finally made it to the silver screen with the feature film *Little Giants of Maple Leaf*. A *Bad News Bears*-style
production short on the intricacies of baseball and long on training montages and
gratuitous animal abuse, the film's main accomplishment was the confirmation of
this capitalist narrative. When the team arrives in Taipei (for their games with the
"world champions" *[sic]* from Japan) they overwhelm hotel management with their
typically Aborigine lack of manners. But eventually the wild but lovable boys win
them over with their irrepressible energy. After driven to great distraction by the
noise coming from the boys' crowded room, a (conspicuously Taiwanese-speaking)
hotel manager is persuaded by the better angels of his nature to laugh, shake his
head resignedly, and decide that "I like their guts—they're like me."[42] The paean to

Taiwan's will to success continues to the "big game," when the privileged and arrogant Japanese manager protests against the Maple Leaf boys' insistence on playing the game barefoot. The PA announcer clears this up for the audience, editorializing that this preference is only because the children are poor and have triumphed over great odds. The money shot of the Maple Leaf victory of course follows, and crowds of Taipei residents flood the field to celebrate once more the powerful ideological structure that these youngsters' baseball skills somehow helped to create in August 1968.[43]

The overall significance in Taiwan of the Maple Leaf success is hard to describe. Virtually all of Taiwanese society was energized by a triumphalism in a way that has few parallels in American sporting history—Joe Louis's 1938 victory over Max Schmeling or the 1980 Olympic hockey team's upset of the USSR are perhaps the closest examples. Professor and novelist Ping Lu, in the public television documentary *The Children of Baseball* (2000) remembered 1968, the year of Maple Leaf's triumph, as a year of liberation and popular rights movements around the globe. But she lamented how these boys' baseball victories actually accomplished "the opposite of the liberation movements" that year. While her fellow citizens of the world were fighting for and winning dignity and rights, the people of Taiwan were being tricked into embracing "one more national myth."[44] To this day, Maple Leaf's 1968 victories against Wakayama are cited as a defining moment in the history of Taiwanese nationalism. A print advertisement for a set of two books chronicling twentieth century Chinese history, published in Taiwan in 2000, featured photographs of the five crucial moments of this century: the 1911 Revolution, the 1945 surrender of Japan after World War II, the Great Leap Forward famine of the early 1960s, Taiwan's withdrawal from the United Nations in 1971, and the Maple Leaf baseball triumphs of 1968![45]

The hubris produced by this win was palpable. Taiwan's urban middle classes, celebrating their own rise, were seemingly obsessed with almost pornographic descriptions of how little the Maple Leaf boys had to eat at home, and how well they could eat in Taipei.[46] An official government newsreel celebrating the squad lingered for minutes on the beautiful and primitive setting of the children's Taidong home village. Filmgoers were taken along rocky and dusty roads to Maple Leaf Village, where they learned through an anthropological gaze about young women washing clothes in a creek, an old woman in a traditional headdress smoking a pipe, and the spare furnishings and rifle racks inside the villagers' homes.[47] Another silent newsreel released weeks later included some of this same footage, but made even more effective ideological use of it. After the same two-minute survey of Maple Leaf poverty, the film showed the boys practicing in a peaceful valley before a stunning mountain backdrop. The film then cut immediately to the team playing before a packed Taipei Municipal Stadium crowd,[48] making a clear point about the fame and riches that awaited any Taiwanese citizen who just tried hard enough. Effectively reproducing this newest "rescue fantasy" was one of the donations received by Maple Leaf Elementary just days after their victories—a pledge from ROC Education Minister Yan Zhenxing to pay for school lunches for all the 150 children of the school.[49] (It is not recorded if anyone asked about helping to feed other poor children whose classmates were not such good baseball players.) The Maple Leaf ideology was powerful enough that just three days after the final game with Wakayama, Taiwan's Central Motion Pictures studio was already working on a script to take this inspirational saga to the big screen. Less than two weeks later, the studio had a title for their film, which they classified as belonging to the "healthy art" genre: *Magic-Ball Youth (Shaonian moqiu)*.[50]

The week after the victories also saw the publication in the *United Daily News* of another celebratory piece titled, "Maple Leaf players' height and weight not inferior to Japanese and American children's of the same age." Doctors at Fraternity Hospital in Yilan County, after consulting the players' biodata, urine samples, dental records, and X-rays, published the inspiring news—after weeks of media coverage on how poorly the Maple Leaf boys ate at home—that they were actually as big and as healthy as Japanese and American youth (the obvious guideposts in 1968 Taiwan).[51] Such was the Maple Leaf triumphalism that its composite narratives did not even have to make sense.

Unfortunately, all of the jubilation and hubris over these victories was soon dampened by an unfortunate revelation. It was soon revealed that on their roster of eleven players, the Maple Leaf team included nine overage boys who were playing under false names provided by their coach, school principal, and head administrator. Suspicions had been raised even before the contests with Wakayama, when Liren Elementary in Tainan, third-place finishers in that year's Students' Cup, came under investigation in August for allowing eight student-athletes to return for a second sixth-grade year. Parents accused of involvement soon pointed to the top two finishers, Maple Leaf and Chuiyang Schools, as having also used "ringers" (*qiangshou*) in the national tourney.[52] (This age differential was extremely obvious in a government newsreel from 1968, which showed the Maple Leaf boys towering over their Taizhong opponents that summer.)[53] Japanese Little League authorities, not pleased at having seen their outstanding team upstaged by a band of cheaters, sent their own investigators to Taiwan that fall.[54] By October, the jig was up when it was publicized that five Maple Leaf star players had "changed their names" before entering middle school that fall.[55] One year later, the Maple Leaf Elementary School principal, head administrator, and baseball coach were all sentenced to a year's imprisonment by the Taidong County Local Court for these gross violations.[56]

Three decades later, one of these players appeared on camera to discuss these experiences for the documentary *The Children of Baseball*. The slugging catcher Jiang Honghui's boyish face may have looked familiar, but his name would not have rung a bell, since his Taipei triumphs of 1968 were achieved under the (slightly homophonous) alias Hu Yonghui. A handsome man in his mid-forties, Jiang wore an embittered expression as he remembered the humiliating truth about his team's epic victories. He remembered the village adults' decisions to have the boys play under false names—names that the children could not even write, that they would even forget to use, cringing each time they accidentally called their mates by their real names. Eventually, the boys decided—in a move that unknowingly reproduced a strategy of the famed Savage Team Nōkō of the 1920s—to call each other by their Bunun Aboriginal names in order to avoid detection of their fraud. On film, Jiang confessed with a bitter smile that he never even admitted anymore to having been one of the shamed Maple Leaf legends.[57]

That these seminal baseball triumphs were defined by cheating, controversy, and embarrassment is significant when one considers how totally they have become part of Taiwanese nationalism. For example, Taiwan's President Chen Shui-bian concluded his 2000 "Bridging the New Century" speech by making reference to an iconic photograph of "a barefoot aboriginal [Maple Leaf] boy at bat." Citing the boy's "full concentration" and his teammates' earnest encouragement, Chen opined simply that "Such a beautiful moment perfectly captures twentieth century Taiwan and is a memory that I will never forget."[58]

Anthropologist Michael Herzfeld has provided a useful framework that can help us start to understand this apparent paradox—which we will see repeated in the way that Taiwan's legendary Little League baseball program has been remembered—of pride and fellowship in humiliation and embarrassment. His book *Cultural Intimacy* makes the case that the strongest bonds of nationalism are often those that lie within a nation's "secret spaces" and in fact are causes and ideologies of "national embarrassment."[59] Although we are used to, especially within the common intersections of sport and nationalism, easy formulas of "victory" and national pride, Herzfeld illustrates how our sites of greatest national or cultural "intimacy" are those "that are considered a source of external embarrassment but that nevertheless provide insiders with their assurance of common sociality."[60] This allows us to ponder how Ernest Renan's oft-cited notion of "forgetting" as "the essence of a nation" is not always sufficient to address what happens to our many collective failures and humiliations. But this work does happen to *confirm* Renan's less-cited thoughts on how, "indeed, suffering in common unifies more than joy does. Where national memories are concerned, griefs are of more value than triumphs, for they impose duties, and require a common effort."[61]

Thus, former President Chen's official Maple Leaf memories posit national shame and pride as not paradoxical but in fact intimately linked. Returning to the Maple Leaf case, the three grown men shamed and sentenced for falsifying official identity documents for the young baseball players eventually received reduced sentences in special consideration of their contributions to Taiwan youth baseball.[62] This gesture makes much more sense if we apply to it Herzfeld's discussion of the links between embarrassment and a nationalism best described as "a fellowship of the flawed."[63]

Since that epic Maple Leaf year of 1968, Taiwanese Little League discourse has scarcely been able to address these many great baseball triumphs without discussing them in the context of embarrassing ethical, if not legal, violations. In 1971, as Taipei prepared to host the Far East playoffs, which the Tainan Giants would win, the newspaper *Chinese Daily* stated that Taiwanese Little League baseball was "walking on fire and going to hell." A piece in *Physical Education Quarterly* summarized thirteen recent newspaper articles covering problems in Little League, including: ticket scalping, expensive ticket prices, school teams neglecting schoolwork in order to spend more time practicing baseball, adults brawling at games or crashing through gates to get into games, troops having to be brought in to restore order at one game, and a team from Jiayi having to sneak back to their hometown and stay in a hotel after losing a big game.[64] Another piece in the next issue described a game where hysterical parents threatened to kill a coach, scaring the children so much that many had to leave the game.[65]

There was most certainly much else behind this media attention to youth baseball—for instance, issues of class, regional, and subethnic difference between upper-middle class Taipei mainlander intellectuals and the working-class southern Taiwanese communities they described. And there was much to be concerned about in Taiwan's burgeoning Little League community. The Tainan Giants' championship run in 1971 was blemished by public charges made by a mother of an opposing player that her son's coach had been paid off to throw the game to the Giants. Before the island championship game, held in Taizhong, the coaches of both teams received so many threatening letters and phone calls that five hundred military policemen were called in to maintain order at the city stadium.[66] Yet one can still see a sense of great pride in these national media reports: the author of the first *Physical Education Quarterly* article also took time to boast of how the 1969 Golden Dragons championship team, "purely Chinese-trained without relying on foreign technical assistance," had "defeated all under heaven and shocked all from the eight directions" and shown that China (i.e., the ROC) was the "future master of baseball."[67]

More recently, a new discourse of shame and embarrassment has emerged in discussions of Taiwan's former Little League supremacy. The aforementioned public TV documentary on the Maple Leaf story, made in 2000, presented footage of their victories over Wakayama over lyrics from the Beatles: "Hey, Jude, don't make it bad; Take a sad song and make it better."[68] Again, with recourse to Herzfeld, this case shows us how the "alleged national traits"[69] of which Taiwanese people are ironically "proud"—clever manipulation of the system, stifling parental pride in their sons, and local, community, and national loyalty—became a valuable framework within which to discuss the abuses of and social problems reflected within youth baseball culture. In the same broadcast, Maple Leaf catcher Jiang Honghui remembered how many of his teammates died as young men, felled by alcohol and disease; the only time he sees the remaining players is when they get together to "drink hard."[70]

In 1999, a novel published by Li Tong, a native of Hualian on the east coast, centered on the life and memories of a fictional member of the Maple Leaf team with reference to this same set of "national" flaws. The novel begins with the dramatic line, "I was a backup player who lost my name"—a fascinating, if maudlin, bit of interplay between nostalgia and true loss. The novel's opening passage continued, "I truly miss the days before we established an official team, when we played on our rocky and bumpy field, without gloves, with just one bat and one ball to use. Our swings, dashes, and slides covered us in sweat. We used our real names when we hit those rocks in our Maple Leaf Valley."[71]

During that same year, a short story called "Hu Wuhan and I" investigated the feelings of the grown-up Maple Leaf boy whose name was taken and used fraudulently by pitcher Jiang Wanxing. Unlike Jiang, who died at age thirty-seven of liver disease, Hu in this story has a nine-to-five office job in the city. But he asks himself, "Who am I? My dad calls me Hu Wuhan, and Hu Wuhan called me the same thing—I'm Hu Wuhan's Hu Wuhan, a body double, an attachment that will be remembered forever and totally forgotten. The mountains sealed my fate and buried my soul."[72] Three decades after the Maple Leaf moment, many in Taiwan still seem to be gripped by a trauma of modernization that is expressed most poignantly through these intimate and shared formulae of nostalgia.

Other scholars of popular culture have studied similar questions of sadness and the loser in Taiwanese popular music. Nancy Guy has looked at Taiwanese-language songs of lament and loss from the colonial and immediate postwar eras and the use of these songs in later (1979 and 2006) protest movements in Taiwan. "Mending Broken Nets" ("Bu powang") and "A Flower in the Rainy Night" ("Yuye hua") are perhaps unremarkable in their portrayal of lost love.[73] But the fact that they have remained politically useful for the last three decades speaks to the power of this narrative of trauma during a time of an unprecedented economic boom. Jeremy Taylor has also put forth the thesis that Taiwanese-language songs—especially those linked to traditions of Japanese music—are by definition more political in content than the Mandopop ones that dominate the airwaves in Taiwan. He shows how the "bar girl" and "wine song,"[74] narratives of loss and the loser, have become the most authentic expressions of Taiwaneseness in all of Taiwanese pop culture.

It is the most worn of clichés to insist that baseball is at the heart of Taiwan's unique culture. We can accept this proposition, as long as we also realize that we have to see what else this national "quality" (in this case, baseball discourse) is supposed to *contest* at the heart of Taiwanese culture as well. If the Maple Leaf legend and all that it said about Taiwan was discovered to be a sham so soon after its very creation, why is this team still such an iconic element of Taiwanese culture? Why would such embarrassment become, in former President Chen's words, a "beauti-ful moment [that] perfectly captures twentieth century Taiwan"?

These Maple Leaf victories galvanized the formation in Taiwan of a formal Little League Baseball (*Shaonian bangqiu*, or *Shaobang*) program in 1969. Although the Nationalist government had invested very little in developing the game over the previous quarter century, these international victories proved that baseball could have real domestic uses for the regime. We might understand the "flawed" ROC nationalism constructed through the Maple Leaf experience to reflect a certain commonality of victimhood, where past mainlander and Taiwanese suffering at the hands of the Japanese, the Communists, and each other, could be best shared through this sort of damaged victory. It is possible to imagine these many groups of people, all invested differently in modern Taiwan and its significance, even un-wittingly sharing a metonymy of associations of pain, suffering, and humiliation—of colonialism, of cultural loss, of war, of exile, of repression and white terror—that could finally come together in this exciting cultural realm that, ironically, could ap-pear to transcend all of this.[75] Finally, this nationalism, as a mutually understood "fellowship of the flawed," was also powerful for its ability to create striking critiques of the national state and community that it also purported to support.

TO AMERICA: THE GOLDEN DRAGONS, 1969

The year 1969 saw Taiwan's first entry into the Little League World Series, operated by the U.S. Little League Baseball (LLB) establishment and held in Williamsport, Pennsylvania. The schoolboys of Taiwan spared no time in making this tournament a yearly blowout of almost any and all challengers. In a tremendous run perhaps unmatched in the history of international sport, Taiwanese teams won ten Little League World Series titles between 1969 and 1981,[76] and seventeen in the twenty-eight-year period from 1969 to 1996. This success brought desperately needed at-tention to Taiwan in a time when its most important ally, the United States, was gradually shunning the island in favor of ties to the People's Republic of China (PRC). These sporting victories could serve both fantasy and reality; the ROC gov-ernment presented them as clear proof of both their right to take back the Chinese mainland from which they had been exiled in 1949 *and* the beneficence of their rule over Taiwan since 1945. But this baseball culture also allowed the playing-out of a very complicated jumble of national and racial tensions that make a study of baseball crucial to a deeper understanding of Taiwanese society during this era.

As described in chapter 3, the Chinese Nationalist government in Taiwan had never seen the promotion of baseball, a game they inherited from the Japanese colo-nial era, as important to their governance. For more than two decades, basketball and soccer continued to serve as the unofficial "national pastimes" as they had on the mainland since the 1930s. A 1966 book titled (in English) *Republic of China To-*

day and published to mark Chiang Kai-shek's eightieth birthday included two pictures of Chiang's Sinicized heirs playing sports—basketball ("Girl students watch boy schoolmates playing basket ball") and soccer—but none of baseball.[77] Another edition of *Republic of China Today* published in 1968, the year of the Maple Leaf triumphs, also featured no baseball photos among its sporting attentions.[78] But even Maple Leaf's inspiring victories, for all of the hubristic nationalism that they achieved overnight, did not change this situation. Baseball became a specific emphasis of the Education Ministry's annual national sporting plan for the first time in 1969, but the 20 percent decrease in the national sports budget for that year erased this symbolic new consideration.[79] Regardless of funding difficulties, the leaders of the ROC Baseball Association continued to aggressively move into the international Little League system. In July 1969, a Taiwan all-star team known as the Taizhong Golden Dragons (Taizhong Jinlong) was sent to Japan to compete in the Pacific Regional Championships.

Just three weeks earlier, a radical opponent of the KMT and an advocate of Taiwanese independence who called himself "Tai-phoon" had penned a harsh article for the journal *Viva Formosa* (published in Tokyo, away from KMT censorship). Tai-phoon attacked "the Chiang dictatorial regime's" sacrifice of the sports belonging to the Taiwanese people, beginning with a claim that resonated strikingly with some forty years of Nationalist rhetoric about sport, democracy, and citizenship: "The prosperity or indolence of a society can be seen in the condition of the sports of a nation and its people." But Tai-phoon challenged the KMT claim that Taiwan was an example of a flourishing society. Instead, the author opined that "the 'Chiang-Dog-Party' (Jiangquandang) had assassinated the sport of the Taiwanese people, degrading the strength of the Taiwanese people so that they are weaker than before . . . something that in all the world only the Chiang father and son could do."[80] The author compared the almost total lack of official support for baseball with the NT$600 million (US$15 million) spent every year teaching kids to throw grenades in the Youth Anti-Communist Corps. Finally, if baseball was starting to get a bit of attention, the author continued, it was only because the regime had resuscitated the game only in order to "buy face" from the Japanese.[81]

This last point—the regime's image vis-à-vis the Japanese—was indeed important for the Nationalists, and did in fact constitute a large part of how the baseball establishment prepared for this first formal Little League venture. In order to prepare for the LLB Pacific Regionals in Japan that summer, Taiwan authorities invited a Japanese team for a friendly two-game series in April 1969. Unlike the previous year, however, this Japanese squad handily defeated an all-Taiwan team of stars from the island's eight top elementary school teams, leaving the children's parents "crying in pain." Even more painful was the opening banquet that showed how much bigger (on average seven inches taller) the Japanese children were. How could this team of "yellow-faced skinnies" (as newspaper reporters put it) help Taiwan compete with Japan?[82] This humiliation, just six months after the Maple Leaf victories of 1968 were revealed to be shams, spurred even more official work to bring together Taiwan's best young players to represent the ROC.

However, the Little League World Series was never meant to be a competition between national teams. The teams that competed in Williamsport every summer were supposed to represent communities (towns or districts) of a maximum of fifteen thousand people. The ROC Baseball Association scoured Taiwan's population of fifteen *million* for talent, testing the skills of hundreds of players (especially those 145 cm [4'9"] or taller) from all over Taiwan, in intense training sessions and scrimmages publicized by national newspapers.[83] But the symbolic rhetoric of unity under benevolent KMT management that was supposed to come out of this process only brought attention to how the adults in charge of Taiwan's LLB program were now cheating in a different way.

The team that arrived in Japan for the Pacific Regionals in July consisted of the finest talent from all over Taiwan, with fourteen players representing six counties in a profound violation of the LLB charter.[84] Among the youth who had trained nonstop for months were Yu Hongkai (who had played for Maple Leaf the previous year!) and Guo Yuanzhi (a pint-size marvel from an impoverished Amis Aborigine family in Taidong, who would go on to star in Japan, but who was best known then for throwing 264 pitches in twenty innings in consecutive scrimmages that summer).[85] Only two players were from the city Taizhong, whose name was attached to the team, while nine were from Jiayi and Tainan in the south. The team was only chosen to represent Taizhong at the last minute because a city assemblyman there, Chen Qingxing, had funded extensive training for the tourney in Japan.[86]

The assistant team leader *(fulingdui)* of this Taizhong Golden Dragons squad was Jian Yongchang, the figure cited and interviewed in chapters 1 and 3 about the Japanese influence on the game. In yet another self-published book, Jian remembered the pressure that faced him and his squad when they got to Japan. In a telling gesture of paternalism that speaks as well to the reach of American cultural hegemony a quarter century after the end of World War II, the U.S. military housed Jian and the team at their Urawa army base north of Tokyo. Jian did not enjoy the digs, however; he could not sleep because if his team lost he would not be able to face his countrymen, and if they won, the under-funded team would not be able to pay for their trip to Williamsport, Pennsylvania.[87] The Golden Dragons ended up winning this tourney overwhelmingly, shutting out all of their opponents.

Reporters at the KMT-run *Chinese Daily* reporters described another great victory against the "Asian baseball kingdom of Japan . . . just a year after a bunch of barefoot angels from Maple Leaf Village in the mountains of Taidong trained using rocks and bamboo poles" had done the same.[88] Perhaps more representative of the government position, though, was "an elderly official of the [ROC] Committee for the Promotion of Sports, who greeted the boys at the airport on their return from

Japan, [and] admitted that he had never seen a baseball game. 'I have no idea how you play baseball,' he exclaimed, 'but I think this is terrific. It's a great day for China.'"[89]

These vague commendations were all that was forthcoming from the KMT government in Taipei. Xie Guocheng, head of the ROC Baseball Association and LLB apparatus, now had to raise on his own the NT$1.7 million (US$42,500) needed to take the team to the world Little League championships in Williamsport the next month. The national sports budget had just been cut by some 20 percent, and the Chiang-era budget that dedicated 80 to 85 percent of national resources to military expenditures left little room for these sorts of affairs. Japanese LLB authorities, whose teams had won the previous two world titles in Williamsport, saw an opening in these Taiwanese funding troubles (as well as a use for the plane tickets to Pennsylvania that they had already purchased) and volunteered to instead represent the Pacific region if the Golden Dragons could not afford to make the trip.[90] Xie turned to his contacts in local governments and business, raising NT$100,000 (US$2,500) each from the Taipei city government and the Taizhong city assembly, NT$200,000 (US$5,000) from a Suzuki Motors agent, and smaller contributions from local Lions Clubs and other businesses. The largest donation came from a source that, again, reinforced the important global and cultural cold war hierarchies of the time. When Xie showed up at a "Reno Night" held at the local American military base, those present were happy to donate all of the cash (US$7,589) atop one of the gambling tables to the cause. (U.S. military advisors, however, had to turn down Xie's request that they fly the Golden Dragons to Pennsylvania by military transport.)[91]

The trip to America was an almost unimaginable experience for the team, most of whom came from impoverished families for whom even a visit to Taipei was an incredible voyage. Aboard the airplane to the United States, one youngster, infielder-captain Chen Hongpi from Jiayi, asked the teammate in the next seat if they were dreaming. Their memories at Williamsport are largely those of typically mischievous but well-mannered boys in an exciting new environment: Chen being chased and kissed by groups of American girls, Maple Leaf veteran Yu Hongkai hitting a beehive with a stick and being covered with stings, playing with the American boys there (Ping-Pong, trading Taiwanese for American currency at thieves' rates, and signing dirty Chinese characters as their "autographs") or not (very few were brave enough to get in the swimming pool at the LLB complex), eating ham and eggs for the first time, and Guo Yuanzhi rubbing chili peppers on his cheeks before the interminable rounds of kisses from proud overseas Chinese.[92] But all also seemed to understand the uniqueness of their opportunities for geographic mobility that eluded all but the most privileged Taiwanese citizens.

The children were not naïve or easily intimidated. Pitcher Guo Yuanzhi later remembered his teammates' initial racial jitters at being the only "yellow" players in Williamsport. They overcame these fears by using the taller physiques of their Western opponents against them, throwing more curve balls that they felt longer-armed

North Americans would have trouble hitting.[93] Chen Hongpi is typical for remembering his teammates' immense confidence after all that they had been through. In 2000, he said, "We knew that no one else could compete with us. We were an all-star team from all over Taiwan. We didn't imagine that anyone could be stronger than us, especially after all that training. . . . We played like we were an army."[94]

Few others (except the Japanese LLB body, which actually sent the manager of the team who had lost to the Golden Dragons to Williamsport to lobby against the team's illegal composition)[95] could have expected a team this disciplined and skilled. In their white-and-red pinstriped "Republic of China" jerseys (except for one child's, which read "Chian"),[96] the squad "surprised everyone from Japan to the U.S." with their easy victories over opponents from Ontario and Ohio. An impressed *Sporting News* described the skill and infectious enthusiasm of "the Orientals":

> Thousands of gong-clanging, cheering fans in the stands at Williamsport adopted the Chinese as their favorite team.
>
> [Pitcher Chen Zhiyuan] captured the fans' imagination when, after every out, he'd turn around and shout to his fielders, raising the ball above his head. In return they yell in Chinese the American equivalent of, "Go men!"[97]

Local newspapers were no less effusive; the *Harrisburg Patriot* called Chen "the best pitcher in the world," and the *Williamsport Sun* followed forty years of KMT propaganda by exclaiming that on the basis of the Golden Dragons' baseball talents, "Asians will not be humiliated again."[98]

The Taiwanese boys' confidence was also boosted by the presence of thousands of delirious flag-waving fans from the ROC. Students from nearby Penn State, hoisting signs reading "Go, China, Go, Uno," and chanting "We are number one!"[99] made up just one of a dozen cheerleading squads organized by ROC citizens residing in the United States and Canada. Although the ROC government had invested almost nothing in the Little League Baseball project (besides sending three thousand ROC flags with the squad for distribution to overseas Chinese fans),[100] the passionate reception given the Golden Dragons in Williamsport made the regime take notice of the convenient gains to be made in the form of popular nationalism. The government decided to broadcast, during the very early morning, the American Broadcasting Company feed of the championship game, which began with a representative of Ambassador Zhou Shukai throwing a ceremonial first pitch to William Shea of the New York Mets.[101]

Returning to Herzfeld on the topic of "cultural intimacy" helps us understand the results of this KMT decision to become involved symbolically in baseball in this way. He writes that when "the state so fully adopts the cultural signs . . . in order to permeate the oppressed citizens' every sentient moment, . . . it exposes itself to greater day-to-day manipulation by these same citizens, who are familiar with the capacity of those signs to bear subversive interpretations."[102] Indeed, the KMT regime's involvement in baseball opened up a whole new space in the Nationalist narrative that was quickly exploited by the state's enemies, in this case supporters of Taiwanese independence from all Chinese rule. Such individuals, eager to publicly recognize the centrality of this Japanese game to Taiwanese society and thereby to negate KMT claims of legitimacy in Taiwan, also made sure to appear in Williamsport in great numbers.

"TEAM OF TAIWAN": CONTESTING NATIONALISMS

Before the LLB World Series even began, Reverend Song Chaon-seng and the Formosan Christians for Self-Determination sent to all Williamsport residents copies of a four-page letter supporting Taiwan independence, criticizing the KMT and Richard Nixon for his overtures to the PRC, and refuting KMT claims that "Taiwanese watchers of the game were communist instigated."[103] But the most amazing coup scored by Taiwan independence activists in Williamsport occurred right before the championship game against Santa Clara, California. During the playing of the ROC national anthem, the ABC television cameras focused in on a sign in the stands that read (referring to the ethnic composition of the Golden Dragons), "TEAM OF TAIWAN, NOT REP. OF CHINA!" Foes of the Chiang government viewing this in predawn Taiwan could only have been ecstatic at this ingenious manipulation of what was to be an easy win for KMT nationalism abroad. ABC announcer Jim McKay only made things better (or worse, depending on one's perspective) when he insisted on referring to the ROC team as representing "Taiwan, or Formosa" during his broadcast of the game.

Representatives of United Formosans in America for Independence also distributed to Little League fans thousands of handbills titled, "Cheers for the Taiwan League." Those who read on would have noted the passage that read, "Taiwan (Formosa) is neither free nor China. The team [here] is the *Taiwan* team, not that of 'the Republic of China.' . . . Taiwanese love baseball, but not Chinese mainlanders in Taiwan."[104] In this last sentence, the modifier could dangle either way and still provide an accurate reading. The official meddling of "Chinese mainlanders," who for twenty-four years had no use for this Japanese game—Taiwanese fans could not believe that the "mainlanders" in attendance in Williamsport were cheering for "touchdowns" when the Taiwanese boys scored *runs*[105]—provided unprecedented new opportunities for Taiwanese people to express their love for baseball and not Chinese mainlanders. For years to come, Williamsport became a "new battlefield"[106] between residents of North America who supported the KMT and those who supported Taiwan independence, and who all found these yearly baseball pilgrimages integral to their diverse expressions of nationalist identity.

Thus, here we can start to see baseball functioning again during this period of Taiwanese history as a realm of glocalization. During the first two decades of KMT rule in Taiwan, the regime was loath to allow the game's many and memorable links to global, colonial, and Japanese flows of culture to be exposed too clearly. But the reentry of Taiwan baseball into an international sphere made it possible for fans attending these games in Pennsylvania to incorporate a rich array of messages and ideas in expressing their particular experiences of Chiang rule.

These "subversive interpretations" brought to bear by anti-Nationalist elements visiting Williamsport also did not pass unchallenged. The *New York Times* reported the next day on the armed battles that took place after one Golden Dragon victory between "two factions of Chinese-speaking fans [who] attacked each other with broken sticks and megaphones." This article was vague about why this violence was taking place, except for a mention that bystanders were holding proudly the "TEAM OF TAIWAN" sign that would have infuriated any KMT loyalists.[107] But the Nationalists' own reports on the ROC triumph explained much more:

> Of all the overseas Chinese living abroad, there were not any who did not greet each other joyfully. . . . But there was one pack of "Chinese people" without any pride who, as the crowd was leaving, held up a "Team of Taiwan" flag, harassing and molesting people in an insanely unscrupulous way. There were several patriotic overseas compatriots who had no use for this, and came together to denounce them and drive them away. But in the foreigners' eyes this was "two groups of Chinese people fighting." These "Taiwan Independence" elements who have exiled themselves to America and make fools of themselves in front of foreigners simply humiliate all of us Taiwan compatriots. Now we simply must ask all overseas compatriots travelling to America to follow the [ROC] government and its conscientious ways.[108]

The ROC government in Taiwan had to totally marginalize those who would challenge their claims of a successful rule of Taiwan that entitled them to take back the Communist-held mainland.

For obvious reasons, the government preferred to concentrate on the reaction to this victory within (a tightly censored) Taiwan. The Golden Dragons' world championship soon took on great importance for the Nationalist regime in its claims to legitimacy, over not only Taiwan, but over China as well. It took only twelve days for a book to be published in Taipei about the Golden Dragons; it began: "Full of wonder and pride, with eyes full of tears, the whole nation from commoner to government official, even those, old and young, women and children, who did not understand baseball, at 3:20 A.M. in the early morning of the twenty fourth of August of the fifty-eighth year of the Republic of China [1969], learned that the 'Unrivalled Golden Dragons' captured for the ROC the twenty-third World Youth Baseball Championship, winning unprecedented glory for our nation on the world sporting stage."[109] Confirming this official account, a radio DJ remembered thirty years later how "the Taipei night nearly boiled over. When the game finished at 3 A.M., the streets of the city erupted with the constant banging of firecrackers, as ordinary citizens opened their windows and yelled out to the night sky, 'Long live the Republic of China!' "[110]

One fascinating thing about this reaction was how quickly the Golden Dragons' victory in Williamsport gibed perfectly with the stalled propaganda needs of the ROC regime. One only needs to consider that even after the Great Leap Forward famine that killed some thirty to forty-two million people in the PRC, and three years into the terror and destruction of the Great Proletarian Cultural Revolution, Chiang Kai-shek's ROC was actually *losing* to Mao Zedong the battle for "hearts and minds" around the world. This Little League triumph appeared as a desperately needed break in this trend, and the government was committed to making the best of it. And best of all, little effort was required at home. After more than two decades of enforced Chineseness—from the Mandarin language to the Nationalist-centered education system to the infinitely repeated vows to "retake the mainland"—this weird Japanese sport of baseball now had the Taiwanese public, of their own will, waving ROC flags, taking to the streets to proclaim their loyalty to Sun Yat-sen's republic, forgetting about the ethnic and political tensions of the time, and embracing the notion that these twelve-year-old boys' victories truly reflected virtues of the "Chinese" nation.

The government's official thoughts on these triumphs were awkward, unsophisticated, and unoriginal. Some propaganda reassured the people of Taiwan that these Little League championships showed the world that "Chinese people were strong and on top of the world, and no longer the 'Sick Man of East Asia' *(dong Ya bingfu)*"[111]—the latter a cliché that had been part of sporting discourse dating back to the late Qing dynasty. Nationalist hubris, just as with the Maple Leaf win a year previous, became commonplace and boundless. (Despite the fact, again, that the ROC Baseball Association had clearly and egregiously cheated.)

An author wrote in the *Physical Education Quarterly* that the Golden Dragon win proved that, thanks to ancient traditions and the power of Chinese medicine, Western children were not always bigger and stronger, although it was true that Chinese kids were more clever (a fact he could tell just from watching "foreign" children's stupid and slow motions). He was even more optimistic about the value of a Little League game, stating that the boys from Taiwan had "gotten the attention of every American" and "had made people in every corner of the world more deeply understand the dynamism of Chinese youth."[112] Another "quickie" book on the Golden Dragons told of how their win had "put the name of ROC in the championship ring" for the first time. This author bragged of the Golden Dragons' popularity in the home of baseball. While the country youth were besieged by attention from American children, reporters, and businesses eager to profit from their skills by using their likenesses in advertisements, LLB head Peter J. McGovern compared catcher Cai Songhui to the Detroit Tigers' all-star Bill Freehan, and said that the Dragons as a whole were the finest Little League team he had ever seen.[113] Meanwhile, the KMT weekly *Newsdom* opined that the victory was simply proof of the success of the nine-year compulsory education system begun one year before. If not for the government's wisdom, their explanation went, the players would have been too busy cramming for examinations to win the previously rare privilege of attending junior high, and their "original baseball skills would be lost beyond the ninth level of heaven."[114] (This odd claim would be repeated by KMT loyalists—clearly able to find no other connection between government efforts and the game of baseball—for years to come.)[115]

The climax of this intersection between Little League skill and nationalistic hubris came on 18 September 1969, after the conclusion of the young champions' exhausting victory tour of Taiwan. The team was taken to Jinmen (Quemoy) Island, the "anti-Communist fort" held by the ROC military just a mile and a half off the coast of Communist China's Fujian Province. Michael Szonyi has described how Jinmen served as a potent "symbol of the government's commitment to national recovery and anti-Communism"; at this time it was home to a population of sixty thousand thoroughly militarized civilians and some eighty thousand ROC troops.[116] There, on the island that had been shelled by the PRC military every other day since the 1958 Taiwan Strait Crisis, the government staged a surreal meeting of two groups of boys and young men fighting on different front lines of Chiang Kai-shek's struggle for Chinese supremacy. All of the predictable gestures were made—a welcome with flowers from bowing girls from Jincheng Elementary School, returned by a gift of baseball equipment from the world champions to the boys of that school, puns about the "ballfield and the battlefield," and interminable liquor-soaked banquets dedicated to the "little heroes"[117]—to link the boys' wins in Williamsport to as many tropes of ROC unity and strength as possible.

But two particular details of the trip made it even more symbolically powerful. The first is that Golden Dragon catcher Cai Songhui's older brother Cai Songchuan was actually among the troops stationed on the ROC's most forward position at Jinmen. The synchronicity of their dramatic meeting was chronicled proudly by a Nationalist media eager to justify the regime's pretensions to work toward reconquering China.[118] But the Cai boys' reunion also highlighted an important fact that few (except for Taiwan Independence activists) mentioned publicly—namely, how much of the regime's effort and bravery was expended by impoverished members of the ethnic Taiwanese population who, generally, had much less to gain from Nationalist "victory" than their mainlander compatriots. This contradiction, at the heart of the regime's relationship with baseball for a quarter century by then, would complicate their uses of the game for decades to come.

A second fantastic element of this trip came at Horse Mountain Observation Point, the northern station closest to the PRC. Pitcher Chen Zhiyuan, when peering across from the observation tower, had remarked, "the mainland is so close, I'd love to throw a baseball over." Military officials had the next best thing in mind. Showing that they took seriously their rhetoric about sharing the news of the victory with "the compatriots of the entire [Chinese] nation," they used massive speakers to make a special booming broadcast to the people of coastal Fujian:

> Our ROC youth baseball team recently took part in the twenty-third youth baseball world championships in America, and beat teams from Canada and the United States to win the world title. This is not only the glory of the entire populace of the Republic of China, but represents a mission of glory accomplished for all the countries of the Pacific region. Mainland compatriots, the ROC youth baseball team's world championship is the [Chinese] nation's greatest sporting accomplishment in history, and is the result of a superior educational system, allowing all of us Chinese people to enjoy this glory together. Just think, what kind of lives are your children living now?[119]

Team members, riffing on this wildly irredentist theater, chipped in on their eagerness to go play baseball before the youngsters of Nanjing, Beiping (the ROC referred to Beijing as Beiping, as they did not recognize it as the official capital), or any other corner of China.[120]

Again, however, the "subversive interpretations" were quick to come. If the Nationalist regime hoped to use the incredible skills of these southern youngsters to unify China, dissident baseball fans saw a very different meaning in the Golden Dragons' triumph. Frenzied Taiwanese fans in Williamsport shouted their challenge to Nationalist rhetoric and authoritarianism at the end of the championship game: "The players are all Taiwanese! Taiwan has stood up!"[121] The September 1969 issue of *Taiwan Youth*, a magazine published jointly by proindependence Taiwanese groups around the world, included three articles on the meanings of this win. One author, in a piece unambiguously titled "Glory of Taiwanese Youth, Victory of the Taiwanese People," scorned the Chinese "gangsters and hoods" who—following Nationalist rhetoric—posed as "pure and true descendants of the Yellow and Yan Emperors" and bored all with their arrogant talk of "five thousand years of culture." Instead, he explained how the Williamsport win was the triumph of three generations of Taiwanese effort, from those elders who learned the game during the Japanese era, to those who funded the trip, to the team's coaches. Hardest of all for these Taiwanese intellectuals to swallow was the fact that the endless Nationalist rhetoric about "China" and Chinese pride actually negated itself, leading some American fans to assume that the Golden Dragons were representing the Communist regime in the real China.[122]

Another article in the same proindependence periodical explained how the groups present in Williamsport made their appeal to locals and baseball fans unaware of the great struggles that the Taiwanese people faced. When Nationalist authorities instructed "ignorant [local] employees and security" to take down dissidents' "Team of Taiwan" signs, members of the United Formosans in America for Independence "argued resolutely that all people in America enjoyed the freedom and rights enshrined in the Constitution," and were able to keep waving their controversial banners. This, they explained, was the opposite of the "Chinese" approach of cursing the Taiwanese people, ripping their banners away, and starting fights. These activists worked hard to clarify what was at stake, distributing thousands of small flags with pictures of Taiwan on them, and the aforementioned "Cheers for the Taiwan League" leaflets, which specified, "All [the Golden Dragons'] players and coaches are Taiwanese (Formosans), born and brought up in Taiwan, not Chinese." It went on to make a very clear case against the legitimacy of Chiang's "exile regime without the consent of the governed" and, of course, the support that the United States granted it, and took advantage of the setting to conclude dramatically: "Like American children, Taiwanese children [have] their dreams. But their dreams cannot come true under the continuing suppression and indoctrination of Chinese Nationalists. Won't you help them fulfill their dreams?"[123]

This aggressive Taiwanese nationalism—par for the course on American college campuses and in large cities, which armies of paid agents countered with often violent pro-KMT responses—was not imaginable in the suffocating authoritarianism of 1969 Taiwan. Resistance to the government's spurious uses of baseball for its ideologies of "conquest of the mainland" and suppression at home could only come in more subtle ways. One famous photo from this year has the world champion Golden Dragons and their coaches posing with President Chiang and his wife Song Meiling in the Presidential Palace. The weekly *Newsdom* featured this image on the cover that September, complete with a long caption passing on what they assumed to be the poor southern boys' gratitude for the First Couple's attention: "[They] all said: This was the most glorious and exciting day of their lives. They will forever hold in their memories the greatest encouragement, and will resolve to give themselves totally to seeking progress."[124]

These recollections were made much more complicated, however, by Golden Dragon official Jian Yongchang's recollections. The lifetime "baseball man"—whose memories of playing baseball in order to express his "not Japanese and not Chinese" identity were examined in chapter 1—is a fascinating and animated man with a gratifying gift for rich and intricate historical memory. In 2004, I had the chance to chat with him in the sitting room of his Taipei apartment. Considering his outspoken and "Taiwanese"-identified odium for the Nationalist regime, I asked him about the presence of a framed copy of this very photo above his sofa. His answer, as usual, was brilliant. He remembered the team's excellence that forced Chiang to finally pay attention to this "Japanese" game of baseball, and was most proud of the fact that he had held up the Generalissimo and his photo session by an hour so that he could squeeze in a celebratory game of golf that morning.[125] The likelihood of this story being apocryphal is not really the point, though. Instead, it is probably most useful if it helps us to imagine the evermore complicated relationship with Taiwanese Little League Baseball that this "ROC" world championship birthed in 1969.

Days after the return of the triumphant Golden Dragons, Taipei's East and West Press published a book compiling news articles, statistics, and player bios for instant consumption. For a personal touch, the book also included pages of letters that the players sent home from Williamsport. The contents were typical of the earnest boys that the players genuinely seemed to be: Catcher Cai Songhui and shortstop Zhuang Kaiping asked their parents to register them for school in their absence, pitcher Guo Yuanzhi urged his parents not to worry about travelling all the way from far-off Taidong to meet him at the airport when he returned to Taipei, and Yu Hongkai told of the comic books he was able to read in the hospital while recovering from his bee stings. First baseman Huang Zhengyi, in between mentioning the camera he was able to buy for his father and reminding his brothers to take care of his pigeons, cited the moving events of the team's stopover in Tokyo. While the team changed planes, Huang was greeted by his father's former teacher, a Japanese man who took his entire family to the airport to greet the son of his former student of a quarter century before.[126] This quick episode, while heartwarming and filial enough to be included in this "Chinese" volume, would have been understood by any Taiwanese reader as one more sign of the profound weight of Japanese colonialism in Chiang Kai-shek's Chinese Taiwan.

These traces of the Japanese presence were everywhere, even advertised on the very caps worn by these young players. The Chuiyang Elementary School team, always a force in their southern home city of Jiayi, wore caps emblazoned with an interlocked "CY" that was a dead ringer for the Tokyo Yomiuri Giants' trademark "YG" design. Even the national team wore caps with a "C" (China) that Americans long imagined was designed to copy the Cincinnati Reds' logo. The typographic and historical inspiration for this flattened but subversive "C," though, was another Japanese professional team, the Hiroshima Carp.

As will be described in chapter 5, the 1970s and 1980s saw Taiwan's Little League Baseball program become known, feared, and suspected around the world. The combination of glory and shame that these dozens of youth teams would generate is explained best with recourse to Michael Herzfeld's work, mentioned earlier in the chapter. The Japanese game of baseball was rooted totally in the "secret spaces" of Taiwanese people's colonial experiences. How better to understand this powerful combination of historical memory, nostalgia, pain, and anti-KMT subversion than with wonder at how yesterday's embarrassments so often have become "today's proud boast"?[127] The Maple Leaf and Golden Dragon boys had probably never dreamed how much their fine baseball skills would mean to their elders, whose lives were totally defined by these colonial and postcolonial legacies.

5

"Chinese" Baseball and Its Discontents, 1970s–1980s

No single sport has established itself as the Chinese favorite. Soccer draws the largest crowds.

JAMES WEI, ROC GOVERNMENT INFORMATION OFFICE CHAIRMAN, 1972

Baseball is everywhere in Taiwan.

LEONARD PRATT, ASSOCIATED PRESS, 1972

After 1969, Taiwan's Little League phenoms would win the next nine of twelve Williamsport Little League world championships. As if this were not enough agony for the youth of America, the Little League Baseball (LLB) establishment also began inviting Taiwan to send teams to the Senior League and Big League world championships held every summer, respectively, in Gary, Indiana, and Fort Lauderdale, Florida. Taiwan's teenage representatives—essentially national all-star teams like the Little League squads—were even more dominant in these competitions. In the Senior League category (called *Qingshaobang*, ages thirteen through sixteen), Taiwan's teams won nine straight world championships from 1972 to 80, and seventeen in all over a twenty-one-year period. The Big League (*Qingbang*, ages sixteen through eighteen) teams from Taiwan won seventeen world championships in a twenty-three-year period.[1] Every summer during the 1970s became a moment for extravagant celebration—with massive parades, scholarships, TV appearances, and presidential visits—of the latest world baseball titles won by Taiwanese boys and young men.

Each of these championships won or lost reveals much about the standing and worth of the once Japanese game of baseball, which was now earning the "Free China" regime recognition abroad. For obvious interests of space, I will refrain from trying to relate all of their stories here; Yu Junwei's narrative work collects more anecdotes and details for those interested.[2] Instead, I will look at two main elements of the history introduced in chapter 4: the tensions and contradictions between nationalist and dissident uses (both ideological and diplomatic) of baseball, and the intense culture of loss and shame that continued to grow around these unending triumphs on the baseball field.

Over the 1970s, this Japanese game became a powerful site for the articulation of Taiwanese and mainlander suffering, degradation, and pain, largely because of its associations with colonialism, war, and cultural loss. Intellectuals in Taiwan revealingly attempted to use Milan Kundera's ruminations on *litost* and longing to describe this pain at the heart of a Taiwan collective identity. At the same time, the unprecedented economic boom in Taiwan was creating entirely new narratives of striving, risk, and failure in an evermore dynamic society. Scott Sandage's book *Born Losers,* on the history of failure and human worth in nineteenth century America, also provides a reference for the existence of "a hidden history of pessimism" and reflections on the "deficient self" within a moment of widespread prosperity.[3] Narratives of loss and victory on the baseball field could easily be conflated with other dominant narratives of failure and success in Taiwan's new business world. Finally, this chapter continues with reflection on Herzfeld's work on "cultural intimacy," the sites of "external embarrassment" that eventually assure a "common sociality,"[4] in order to explore how baseball became an essential element of the traumatic experience of modernization and its many narratives in 1970s and 1980s Taiwan.

LITTLE LEAGUE BASEBALL AND A CHINESE/TAIWANESE NATION

Overwhelming yearly youth victories achieved in Pennsylvania, Indiana, and Florida had very little impact on official Nationalist support for what they saw as a Japanese game. Official media and state-friendly intellectuals did their best to maximize the ideological impact of these teams' dominance, but it seems that it was truly difficult for the Nationalist regime to actually support the game. In 1976, the International Baseball Association (IBA), in recognition of the island's excellence in the game, awarded Taiwan the right to hold the twenty-fourth IBA World Cup. The ROC government did not fund the tourney at all, though, so it was eventually held in Colombia instead.[5] That same year, ROC track and field, soccer, swimming, handball, boxing, and gymnastics coaches were all sent abroad for four months of technical training—but not baseball coaches.[6]

This refusal to fund baseball could only have been a function of the state's utter inability to understand the historical (read: Japanese) legacy of the game. One official chronicler repeatedly tried to describe the significance of Taiwan's baseball victories by using an essay written by Chiang Kai-shek in September 1942 for the national Sports Day holiday back in Sichuan Province.[7] In 1971, Chiang's only advice for the Tainan Giants before they left for America was to "be true and pure Chinese" *(tangtang zhengzheng de Zhongguoren).*

This team won the world championship in Williamsport—an event viewed on early morning (2:00 to 5:00 A.M.) television by some ten million people in Taiwan, a staggering two-thirds of the island's population. (This audience did not include Chiang Kai-shek, who, according to the team's coach, went to bed in anger after a first-inning home run put the opponents up by three runs. Song Meiling, accompanied by other officials, did watch the entire game, rousing the President-for-Life only after victory was sealed in the ninth inning.)[8] But even with the benefit of all this rest, Chiang could only phrase his enthusiasm by pointing out, "I trust that all the compatriots of the nation will be moved and excited by the Giants Little League team, in each person's own way, to work to quickly retake the mainland and restore glory to the motherland."[9]

Members of official ROC media took this trope even further. One columnist leapt from the 1971 Giants' extra-innings championship win to the current "standoff" across the Taiwan Straits in a far-fetched piece called "Revelation: Victory": "The officers and troops of the Nationalist Army are defending Taiwan, Penghu, Jinmen, and Mazu [islands], in a situation that could be said to be like the sixth inning. We trust that the ninth inning of our seizing of prisoners, capture of the capital, and retaking of lost territory is not too far away. . . . We will be victorious because our benevolence is unrivalled. . . . All the people of the nation, overseas Chinese, and all members of the armed forces await the coming victory."[10]

Members of Taiwan's intellectual class were not left out of the national (and even racial) self-congratulation that these boys' baseball skills helped them to understand. One author wrote in *The Intellectual* that the 1973 Tainan Giants' sweep of their opponents proved that Chinese people had higher moral standards and enjoyed better inherent physical development and leadership skills than did Westerners. Reveling in this "smashing [of] white feelings of superiority," he continued wildly: "We are the most outstanding nation and race *(minzu)* in the entire world. . . . Chinese leadership of the world begins with Little League Baseball! . . . Now begins the glorious moment of our Chinese people rewriting the history of the world!"[11]

An author in the government's *Central Monthly* began his commentary with an awful poem that concluded:

> "I warmly love my country,
> I promise to abide by the umpire's decisions."
> Listening, listening, this is the grand vow and the heart of the new generation.

This fantasy of the benevolent authoritarian regime was followed by maudlin and prideful chest-beating that also betrayed decades of anxiety about the fate of the Chinese race and the Republic:

> The Chinese nation-race is a superior nation-race!
> The ROC must become a first-rate power! . . .
> The descendants of the Yellow Emperor always as one heart!

The Chinese Republic and the Chinese race must be revived!
Finally we will be giants of the world![12]

These discussions, or as they often were, chants, obviously beg two different questions about these boys' baseball skills and the central role imagined for them in these irredentist dreams of a revived ROC empire. On the latter, it is important to understand that some loyal Nationalists in Taiwan may have seen the goal of "retaking the mainland" as realistic, considering the often brutal, failed, and disastrous record of the PRC state over two decades of Maoism. The championship tours of the Nationalists' forward positions in Jinmen (covered in chapter 4) and the publicity directed toward the mainland just miles away seemed valid steps toward ultimate victory—if only they could alert enough "compatriots" about the tremendous victories won by the boys of the enlightened ROC on Taiwan.

For that matter, then, the Golden Dragons, Giants, and Braves dominating world baseball fit perfectly within these dreams of empire—but not simply for the instrumental reasons that the boys were seen as "future leaders" of the ROC. There is also the fact that boys in particular have been good for thinking about nation-states, in the same way that Darnton makes the case that cats happened to have a particular "ritual value" (as opposed to cows or sheep) that made them "good for staging ceremonies" in early modern Europe. Like cats, boys "straddl[e] . . . conceptual categories."[13] Boys are both the fruit of citizens' reproduction and almost male citizens themselves, and therefore present a fertile site for the imagining of work and conquest. Jonathan Rutherford has reflected on the British Empire as one of "mother's boys," a culture that was taught to fetishize the "boyishness" that bridges conservative domesticity and imperial fantasy.[14] This is a useful tool in understanding the Taiwanese boys' position with regard to the dreams of an ROC empire. Paul Hoch's explanation of a puritan "production ethic masculinity," one of duty and disciplined toil,[15] also helps us—especially considering Taiwan's cult of industry at this moment—to fill out a picture of the pressures, desires, and fantasies that centered upon the baseball players in Taiwan during the 1970s and '80s. As another author in *Central Monthly* concluded, the Tainan Giants' baseball skills, strong bodies, and "refined dignity" were merely the "newest fragrant" product of thousands of years of Chinese culture. In this piece titled "The Baseball Movement, The National Movement," the writer also took the opportunity of these victories to engage in that most lasting and longing Chinese dream of the twentieth century—unity, finally, and a society that "would not be divided by age or hometown."[16]

To most of the people of Taiwan, the attraction of this Little League championship run had little to do with these ideological performances. The glory won by Taiwan's Little, Senior, and Big Leaguers during the 1970s came at the exact same time as two other significant developments—the flowering of Taiwan's "economic miracle" and the island's increasing isolation on the international stage. Taiwan was becoming an economic powerhouse in its own right, a proud Little Tiger that had made the most of the billions of dollars of American aid sent its way, and these triumphs helped feed this hubris. At the same time, the Nationalist regime was also quickly learning that fewer and fewer people around the world viewed their rule of Taiwan as legitimate, let alone moral or humane. The greatest humiliation came in 1971, when the government forfeited its seat in the United Nations, sending Taiwan into four decades of near-total diplomatic isolation from which it has little hope to emerge even today.

The sting and disgrace of leaving the UN was lessened somewhat by the fact that, at the very least, Taiwan's teens and preteens played the most skilled and disciplined baseball the world had ever seen. And, of course, these youth were winning international glories that Taiwan could not hope to match in any other cultural field. What other groups of Taiwanese people ended up with annual invitations to the White House to meet with Richard Nixon, Spiro Agnew, or Gerald Ford? The Nationalist government's reluctance to embrace baseball, then, can only be explained by the game's complicated history and the utter impossibility of essentializing it as an artifact of "Chinese" tradition or endeavor. (Perhaps the only exception to this was the Taipei Municipal Baseball Stadium, which in 1971 "was rebuilt for [the Far Eastern LLB playoffs] and became the only ball park in the world with a handsome Chinese palace-style exterior.")[17]

Nevertheless, in their annual predawn Little League jubilation, the flags people waved were ROC ones, the nation they wished ten thousand years to was the ROC, and so on. Clearly, in just a matter of years, and truly despite itself, this mainlander-dominated regime had managed to achieve a total identification with the Japanese legacy of baseball. As we saw in chapter 4, however, this made it convenient for dissidents seeking to hang subversive signifiers on state symbols. Taiwanese poet Lin Huazhou, a former political prisoner, took biting measure of this ideological overreach with his sarcastic poem "Little League Baseball":

> Little League Baseball! Little League Baseball!
> Saving stars of the race, the new hope of the nation.
> Little League Baseball! Little League Baseball!
> The modern Chinggis Khan, the young Boxers United in Righteousness.
> How much national shame we are counting on you to wash away,
> How many national disasters we are counting on you to reverse.[18]

Unfortunately, one assumes that not every reader got the joke. But the source of material was rich; when Taiwanese youth took the field at Williamsport almost every year, these subversive interpretations reemerged.

The activities by anti-Nationalist and pro-independence activists, who seized precisely and aggressively on these very contradictions between a "Chinese" state and a game learned from the Japanese and played almost exclusively by Taiwanese, became even more audacious and antagonistic as the decade progressed. In 1971, the Tainan Giants swept to a world championship, defeating opponents from Puerto Rico, Hawai'i, and Indiana by a collective score of 30–3 to capture the world title. Meanwhile, above this field of American nightmares, an airplane hired by Taiwan independence forces flew over the stadium brazenly towing a bilingual banner that read, "*Taiwan duli wansui* (Long Live Taiwan Independence), Go Go Taiwan."[19] And raising the stakes even further, the Chinese on the banner was written in PRC-style simplified characters that were illegal to use in Taiwan! The provocation was successful, and the fighting that erupted between independence activists and ROC loyalists was so vicious that state police had to bring in reinforcements by helicopter in order to gain control of the facilities—until the following year, when the two sides would face off again, celebrating another Taiwan/ROC Little League triumph by fighting with baseball bats outside the left-field fence.[20]

The Taiwan teams' games attracted fans from all points of the political spectrum, so that each Taiwan independence flag or banner (for example, "Taiwanese Brothers, We Love You," "Overthrow the Chiangs, Build Taiwan," "End Martial Law in Taiwan," "No Secret Police," and "Chiang Get Out, Mao Stay Out")[21] was matched by a pro-Nationalist mainlander fan waving a national flag and chanting, "Go Go China." The pro-ROC forces had an advantage, however, in the dozens of paid spies[22] and New York Chinatown thugs hired by the Guomindang to intimidate the "Taiwan" fans in the stands. In 1971, the championship game was interrupted when a dozen of these toughs ran across the field to rip down a banner reading in English and Chinese, "Team of Taiwan, *Jiayou Taiwan dui* (Go Team of Taiwan)."[23]

In 1972, when the Taipei Braves challenged for the world title in Pennsylvania, the KMT was better prepared, renting every single commercial aircraft for miles around to keep the Taiwan Independence crowd from repeating their airborne coup of the year before.[24] Some seventy to eighty military cadets training in the United States were also recruited to Williamsport, where they beat Taiwanese male and female supporters with wooden clubs while shouting, "Kill the traitors *(Shasi Hanjian)!*" This war was only quelled by the intervention of police helicopters, but not before making a distinct impression on fans around the world as to just how hotly and violently disputed Taiwanese/Chinese identity was at the time. (The author of one account in *Viva Formosa* urged Taiwanese fans to consider bringing guns to Williamsport the next year!)[25] The joy and determination that Taiwanese fans seemed to exhibit in challenging Nationalist hegemony in Taiwan reminds us that more was at stake here than Chiang Kai-shek's "Free China" ideology. These fans were merely continuing a contest over the significance of Taiwanese baseball that was half a century old.

One interesting difference between these yearly battles and European soccer hooliganism, the best studied field in the larger genre of sporting crowd violence, appears within "the play through which people try to turn transient advantage into a permanent condition."[26] English soccer hooligans, as Buford describes them, for example, seem to take part in grand acts of street and stadium violence simply for the sake of violence, "the exalted experiences that by their intensity, their risk, their threat of self-immolation exclude the possibility of all other thought except the experience itself."[27] There seems to be no sense that their brutal fighting would lead to a new social order or condition. Indeed, these English hooligans *need* their rival club supporters, their "foreigners" and "wogs," against whom to fight even more bestially the next time. The Taiwan case at Williamsport is much more clearly about independence activists using this unique annual stage to make their best argument against the KMT regime and hopefully to "turn transient advantage into a permanent condition" of a Taiwanese-led Taiwan.

The variety of methods that Taiwan Independence and anti-KMT activists used to spread the message about the Chiang state can be seen as a "creative mischief [that] both subverts and sustains the authority of the state."[28] Indeed, these mischievous acts stung the ROC state. The "ignorant and shameless" "traitorous thieves" *(maiguozei)* who "humiliated the people of Taiwan" with these stunts, one official magazine stated, would pay the price at the hands of "patriots . . . rising as a group to denounce and drive [them] away" for their clever subversion.[29]

Taiwan's continued victories in Williamsport and Gary, each seemingly more decisive than the last, seemed only to invigorate dissidents and critics of the Chiang regime thirsting for tangible measures of uniquely "Taiwanese" accomplishment. It turns out, though, that these Taiwanese activists often also had to deal with American authorities in Williamsport who were taking instructions from the KMT. In 1973 at the Senior Little League Championships in Gary, Indiana, ROC officials present were able to have arrested as "terrorists" four activists wearing T-shirts that read in a row, *Tai-Du-Wan-Sui* ("Long Live Taiwan Independence"). Two years later in Gary, Taiwanese activists floated a balloon with this same independence message, and thanks to the generous and curious ABC cameramen on the scene, this sky-high subversion flashed across millions of Taiwan's television screens for the first time in history. But, again, the ROC was able to force ABC Sports to stop broadcasting any Chinese-language messages after this disaster.[30] These activist fans were able to take advantage of the "ROC" entries in the United States, where the liberty to criticize the hated KMT was supposedly protected, in order to embarrass the regime. But this tension between opposing the state and invoking and provoking it at every turn[31] became an inseparable part of their yearly Williamsport physical and psychological experiences, perhaps even making the KMT even more of a hegemonic force from half a world away than it ever could have been before.

Finally, the world of baseball also continued to serve as an important site for the expression of strength and pride among Taiwan's Aboriginal tribes. Many of Taiwan's early youth championship teams featured players originally from the Aboriginal areas of eastern Taiwan. These youngsters and their adult followers could only have taken an ironic pleasure in winning such great honors for, and being feted by, a state that only continued to ignore and impoverish the representatives of a pre-Chinese Taiwan past. In fact, their baseball and sporting success in general became one of the most important ways in which Taiwan's Aboriginal citizens represented and understood their identity and position in Taiwan society.[32]

Yet this gratifying annual attention paid to the original inhabitants of Taiwan and their baseball prowess unfortunately was not enough to truly sustain the Aboriginal populations. It is telling that Taiwan's two greatest exports to Japanese baseball, Guo Yuanzhi (Kaku Genji) and Guo Taiyuan (Kaku Taigen), were both Little League icons of Aboriginal descent. Both Guos left Taiwan as very young men, settled and married in Japan, and only returned to the Taiwan baseball world in the late 1990s after their careers in Japan came to a close.

"FELLOWSHIP OF THE FLAWED," PART I: MURDERERS

In 1971, after collecting Taiwan's second LLB championship, the Tainan Giants enjoyed the American celebrity life for the next several days, posing for photos with Vice President Spiro Agnew in the White House and baseball legend Ted Williams in Yankee Stadium, and feasting at Chinatown banquets from New York to Los Angeles to San Francisco. On their way home, they made one more stop in Tokyo, where they were greeted by several hundreds of ethnic Chinese residents, and then formally received by ROC ambassador Peng Mengqi.[33] These boys perhaps had no idea who this kindly ambassador was, and even those precocious enough to know would surely have been too polite to bring up the events that led to Ambassador Peng being dubbed "The Butcher of Gaoxiong" and "The Murderer King."

Peng Mengqi had been commander of the army garrison at Gaoxiong at the time of the uprising on 28 February 1947. He has long been held responsible for his army's murderous assault on the civilians of that city and was despised by many even within the ROC's leadership for his brutal command. Chiang Kai-shek appreciated Peng's loyalty, however, and the Butcher enjoyed a long and prosperous career in the Nationalist army and government. But one does wonder whether, as he greeted these southern Taiwanese children whose parents' teachers, doctors, and community leaders he had commanded to be shot twenty-four summers earlier, Peng's thoughts drifted at all to the public and private executions he had conducted back down south during his rise to the top.

This was just one event in the busy lives of these child champions; after this visit there were still parades, TV shows, press conferences, more banquets, visits to martyrs' shrines, gifts to receive humbly (including a scholarship totaling NT$3 million [US$75,000] presented by Chiang Kai-shek and the KMT Central Committee, to be distributed every year on the Generalissimo's birthday),[34] and a future military invasion to inspire (this was the team whose victories Chiang hoped would inspire all "to quickly retake the mainland"). In Ambassador Peng, what was one more funny-talking mainlander who knew nothing about baseball showering the team with gifts and speeches? Yet to the historian, this chilling incident cries out for more analysis.

One wonders if there was in fact a crueler irony that the Nationalist government could have perpetrated upon the game of baseball—this modern legacy of Japanese colonialism—than to fold it into the same KMT world that honored those (like Peng) who had massacred thousands in 1947 for serving as walking legacies of modern Japanese colonialism. It was one thing to deny the Japaneseness of the game, either in print, which the official *Free China Review* did that month,[35] or physically, as in the "handsome Chinese palace–style exterior" on the Taipei Stadium. And it was not surprising that the government would hire dozens of New York Chinatown thugs to beat up Taiwanese activists at the games in Pennsylvania. But how does one explain this meeting with the Butcher of Gaoxiong?

In the end, it perhaps explains much more about the Nationalist uses of baseball than do the iconic pictures of poor Aborigine children playing baseball barefoot or smiling in victorious celebration. The gambit could not have been that no one would remember what Peng had been up to twenty-four summers before; indeed, the point almost seems to be that any conscientious adult *would* know that Peng had been behind the murders of a previous generation of southern Taiwan standouts. Yet to write this event as a cruel flaunting of Peng's murderous guilt and the Nationalist government's total complicity in rewarding him with a long official career seems to miss an important prop in this production. Only an understanding of how "national embarrassment can become the ironic basis of intimacy and affection, a fellowship of the flawed,"[36] can explain the true logic of such a gesture.

The Chinese rock star Cui Jian, in his powerful 1991 song "A Piece of Red Cloth," sang, "I want to always accompany you this way, because I know your suffering best."[37] While the modern histories of the PRC regime that Cui addressed and Taiwan are unmistakably different, his vivid language explains very well this "fellowship of the flawed" that existed between the Nationalist regime and the Taiwanese public for four decades, through the 1980s. If we begin with presumptions of some sort of "authentic" Taiwanese state of rebellion against the KMT, or its converse, a profound inauthenticity characterized by "selling out" to this mainlander regime, it is simply difficult to understand the workings of martial law-era Taiwanese ROC nationalism, anticommunism, and pride in the economic "miracle" presided over by the KMT.

Instead, we imagine the complexities, but ultimate convenience, of this relationship between actors who know each others' suffering best. The shared discourse of suffering (even though some clearly suffered more than others) that would have been apparent to all upon seeing this ritual in Tokyo explains much more clearly the traumatic and ironically proud ways in which this island of former Japanese colonial subjects became the KMT's "Free China." Instead of a *rupture* in the early 1970s discourse about baseball and ROC history, this visit to the butcher served as the ultimate capstone to this championship voyage and reinforcement of what baseball really meant to Taiwan.

HOW CAN A LOSER EVER WIN?

The researcher of Taiwan's baseball history is blessed by a Taiwanese population that seems to love recollecting the old days when people experienced as one these many triumphs and defeats. However, an accompanying problem is the fact that these memories are almost inevitably phrased in explicitly nostalgic terms of family, community, and nation—staying up all night, eating instant noodles while listening to or watching the games, and then going outside to enjoy the firecrackers and national flags. Even those who use language generally associated with critiques of this nostalgia—like professor and former national team coach Lin Huawei's talk on baseball and Taiwanese "collective memory" (*jiti jiyi*) at the Presidential Palace in July 2004[38]—often employ it only to encourage this nostalgia even further. Indeed, the longing for such state-centered artifice—even if one understands that it also marks a nostalgia for the "simpler" era of Nationalist rule—is troubling. Herzfeld's investigation of "cultural intimacy," described in chapter 4, constitutes an excellent theoretical way through these sets of collective memory.

The chronology of the Tainan Giants' 1971 championship is even more revealing; it followed Nixon's announcement of his upcoming visit to the PRC by six weeks, and preceded the ROC's withdrawal from the United Nations by eight weeks. If ever "national embarrassment" and humiliation was palpable in Taiwan, this was that moment. Most Americans were likely not stung by Chiang Kai-shek's speech lamenting "an age of agony in which there is no distinction between justice and injustice . . . [when] some people have even lost their moral courage. . . . [and] become the lackeys of Mao Tse-tung."[39] But many in Taiwan hoped the Yanks would feel for once the hurt of the ROC team beating the American team led by "that big gorilla Mc-Something" (star Lloyd McClendon of the all–African-American Gary, Indiana, team, as a wistful *China Times* piece described him in 1993).[40]

The "embarrassment" trope in memories of Little League baseball is so strong that it sometimes trumps actual chronology. In his 1997 memoirs, cartoonist Cai Zhizhong remembered, "During the summer of 1970, my third year in the military, the worst disaster for Taiwan was not our withdrawal from the United Nations, but the [Jiayi] Seven Tigers Little League team's loss to Puerto Rico at Williamsport."[41] The fact that Cai seems to remember so clearly (if doubly incorrectly—the ROC left the UN in 1971, and Jiayi lost to Nicaragua) these humiliations both occurring during the same summer hints at how the most "intimate" national memories can be those of failure.

The Jiayi Seven Tigers, winners of the ROC national championship in 1970, were yet another of the "all-star" teams compiled for victories abroad. The ROC Baseball Association made much of the fact that the children were all under age twelve this time, after satisfying an official LLB delegation's investigation in June. (The *United Daily News* also proudly cited LLB head Peter J. McGovern's delight that, unlike in the United States, he did not see any Taiwanese boys with long hair.)[42] Instead, the Seven Tigers merely were cheating in another way; the squad included only seven boys from the baseball-mad town of Jiayi, supplemented by five standout ringers from Tainan and two more from Gaoxiong.

The Seven Tigers' 12–0 victory over the Japanese champions from Wakayama clinched the Asia Pacific title and showed them to be yet another world-class entry in the LLB World Series in Pennsylvania. The team returned to Taipei for more training, and were treated as the latest champions of Chinese Nationalist heroism. One psychologist saw in their recent wins a "renewal of the promise of the [Chinese] nation and race." This could only be achieved, though, with a strong-willed coach able to guide his charges away from the cowardice, dishonesty, irresponsibility, and wildness that they were too ignorant to avoid on their own.[43] A more patent and transparent paean to authoritarian rule has seldom been written, but we see once more a striking willingness to co-opt baseball for the express purposes of the state.

Official media also issued all fourteen boys comic book-style nicknames, like "Tornado Tiger" (third baseman Huang Yongxiang), "High-Flying Tiger" (pitcher Huang Zhixiong), and "Lightning Tiger" (catcher Hou Dezheng). Three decades later, star player Lu Ruitu, the "Concealed-by-a-Ridge Tiger," remembered the hundreds of fan letters he received and the beautiful and forward Taipei girls who followed the team around for days.[44]

But in their first game in Williamsport, the Seven Tigers ran into another fine team from Nicaragua, who topped the Seven Tigers 3–2, the painfully close game ending on a hard ROC line drive caught with the bases loaded. Taiwan Television broadcaster Sheng Zhuru cried on air, joined in tears by Nationalist loyalists and Taiwanese nationalists in the Williamsport stands sharing the pain, shedding tears underneath their flags of enmity.[45] Once in the loser's bracket in Williamsport, the Seven Tigers took out their revenge on opponents from Tennessee and West Germany, dominating both to capture the least satisfying fifth-place finish in LLB World Series history.

This loss in the 1970 Little League World Series was experienced in Taiwan as the truest, yet most profoundly bonding, form of embarrassment. The next day's "In Black and White" column in the *United Daily News* began this narrative. Titled "Sorry," the column issued both faint and fervent praise for Coach Wu Mintian's dignity in immediately apologizing to the nation after the loss: "This spirit of taking responsibility for a national humiliation and insult is truly moving!"[46] A film on public television in 2000 showed the painful details of the 3–2 loss, set to background music by the Bee Gees: "How can you mend this broken man? How can a loser ever win?"[47] While Taiwan's Little League teams won seventeen world titles about which to boast, this *loss* in fact remains at the heart of nationalist memories of Taiwan baseball's golden age.

Since then, the official Little League narrative in Taiwan—shared by Chinese Nationalists and Taiwanese separatists alike—has come to center on the artifacts of the fifth-place Seven Tigers' moving return to Taipei. Chiang Ching-kuo greeted the children at Songshan Airport in the rain, doing his best to cheer them up with kind questions and comments: "Did you have fun in America?" "Did you make some new friends?" "Losing is OK; there's always next year." The Tigers' players behaved with stoic dignity, presenting to the Generalissimo's son deep bows that would be cited in Taiwan for decades to come.[48]

But the most moving event was to follow. Coach Wu apologized once more for the team's loss, only to have Xie Guocheng, head of the ROC Baseball Association and the "father of Taiwanese Little League baseball," seize the microphone, his eyeglass frames dripping with tears, and (ignoring a certain Nicaraguan pitcher's expertise) state that "Responsibility for the Seven Tigers' loss is mine and not the coach's."[49] One perhaps can only understand the power of the phrase "fellowship of the flawed" by seeing how a writer for the *China Tribune* twenty years later, in a piece titled, "The Beauty and Sorrow of Baseball," identified this noble fight to accept blame as the moment when youth baseball truly became part of ROC nationalism.[50] Or, to cite another medium, the only picture of a Little League player in Taiwan's official baseball "Digital Museum" is one of these sullen Seven Tigers players, Li Zongzhou (the "Beastly Fanged Tiger"), sheltered from the rain by Vice Premier Chiang's umbrella and wide smile.[51]

Finally, even more spectacular was the speech that the Jiayi losers received from President Chiang Kai-shek three days later. The *United Daily News* account started predictably enough, given the personality cult of the day: "The children stood on their toes and craned their necks in order to see the greatest leader and man residing in their hearts." But his thoughts that day were on matters that the *UDN* seldom would have mentioned in this age of the "economic miracle"—Chiang's own defeats: "The President pointed out, for anyone and in any matter, the road to success will inevitably include some failures. Only one who has failed can truly appreciate the precious value of victory. . . . Winning every time would only have taught you arrogance, and that is the biggest failure."[52]

It was difficult for Chiang to revisit publicly his failures of twenty-five years earlier, when he ruled all of China and the stakes were much higher. And it is hard to imagine him truly believing that he would live to appreciate success in retaking the mainland. But his humble candor in this emotional meeting represents one more unlikely example of his cultivation of a "fellowship of the flawed."[53] It seems that, while anyone can *win* a championship, the ability to lose with grace and, with only the purest of motives, to still stand together with others who suffered pain and embarrassment, became the quality of which Taiwanese people and their Chinese government were most proud. Three-quarters of the way through a twentieth century marked by acute Taiwanese and Chinese trauma, the shame and failure at the heart of baseball provided a powerful and shared pathos in which all in Taiwan could express their own histories of loss.

LOSS AND *LITOST* IN BASEBALL FICTION AND FILM

The first literary representation of the youth baseball phenomenon in Taiwan came in a comic serial, *Little Baseball Hero (Bangqiu xiao yinghao)* published in *Prince* magazine in 1970 (see figure 5).[54] The comic follows the adventures of a boy named Wei Xinwu (literally "Mighty New Weapon"), who stars for "Golden Tiger Elementary School" and is taken by a strange hermit to the rugged woods to engage in "crazy training." The cruel natural-style training exhausts him to the bone, but eventually produces incredible skills; Wei learns to use rocks to knock birds out of the sky, or even to fell a crazed boar, with his strong arm.[55]

Wei ends up performing good deeds for the baseball world and the larger community all over Taiwan, but the most stunning part of the story comes in part 3 of the comic, when the mysterious hermit reveals his story to Wei. His name is Wang Yuanxuan ("King of the Original Players"), and thirty years before (i.e., in 1940) he had been one of the many Taiwanese students in the colonial metropole of Japan. In an impossibly chronologized and strangely imagined episode, Wang was inspired to join a Japanese all-star baseball team that would be playing a visiting American squad. He met Wei's father that summer in Taiwan as they both trained for the team. Tragically, though, all nine of the players on this team were drafted by Japan's warlords into the military. They all were wounded, losing arms and legs, and were no longer able to play baseball. But they all had sons, and Wang's mission now was to keep his promise to Wei's dead father—to find these eight remaining boys in order to form a baseball team that could win revenge once and for all. (And for assistance in this—not to mention ideological cover for the magazine—hermit Wang is accompanied in the woods by Mr. Zhang, a bespectacled bureaucrat from the ROC Baseball Association!)[56]

This storyline amazes as it tries to traverse territory between Chinese (anti-Japanese, even anti-U.S.) nationalism and statism (see also Wei's "China" jersey) and Taiwanese collective nostalgia of community and struggle as Japanese subjects. The wild-haired (almost shoulder-length; it *was* 1970 Taiwan) Wang's character—which combines Rip Van Winkle, the ultimately assimilated colonial subject, and the avenging anti-Japanese mensch—was a brilliant way for *Prince* magazine to sell a story of such postcolonial pathos to a Chinese Taiwan. One also might wonder about the reasons for a children's magazine to include such a heavy story—unless, of course, the only story that one *could* tell through baseball was one of alienation, longing, and loss.

The year 1977 saw the first formal entries into what would become a burgeoning field in Taiwan, baseball literature. It is also telling—given the incredible performance of Taiwan's youth baseball teams for almost a decade by then—that these two short stories were written from within explicit notions of humiliation and loss.

The first, "Forced Out," is an imagination of a poor boy's traumatic participation in elite-level baseball. It won first prize in the United Daily News Literature Competition and the author, Xiaoye, won that year's Belles-Lettres Medal from Taiwan's China Art and Literature Association. In other words, this story did not appear as a minor work, but clearly spoke to dominant notions of how baseball fit into national and personal imaginations at that moment.

The entire story takes place during the course of a single at bat, as the reader experiences with protagonist A-cai his painful recollections and reflections on his involvement in the game. When A-cai comes to bat with the chance to win the Taiwan championship for his Divine Eagles, he has much more on his mind. There is A-cai's understanding that winning this title would be his only chance to ever visit America. But much weightier were the knowledge that his father had bet NT$200,000 (US$5,000) on the *opposing* team to win, and the horrible memory of his sister being given away to an evil neighbor to settle his father's previous gambling debts, only to die a horrible death soon after. A-cai seethes with feelings of powerlessness, regret, humiliation, and dreams of revenge as he finds himself in a full count.

Even after he hits the ball into far left field, though, the horror pursues him all the way around the bases—"Far away America. . . . I'm going to whip them all!" "Father don't blame me. I'll be a good filial son," "ox-headed and horse-faced demons . . . calling home the souls of the dead," "a terror of death, like looking at A-Jin's mutilated little corpse"—until he is, of course, thrown out at home plate.[57] The story is a painful one to read. But our main concern is the thoroughness with which the many miseries and humiliations suffered by those residents of Taiwan not lucky or savvy enough to take advantage of the island's "economic miracle" could be understood, and in medal-winning ways, through baseball.

Finally, the author's notes in a 2005 anthology clarify even more. Twenty-eight years after the publication of this landmark story, Xiaoye came clean with an apology for technical mistakes he had made in the story. He admitted that he had since learned that in the situation he had imagined, A-cai could only have been tagged out at home plate and not "forced out" (an awkward mistake since this was the title of the story). He also had "learned" that baserunners are not allowed to leave their bases until after a ball hit in the air falls to the ground.[58] I include this point here only for its absurdity; no one with the slimmest acquaintance with the game could think that this was true. The author who wrote as "Xiaoye" was a graduate biology student from Taipei named Li Yuan who seemed to know nothing about baseball, other than its unmatched power in summoning the humiliation, fear, and violence of Taiwan's recent history.

Another important baseball short story—"The Invader," by Hsien-hao Liao, now a renowned professor of literature at National Taiwan University—was published during this same year of 1977. This story is written from the perspective of a standout young pitcher, whose childhood is scarred forever by baseball in a different way. The boy is named Taisheng, literally "born in Taiwan," a common name for children of postwar mainlander émigrés. He has a child's awareness of the postcolonial tensions in Taiwan surrounding the Japanese and their lasting cultural presence in Taiwan. The story is set in 1970 (the year of the Seven Tigers' epic defeat) in a Taipei military housing complex (juancun)—likely a device that would allow this second-generation "mainlander" to come into contact with the "Taiwanese" game of baseball.

The main narrative follows Taisheng over the course of his preparation for a big game with a visiting Japanese youth baseball team from Ise (home to the most sacred of Japan's Shintō shrines) and the blossoming of a childhood romance with the Taiwanese girl next door. He hurts his left shoulder practicing, and prays at the household altar that he will still be able to pitch well and to "awe" Yingzi next door. She dresses up like a beautiful bride for the big game, which Taisheng's team loses. At the postgame party, Yingzi has little to say to Taisheng and ends up talking to the winning pitcher of the Japanese side. When he can take no more, Taisheng screams at her, in Taiwanese, to go marry the guy. Soon after, his father is transferred, the family moves, and he never sees Yingzi again.[59]

A Taiwanese author in 1992 went so far as to use the Czech word *litost*—defined by writer Milan Kundera as "the synthesis of many [feelings]: grief, sympathy, remorse, and an indefinable longing. . . . a state of torment caused by a sudden insight into one's own miserable self"[60]—to describe the history of Taiwan baseball. Only this concept of *li-tuo-si*, the author claimed, could help us make sense of a history that included Taiwan's love for and resistance against the Japanese, and so many players' later suicides and deaths due to alcohol and drug abuse. Even Wu Mintian, the celebrated championship coach mentioned earlier, died estranged from his family, poor and alone on the island of Jinmen, to the everlasting *litost* of his hometown Jiayi.[61] This *China Tribune* piece was titled "A New Formulation for Identity"; it is telling that this author sought to frame Taiwanese history, culture, and identity within this Kunderan condition.

This Taiwanese *litost* also helps to explain two baseball-related films that were released in Taiwan in the mid-to-late 1980s. The first is *Taipei Story (Qingmei zhuma)*, a 1985 film made by Edward Yang about Taipei modernity and its discontents. The film costars singing idol Tsai Chin as A-zhen, an employee of a modern architectural firm who is laid off and soon engages in a seedy race to the bottom of Taipei's "miracle." Yang makes the striking choice to have this depressing scenario also revolve around the saga of A-zhen's boyfriend A-long, a washed-up former Little

League Baseball hero (played by the legendary director Hou Hsiao-hsien). A-long is useless, good for little more than dreaming of moving to Los Angeles, watching old videotapes of Japanese and American professional baseball games, and starting fights with yuppies who ask him about his former stardom. His only friend is an old teammate (played by director and screenwriter Wu Nien-jen) who destroyed his arm throwing curveballs as a young boy. They play sad games of catch in empty concrete rooms, and the friend, who is being cuckolded conspicuously and is having problems even feeding his many children, can only remember: "Practice! Practice! Williamsport! . . . Been all downhill since I left the army."

Hou plays this sadness and alienation well (although shots of him swinging imaginary bats in quiet sadness reveal truly poor technique), and Tsai's own sad and flawed beauty seems appropriate to the story. Shots of a Presidential Palace lit up for national celebration and of wild youth riding motorcycles and frolicking to Kenny Loggins's "Footloose" create an image of Taipei prosperity and happiness that evades the losers of 1985 society, represented revealingly here by former baseball players. For a film that contains such long and probing shots, A-long's end comes fairly suddenly; he is stabbed twice in the back by a young man who is stalking A-zhen. Stuck out in the suburbs that represent this new prosperity, all A-long can do is sit down on the curb, bleed, smoke a cigarette, and finally die as he imagines images of his Little League victory parade playing on a TV set left out for garbage pickup.[62]

Edward Yang was not ethnically Taiwanese, and it is possible that as such, he had little personal engagement with the game of baseball. The film *Taipei Story* in itself had very little to do with baseball; the story of loss and alienation that Yang wants us to understand as a real part of Taipei's miraculous modernization could have been told perfectly well using any number of professions or back stories. Yet clearly, given the power of the "national game" to metonymize virtually any memory of suffering, it made such perfect sense for Yang and screenwriter Chu Tien-wen to give A-long this particular experience as the archetypal failure, a former baseball player.

A final example to investigate here is the Taiwanese film *Struggle,* made in 1988 as an oddly conceived fictional biopic of Taiwanese baseball star Guo Yuanzhi. Guo was a former Golden Dragon LLB star then in the eighth year of his career with the Chunichi Dragons in Japan, and played "himself" in the film. It begins with an extended shot of a man bitterly watching Guo's pitching and hitting exploits on television. We soon learn that the voyeur is Guo's fictional childhood friend and longtime catcher A-de, who is quitting baseball after being cut by Chunichi. The next Guo hears about his friend is from their childhood teacher, who has to break the news that down-and-out A-de has committed two gang murders back in Taiwan and has been sentenced to death.

Most of the film consists of long flashbacks of the two men's childhood friendship and baseball toils, and plays as a much more typical rags-to-riches, poor-kids-hitting-a-tire-with-a-bat version of the Taiwanese Dream. We learn how the two learn true discipline—continuing the capitalist narrative of individual effort and success discussed in chapter 4—from a crusty old coach and come to excel as a pitcher-catcher battery for all time. Once more, though, the viewer is amazed to see how this more staid "baseball" story is shoehorned into such utter tragedy, the film ending with Guo falling to his knees on a Japanese beach when he "hears" the government's bullets fired into his lifelong friend back in eastern Taiwan.[63]

These examples help to provide a full reading of the baseball triumphs of the 1970s and '80s. Beyond the predictable triumphalism of the state and its ideologues, Taiwan's artists and consumers seemed most comfortable with narratives that included within baseball the pain, loss, and humiliations that members of modern Taiwanese society had experienced over the last several decades—"equal treatment under the emperor," "Free China," "economic miracle," or not. In modern Taiwan, it seemed that the only honest historical narrative was one that accounted for all the sadness, regret, violence, hubris, and lies of these experiences. Could any subject encapsulate these "secret spaces" and national embarrassments more than baseball?

"FELLOWSHIP OF THE FLAWED," PART II: CHEATERS

1981: Taiwan credits their fifth Little League World Series championship in a row [to] their ability to retain most of the same players from their 1977 squad.
"GREAT MOMENTS IN LITTLE LEAGUE WORLD SERIES HISTORY,"
THE ONION, 2006

In 1971, "Legendary Lloyd" McClendon and his team from Gary, Indiana, faced the Tainan Giants in the championship game in Williamsport. The five-foot, eight-inch McClendon put Gary in front with an early home run (his fifth in five LLBWS at bats!), but the Giants' own phenom, five-foot, four-inch pitcher Xu Jinmu, known throughout Taiwan as "Buckteeth" *(nng-khi-a)*, was able to overpower his opponents and lead Tainan to a nine-inning victory.[64]

The lanky Xu towered over his teammates and with his thick black eyeglasses was an imposing presence on the mound. He was a familiar presence as well for Taiwanese fans; he had played on Taiwan's 1970 LLBWS representative Seven Tigers squad (from Jiayi) as well, when he was dubbed the "Descended Demon Tiger." In 1971 Xu was no longer a ringer, but leader of his hometown Tainan Giants. But one of his former teammates explained to me that Xu's 1971 participation in the Little League World Series was dubious as well. In the rural, not-yet-"miraculous" Taiwan of the late 1950s, many families were late to report births to the state, so that even before world Little League dominance was a gleam in any Taiwanese eyes, the island happened to have a surfeit of rural boys and girls older than the official records said they were. By the 1970s, this common rural resistance to state surveillance was coming in handy for Taiwan's youth baseball program.[65] Xu never grew much at all past his Little League height, an indication that he had enjoyed more days and years in the Tainan sun than said his household registration. It is perhaps for this reason that Xu is now so reclusive today, a factory worker who refuses to talk to the media or even to admit that he was the legendary "Buckteeth" Xu of 1971.[66]

Xu was not the first Taiwan player to enjoy several turns in the spotlight. Yu Hongkai starred on both the 1968 Maple Leaf and 1969 Golden Dragons teams, representing schools on opposite sides of the island, and then in 1970, for good measure, played for two different Taipei school teams challenging Jiayi for the title. This "all-star team" trend, despite the warnings from American Little League officials, would not end soon. As late as 1979, the Puzi Elementary School Tornadoes world championship team included two ringers from elsewhere in Jiayi County.[67]

These teams, and it turns out rightfully so, generated great suspicion on the part of an American public unable to fathom the source of this invincible Taiwan baseball dynasty. Yet this view of their Little League program mattered little to the Taiwanese public of the time. Baseball stardom became an almost universal aspiration among the boys and young men of Taiwan. Li Kunzhe, who starred professionally for the China Trust Whales in the late 1990s, remembered: "I grew up watching baseball. . . . I remember the days when everyone would wake up in the middle of the night to watch our national teams perform in the international competitions. They were national heroes. We all wanted to represent our country and be a hero."[68]

These triumphs were especially thrilling for Taiwanese people given the island's unique geopolitical squeeze described earlier. The sight of these Taiwanese boys annually making mincemeat of strong and confident American teams was rewarding to anyone hoping to strike back and prove the strength and general worth of Taiwan to their American "allies" so busy selling them out in favor of relations with the PRC during the 1970s. Baseball became one of the few ways that the ROC state could make its case against the "commie bandits and their fellow travelers, who are undertaking plots to win the support of . . . government[s], overseas Chinese and scholars."[69]

Originally, Americans in Williamsport had cheered enthusiastically for the Taizhong Golden Dragons and Jiayi Seven Tigers, proud that, as *The Sporting News* put it, the great American game had "reached base in another nation."[70] No doubt also influenced by cold war notions and horror stories of Chinese communism, they took to the ROC teams and their "classy" spirit.[71] But by 1971, American fans were beginning to boo the Taiwanese Little Leaguers for winning in such expert fashion.[72] A cute "Oriental" underdog (also *The Sporting News*) sent by a reliable cold war ally was fun to root for; a "big yellow machine" (as the *New York Times* saw the Taiwan Little League program)[73] that rolled over American twelve-year-olds every summer was a different story.

By 1973, it was altogether too much to take, as that year's Tainan Giants (see figure 6) swept their three Williamsport opponents by a total score of 57–0, and on three no-hitters![74] (Just days earlier, in the Senior League world tourney at Gary, the team from Huaxing Middle School in Taipei won their five games by the combined score of 26–0.) Now, American fans booed these Taiwanese youngsters as they took the field against boys from Tucson who, along with devastated players from Bitburg and Tampa, just seemed to be playing the game more fairly. The losing Tucson manager stated, "There's no way they're that good following the rules," and "bitter" LLB officials planned to investigate whether Taiwan's program was violating rules on "eligibility, district size, and practice time."[75] We now know, of course, that these accusations were true, and that little effort was made even to hide the fraudulent practices. An article by Fang Junling, who coached the Giants in 1971, described his club's workout schedule as they prepared for that year's championship run. He ran his twelve-year-olds through what was quite simply a daily regimen of child abuse; ideally practicing for nine hours and twenty minutes a day, and his pitchers throwing up to three hundred pitches a day (including, on some days, one hundred curveballs).[76]

That same week, the *Los Angeles Times* published a cartoon showing an "Official U.S. Little League Baseball" to be "Made in Taiwan,"[77] summing up frustrations at American baseball and economic losses of the time. The official probe somehow turned up none of the serious violations of rules that we now know to have occurred; Taiwan's baseball officials were let off in exchange for promises to run their baseball program "in close conformity" with LLB regulations.[78] But allegations of cheating were regular for the next two decades as Americans remained suspicious of continued Taiwanese supremacy. Indeed, a *Philadelphia Inquirer* columnist put it most memorably in a piece titled, "Taiwan Plays Ball like It's Tong War," citing a popular belief that "Chiang Kai-Shek had hired a band of professional midgets just to humiliate the U.S."[79]

In 1974, *Rolling Stone* featured an article on this "Chinese juggernaut" that every summer provided the rare "moments of glory Chiang Kai-shek's government ha[d] experienced of late." That year's world championship (Taiwan's fifth) won by Lide ("Establish Virtue") School in Gaoxiong brought Taiwan's record in Williamsport over the last six years to 15–1 (including thirteen shutouts); they had outscored their opponents 171–11. Now LLB officials used predictable analogies such as the "sneak attack at Pearl Harbor" to describe Taiwanese perfidy. White fans shouted "Beat those chinks!" at the (mostly black) New Haven team that faced Taiwan in the first round (and lost 16–0). Before the final game (Lide 12, Red Bluff, California, 1), one fan avowed, "This is where we make our stand. We've got to stop the Yellow Peril now."[80]

Influential journalist Anthony Lukas provided an appropriate twist to this piece as he also worked to find the voices of resistance to this white racist discourse. He described the "roving pack of thirty Williamsport girls . . . [who] transferred their allegiance to the mysterious Chinese," following the Taiwanese boys around and chanting "Taiwan, Taiwan is the best, you can forget about the West." And after absorbing a thorough first-round defeat, the coach of the New Haven squad became another convert. He and his players figured out quickly that the same Williamsport fans who called the Taiwanese "chinks" were the same ones who called his team "niggers." By the day of the championship, he was wearing a Taiwanese-style "coolie" hat, waving an ROC flag,[81] and fully enjoying an ironic version of the international friendship that LLB professed to promote. As was Lukas's point, though, this coach was in the minority. Americans became obsessed with Taiwanese "hyperconformity" that they fantasized as being the opposite of the healthy upbringing they provided their children in the United States.[82] In 1975, the American Little League establishment went so far as to ban all foreign teams for a year in order to guarantee an American "winner."[83]

These questions of cheating, or other disturbing questions of violence, do not usually emerge in Taiwan's glossy official narratives of "Chinese baseball world champions." However, besides the many literary and cinematic examples cited earlier, most historical and analytical studies do bring up the question, often as "a source of external embarrassment . . . that nevertheless provide[s] insiders with their assurance of common sociality."[84] This discourse often borders on the masochistic; one Taiwanese PhD student wrote in a 2002 online book review, "I am writing a thesis about Taiwanese amateur baseball under which many appalling conditions occurred, including over-training, fabrication scandals, vicious under-the-table recruitment, lack of education, just to name a few, all of which will subvert the beautifil [sic] images held by common people. . . . My intention is to expose the dark sides of Taiwanese amateur baseball."[85] The cutting humiliations and guilt associated with Taiwan's Little League Baseball program have made this outwardly glorious era one that can only be remembered in terms that tie into the degradations and abuses suffered by Taiwanese people under both of its twentieth century authoritarian regimes.

Under the Nationalist government's four decades of martial law in Taiwan (1948–1987), baseball was an important realm in which Taiwanese people, especially the poorer residents of the south and east, could register their own contributions to Taiwan culture and society. A provocative and fun mixture of mild pro-Japanese nostalgia, resistance against KMT hegemony in Taiwan and American hegemony in East Asia, and even Aboriginal resistance to the double oppression of the mainlander and Taiwanese Han presence, could all be voiced in the language of baseball. So could, as shown in this chapter, virtually every kind of Taiwanese *or* mainlander memory of trauma, loss, and humiliation of the colonial, wartime, or cold war eras. And what made this space for dissent and reflection safe was the Nationalists' own understanding of the role of sports in modern society. Their standard two-part philosophy, developed when the party ruled China in the late 1920s and 1930s, was that popular participation in sport served to integrate a diverse population into a single nation-state, and that outstanding sporting performances on international stages were valuable opportunities to win national face, sympathy, and even allies in the ever-changing world of the twentieth century. Baseball thus represented a table of negotiation, where Taiwanese baseball communities exchanged measures of integration for measures of independent expression, measures of "Chinese" identity for measures of pro-Japanese nostalgia, and measures of martial-law autocratic Nationalist statism for measures of an independent Taiwanese culture and society.

Allen Chun, in a discussion of KMT rule in Taiwan, described Chinese "national culture" as an ideological move, "a hegemonic presence whose fate is linked inextricably to the very mechanism of political domination that has served to perpetuate the authority of the state."[86] The KMT's "Chinese culture" was based on myths of shared ethnic-cultural origin, fantastically irredentist education and images of the world, and the protection of mainland antiquities. However, its doppelgänger, the "Taiwanese" culture that grew within it, and which was centered to a large degree on the culture of baseball, was a much more personal, intimate, even existential affair that gained much of its power from the shared pain and humiliation of its members. This culture of baseball—and its power to bring out and recall the worst (as well as the best) in its participants over a century—thus stands as an important example of how "cultural intimacy" must inform any functioning model of Taiwanese culture.

By the end of the 1970s, the fantasies of living out the equally fictional "Chinese culture" or "Taiwanese nation" through children's baseball were disappearing. The one-sided victories in Williamsport, Gary, and Ft. Lauderdale every summer were just not very interesting anymore, now that the best youth baseball tournament in the world was Taiwan's own.[87] Now, the dominant sense among the young players and Taiwan's public alike was that their teams would not and could not lose in the United States. Decades later, many players remembered how this made for extremely tense training sessions and almost unenjoyable victories.[88]

By then, the commercialized and globalized attentions, fascinations, and desires created by Taiwan's economic miracle called for a new site for the national game. By the mid-1980s, these exquisitely talented and disciplined boys who won so much fame a decade before were now of an age to play for pay and for entirely new and worldly measures of achievement.

6

Homu-Ran Batta

Professional Baseball in Taiwan, 1990–Present

I am sure that the league will enhance the nation's baseball standards.
ROC PRESIDENT LEE TENG-HUI, ON THE FOUNDING OF THE CHINESE
PROFESSIONAL BASEBALL LEAGUE (CPBL), OCTOBER 1989

Bad league. Good pitchers, though. They gave me a lot of money.
MELVIN MORA (EX-MERCURIES TIGERS PLAYER THEN PLAYING FOR
THE NEW YORK METS) ON THE CPBL, OCTOBER 1999

PLAYING ABROAD (OR NOT), 1970s–1980s

The 1980s and '90s saw Taiwan's baseball talent succeed at the professional level for the first time since Taiwanese players joined Japan's professional leagues in the 1930s and '40s. After World War II, several decades passed before Japanese professional teams showed interest in Taiwanese players—a fact understood in Taiwan as proof of the harm done the game by the ruling Chinese Nationalist Party—until pitcher Chen Xiuxiong defeated Japan's national team in the 1971 Asian Championships and the 1972 World Cup.[1] One month after the second defeat, Japan's professional Seibu Lions club sent a representative to Taipei to start wooing Chen (and his chaperone Jian Yongchang, the "baseball expert" whose attachments to Japanese culture and baseball have been outlined in previous chapters).[2] The Lions held their spring training in Taizhong in February 1973, hoping while on the island to become reacquainted with Taiwan's talented ballplayers—many of whom, like Chen, after all, were born Japanese subjects.[3]

The negotiation process clearly was hurt by the negative pronouncements of Nationalist media and military leaders still resentful of this organic Japanese connection within the game of baseball. Eighty-five-year-old General Yang Sen, whose military career started with anti-Qing efforts in Sichuan Province and included brave fighting against the Japanese in central China, was serving out his days as head of the ROC National Amateur Athletic Federation. He publicly forbade the idea of Chen going to Japan, citing imagined "hardships" suffered by previous Taiwanese athletes who had done the same.[4] A *United Daily News* reporter made the strange case that Chen should "think carefully" about such a decision, since he would only be an "unimportant" relief pitcher there and that the main reason for Seibu's attentions was merely to get him off of the ROC national team.[5] There seems to have been immense pressure against Chen's signing with Seibu; the *United Daily News* made their case against the move by repeatedly denying that he would train with the club. His confidante Jian Yongchang had to deny explicitly to the *UDN* that his travels in February were related to the Chen negotiations.[6]

The late author Gao Zhengyuan records that Chen was secreted to Tainan for a tryout with the Lions, after which their coach offered him a contract with a signing bonus of US$300,000.[7] One blogger was recently told by reporters of the time that Chen actually boarded a flight for Japan before being confronted by General Yang, who made specific threats to Chen and then promised material rewards for remaining in Taiwan.[8] Whether the actual story is this dramatic is not certain. But Chen did not go to Japan, instead staying on in Taiwan where he eventually served as manager for two professional clubs. It is likely that this chance to make history was derailed in some way by KMT elders who (once again) could not accept the ties to Japan that lay at the heart of the game.

American major league teams were also tempted by the ever-more talented players coming of age in Taiwan. The Cincinnati Reds, then the pride of the National League, tried for years to obtain the rights to Eng-jey Kao and Lai-hua Lee, known even today as the finest pitcher-catcher battery ever produced in Taiwan. In 1974, when the two were nineteen and eighteen respectively, the *United Daily News* was already complaining that American scouts were "constantly pursuing [them] and will not give up."[9] The two, who had been teammates since their days at the East Asia Vocational School in Jiayi County, eventually signed contracts with the Reds in 1975 (although the *New York Times* seemed to think that "Chinese" players could only be acquired as part of some odd "publicity stunt"). The only catch was that Kao and Lee would not be available until 1976 because of mandatory military service requirements;[10] this detail ruined their American dream. Over the next several months, the ROC government refused to give Kao and Lee exit permits until they completed, depending on when the Reds asked, three years of military service or six years of educational and military commitments.[11] The Cincinnati club, like the Seibu Lions before them, eventually left empty-handed, as ROC sports authorities preferred to have Kao and Lee excelling on the Air Force team than in someone else's National League.[12]

Kao and Lee eventually would become the first Taiwanese players in three decades to retrace the steps of several of their Jiayi elders and play professionally in Japan. By late 1979, their military service in the ROC Navy (which consisted mostly of playing baseball for the Air Force team) was finally completed, and the anti-Japanese hardliners who had enjoyed the final word for decades had passed on. Kao and Lee were able to sign with the Nankai Hawks of Japan's Pacific League,[13] where they played from 1980 to 1983. Neither was a standout, but their signing reignited Japanese teams' interest in Taiwan as a source of talent.[14] Also, the attention they received made it possible for more Taiwanese players to dream of taking their skills—more often than not taught to them by men who had learned the game under the Japanese—to the former metropole.

Guo Yuanzhi, an Amis Aborigine child star and former Little League champion, was the first of this generation of Taiwanese players to become successful in Japan. He was an appropriate figure for this role; his father had served in the Japanese Navy during World War II and had named his son for a Japanese comrade named Genji (Yuanzhi in Chinese).[15] Guo had an uncle who had played as Hamaguchi Mitsuya for the triethnic Kanō baseball teams during wartime, and seems from a very young age to have been very familiar with the Japanese essentialist fascination with Tai-wanese Aborigines' "superior athletic abilities."[16] His signing with the Chunichi Dragons from Japan's Central League in 1981 was a dramatic affair; Guo's father and the Chunichi representative, a Mr. Ōkoshi Kanji, exchanged deep and solemn bows as former imperial subjects now joining again to revive the deep ties between Japan and Taiwan.[17]

Guo is the player who was featured in the 1988 biopic *Struggle;* his Japanese identity was made official in 1989 when he took Japanese citizenship and a new officially Japanese surname (Kaku).[18] This complex Taiwanese-Amis Aborigine-Japanese identity (captured most literally in figure 7), along with his brilliant pitching skills, made Guo/Kaku the focus of much desire and attention in both Japan and Taiwan during his excellent sixteen-year career with Chunichi.

These Japanese connections were made even more firm by Guo Taiyuan, another extraordinary Taiwanese pitcher who starred for the Seibu Lions from 1985 to 1996. His talents were apparent at an early age; while Guo was in high school the Toronto Blue Jays expressed their interests in his preternatural fastball. But Guo had also learned at a young age to point his aspirations and desires toward Japan. In 1980, when Guo was just eighteen, Seibu sent a scout to meet with Guo; his chaperone was Chen Runbo, another Japanese-era player who by this time was coach at Chinese Culture University.[19] Chen helped Guo make his commitment to Seibu—to be renewed once he was finished with military service (in his case, playing for the ROC Army baseball team)— as one more link in this old colonial relationship was made anew. Guo's career began with an excitement perhaps never seen before in Japan; during his first month pitching for Seibu he was named April 1985 MVP, and two months later the "Oriental Express" *(Dongfang tekuaiche)* threw a no-hitter. He soon became an all-time fan favorite, although Guo never took Japanese citizenship during his twelve years there.

These performances, mainly by "the two Guos," as the two Kakus were known in Taiwan, cemented Japan as a natural and historically relevant site where Taiwanese baseball players could continue their careers professionally. Some were high profile: Lü Mingci, who was also pursued by the Baltimore Orioles, was given a signing bonus of ¥50 million (US$333,000) by the Yomiuri Giants in 1987 in the hopes that he could replace their departed star Oh Sadaharu.[20] Many more standout Taiwanese players went to Japan in the 1980s to play in the Industrial Leagues, the parallel (and very high-level) professional baseball structure that is not "major league" in name but in fact is often able to outbid Nippon Professional Baseball teams for players.[21] (The fact that many NPB teams chose to use their two-player "foreigner" quota on American sluggers hurt many Taiwanese players' chances of playing in Japan's most celebrated leagues.)

For all of these postcolonial Taiwanese dreams that were fulfilled in Japan, however, there was often an acute sense that these talented exports did not always receive fair treatment as the sons of former second-class imperial subjects. Chen Dafeng, after starring for the Huaxing Middle School and Fu Jen Catholic University teams in Taipei, transferred to Nagoya University and was able to take Japanese citizenship as Yasuaki Taihoh (notably keeping his Chinese given name as his Japanese "surname"). He enjoyed an excellent fourteen-year career in Japan with the Chunichi Dragons and Hanshin Tigers, but a teammate and good friend of his, Alonzo Powell, remembered years later that Chen still was treated as such an outsider that he still "saw himself as a foreign player even though he had Japanese-player status."[22] Years later, a self-identified Aborigine author cited Guo Yuanzhi's initially low salaries with Chunichi as an example of the exploitation of Aborigines through baseball.[23] The *United Daily News* took a more predictably nationalistic stand, pointing out that besides Guo and Li Zhijun of the Kumagai Gumi Construction team, none of the other seven Taiwanese players in Japan in 1982 were being "used properly" by their neglectful Japanese managers.[24]

Some Taiwanese players in Japan experienced more unpleasantness than just neglect. Pitcher Liu Qiunong, whose father Liu Canglin was another former great from the Kanō teams, played for Yamaha's industrial league team in the early 1980s. Lin Huawei, a fine third baseman who had played for Taiwan's national teams at four different levels, was playing for the Kawai Musical Instruments baseball team at the same time. When the two teams met in the highly publicized 1984 Intercity Baseball Tournament, Liu pitched a three-hitter against Kawai. Lin had two of these hits, and the Japanese media accused Liu of "feeding" easy pitches to his fellow Taiwanese national.[25] I asked Lin about this event twenty years later, when he was a professor at the National Taiwan College of Physical Education. He dismissed it, maintaining that this was just a case of reporters "having fun."[26] But I could tell that such a charge of cheating had constituted a vicious slur against the reputation of one of the most decent men I have ever known.

It was no doubt for reasons such as these that by the late 1980s, many Taiwanese players, as well as corporations and fans, were dreaming of the day when Taiwan could support its own professional leagues. As early as 1985, an author wrote in the pages of *Free Youth* about how the excellence of so many Taiwanese players on the Japanese baseball stage—"talent from our nation being employed by another"— was "both joy and misery" to see.[27] Another writer, in *Japan Digest*, was similarly ambivalent about Taiwan's role as a "treasure-house of talent" *(rencai baoku)* for the Japanese, who never quite appreciated these Taiwanese players who provided "beautiful merchandise at a bargain price" *(wumei jialian)*.[28]

The fact that it was Japan where Taiwan's players starred caused great ambivalence among the Taiwanese baseball public. As Taiwan's professional league finally was being organized in the late 1980s, one reporter mixed revealing gendered metaphors to write an article called, "Taiwanese pro baseball—After twenty years the daughter-in-law has proudly become a mother-in-law," discussing how baseball will allow Taiwanese "never to have make bridal gowns *(zuo jiayishang)* for the Japanese again."[29] While many Taiwanese held on to nostalgic memories of Japanese colonialism and baseball, others, like this writer, had imbibed Chinese Nationalist portrayals of "slavery" and gendered subjection to the Japanese "occupiers," and could take little joy from Taiwanese players' successes in Japan.

Some did not support a move to professional baseball, fearing that Taiwan's amateur national team—the source of so much recognition for Taiwan for years— would be irreparably weakened by such a development. One author urged baseball authorities not to feel that they had to "blindly follow" America, Japan, and Korea in establishing their own league, suggesting instead that one Taiwanese professional team, which could join one of these three nations' professional leagues (!), would be sufficient.[30] But authors like this one were characterized as "conservatives." As many in Taiwan looked forward to more explicitly commercialized forms of their "national game," more typical was the outlook expressed in the 1988 article "Pro Baseball—Can't Delay another Day."[31]

TAIWAN AND BASEBALL IN THE WORLD

In August 1987, P. P. Tang, director-general of the Chinese Taipei Amateur Baseball Association and president of the Broadcasting Corporation of China, told an Indianapolis audience that the Republic of China would "strive to promote international friendship, mutual understanding and cultural interflow through baseball . . . [and] to promote world peace and harmony through baseball."[32] Planning for a Taiwanese professional baseball league began in late 1987[33]—a momentous year in Taiwan's history which marked the end of four decades of naked authoritarian rule by the Chinese Nationalist Party. Taiwan's "long 1987" began in October 1986, when President Chiang Ching-kuo famously told Katherine Graham of the *Washington Post* of his intentions to begin working toward true democracy in

Taiwan. In July he ended thirty-eight years of martial law, and in January 1988 the Generalissimo's son was dead at age seventy-seven. Sixty years of his family's leadership of the ROC and KMT came to a sudden and shocking end.

This all signaled a new era in Taiwan, where there was now space to redefine identities and historical memories once officially defined by Japanese, Chinese, and American hegemony. By the late 1980s, two different movements had emerged in this new Taiwan. The first was the quest to define a unique identity for the Chinese-but-not-really-Chinese island nation. This uniqueness in turn would aid in the second, the scramble to ensure Taiwan's inclusion in a new globalizing world order more and more defined by PRC diplomatic fixations. Both of these impulses, along with the entrepreneurial drive perfected in 1980s Taiwan, came together perfectly with the 1988 public announcement that a Chinese Professional Baseball League (CPBL, Zhonghua zhiye bangqiu lianmeng) would begin play in 1990.[34] Tellingly, one of the first public statements made by the ROC Professional Baseball Preparatory Committee was that the new league was "aimed at stemming the import of Taiwan's best players by Japanese teams."[35]

I have written elsewhere[36] on professional baseball in Taiwan as a powerful, self-conscious, and dialectical hybrid of globalizing forces and local cultures. Indeed, with a PRC eager to bring Taiwan under its rule, perhaps nowhere is there as much at stake as there is in Taiwan in proving to the world the inherent value of one's nation, society, and culture to a globalized twenty-first century. A piece of bureaucratic terminology from Chen Shui-bian's second term is thus very telling. In 2004, the Government Information Office provided these "Important Chinese Terms and their English Translations Used by the President":

> Chinese Term: *Shen geng Taiwan, buju quanqiu.*
>
> English Translation: Richly cultivating Taiwan while reaching out to the world . . . "cultivating localization while promoting globalization" for Taiwan.
>
> Chinese Term: *Taiwan youxian, quanqiu buju.*
>
> English Translation: Putting Taiwan's interest first, while maintaining a global perspective.[37]

In the early twenty-first century, these globalizing notions are crucial to the national survival of Taiwan. Four decades of authoritarian Chinese Nationalist rule, combined with the fear of real military action by the PRC, have led Taiwanese to fervently and enthusiastically celebrate their uniqueness—culturally, linguistically, politically, socially, and otherwise—vis-à-vis the "Chinese mainland."

Pride in the unique aspects of Taiwanese culture, and in the unique contributions that an independent Taiwan can make to today's world, justifies a place for Taiwan in the international community. Likewise, the pursuit of "international" trends and symbols can also be understood as solidifying a status for a Taiwan independent of the PRC and its threats of forced reunification. This dialectic between the uniquely Taiwanese and the international or universal has been a notable characteristic of virtually any cultural, social, commercial, or political enterprise in Taiwan since the early 1990s.

However, discussing this history in terms of "glocalization" actually helps us to see much greater continuities between the Japanese, Nationalist-centered, and professional eras. Baseball in Asia (like contemporary culture in general) is often analyzed using more classically defined categories of "globalization." For example, Cvetkovich and Kellner, in their *Articulating the Global and the Local,* describe how "countries like Japan play baseball but in ways that reinforce traditional Japanese values and structures."[38] Guevara and Fidler write on Major League Baseball's history of "rapacity toward Latin children," and discuss Japanese and Korean agreements with MLB designed to "[protect] the Asian leagues from 'American baseball imperialism.'"[39]

However, as Craig Stroupe writes, this discourse suffers from its assumption of the power of cultural imperialism: "'*Global*ization' is often used as a term to suggest the historical processes leading to a more one-way relationship between the 'global' realm inhabited by multinational corporations, the entertainment industry, CNN, the Web, etc. and a subjugated 'local' realm where the identity-affirming senses of place, neighborhood, town, locale, ethnicity, etc. survive (if just barely) against the global onslaught of global capitalism, media, and network identities."[40] However, this brand of analysis, which is far too quick to assume the unidirectional imposition of global forces onto a subjugated local realm, ill fits a place like Taiwan. There, domestic films are often seen as exotic oddities and young people now use terms like "Taiwanese" *(Tai)* or "local" (in English) to poke fun at peers or celebrities whose behavior, wardrobe, or diction are not cosmopolitan or hybridized *enough* for their long-jumbled tastes. Indeed, in the end an examination of Taiwanese baseball shows that attention to, in Gabardi's words, glocalization's "development of diverse, overlapping fields of global-local linkages"[41] is a much more accurate picture of the ways in which the game has functioned since in Taiwan since the 1990s.

THE CHINESE PROFESSIONAL BASEBALL LEAGUE: NINJA CATCHERS AND MILLER DARK, 1990–1994

The new Chinese Professional Baseball League consisted of four corporate-owned teams: the Weichuan Dragons, Brother Elephants, Uni-President Lions, and Mercuries Tigers. Weichuan, a food products firm, and Brother, a Taipei hotel, had sponsored semipro teams since 1979 and 1984 respectively; Brother CEO Hong Tengsheng was instrumental in moving to a fully professionalized format. Uni-President, another food company, inherited much of the personnel of the Taiwan Electric semipro team, as well as their Tainan base that automatically provided for a convenient north-south rivalry. Finally, after Hong was not able to convince the Evergreen shipping conglomerate to join the new league, he turned to former National Taiwan University classmate Chen Hedong and his Mercuries department store and restaurant group to operate a fourth team.[42]

These teams' uniforms sported a pleasurable mix of English and Chinese lettering in displaying team and player names and a crazy quilt of corporate sponsor patches and logos (as seen in figure 8). The four corporate-owned teams did not represent cities, as teams do in most professional leagues; instead, the teams toured up and down the island's west coast together, playing weekly round-robin series in Taipei, Taizhong, and Gaoxiong. Each of these cities (plus Tainan, Xinzhu, and Pingdong, where a few games were scheduled every year) had their own fan clubs (*houyuanhui,* from the Japanese *kōenkai*) organized to support each of the CPBL's four teams. The majority of these fan club members were male high school or university students, but these fan clubs were also filled with significant numbers of female students, businessmen, and laborers.[43] Their enthusiastic rooting could at times turn violent. The sight of angry fans—Lions fans in the Uni-President Corporation's hometown of Tainan were particularly unruly—hurling bottles, cans, eggs, and garbage at opposing players, or even surrounding the opposing team's bus in a mob, was not uncommon in the league's early years, giving the lie to the notion of a united Taiwan cheering on a united CPBL.

The first year of play, 1990, saw several incidents where the "street movement," a relatively new development in Taiwan after several decades of martial law, was imported from the realm of opposition politics to that of baseball fandom. In May, thousands of fans arrived at Taipei Municipal Stadium unaware that that day's Elephants-Tigers game had been cancelled by rain. Many were persistent enough in their threats of violence toward league personnel that the teams had no choice but to play the game (less several players who could not be reached after the stressful rescheduling).[44] Just ten days later, after another game was cancelled in Taipei, some two thousand fans refused to leave and physically blocked the Elephants players from leaving the premises. Eventually the diehard fans' desires were satisfied when Elephants players agreed to play a "friendly match" in the mud with nine barefoot fans, and to put on a home run contest with Dragons players who were called back to the grounds. The *United Daily News* thought that this was cute the first time, using a term from traditional opera patronage to describe how the fans had "selected a performance" despite the league's plans. This second and more threatening time, however, the state-sponsored paper referred to the mutiny as "a joke" and asked sarcastically in a headline if the CPBL schedule should really be determined by "referendum"[45]—a threatening notion in a Taiwan ruled by a KMT slowly watching its opposition gain public support and sympathy.

Another glocalizing element of the new Chinese Professional Baseball League was the presence of foreign players (usually called *yangjiang,* or "foreign talents") culled largely from the rosters of American Double-A minor league teams.[46] Twenty-three players, American and Latin American in origin, went to Taiwan in the winter of 1989 for tryouts. Sixteen were selected to join the CPBL (with a league limit of four *yangjiang* per team). The presence of these players was meant to add an international flavor to the league, and also to provide an external stimulus for the improvement of the quality of CPBL play. In a 1993 conversation, Jungo Bears pitcher Tony Metoyer described to me how these foreign players also served as "silent coaches" who could share their knowledge of American strategies and training methods with the Taiwanese players.[47] Their many contributions allowed the Taiwanese game to become closer in strategy to the more open or risky style of baseball played in the Americas, and less like the conservative game that suited Taiwan so well in its years of Little League dominance.

Steps were also taken to Sinicize the identities of these foreign players. Each of the players was given a "Chinese name," usually sounding something (if only vaguely) like the player's original name, and which often bestowed fine and admirable qualities on the foreigner. Elvin Rivera, a Dominican pitcher for the Tigers, became Li Wei, Li the common Chinese surname and Wei meaning "great" or "mighty." Freddy Tiburcio, the Elephants' star Dominican outfielder, was called Dibo, or "imperial waves and billows." Luis Iglesias, the Tigers' home run champion from Panama, was called Yingxia, or "chivalrous eagle." These players were photographed for magazine covers dressed in "traditional" Chinese scholars' caps and robes, as Taiwan's baseball public came to thrill in the unexpected mixtures of "East" and "West" that made the game much more complicated than either of these Kiplingian categories.

However, this two-way "assimilation" was often subject to the very crassest of corporate motives, as many of the foreign players' "Chinese" names were just advertisements for products sold by their team's parent corporation. The Tigers awarded names of noodle dishes (Qiaofu, Quanjiafu) from their chain restaurants to pitchers Cesar Mejia and Rafael Valdez. The Lions, whose parent company specialized in convenience stores and prepackaged foods, did the same with the names Shengmaige (San Miguel beer) and Baiwei (Budweiser) for pitchers Aguedo Vasquez and Ravelo Manzanillo. Later, the China Times Eagles resourcefully used names from their minor corporate sponsors, dubbing pitcher Steve Stoole "Meile" (Miller Beer), calling the Afro-Dominican outfielder Jose Gonzalez "Meilehei" (Miller Dark!), and former New York Mets infielder Brian Giles "Aikuai" (Alfa Romeo). However, none of these names even approach the glocalized complexity of the moniker given to the Lions' Jose Cano, a former Houston Astros pitcher who became beloved in Taiwan as "Ah Q." Ah Q is the protagonist in the 1921 eponymous classic story by Chinese social critic Lu Xun, but in the mid-1990s the distinctive name came in handy as a reference to the Taiwanese word for Uni-President food items distinctive for their "chewiness" (*khiukhiu*, or in modern parlance, "QQ").

Clearly, too many historical, corporate, and cultural trends were intersecting here to classify these trends simply as "global" or "local."

Real outsiders from the larger world of baseball came to Taiwan to endorse the CPBL enterprise as well, as the league in its early years won several valuable publicity coups. The Chunichi Dragons[48] and San Diego Padres sent minor league teams to Taiwan for exhibition series against CPBL teams after the 1991 and 1992 seasons. Then in 1993, the Los Angeles Dodgers major league squad visited, only to be beaten in two of three games by Taiwan's CPBL teams. The presence in Taiwan's ballparks of these representatives of the great American and Japanese baseball traditions only boosted the status of the CPBL in the eyes of Taiwanese and foreign baseball communities. Besides this conscious effort to connect Taiwanese baseball and culture to the greater baseball and cultural worlds of the international, efforts were also made to emphasize the CPBL's local composition in marketing the league. The most direct connection was the presence of former Little League heroes who had won such great honors for Taiwan in the 1970s. During their prime years in the 1980s, before the Chinese Professional Baseball League was founded, these heroes could only play in Japanese or Taiwanese semipro leagues. The CPBL was extremely fortunate to have begun play while this celebrated group still was in command of most of their skills; their presence in the first years of play was crucial in making the league a viable enterprise.

Other accouterments of "traditional Chinese culture" helped cement the league's special Chinese characteristics as well. Fan favorites like Dragon pitcher Huang Pingyang and Lion captain Zeng Zhizhen (known as "The Ninja Catcher") were often featured in magazines that told of their pursuits of self-consciously Chinese or Taiwanese customs, like drinking fine tea, taking in traditional Taiwanese puppet theater, or collecting teapots or Buddhist paintings. Popular television variety shows even featured noted numerologists and geomancers using these "traditional" Chinese sciences to predict the results of upcoming baseball seasons.

Thus, the roots of the CPBL's early success lay in this important effort to celebrate this exciting glocalized culture. This strategy is strikingly different from the model by which Tokyo's Yomiuri Giants became such a powerful symbol of Japanese pride and strength during the late 1960s and 1970s. Anthropologist William Kelly has outlined the history of the Giants' nine-year run of consecutive championships won from 1965 to 1973, a reign that "precisely mapped postwar Japan's double-digit boom years that catapulted the country to the first rank of industrial powers." The Giants organization insisted on maintaining a "pure" Japanese team, refusing even to allow the great Japanese-Hawaiian star and three-time batting champion Wally Yonamine to remain a Giant. The Giant cult was constructed atop beliefs of "uniquely Japanese" elements of a "fighting spirit" (konjō) and strategies of "managed baseball" that mimicked new forms of corporate organization, and became an important brick in the wall of an essentialist, culturally- and racially-defined postwar Japan.[49]

Yet there is literally no analogue between the cult of the Yomiuri Giants and the rise of professional baseball in Taiwan. For an island that has always been so politically and ethnically complicated, this kind of national or racial chauvinism was impossible. There was tension, however, between notions of a uniquely "Taiwanese" identity emerging in 1990s Taiwan and some of the essential "Chinese" gimmicks used to show how baseball was being assimilated into Taiwanese/Chinese culture. In the CPBL, explicit "Taiwan consciousness" took second stage to the exaggerated "Chineseness" of the league's image, and this crack in the CPBL's fun mixture of international and local cultures would be exploited by later competitors.

MINOR-LEAGUE FOREIGNERS
AND TENSIONS IN "CHINESE" BASEBALL

The CPBL reached its peak popularity, measured by crowd attendance, in its third through fifth seasons, from 1992 through 1994. In 1993, the league was joined by two new teams—the Jungo Bears and the China Times Eagles—each loaded with seven young, popular members of Taiwan's 1992 silver medal Olympic baseball team. That same season, the all-sports station TVIS paid NT$90 million (US$3.6 million) to broadcast CPBL games over the next three seasons—hardly American network money, but a great improvement over the NT$3,000 (US$120) per-game fee paid by Taiwan's major broadcast stations before that point.[50] CPBL games were now televised in thirty-eight different countries covered by Rupert Murdoch's STAR-TV enterprise.[51] At the same time, the league also actively expanded its schedule into the Xinzhu, Tainan, and Pingdong markets, bringing quality baseball to the hometowns of more baseball-starved Taiwanese.

But somehow, despite all these signs of vigorous growth, the league's popularity began to wane seriously by 1995, as the game began to lose the local significance it had worked so hard to create. The CPBL mishandled the important balance between the local and the international that was so crucial in sustaining public interest in the league, as owners developed a dependence on international networks that made the league less "glocalized" and simply less appealing.

The most visible form of this dependence was the CPBL's reliance on the foreign ballplayers invited to Taiwan to supplement the native rosters. From 1990 to 2009, some 823 foreign players played professionally in Taiwan,[52] and it soon became apparent in the league's first year that a team's success could depend heavily on the performance of their foreign supplements. Many of these "foreign talents" became fan favorites in Taiwan—typically solid players like Tigers third baseman Luis Iglesias, Elephants outfielder Freddy Tiburcio, Dragons pitcher Joe Strong, Elephants pitcher Jonathan Hurst, or Sinon Bulls pitcher Osvaldo Martinez, who were not quite talented enough to make it far in the American major leagues, but were able to excel in Taiwan, willing to learn Chinese or Taiwanese languages and to spend many years overseas. Several *yangjiang* rank among the most beloved of Taiwan pro base-ball's stars. The late Milt Harper (see figure 9) was one of these individuals, a big, kindly power hitter who drew crowds of admiring children wherever he appeared. George Hinshaw, formerly of the San Diego Padres and Chunichi Dragons, re-membered very fondly the bonds that the game he calls "an international treasure" created between him, his teammates, and Taiwanese fans of the game when he played for the China Times Eagles in the mid-1990s. (Interestingly, he described Taiwan to me as "a miniature Japan with an outpouring passion for the game.")[53] And when the Taizhong Robots of the Taiwan Major League cut American second baseman Lonnie Goldberg in 1998, members of a "Goldberg Fan Club" wrote enough letters to the team and league that the team was convinced to resign him to a contract.[54]

However, many seemed to tire of this foreign (usually American and Domini-can) presence as teams became too visibly dependent on these foreign networks—that is, when baseball became more a problem of one-way "globalization" than a fun rehearsal of "glocalization." Teams began putting more emphasis on the foreign element of their roster, seeing it as the quickest path to improvement—it was cer-tainly easier to wave money at a foreigner with proven skills than to dedicate sev-eral years to developing a Taiwanese player from scratch. The situation was exac-erbated when, in 1994, the board of CPBL owners raised the foreign player maximum to seven per team. In 1995, this ceiling was raised to ten foreigners per team, and in March 1997, the league owners voted to eliminate all limits whatso-ever on roster composition.[55]

Public interest in the league fell consistently as the CPBL became less and less "Chinese" or Taiwanese, and more and more reliant on American and Dominican players. By 1995, 44 percent of the CPBL's players came from outside Taiwan! Many of these *yangjiang*—who seemed to imagine their experiences in terms more redo-lent of a one-way "globalization" than the startling hybridity that the Taiwanese pub-lic had come to expect—contributed to these tensions with their own actions. Some admitted far too candidly to being baseball mercenaries in Taiwan solely for the relatively high salaries they could demand there, while others alienated local soci-ety with their sometimes ill-considered, promiscuous, and even brutish behavior. One example of this disrespect can be seen in an early internet blog maintained by an American pitcher in 1995 upon joining the China Times Eagles: "I finally flew down to Pingtung . . . and it is worse than I imagined . . . It is like something from a war movie or a MASH episode . . . there are people who have never had a Big Mac. . . . Even the TV is bad here . . . we get 2 american stations . . . both show I dream of Genie and old Pettycoat Junction re-runs."[56]

In turn, this lack of consideration brought forth Taiwanese attitudes that were much less tolerant and much more harshly (if often hypocritically) judgmental than before. In 1995, many in the baseball world acted shocked when the Jungo Bears' foreign players threatened to go on strike during the heat of the pennant race in order to lodge a protest with their team. Despite this outrage, it is unlikely that many in Taiwan would have defended the club's actions that brought this on in the first place—namely, their failure to reimburse pitcher Tony Metoyer for medical expenses or the back wages owed after suddenly cutting the injured player from the roster.[57] Another issue that also morally exercised the public came out in a 1997 book entitled *Foreign Pro Baseball Players' Sex Scandals*,[58] even though, as Marc Moskowitz has explained, much of this judgment is based on powerful myths of "Western decadence" that ignore the Taiwanese participation that by definition makes up half of these "scandals."[59]

These concerns converged most dramatically and unfortunately in the case of Milt Harper, a power-hitting first baseman who played three years in the CPBL. Harper had played in the Cleveland Indians organization before arriving in Taiwan, where he became a beloved member of the Uni-President Lions' 1991 championship team. Two years later, however, Harper was dead, found in a Taipei parking lot after falling from a fourteenth-story apartment window. What is incredible about the news coverage of this terrible event in October 1993 is how quickly it became one more proof, in the words of several different reporters during the first four days after Harper's death, of how "hard it is to supervise foreign players," of the players' "inappropriate behavior and use of their power to take inappropriate advantage," of the need to teach them "discipline," of what a "headache the supervision of foreign players becomes for coaches and the front office," and of how important it was for Taiwan's baseball clubs to address "the problem of managing foreigners," and for the players' union to establish a "Committee for the Supervision of Foreign Players."[60] Harper's death was ruled a suicide, despite the fact that he recently told family members that he feared for his life.[61] The very real possibility that Harper was murdered by the Taiwanese mob seemed less appealing to the media, which was obsessed with the traces of amphetamines reportedly detected in his bloodstream and his disorderly "American ways and views." The fact that he had earlier been stabbed by a Taiwanese man in a bar on the eve of the Lions' 1991 championship series?[62] Merely further proof of Harper's guilt. This tragedy somehow reinforced in the minds of many Taiwanese images of lawless, ignorant, and wild Western men. There were easily accessed historical precedents to that, and racially-charged memories of Western imperialism in Asia seemed largely to cancel out the exciting glocalized interactions that baseball had provided for so long in Taiwan.

In 1998, commenting on the dominance of foreign pitchers in the CPBL, a *Liberty Times* columnist summoned up specific ugly images from modern Chinese history in calling the league's pitching mound a "foreign concession" *(waiguo zujie)*.[63] Indeed, the predominance of foreign pitchers that season was ridiculous. Of the one hundred CPBL pitchers who took the mound that year, only twenty-two were Taiwanese. The 1998 CPBL champion Weichuan Dragons carried twelve foreign pitchers on their roster (combined record fifty-six wins, forty-eight losses, and one tie), but only two Taiwanese pitchers (combined record 0–0–0).[64] This, in fact, is when the more one-sided picture of "globalization"—an impersonalized far-off assembly-line process, in this case creating an endless string of "foreign talents" without the least connection to Taiwan's cosmopolitan society—began to become more relevant, as the league began to seem less so.[65]

The baseball community's mixed feelings about these foreigners who took over their league were manifested in many ways. Chen Dashun, a Dragon star first-baseman-turned-columnist, reflected on the difficulty of creating a "local *(bentu)* baseball culture" in a league dominated by foreign players, and described Taiwan baseball culture as ultimately and frustratingly "not Chinese and not Western" *(bu zhong bu xi)*.[66] Former Jungo Bears owner Chen Yiping wrote a piece in which he fantasized about ending American "colonialism" in Taiwan and beginning an era of "pro baseball with zero foreigners."[67]

Popular baseball cartoons drawn by artist Ao Youxiang demonstrate aspects of this ambivalence in a baser way. Some cartoons show foreign players (particularly players of African descent) as simply big and dumb, unable to comprehend any but the most corporeal of sensations. In one, a black batsman (with absurdly exaggerated "Negroid" facial features) is hit in the groin by a pitch. As the batter rushes the mound, players of both teams follow, fearful of the damage to be done to the Taiwanese pitcher by this enraged behemoth. But all are stunned when he arrives at the mound, evidently unfazed by pain that would fell any normal man, and thanks the pitcher for breaking up his kidney stones.[68] Another cartoon (figure 10) shows a black baserunner styling himself "the American stolen base king," vainly assured in his attempt to steal second base. But he is fended off by a wily Taiwanese shortstop, who turns the silly American scampering back to first base by waving a plate of "stinky tofu" his way.[69] These stereotypes of the clever and rational Chinese versus the physically gifted but dim-witted black man were tired and ignorant, but these cartoons did show the degree to which many felt betrayed by what was supposed to be Taiwan's own baseball league.

Fans' own wishes for a more Taiwan-centric CPBL could be seen in voting for the annual All-Star Game. In a 1997 season marked by more foreign dominance than ever,[70] fans did not select a single foreigner to the All-Star teams, selecting marginal (at best) players like Whales outfielder He Xianfan (batting average .218) and pitcher Huang Qingjing (one win and nine losses, 5.65 ERA), over the many foreign players who were more deserving by any statistical standard. From artists and columnists to fans themselves, the CPBL community made explicit statements about the kind of local flavor they wished the league had retained since its more successful early years. The presence of these foreign players and managers achieved one of the original goals of this *yangjiang* strategy, in that the quality of CPBL play improved greatly over the league's first few years. However, it is telling that as the CPBL

improved in technical terms, it simultaneously became a subject of such little interest to Taiwanese baseball fans.

Even the baseball clubs themselves seemed to mock the foreign players who had
overtaken the CPBL game. In 1998, after the practice had been prohibited for years,
some teams resumed the awarding of outright, even crudely, commercial Chinese
names to foreign players. Al Osuna, who pitched for the Astros, Dodgers, and Padres
in the American major leagues, was signed by the Mercuries Tigers in 1998, and
given the Chinese name *Napoli*—the same name as the local pizza restaurant which
gave away one hundred free pizzas every night Osuna started a game.[71] The Sinon
Bulls (formerly Jungo Bears), owned by the huge Sinon Agrochemical Corporation,
in 1997 named several of its foreign players after the conglomerate's best-selling pesticides.[72] This meant that former Oakland A's starting pitcher Joe Slusarski, for example, was now known as *Tieshazhang,* Sinon's commercial name for 1-((6-Chloro-
3-pyridinyl)methyl)-N-nitro-2-imidazolidinimine, a chemical useful in killing
aphids, mealy bugs, and whiteflies. Luis Quinones, who just seven years before
played infield for the champion Cincinnati Reds, was known as *Tiebushan,* for
Sinon's best defense against silverleaf whiteflies and beet armyworms.[73]

There were other ways in which an overdependence on international parties and
networks hurt the CPBL in the eyes of its fans. In late 1996, after a disastrous 28–
69–3 season, Sinon Bulls management was proud to announce formal ties with the
Los Angeles Dodgers and president-owner Peter O'Malley. Lessons in new management styles, several loaner foreign players, and the privilege of holding spring
training at the famed Dodgers Baseball Academy at Campo Las Palmas in the Dominican Republic came at a cost (NT$10 million [US$364,000]), but Sinon insisted
these changes would save the franchise and would deliver a championship within
two seasons.[74] In February 1997, the Bulls announced that they and the Dodgers
planned to cooperate in building a Professional Baseball Academy in Xiamen in
the PRC based on the model of the Dodgers' Dominican facility.[75] A week later,
O'Malley attended the CPBL's opening night in Tainan and addressed the crowd,
calling the game "the 1997 Opening Game for professional baseball the world over."[76]

This Dodger influence, however, was viewed by many Taiwanese fans as more
threatening than the all-American franchise would have liked. In May 1997, when
the Bulls decided to fire Korean manager Kim Yong Woon and his coaches, hiring
outfielder Wang Junlang as player-manager, rumors flew through the CPBL that a
group of Dodger coaches soon would come to take over the team. This instance
showed just how fragile the public imagined Taiwanese control of the team to be. If
the imagined Dodger takeover did not in fact take place, it is still useful to see just
how much power the Dodger organization, one of the most fitting symbols of American paternalism and cultural hegemony, was imagined to have in this Taiwanese
league on the other side of the Pacific Ocean. This ominous view of the Dodgers did

soon prove to hold much truth when, in January 1999, the team signed twenty-one-year-old Taiwanese superstar Chin-feng Chen to a seven-year contract in clear violation of all Chinese Taipei (ROC) Amateur Baseball Association regulations.[77]

The CPBL was established at an important turning point in modern Taiwanese history, when society, culture, and identity were being redrawn, and the league was originally able to capitalize on and define the trends of the times. It held great appeal for many in Taiwan, who sought both to explore and to learn more about the world that was now so much more accessible to them, and also to finally establish what it really meant to be "Taiwanese." The league's attempt to establish connections with international baseball and cultural networks, while at the same time retaining a self-consciously local identity, was a perfect strategy for the time. However, after just five seasons, the league's popularity went into decline when this fine balance was lost by short-sighted team owners entranced by the quick-fix talents of American and Dominican players. This overdependence on the foreign only served to make the CPBL seem a slave to the hegemonic forces of American sport that the league was supposed to mediate and resist in the first place, and extinguished much of the enthusiasm so evident in the glocalized early 1990s.

THE TAIWAN MAJOR LEAGUE

In December 1995, a group of investors, led by Qiu Fusheng and Chen Shengtian of the Era Communications and Sampo Electronics dynasties, announced the formation of a new Naluwan Corporation that would operate a Taiwan Major League (TML, *Taiwan dalianmeng*) to begin play in 1997. Qiu, a major figure in the Taiwan baseball world ever since his sports network TVIS began broadcasting CPBL games in 1994, gambled that one baseball league was not enough for the island.

The TML, which lasted for six years before being merged into the CPBL in 2003, was designed to trump the old league, not with better quality baseball, but with a media-savvy and authentically "Taiwanese" approach, which also helps clarify our glocalized approach to the game. This explicitly politicized strategy would fit perfectly within the dialectic between globalization and local Taiwanese identity that drives so much of contemporary Taiwan society and culture.

Contacts to foreign baseball networks, as with the CPBL, were an important priority for the Taiwan Major League. In April and May 1996, top TML officials traveled to Japan and the United States, making important top-level connections with representatives of league offices and teams like the Orix Blue Wave, Seibu Lions, and Atlanta Braves.[78]

Even though TML teams employed a high number of American and Latin American players, the league made much of its preference for what it called a "Japanese way" *(heshi fengge)* or "Oriental wind" *(dongyang feng)* in recruiting Japanese coaches and players.[79] As appendix 2 shows, Japanese players actually constituted only 9 percent of the league's foreign players. Yet TML officials conspicuously praised Japanese players' skill and personal discipline that made them "more manageable" than Latin American ballplayers.[80] These gratuitous gestures to a shared Taiwanese-Japanese past and future served both as a marker of the TML's cosmopolitan distinctiveness, and as a claim to a proud supranational corporate Asianism for the twenty-first century,[81] but also as a self-conscious marker of a cosmopolitan (if still racist) culture of Taiwan baseball.

Where the CPBL utilized static stereotypes of "traditional China," the TML's identity was squarely based in Taiwan's unique culture and history. The name of the Naluwan Corporation which ran the TML, and the names of the four teams—Agan (*Jin'gang*, Robots), Fala (*Leigong*, Thunder Gods), Gida (*Taiyang*, Suns), and Luka (*Yongshi*, Braves)—were taken from the languages of several of Taiwan's Aborigine tribes who made such great contributions to the history of Taiwan baseball. Team uniforms were designed to reflect "the special characteristics of the Aborigine peoples," but also only after "consideration of the colors and design of professional baseball uniforms of other nations"[82]—a move that speaks to nothing better than the swirling environment of "global" and "local" forces that the term *glocalization* represents. In case these measures did not make the Taiwan-centric flavor of the league distinctive enough, the TML chose as its 1999 league slogan: "Focus on Taiwan, the Local Comes First" *(Taiwan youxian, bentu di yi)*.[83]

Another important choice made by the Taiwan Major League was to follow what it called a "territorial philosophy" *(shudi zhuyi)*, where each team had a city or region which it called home,[84] again unlike the CPBL. The "territorial" doctrine of *shudi zhuyi* dictated that teams take these "home" connections seriously. Before the 1997 season, teams took part in New Years' ceremonies in their home cities, and took oaths before city officials to serve as loyal and morally upright representatives of these cities. The Robots' team oath, taken on 17 January 1997 before the Taizhong Municipal Assembly, went as follows:

1. We will love and cherish Taizhong, and will work together with our Taizhong neighbors to promote the baseball movement.
2. We will sink roots in Taizhong, and will join together with our Taizhong neighbors in working for the public good.
3. We will have the fervent spirit of a rainbow, and are determined to win the highest glories in this first baseball season for our Taizhong neighbors.
4. Our hearts are full of sincerity, and we will work together with our Taizhong neighbors to create a healthy baseball movement.
5. We will play conscientiously and diligently, vowing to work with our Taizhong neighbors to make this the new home of "power baseball" *(qiangli bangqiu)*.[85]

These hometown loyalties took on more significance with the tragic earthquake that struck central Taiwan in September 1999. The Robots quickly dubbed themselves

"The Disaster Area Team," and set up their own Robots Van that delivered disinfectants, vitamins, and medicines to the residents of the epicenter in Nantou County.[86]

The Jiayi-Tainan Braves took their municipal vows seriously as well, canceling one of their 1997 preseason games against the Thunder Gods so that players could attend *miaohui* temple festivals in Beigang, Xingang, Puzi, and Dongshi during the Lantern Festival in late February.[87] That fall, during Jiayi County Magistrate Li Yajing's bid for reelection, Braves Manager Zhao Shiqiang (a second-generation mainlander) registered as an official member of Li's campaign team. He and his coaching staff put in tireless hours drinking with, fêting, and entertaining Jiayi County's many power brokers, as well as participating in local religious festivals.[88] The Braves' capturing of the TML championship in early November certainly did nothing to hurt Li, who soon recaptured the magistrateship for the KMT by a comfortable margin.

This anecdote is an example of the TML attempts to form explicit ties to local and national politics, and thus to an "authentic Taiwanese" credibility that—oddly enough—betrayed the same statist essentialism against which so many Taiwanese people chafed during the era of Chinese Nationalist hegemony. In February 1996, the TML named Jian Mingjing, Taiwan Television chairman and former Taiwan Provincial Assembly Speaker, as League Chairman, and Wang Jinping, vice chairman of the Legislative Yuan, as TML Vice Chairman.[89] These explicit political connections continued, and even intensified, during the TML's inaugural 1997 season, extending even to ROC President Lee Teng-hui. He was no stranger to the loaded language of Taiwanese baseball politics and its usefulness in clarifying Taiwan's historical ties to Japan.[90] In 1997 President Lee threw out the ceremonial first pitch at the TML's Opening Night, held in Jiayi on the arresting date of 28 February, after ignoring the CPBL's repeated invitations for him to appear at their opening game as he had in 1996.[91] For the next two weeks, the league's inaugural games in Taiwan's other baseball cities were graced by the presence of political heavyweights like Provincial Governor James Soong, Gaoxiong Mayor Wu Dunyi, and DPP Chairman Xu Xinliang. As one *Liberty Times* writer summed up these connections, "Politics + Baseball = Taiwan Major League."[92]

It did not take long in this election year for an even more powerfully symbiotic relationship to develop between the TML and Taiwan's ambitious city- and county-level politicians. As early as April, more than seven months before the elections were held, politicians began "chartering" *(baochang)* TML games held in their local baseball parks, buying up hundreds or thousands of game tickets and distributing them to their constituents.[93] Politicians all over Taiwan used this tactic in order to cash in on the votes of the island's baseball fans, and also to "show their power" *(zaoshi)* by their ability to fill a ballpark with their supporters. Even two of the TML's Championship Series games were chartered, one by Taidong County Magistrate Chen

Jiannian, the son of the Kanō baseball legend Akawats (aka Uematsu Koichi or Chen Gengyuan), who was described in chapters 1–3.[94]

The most spectacular demonstrations of the Taiwan Major League's distinctively Taiwanese character came in two of the league's trademarks. The first was its tradition of holding its season openers on 28 February at the Jiayi Municipal Stadium. Little explanation needs be given of the colossal significance of this date in Taiwan's history. Yet the TML stripped the powerful date of the anti-Nationalist/mainlander acrimony that marked private, subversive observances of the 1947 massacre for almost five decades. Instead, it transformed 28 February into a celebration of everything truly "Taiwanese." As one *United Daily News* scribe reported, perhaps a bit too glibly, this event now promised to "turn the tragic 228 into a joyful 228."[95] In addition to President Lee's ceremonial first pitch, leaders of Taiwan's nine official Aboriginal tribes also were honored in the game's opening ceremonies. The decision to honor Jiayi with this tradition (and with the TML's marquee team, the Braves), was a very conscious one as well, as the TML paid its respects to the historic "baseball capital" of Taiwan.

Where the CPBL, perhaps constrained by the politics of the late 1980s and early 1990s, presented itself as a "Chinese" baseball league, the TML did everything it could to be a truly "Taiwanese" league. Local politics, local religion, a tribute to the aboriginal tribes of Taiwan, and even modern Taiwanese history's most sacred date, 28 February, were all included in the elaborate rituals of the new Taiwan Major League. And their ability to present a cosmopolitan image at the same time it boldly celebrated the local paid off. Even though the new league offered an inferior quality of baseball than the old CPBL, the Taiwan Major League consistently outdrew its rival at the gates. One random (but telling) example was a night in September 1998, when 14,385 Jiayi fans attended a TML Braves-Robots game, compared to crowds of 629 and 1,113 that showed up for CPBL games in Taipei and Gaoxiong.[96]

Finally, the Taiwan Major League's official theme song, "Naluwan—True Heroes" (*Naluwan—chia^n-kang e eng-hiong*) was perhaps the finest example of the fascinating mixture of historical and cultural legacies typical of contemporary Taiwan, those so difficult to fit within most standard models of historical, economic, cultural, social, or political development. The TML anthem, supposedly based on rhythms and patterns of several types of Aboriginal tribal songs,[97] consisted of lyrics in Mandarin, Taiwanese, English, Japanese, and Aboriginal languages:

"NALUWAN—TRUE HEROES"

Take charge—the fervent spirit of the rainbow,
Our hearts are filled—with great fire shining bright,
Struggle on—with hopes that never die,
Start anew—a space for us alone.

> Fight! Fight! Fight, fight! Speed just like the wind,
> K! K! K! Power stronger than all,
> *Homu-ran batta*—truly strong and brave,
> Aaa . . . Na-Lu-Wan, the true heroes![98]

Each singing, each playing of this league anthem became a neat and tidy re-creation of the last several centuries of Taiwan history and culture. To be sure, little room for critical analysis of, or retrospection on, this history was allowed in this rousing, commercial theme song. But the tune was one more way in which the TML sought to portray itself as the true heirs, and "the true heroes," of the proud, complicated, and glocalized history of Taiwan.

"YOU'VE GOT THE F—ING TROUBLE": THE FALL OF TAIWANESE PRO BASEBALL, 1997–2001

In the winter of 1997, the future of Taiwan's pro baseball enterprise looked bright. The CPBL was beginning the first year of a rich new television contract with the China Trust conglomerate worth NT\$1.5 billion (US\$60 million) over three years, seventeen times more than the league's previous deal with TVIS. The new Taiwan Major League, while stirring up controversy by stealing some of the CPBL's best players, promised to provide healthy competition for the old league.

The CPBL enterprise was also newly energized by the revival of Jiayi, the traditional home of Taiwanese baseball. Jiayi's new fourteen-thousand-seat municipal baseball stadium was completed in 1997, and the new China Trust Whales, the CPBL's seventh team, chose Jiayi as their home base. This city also happened to be the hometown of Whales manager Lai-hua Lee, the brilliant catcher who was hounded by the Cincinnati Reds for years, eventually played pro ball in Japan, and then managed Taiwan's 1992 Olympic team.

Unfortunately, 1997 would bring only disgrace, both domestic and international, to the CPBL. In late January 1997, law enforcement uncovered a gambling scandal that revolved around the fixing of CPBL games by ballplayers in return for huge payoffs, often double a player's monthly salary. The nation was shocked by the front-page news that some of the game's greatest and most popular stars had accepted payoffs of NT\$300,000 to NT\$500,000 (US\$11,000 to US\$18,000) per game that they threw for the local gangs handling the "gambling" on each team. The China Times Eagles were the most spectacular culprits; it was revealed that the entire team was bought off regularly for a single team fee of NT\$7.5 million (US\$270,000) per game![99]

This scandal, later found to be linked to gambling interests in Hong Kong and Macao as well as southern Taiwan, led to the near-unraveling of the league as the baseball public learned the sordid details of the enterprise. And unfortunately for the home of Taiwanese baseball, the scandal was centered in the city of Jiayi. Three

Eagles players from Jiayi[100]—all members of the 1992 Olympic team—were at the core of that team's game-fixing plans together with the powerful Xiaos, a home-town crime gang run by three brothers who also held high posts in the municipal and county government.[101] Jiayi native Jiang Taiquan, the 1992 Olympic team captain and a Lions star outfielder who was to join the Whales for their inaugural season, was also indicted for fixing games.[102] This was a risky business; Jiang and star pitcher Guo Jinxing lost some NT$200 million (US$7.3 million) of the Xiaos' money in one game (Lions versus Bulls, 28 August 1996), by "accidentally" winning after assuring gamblers that the Lions would lose.[103] The powerful Xiaos were not men to suffer gambling losses like this gladly. Another Lion outfielder and Jiayi native may have learned the lesson the hard way; Wu Linlian went missing without a trace after he became a target of investigation in the scandal in February 1997.[104]

In all, investigators estimated that at least twenty CPBL games (out of the league's three hundred-game schedule) were fixed, with some NT$200 million (US$7 million) typically bet on each game.[105] No team or player was safe from these gangs when their favorite teams won. Loyal Elephant gamblers furious at their team's winning ways kidnapped five Elephant players, pistol-whipping one and shoving a gun down the throat of another. Seven Tigers players (including two Americans and two Puerto Ricans) were abducted at the Gaoxiong Stardust Hotel by gun-packing thugs who used similarly violent ways of requesting the players to throw games.[106] And one day, after dropping his daughter off at school, Dragon manager Xu Shengming was stabbed several times in the in the lower back, thigh, and arm by three or four representatives of yet another gambling outfit.[107]

Understandably, fewer and fewer fans decided to pay much attention to a league whose games were being decided by sleazy mob kings. A bad sign was when fans started circulating jokes that the CPBL's initials really stood for the "Cheat People Baseball League." Attendance fell by 55 percent in 1997, a change also due to the easier availability of American and Japanese baseball games via Taiwan's growing cable TV market. It was hard for the league to know where to start addressing this gambling problem; predictably, they began by blaming the mess on the foreign players and their "desire to come to Taiwan and do whatever it takes to get paid *(hun kou fanchi)*." Four foreign players were suspected of colluding with these gamblers and had their contracts cancelled—far fewer than the number of Taiwanese players who were banished from pro baseball. But one *Liberty Times* reporter, in describing the problem, felt comfortable starting from the assumption that "all the foreign players want [in Taiwan] is money" in praising the league's weak solution to a massive structural problem.[108]

Although no one admitted it at the time, the underworld connections and violence associated with the CPBL were a main factor in the defection of so many of the league's stars to the new Taiwan Major League before the 1997 season.[109] Over the next two years, the CPBL tried to find new ways of appealing to Taiwan's increasingly inattentive public. Yet neither new slogans for the league like "Continuing our traditions and looking to the future" and "Exciting and good baseball, extremely lively,"[110] promotional events with movie star Kevin Costner and vice president Lien Chan,[111] nor even plans for the Sinon Bulls and Weichuan Dragons to play China's national team in Xiamen,[112] were enough to convince Taiwan's baseball public of the league's continuing relevance. By the 1999 season, fan attendance for most games was below one thousand. One day in October 1999, the two scheduled CPBL games, both crucial to the late-season pennant race, drew just 176 and 116 fans respectively.[113] During the winter after the 1999 season, the league lost two more teams, as the Mercuries Tigers and three-time defending champions Weichuan Dragons both cited financial pressures in folding their baseball operations.[114]

Meanwhile, the rival Taiwan Major League originally had profited greatly from the CPBL's gambling problem, although it was later revealed that Taiwan's gangs had been able to infiltrate the new league just as easily. Before his later success with the Anaheim Angels, American pitcher Ben Weber spent two seasons with the Taipei Suns of the TML; he later recalled in a *Los Angeles Times* interview how he "would go out on the street and people started calling . . . 'Way-bo, Way-bo.'"[115] Although he appreciated the ways that this intense fan involvement prepared him for the major leagues, Weber was not one of the foreign players who immersed himself in the local culture. He and his wife "didn't really like it there . . . we just kept reminding ourselves we were only there for the money."[116] Weber "couldn't swallow any of [the Taiwanese food]. . . . We had three days off a week and there was really nothing for me to do but sleep."[117] But what shocked him were the massive cash payments that he discovered his Suns teammates received for throwing games, including individual payoffs of US$100,000 after they blew the final game of the TML championship series by the ludicrous score of 18–0. Weber's conclusion was that, as he told the *Fresno Bee,* "All morality in baseball just goes out the window over there."[118]

In 1999, a *Baseball World* author reflected on the general state of disinterest in Taiwan in the game of baseball—for so many decades their "national game" (*guoqiu*)—concluding that the game now could only be called Taiwan's "national stench" (*guochou*).[119] A longer-term implication of the dramatic fall of professional baseball in Taiwan was that it came at the exact moment when American and Japanese major league teams were beginning to aggressively scout young Taiwanese baseball talent. In 1999 and 2000, seven young players who would have starred in Taiwan signed lucrative contracts with American and Japanese teams. The Los Angeles Dodgers, well connected in Taiwan, struck first by signing outfielder Chin-feng Chen, who they believed to be "a baseball slugger nonpareil with a blindingly bright future."[120] Chen was named League MVP in his first U.S. minor-league season for the San Bernardino Stampede (California League, Class A) in 1999, and had his uniform number retired by the club when he moved on to Class AA.[121] At age twenty-four he made his celebrated major-league debut in September 2002,[122] although he was never able to catch on with the Dodgers for good.[123] Chen was released by the team in 2005 and has played for the CPBL's La new Bears since 2006.

At the time, the loss of Chen was crippling. And the Dodgers did not stop there, secreting seventeen-year-old pitcher Hong-Chih Kuo (Guo Hongzhi) away from his national youth team dormitory and signing him to a US$1.25 million contract in 1999. This highly controversial (if not immoral) signing infuriated and saddened many in Taiwan, who saw in this event many signs of the fall of Taiwanese baseball. One author identified six "manifestations of chaos" *(luanxiang)*—including greed, dishonesty, exploitation of young men, increasing power of professional agents, and disregard for law—that now doomed the game in Taiwan.[124] Two *United Daily News* reporters, making explicit comparisons to the days of the late Qing Dynasty, when "the Imperial Palace valuables were sold to the West," asked pointedly, "who is slicing away the roots of Taiwan baseball?"[125]

The Colorado Rockies stepped in to answer this question next, bagging eighteen-year-old Chin-hui Tsao, toast of the 1999 World Junior Championships, with a US$2.2 million contract in 2000. Tsao, who had been scouted by major league teams since junior high school, became "the Hope Diamond of the Rockies' minor league system";[126] one reporter suggesting that a pitcher so good could only have been designed by "a sentient supercomputer."[127] (However, shoulder injuries limited Tsao to just fifty appearances for the Rockies and the Dodgers from 2003 through 2007.) The New York Yankees, Seibu Lions, and Chunichi Dragons also invested heavily in young Taiwanese players whose talent the CPBL and TML, already crippled by the events described earlier, had to go without.

The disillusionment that so many felt was phrased most poignantly by a middle school student from Tucheng, Taipei County, who wrote the *United Daily News* with his pleas: "I once loved baseball. I loved it to the point where I would even neglect sleep and meals. . . . But since the gambling case, my impassioned bosom has frozen to ice, and I now understand what it is like to want to cry but lack any tears. Baseball culture now has no morality of which to speak. . . . Oh, my beloved baseball! How many more hearts will you break? . . . Fans are not returning—this is our silent protest!"[128] If this boy's appeal was a bit melodramatic, there is no question that his sadness reflected many Taiwanese citizens' real doubts that baseball could ever matter to their society again.

One more humiliation came in March 2001, on the opening night of the TML's fifth season of play. The Taiwan Major League also had seen the popularity of its inferior quality of baseball wane since 1997. By 2001, the two rival leagues, both plagued by several consecutive money-losing seasons, were seriously considering a merger and a further downsizing of the baseball enterprise. For 2001, the TML shortened team schedules to just sixty games each (from eighty-four), and desperately tried to attract fans with a new marketing gimmick, naming four pop stars as official "spokespeople" for each of the league's teams. Rapper Chang Chen-yue, spokesman of the Gaoxiong-Pingdong Thunder Gods, was scheduled to kick off the festivities at Chengqing Lake Stadium, along with ROC Legislative Yuan speaker and TML chairman Wang Jinping, plus Ronald McDonald. The game itself was to be a milestone in TML history, marking the debut of Taipei Suns Manager Li Juming, the former Little League and Brother Elephant star idolized as Taiwan's "Mr. Baseball." The season got off to an unbecoming start, however, when Chang enthusiastically performed his song "Trouble," repeatedly screaming in English before the sellout crowd and a national TV audience, "You've got the f—ing trouble! You've got the f—ing trouble!"[129] His words were a very accurate diagnosis of the state of Taiwanese pro baseball at the beginning of the twenty-first century.

Conclusion

Baseball's Second Century in Taiwan

100 Years of Taiwan Baseball Glory
Wherever there is baseball, there are Taiwanese.
Taiwanese use baseball to write history! Baseball is not dead; the story still continues!
SLOGANS ON THE FRONT COVER OF ZENG AND YU, *BASEBALL KING OF TAIWAN*, 2004

On 31 December 2000, Taiwan's president Chen Shui-bian made his first New Year's address to the nation, remarks meant to sum up his first seven months in office and also to "Bridge the New Century." Chen had much to discuss, from the political revolution completed by his own victory and his once-illegal party's climb to power, to the world economic recession and Taiwan's entry into the World Trade Organization, and tense relations with China and the increasing possibility of an armed conflict across the Straits. The president summed up his remarks with comments on the unique "Taiwan spirit" forged during the twentieth century, and closed his address with a vivid symbol of the Taiwan experience: "My dear fellow countrymen, history has passed the bat to us, and it is now our turn to stand at the plate. The twenty-first century will undoubtedly throw us several good pitches, as well as one or two dusters *(huaiqiu)*. Regardless of what is thrown to us, however, we must stand firm and concentrate all of our strength and willpower for our best swing."[1]

It is no accident that Chen chose this imagery to encapsulate Taiwan's history and identity. (Although he may have understated the case by calling a possible Chinese invasion of Taiwan a mere "duster.") I have tried to theorize here that a history of Taiwanese baseball is an appropriate and crucial window for understanding the complicated histories and cultures of modern Taiwan. Starting with the game's Japanese origins, and then the high-profile successes of Taiwanese Little League baseball from the 1960s to the 1980s, baseball was an important avenue by which Taiwanese people have navigated their traumatic historical relationships with the

Japanese, the Chinese Nationalists, and their American allies. Now, in the early twenty-first century, as the search for a uniquely Taiwanese identity is given official sanction, baseball remains a crucial element of this identity, in ways that by turns continue and depart from the meanings of the game's first century in Taiwan.

BASEBALL AND NOSTALGIA IN TAIWAN

> I wanna take you to my grandma's home, to watch the sunset until we sleep.
> I wanna hold your hand always—could love always be pure without
>   sorrow?
> I wanna ride my bicycle with you, I wanna watch a baseball game with
>   you.
> Wanna be carefree, singing, and walking, I wanna hold your hand always.
> JAY ZHOU, "SIMPLE LOVE," 2001

Taiwanese pop superstar Jay Zhou's allusion to baseball as a central element of the Taiwanese pastoral was hardly original, although other nostalgias centered on the game have evolved over the last century. Romantic Japanese colonists waxed about the good days before World War I when they played baseball in Taiwan unmolested by ignorant islanders, until the dominant imagining of an "authentic" Taiwan became one where Japanese, Taiwanese, and Aborigine subjects could give their all on the baseball diamond under the eye of imperial fairness and favor.[2]

After 1945, baseball was home to a uniquely Taiwanese nostalgia for this era of Japanese fairness before the crippling corruption, forced Sinicization, and anti-Taiwanese discrimination of the Chinese Nationalist era. One example of this is the cult of Kanō, the one-time agriculture and forestry vocational school now known as National Jiayi University (although the school still makes strategic use of the Japanese "Kanō" nomenclature). In 2001, then President Chen joined a solemn ceremony on this campus to unveil a large silver monument to the Kanō team whose play gripped the Japanese Empire in 1931 (see figure 11).[3] The monument, inscribed "Kanō, Champions of All under Heaven" (Tianxia Jianong), is a massive replica of the plaque (the original of which went missing in the chaos at the end of World War II) that the school received for their stirring second-place finish that year. Indeed, Kanō graduates—even those who have matriculated in recent years—speak proudly of the Japanese legacy and ethos that they see their school as uniquely transmitting more than six decades after the departure of those colonial masters. And this legacy is important at the highest levels of politics as well. It is no accident that Chen went out of his way to don white gloves for this important remembrance of an essentially Japanese (and therefore, not Chinese) Taiwan in 2001. Another instance: in August 2007, I visited the home of Kanō Alumni Association president Cai Wuzhang exactly one week after Ma Ying-jeou, the Nationalist Party (and eventually successful) candidate for president in 2008, did so (albeit with more media attention).

While baseball stands in so well for memories of Japanese imperial benevolence, the KMT regime saw the usefulness of the sport as a way of representing the pride, excellence, and glory of Chinese culture (especially as opposed to the despoiling influences of [paradoxically] Japanese or Communist "slavery"). By the turn of the century, the game had become an easy way to summon nostalgia for the heady days of the yearly Little League championships and the last moment (paradoxically again) when the Republic of China had been allowed to stand and excel among the community of nations. (Former President Chen went so far as to invite members of the Jiayi-Tainan Braves to perform a skit about Taiwan's 1969 Little League world championship team on stage at his 2000 inaugural celebration.)[4] The Taiwanese pastoral (baseball, boys, and old country home) is one that bears clear relations to the American and Japanese versions from which it sprang, although it has also been marked indelibly by the unique changes that Taiwanese people experienced under Japanese and Chinese Nationalist colonialism for almost a century.

"NOBODY BUT ME!" "NOW YOU KNOW WHO I AM!": BASEBALL, IDENTITY, AND THE INDIVIDUAL

We have a special relationship. ·
I am me. You are you.
I play ball. You cheer me on.
UNI-PRESIDENT LIONS FIRST BASEMAN GAO GUOQING'S SPOKEN-WORD
CONCLUSION AFTER SINGING A POP SONG ON THE FIELD BEFORE A
CPBL GAME, TAIZHONG, 30 JULY 2004

The first eight decades of baseball's career in Taiwan were recorded during eras of colonial and authoritarian rule by the imperial Japanese and Chinese Nationalist regimes. While baseball was a game that certainly brought great enjoyment to the many millions of Taiwanese people who played it during these many years, there was little space for expression of individual interest in or attachment to the game. Indeed, the notion of one's baseball aptitude or involvement being part of one's individual identity was nearly a moot point when the game meant so much politically to these modern regimes. Baseball could be about *isshi dōjin* ("impartiality and equal favor," or not) under the watchful gaze of the emperor, or it could be about Japanese-Taiwanese-Aborigine racial harmony, the 1930s process of *kōminka* ("imperial-subjectification"), or even tribute to "white-robed warriors" recuperating in Taiwan from the hell of World War II.

Under the KMT, baseball was supposed to be about (once more, paradoxically) fealty to a regime that allowed Taiwanese people to live in "Free China" as opposed to colonial slavery. Or it could be about a potent cold war commitment to the game that the ROC shared (this time ironically) with Japan, South Korea, and the Philippines, the former members of the Greater East Asia Co-Prosperity Sphere who now made up America's anticommunist "crescent" set up to contain the supposed Bol-shevik monolith in East and Northeast Asia. We know that many Taiwanese rejected this categorization, but largely for a pro-Japanese nostalgia that simply constituted the mirror image of the KMT obsession. By the 1970s and 1980s, the game of base-ball in Taiwan revolved around the Little League dynasty—although we know that this too was subject to even more urgently competing interpretations. Many in the Nationalist camp, upon seeing Taiwanese youngsters triumph year after year in this once-Japanese game of baseball, somehow were reassured of the superiority and sustainability of their Chinese "Cultural Renaissance" in Taiwan, as opposed to the Communists' hysterical and destructive Cultural Revolution on the mainland. At the same time, though, Taiwanese people who felt much less loyalty to the Chiangs' regime saw these baseball triumphs even that much more clearly as a Taiwanese (read: partly Japanese) rebuke to the KMT's overwhelming "Chinese" presence and a final nail in the coffin of this illegitimate mainland occupation of Taiwan.

So although the Western assumption (against most available evidence, of course) is that sports' "natural" orientation is to be *depoliticized,* it turns out that it is an aberration in baseball's long career in Taiwan to be about and directly accessible to the depoliticized "individual." Taiwan's professional baseball establishment and me-dia have worked hard to position baseball since the 1990s as an appropriate, healthy, fun, consumptive activity—which is perhaps why recent appeals to re-politicize baseball have seemed so ham-fisted. Since the success of capitalism lies in its positioning of itself as the only natural option or regime, baseball's 1990s pro-fessional turn has also resulted in the distinct presentation of baseball players and their bodies as representatives of capital, as opposed to representatives of Japanese, Taiwanese, or Chinese nations, states, or cultures. The Chinese Professional Base-ball League's fuzzy mascots, explicitly corporate ownership, and over-the-top pro-motional schemes—let alone the labor rights common to most professional ath-letes that CPBL players have never enjoyed[5]—have all worked to create an image of baseball that seems quite divorced from the political considerations under which the game thrived in Taiwan.

Where the game once stood for the loftiest goals of multiracial cooperation un-der the emperor, or for the salvation of the starving multitudes on the Communist mainland, professional baseball has become just one more way to sell 7-Eleven Big Gulps or McDonald's hamburgers (see figures 9 and 12). If Elephant star first base-man Peng Zhengmin was not wearing a uniform almost literally covered with cor-porate sponsorship patches,[6] he was dressed as a caveman with a bone in his hair in a Bomy Fruit & Vegetable Drink advertisement. This all reached a logical ex-tension when former L.A. Dodger Chin-feng Chen, upon returning home to play in Taiwan in 2005, appeared in a series of MasterCard promotions and commer-cials ("[With MasterCard] everything can be achieved, only friendship is priceless") wearing a jersey with his own given name splashed garishly across the front.[7]

Baseball now stands as a great representative of the triumph of the plurality of identities that capitalism always suggests. *Baseball World* magazine's October 1999 cover story was a feature on the "Prince of the Forkball," star pitcher Cai Zhongnan. Although Cai himself appeared apprehensive, even sullen, in the darkened photograph, it somehow made sense for the cover to bear, in large English lettering, the phrase "Now You Know Who I Am!" Although Ichirō Suzuki scarcely needed *Baseball World*'s help in announcing so, the Taiwanese magazine's next cover featured the Orix Blue Wave star on the cover with the English phrase "Here I Am!"[8]

The baseball establishment's bet has been on this mode of attributed self-expression as they have positioned the game as part of a more individualistic Taiwan. In 2002, the Taiwan Major League's final season, the official TML slogan was (in English) "It's My War." This was meant to represent how "on the field, baseball players spare no effort to show their individual skills . . . allowing themselves to sparkle and shine on the diamond! . . . [It is] a new kind of military campaign for the baseball fans of Taiwan."[9] Six years later, the CPBL borrowed from the lyrics of a popular song by Hong Kong idol Leon Lai in formulating their league slogan for 2008, "Nobody but me!" *(fei wo mo shu)*. A commercial for the league showed their biggest stars making outstanding plays in the field or waving forefingers aloft after hitting home runs, to the backdrop of a pop song with the aforementioned title:

> My pledge will never change, I believe I can make it happen,
> Nobody but me! Standing on the top of the world,
> Nobody but me! I sing to celebrate,
> The rhythm of our heartbeats cry out, you're my finest partner,
> Oh, nobody but me![10]

Baseball in Taiwan thus clearly has been reoriented to define the striving individual—working with others when necessary, but also conscious that he or she can count on "nobody but me" to really accomplish anything. This individual is of course the star of the capitalist narrative, be it player as product or fan as consumer.

The fan's own role has changed as well. It is no longer enough just to wave banners and chant slogans in support of one's favorite team (based on the Japanese model of fan behavior); now, fans can make themselves the center of the game. The CPBL's official video game by 2008 had evolved into a sophisticated animated online site, "Everybody Play Baseball" *(quanmin da bangqiu)*. Here, the fan becomes a fierce but cute *anime* version of one's favorite CPBL players and adopts the (by now predictable) slogan, "I want to be the ace!" *(Wo yao dang wangpai!)*.[11] And in case the video game ace is not sure which player's personality most closely fits him or her, the site even includes a "psychological test" to calibrate and correlate one's most individual qualities.[12]

It is worth noting, though, that little of this seems to be working for the ledger sheets of Taiwanese professional baseball. In 2008, the owners of two of the CPBL's finest teams, the Brother Elephants and La new Bears, stated publicly that low attendance was causing financial losses that may cause their corporations to shut down their baseball operations.[13] During the summer of 2007, I was interested to note that baseball—ostensibly Taiwan's "national game"—was actually featured on television less than international billiards (a field in which Taiwanese women have done especially well). This even took into account, besides almost-nightly CPBL broadcasts, broadcasts of every game played by the New York Yankees and Rakuten Golden Eagles, who both featured excellent Taiwanese players. And baseball fared even worse in the print medium; I was much more likely to see young people engrossed in basketball magazines (of which there are five or six sold at many newsstands: *Sports Plus, SLAM, XXL, DUNK, American Pro Basketball,* and *Ace Combat*) than reading either of the two baseball magazines that are still published— the CPBL's own official *Professional Baseball* (now a monthly after sixteen years of operation as a biweekly), and *Passion (Bang bangqiu),* a hard-to-find vanity publication by construction magnate, political gadfly, and former Jungo Bears owner Chen Yiping.

Finally, Little League Baseball, the heart and soul of Taiwan's baseball culture for two decades, now seems to carry very little significance. As discussed in chapters 4 and 5, Taiwan's Little Leaguers won a total of seventeen world championships in twenty-eight years from 1969 to 1996. But in 1997, Taiwan gave "hope for the seven thousand other teams across the world"[14] when they decided to leave the Little League structure because of "difficulty in implementing completely *[sic]* in compliance with LLB's regulations."[15] Taiwan returned to the LLB system in 2003, but to little fanfare, since professional baseball had become the new focus.

In 2007, a team from Diligence *(Lixing)* Elementary in Taizhong qualified for the Little League world championships in Williamsport, Pennsylvania, home of a quarter century of triumphant Taiwanese memories. The 2007 team reminded one of their 1970s and 1980s predecessors in one way—the Taizhong school did not have, and until the very last minute were not granted by Taiwan baseball authorities, the NT$1 million (US$30,500) that it cost to get the team to Williamsport. However, it was also very different, in that this time, instead of seeing these boys as saviors, no one really cared. The *United Daily News* carried news of Diligence's win in a short piece on page D8, a far cry from the *four-page* special front section devoted to the news of New York Yankee pitcher Chien-ming Wang's victory over the Tampa Bay Devil Rays the very next day.[16] The *China Times* devoted about three column inches on page D8 to the story, again in contrast to their own four-page pullout on Wang.[17] As I completed this manuscript in August 2009, Taiwan's young LLB representatives, an Atayal Aborigine team from Turtle Mountain Elementary in Taoyuan County, qualified for Williamsport. They too had to take to the media to ask for handouts, eager politicians posing with utterly disillusioned-looking boys, who were likely wondering why no one seemed to care anymore about the heroes of the national game.[18] It is hard to imagine a more telling sign of how little Taiwanese baseball has come to matter in many spheres of contemporary society. But Taiwanese baseball's loss of popularity has not necessarily represented a loss of popularity for baseball as a whole in Taiwan; by 2009 it was universally accepted that Taiwan had a new "national team"—no longer diligent twelve-year-olds, but Wang's own New York Yankees.

BASEBALL AND THE NATION, ONCE AGAIN

"FREE TAIWAN!"

SIGN AT DODGER STADIUM ON THE OCCASION OF CHIN-FENG CHEN'S
MAJOR LEAGUE DEBUT, SEPTEMBER 2002

New York taxi driver to Chien-ming Wang: "Ya wanna tell me where is Taiwan?"
Wang (dreaming about his pitching exploits for the Yankees): "I will show you."
TELEVISION COMMERCIAL FOR TAIWAN TOURISM PROMOTIONAL
CAMPAIGN, 2007

The way that baseball has remained relevant in Taiwan, despite all of the problems just mentioned, is the ease with which it attaches to events and issues of national concern. That is to say, for all the marketing about "me" and "my" skills on the baseball diamond, the game's DNA remains one that swirls in nationally defined helixes. And the nations (besides Taiwan) that are most relevant to this inheritance are the obvious ones—Japan, the United States, and China.

During the 2004 Olympics—popular in Taiwan mostly for the baseball competition, in which Taiwan finished fifth of eight teams—the evening television program "Big Talk News" (Dahua xinwen) hosted a discussion of Olympic baseball and the Athens Games in general. The roundtable included several guests: Democratic Progressive Party (DPP) Legislators Cai Huanglang and Hsiao Bi-khim, KMT spokesman Justin Chou, and ex-pitcher Chen Yixin, formerly of the Chunichi Dragons, Brother Elephants, and Jiayi-Tainan Braves. The DPP's Cai spoke only in Taiwanese, while Chou also played to script and spoke only in Mandarin. Chen, an Amis Aborigine, spoke mostly in his own Hualian-accented Mandarin, but also naturally interspersed his speech with the kinds of Japanese-English terms (*kurosu pitcha* [closer] and *homuran*) discussed in the introduction.[19] The production was notable for, in an unrehearsed way, showing just how complicated the jumble of language and ethnicity can be in Taiwan. But these languages—Taiwanese, Mandarin Chinese, Japanese, and English—were hardly spoken in some ahistorical vacuum; there are very distinct reasons why baseball and the Olympics and, more generally, virtually any cultural or political issue in Taiwan will be discussed between these several reference points.

The historical connections between baseball in Taiwan, Japan, the United States, and China—and many Taiwanese still insist that baseball is totally foreign to the mainlanders—provide the lasting resonance for the game. In the case of the United States, we have already seen in chapter 5 the multiple meanings that Taiwanese people gained from seeing their Little League teams annually thrash America's finest youth teams during the 1970s and 1980s. By the end of the first decade of the twenty-first century, though, the American connection had switched totally to Major League Baseball and the Taiwanese players, most spectacularly Chien-ming Wang, who have thrived there. It is barely an exaggeration to say that Wang by 2008 was a national obsession. When he played for the Yankees through 2009, every one of his team's games was shown live on Taiwanese television, usually on two networks, and then replayed at least once later that day, leading many to joke, as was noted above, that the Yankees were Taiwan's new "national team."[20] Taiwanese people reserved the right to withdraw this mandate, however. In December 2009, the Yankees declined to offer Wang a new contract, and within days one television show in Taiwan was referring to the Yankees as an "evil empire."[21] The sight of the tall (six feet three inches) and handsome Wang becoming one of the very finest pitchers in the American League was a joy for Taiwanese fans, although at times to an unhealthy extent. In September 2007 a man in Taoyuan was clubbed to death for trying to steal one of the four-page newspaper supplements cited earlier, in this case celebrating Wang's nineteenth win of the season.[22] For most people, however, the triumphs of Wang and other Taiwanese players, like Dodger pitcher Hong-chih Kuo or Detroit Tiger pitcher Fu-te Ni, are imagined to remind Americans where and what Taiwan is in a world increasingly dominated by PRC economic and political interests.

In 2006, the Taiwanese government and media celebrated "a century of baseball" in Taiwan. The observances clearly were designed to appeal to and to construct a Taiwanese nationalism, but they also were meant to spotlight memories of Japan's "contributions" to Taiwan during their fifty-year occupation of the island. Firstly, the fact that Taiwan's national game is Japanese—and, the point being, *not Chinese*—in origin is of inestimable propaganda value for supporters of Taiwan independence. This obsession is stifling and self-defeating, though. By the early 2000s, it became far more important for the Taiwanese to beat China's baseball team than to be able to knock off powers South Korea or Japan. The norm for Taiwanese managers was to send their best pitchers out against China's weak team—hurting their chances against other rivals but guaranteeing at the very least that they would not be the manager to suffer the shame of losing to the PRC.[23] It worked for many years, until the Beijing Olympics of 2008. Despite vowing in the media that "on Chinese soil, no matter what we cannot lose,"[24] and despite (once again) sending their finest pitcher, Pan Wei-lun, against the underdogs, the ROC team gave up five runs in a breathtaking twelfth inning to lose to the PRC team for the first time ever, 8–7.[25]

Within hours, Taiwan's media was calling this "the most humiliating day in Taiwan baseball history,"[26] "the most sorrowful and insulting defeat,"[27] and "the most embarrassing battle in history."[28] Bloggers, of course, went further, calling for observation of a "Day of National Humiliation" every 15 August hereafter and asking their government to lower the national flag to half-mast. Another screamed the players' way, "A deathly loss of face! Tell [American gold medalist Michael] Phelps to teach you how to swim home!"[29] This anger and humiliation, tied so closely to one of the most crucial pillars of Taiwanese identity for almost a century, was not just harmful to a collective psyche. One elderly woman from Taizhong, upon seeing the PRC outfielder Sun Lingfeng score the winning run, suffered chest constrictions, became unable to breathe, and had to be hospitalized. A countryman of hers from Gaoxiong was not so lucky, however, dying of a heart attack at that same fateful moment. After these tragedies, psychological and heart specialists were interviewed in the United Daily News for advice that they could pass on to an angered and exhausted nation.[30] No wonder, then, that one more blogger could only ask his countrymen to stay inside the rest of the day, since "only Heaven knows what other inconceivable things might happen."[31]

However, it was entirely conceivable and revealing—if still depressing—what happened next: accusations from the government and media that the Olympic baseball team had purposely *thrown* their game against China for their own illicit financial gain! (Prosecutors in Taiwan now believe that this indeed was the case.)[32] Just one month later, it was revealed that the d-Media T-Rex were the latest CPBL club to be suspended for illegal game-fixing. At least this operation was thorough; mafia members allegedly helped d-Media CEO Shih Jian-hsin purchase the team so that they could control players and game results more directly and efficiently than they were able to with their previous stabbing and pistol-whipping tactics.[33] Indeed, baseball is back—but not at all in the way that the typical triumphalist narratives would have it.

If baseball for so long helped Taiwanese to imagine China as other, backward, and so on—and the loss of this certainty does seem crippling—the game also has helped Taiwanese to reflect on their longstanding connections with Japan's "advanced" culture. In this case, the postcolonial signifier works in a way that also follows Herzfeld, whose culturally intimate history has established "yesterday's embarrassments [as] today's proud boast."[34] The fact that many people in Taiwan still refer to baseball as *yakyū* and not *bangqiu* is not coincidental. Nor, for example, is the fact that the world champion Tainan Giants team took their name from the *Tokyo* (not San Francisco) Giants. Obviously, in this case the colonial legacy is much more complicated than simply a stigma, or, for that matter, a nostalgic object of desire, but a readily available device for the instant creation of a Japanese (and therefore authentically Taiwanese) heritage in Taiwan. Just days after his party's disastrous showing in the 2005 elections, President Chen Shui-bian made an ostentatious show of welcoming Oh Sadaharu to Taiwan, and calling the upcoming World Baseball Classic game between Japan and Taiwan a "meeting of gentlemen."[35] Again, while the cliché is always that sports develop most purely and authentically when "politics" is left out of the recipe, the recent history of baseball in Taiwan tells us that the nation is still, a century on, a key ingredient.

MANUFACTURING CONTENT:
THE "BASEBALL IS BACK" DISCOURSE

One of the most celebrated events in the recent history of baseball in Taiwan was the hosting of the Thirty-Fourth Baseball World Cup in 2001. The tournament was marred by quibbles both international—the PRC insisting that Taiwan only compete as "Chinese Taipei" and that they not be allowed to display their own ROC national flag during the tournament[36]—and domestic, like President Chen Shui-bian's public suggestion that the recently defeated Nationalist Party should learn about sportsmanship and "polite behavior" from the games.[37] Most media attention was devoted to Taiwan's thrilling bronze-medal victory over Japan. But the *Liberty Times* took a larger view, concluding that the tournament "serves as a reminder that Taiwan's entry into the global community cannot place hope on China's goodwill, but rather Taiwan must rely on its own strengths."[38]

Some of the biggest stars of this media event were several university students, who, seemingly independently, brought tongue-in-cheek banners to Taiwan's quarterfinal game against Holland, imploring the assistance of Zheng Chenggong (Koxinga), the Ming dynasty loyalist and military leader who defeated the Dutch in Taiwan in 1662.[39] Copycats abounded, with, less cleverly, portraits of Generalissimo Chiang Kai-shek waving for the bronze-medal game against Japan, and (tastelessly, just ten weeks after September 11) a picture of Osama bin Laden exhibited by fans rooting on Taiwan against the Americans in the semifinals.[40] The Koxinga posters became the longest-lasting symbol of this tourney, their over-the-top nationalism amusing many, but also deeply inspiring many others. A page two op-ed in the *United Daily News* two days later reflected on these posters and the instant "*women gan*, We Feeling" (using both Chinese and English) that they created in Taiwan. The author could only (and significantly) compare this sense of unity to the feeling of watching the national flag go up every New Year's Day (the anniversary of the ROC's inauguration in 1912).[41]

Three important facts emerged from this discourse. The first was that baseball seems to possess the most resonance in Taiwan when it can be used to talk about nations—and paradoxically, in this case, it was the old ROC-style (and not Taiwanese) nationalism that was tapped most explicitly in remembering "Chinese" triumphs over former imperialist enemies. (And if pressure from the PRC forced the Taiwanese team to wear their customary "Chinese Taipei" uniforms, the scoreboard at Tianmu Stadium still used Roman and Chinese script to restore, at long last, the "ROC [Zhonghua minguo]" to the world of international baseball.)[42] The second point that emerged from all of this was the degree to which so many around the island seemed to hope that baseball could "come back" and inspire a now-jaded Taiwanese population. The third point was that this dramatic baseball "comeback" was a patent fiction. Television broadcasts of the World Cup showed thousands of empty seats for games not involving Taiwan; in the early days of the tournament the *Taipei Times* called it a "dud" when just thirty-five spectators attended the game between South Korea and South Africa, despite the low (NT$150 [US$4.30]) ticket prices.[43] But not even every game featuring Taiwan's national team sold out the island's small stadiums. A temporary hysteria during the last days of the tourney was misread— optimistically by some, purposely by the baseball establishment—as some intrinsic interest in the "national game" that could unite the twenty-three million of Taiwan once again.

Yet, it has become an article of faith—against most available evidence—that this 2001 Baseball World Cup represented a "comeback" for the game after the humiliations of the late 1990s. Indeed, the speed with which this narrative was created speaks to how badly Taiwanese people have hoped for the "degraded" culture of baseball to become a form of national salvation once again. The *Taipei Times* called the final day of the tournament, when Taiwan won the bronze medal against Japan, "a wonderful day in Taiwan—a rare day without unification-independence disputes, ethnic grudges, or wrangling between political parties." The seeming desperation for a long-lost unity came through very strongly in passages like this: "The baseball tournament and the performance of the Chinese-Taipei team became the key to a collective psychological healing during a frustrating period for the nation— in the same way the Yankees helped New Yorkers emerge from the gloom cast by the Sept. 11 attacks. Taipei City's hosting of the Baseball World Cup tournament won back the hearts of Taiwanese fans, who cheered for their team regardless of age, gender, ethnic background or party affiliation."[44] The same newspaper, an important bellwether of Taiwanese nationalist sentiment, felt confident enough to declare simply that Taiwan's "baseball buzz" was back.[45] By December, *Sinorama* Magazine featured a piece titled "Baseball Fever: Taiwan Catches It (Again) from Baseball World Cup," echoing this discourse of a Taiwanese people revitalized by the game.[46]

Since then, almost any mention of the 2001 Baseball World Cup hosted by Taiwan inevitably and formulaically cites this revitalizing effect—a discourse made even more resonant by the decision just one year after the World Cup to merge Taiwan's two competing professional leagues into one unified organization, the Chinese Professional Baseball Major League (Zhonghua zhiye bangqiu dalianmeng). League commissioner Harvey Tang remarked that the unification meant that "Baseball's coming home," while Chen Shui-bian, who made much of his own involvement in this process, declared that this unity was "what all the people have hoped for."[47] This narrative has even become part of English-language scholarship on Taiwan baseball; in a 2006 article, Yu Junwei recorded how in 2001 "with the efficiency of a miracle drug, nationalism had resuscitated the ailing professional leagues,"[48] and in his 2007 book, he wrote on the "renaissance" and "rebirth" of baseball created by the World Cup.[49]

Unfortunately for these prognosticators, this revitalization was fleeting, the "miracle drug" merely one more round of DPP and corporate ideological snake oil. As of 2010, Taiwan's entire baseball enterprise is now in doubt. It was discouraging to see how quickly this 2001 enthusiasm became one more piece of far-off nostalgia when troubles returned, as in further gambling scandals in 2005, 2008, and 2009 that involved several CPBL teams.[50] (This included, allegedly, one Australian pitcher who was convinced to throw games by gangsters supplying him "special entertainment" at Taipei girlie bars.)[51] It is important, then, to wonder why there was such an investment—popular, corporate, and even scholarly—in manufacturing this notion of a renewed "national game."

The significance of this discourse is best understood when one takes into account the geopolitical and economic realities at the turn of the twenty-first century. Taiwan's perilous status as an independent democratic entity is never far below the surface of most contemporary discussions of society and culture; this surely includes baseball. Taiwan's national game comes to figure in almost any calculation vis-à-vis their rival on the Chinese mainland; the PRC's far-from-peaceful rise is very easily imagined as a direct threat from the other side of the Taiwan Straits. Thus, this helps us return to ideas of baseball's glocalized legacy and significance. Once again, instead of discussing the game as part of the trend of "globalization . . . like a tidal wave erasing all the differences," it is much more helpful to see how events like the 2001 World Cup make "some local ideas, practices, institutions global" and incorporate "certain global processes into the local setting."[52] Of all the things that baseball represents in Taiwan, it has really nothing to do with the "isolation" cited by Yu Junwei in the title of his 2007 book on the game.

The idea of the local in Taiwan, as the present study demonstrates, seemingly can only be expressed with explicit reference to the national and the global. Thus, two decades of prosperity—cultural, economic, and democratic—can be experienced with profound regret when one considers the relative powerlessness of Taiwanese people to control their political fate today. It is not hard to see in Taiwan's culture "intimations of a collective mortality"[53] as these twenty-three million people crowd within the target sights of one thousand ballistic missiles in Fujian and Zhejiang. In a world already scarred by twenty-first-century fascism, violence, and irredentist fantasies of imperial might and vengeance, a "deep sense of a shared fatality"[54] seems an altogether appropriately existential response to the absurdity of Taiwan's national condition. It is telling, then, that of all things, one of the key cultural weapons with which former president Chen Shui-bian chose to combat this PRC threat is baseball.

On 20 March 2004, Chen's government asked the electorate to vote not only for his reelection as president, but also for a referendum that would openly renounce the PRC's bellicosity and threats. And as he did time and time again, Chen used symbols of baseball (in this case, the campaign button pictured in figure 13) to frame the populist Taiwaneseness of this position (pushed over the top with the gratuitous reference to the 28 February "Hands across Taiwan" event). Whether it was Chen's first public appearance as president-elect in 2000 (at the Taiwan Major League opening game in Gaoxiong), his habit of turning to baseball to score easy political points (promising a dome for Taipei and welcoming Oh Sadaharu to Taiwan just days after his party's disastrous showing in the 2005 elections),[55] his hiding behind baseball patriotism to avoid criticism of his disbanding of the National Reunification Council on 28 February 2006,[56] or his urging DPP supporters to wear Chienming Wang New York Yankees jerseys when marching to protest corruption charges brought against his family and friends later that year,[57] it has been a consistent policy over the last several years in Taiwan to use the colonial legacy of baseball as the ultimate official defensive "cultural cringe."[58] Only in Taiwan could a Human Rights Parade—led by the Presbyterian Church in Taiwan (Taiwan jidu changlao jiaohui) in August 2007—take as its central symbol (that is, after the massive wooden cross in the first float) a huge inflatable baseball some six feet in diameter.[59]

However, this level of cynicism and instrumentality is not necessarily new. For many decades, baseball also has been an important element of much more complex notions of "public culture" in Taiwan. From its colonial origins and its position within Japanese educational, business, and bureaucratic institutions to the Nationalists' cold war uses of the game, to 1970s and 1980s corporate sponsorship and cooperation with colleges and universities, to the official positioning of the game within Taiwanese ethnic politics in the 1990s and 2000s, baseball—many times more so than tennis or rugby, other sports imported by the Japanese—has been an important element in fashioning public identity in Taiwan.

When Lee Teng-hui, a native Taiwanese, was president in the 1990s, he occasionally appeared at political rallies in a kitschy bright blue-and-red "KMT" uniform and cap, swinging a red inflatable baseball bat. Lee, especially later in his political career, enjoyed making much of Taiwan's Japanese heritage—including, to the infuriation of 1.3 billion PRC citizens, his 1995 confession to a Japanese interviewer (Shiba Ryōtarō; see chapter 1) of his fond memories of Japanese rule of Taiwan—so his political use of baseball is probably to be expected. But even current president Ma Ying-jeou, an ethnic mainlander, felt obligated, during his election campaign of 2007 and 2008, to appear on stage swinging a cartoon-like eight-foot-long inflatable baseball bat stenciled, "The Light of Taiwan" (*Taiwan zhi guang,* i.e., pitcher Chien-ming Wang's all-but-official title).[60] The sheepish look on Ma's face hinted at his discomfort in plumbing the depths of Taiwanese "local" populism, but that didn't stop him from trying. Ma's campaign maintained a website (baseball.ma19.net) dedicated to explaining the KMT candidate's commitment to support the national game, to "sincerely invite everyone to support the ROC national team," and to urge all to "get back to the baseball park!!!"[61] On 22 March 2008, Ma fulfilled most expectations by winning the presidency with 58 percent of the vote. Nine days later, political mission accomplished, his baseball website had already been taken off the internet.

Playing baseball as an exclusively "local" device has the effect of appearing unseemly and cynical, because it is so simply a product of the global and national as well. Understanding these different "global" influences on baseball in Taiwan—Japanese, PRC Chinese, and American—helps us to see more in these complex twenty-first-century cultural projects than a bleak (and oddly, ethnocentrically conceived) America-centered "Cocacolonization" of world culture. Indeed, a time when histories, "traditions," commodities, and cultures are so fluid deserves more nuanced consideration than discussions of essentialized and static conceptions of "local" and "global." For nearly a century, baseball in Taiwan, an intensely local aspect of Taiwanese culture, has succeeded most as an avenue of engagement with Japan, the United States, the PRC, and the world—truly a national pastime worthy of the name.

TAIWAN'S AUSTRONESIAN ABORIGINES AND TRACES OF EMPIRE IN TWENTY-FIRST-CENTURY BASEBALL

[Han Taiwanese people] act so pleased that [Aborigines] have been able to show their talents and assimilate into society through sport, but we also know that sports are one of the only choices they have. Success in sports actually just solidifies the structure and the stereotype of the Aborigines as dominated people among whom the men sell their strength while the women sell their bodies.
WRITER NANFANG SHUO, 1995

[Former President] Chen said Aborigines have often been ignored in the past, but their talents and achievement in sport, music, arts and culture cannot be overlooked.
TAIPEI TIMES, 2003

Hongyeh Youth Baseball Team is Taiwan's first worldwide famous baseball team. The folk songs of the Bunun tribe are very beautiful and euphonious.
"TAITUNG TOURISM" WEBSITE, 2002

Every summer in Taiwan, as the August anniversary of the Hongye (Maple Leaf) youth baseball team's epic 1968 triumphs approaches, the newspapers fill with remembrances of that moment and of the now middle-aged Bunun Aborigine men who created it some four decades ago. In 2004, the media reported heavily on the 1111 Job Bank employment firm's study of former Little League national team members and their often sad lives as adults. Only 44.44 percent of these childhood stars now had steady work; 67.22 percent felt that their extended childhood baseball careers had made it harder for them to develop their own adult careers; 46.43

percent said that old baseball injuries still made their careers harder; and 31.11 percent even admitted to regretting their involvement in Little League at all. From here it was a short leap to the fate of the twelve former Maple Leaf standouts that made so many in Taiwan so proud; fully half of these men died before or around the age of forty, while all but one of those who were left had been working low-paying manual labor jobs for decades.[62] The subtitle of an article the next summer was more explicit: "Catcher Jiang Honghui in a factory for twenty years, Third baseman Hu Mingcheng a janitor in Taizhong, Outfielder Qiu Chunguang a taxi driver back in the village."[63] Indeed, to recall the discussion in chapter 5, it seems that these memories of baseball triumph can only be considered through a mist of tragedy and regret.

The dissonance between the nostalgia that so many in Taiwan feel for the heady Maple Leaf days of 1968, and the real misery that has plagued almost every member of that all-Aborigine team since, is significant. As has been true of Taiwan's Austronesian Aborigine population for more than a century, these Maple Leaf men are most valued in the media for their value as metaphors and symbols—in this case, as the most poignant possible metaphor for the failure of Taiwanese society to take care of the weakest and most vulnerable among them. A half century of capitalist development under the ROC government has created unimaginable wealth for many in Taiwan, but has left behind many others. This societal scar that the Maple Leaf discourse is meant both to represent and to conceal also can be understood through baseball in contemporary Taiwan.

Aborigine young men were at the center of the Japanese colonial "harmonious triethnic" baseball discourse in the 1920s and 1930s, and younger Aborigine boys constituted an important part of the Little League dynasty that was used to buttress both Chinese and Taiwanese nationalisms. Chapter 4 also described the ways in which the successes of the 1968 Maple Leaf baseball team of poor Bunun Aborigine boys came to stand as an important metaphor for the capitalist development of Taiwan occurring at that same moment—even when Taiwan's Aborigine population has yet, four decades on, to truly benefit from this national progress. Today, young Aborigine boys and men still dominate Taiwanese amateur and professional baseball, providing both the truest continuity of Taiwan's baseball century and a painful reminder of Japanese, Chinese, and Taiwanese elites' failures to create equal educational, health, employment, and cultural opportunities for the 450,000 descendants of Taiwan's first peoples.

Former ROC President Chen Shui-bian's pandering remarks in the section epigraph hint at the condescending "admiration" that many Han Taiwanese profess for the physical abilities, natural rhythm, ad nauseam that they imagine and fantasize their Aborigine countrymen and women to possess from birth. Essentialized reminisces in the official magazine *Sinorama* of the "unrestrained and carefree Bunun children"[64] who played baseball barefoot and joyously despite their crushing poverty are representative of the stereotype of the poor but cheerful baseball-playing Aborigine boy that corroborates myths of relative Han sophistication, learning, and culture. Indeed, it is hard to imagine this staid magazine publishing a picture of nine naked twelve-year-old Han Taiwanese boys scrubbing their underwear together, as they did of a Puyuma Aborigine baseball team in 1992.[65]

Thus, mainstream expressions of unique Aborigine baseball gifts and abilities are best understood as damning, if not faint, praise. The "miraculously brave" Amis Aborigine Lin Zhisheng's towering home run in the 2006 Konami Cup at the Tokyo Dome, for example, according to the CPBL's official magazine, "truly showed everyone how ferocious *(lihai)* Taiwan's Aborigines are."[66] The media's early twenty-first century use of the collective nickname the "Three Savage Blades" *(san fan dao)* to refer to the Sinon Bulls' trio of star Amis Aborigine players Huang Zhongyi, Zheng Zhaohang, and Zhang Taishan is a bit too glib. So is the ease with which the CPBL's official magazine can refer both to China Trust Whales star Wang Guojin's supposedly "inborn *(yu sheng ju lai)* Aborigine good-naturedness and explosiveness" that has allowed him to become a great fastball pitcher, and his "inherent *(tianxing)* Aborigine optimistic and cheerful nature."[67]

The league website's description of the Changle Elementary School team in the far southern city Pingdong, where "[cross-]racial cooperation" *(minzu gonghe,* a term that clearly connotes colonial models of the same) is the order of the day,[68] suggests that little thought has been given in the eight succeeding decades to all that a term like this can obscure in truly understanding contemporary Taiwanese society. The league betrayed their tin ear again in 2007 when they broadcasted the news that seven of the ten top league salaries were earned by Aboriginal players, the "rich folks *(ho ia lang)* of professional baseball," who thankfully were "destroying the common idea that 'Aborigines are poorer [than Han Taiwanese].'"[69]

The other shoe is never too long to drop in this public discourse of Aborigine baseball excellence. Chen Yixin, the winningest pitcher in Taiwan professional baseball history, was famously infuriated by the Taipei Suns Fan Club's coordinated chants of "Savage *(hoan-a)* get out!" directed at him during the 1997 Taiwan Major League Championship Series.[70] The "savage incident" was a hot topic of discussion for several days in Taiwan, although it quickly became much more about fan etiquette than about the kind of Taiwan where it could still be acceptable for hundreds of educated people to chant the cruelest of racial insults.[71] Also egregious were the comments made by Chen Zhixin, coach of the National Taidong Junior College team, in a 2004 *HIT!* magazine special issue on Aborigine baseball. Chen, formerly a catcher for the China Times Eagles, was banned from the CPBL for life for his involvement in the 1997 gambling scandal. But he still felt qualified to tell *HIT!* that his Aborigine players had more "natural gifts" than Han Taiwanese, except in the category of "brains," where they simply were "not up to the level" of Taiwanese.[72]

However, as the thoughts of writer Nanfang Shuo indicate in the section epigraph, there are critical voices in Taiwan that attempt to bring this history of Aborigine excellence and exploitation in baseball to light. Scholar Chang Li-ke writes about the "colonialist biology" invented by the former Japanese masters of the island and still employed by Taiwanese observers to "explain" the Aborigine presence in baseball while ignoring the often painful historical contingencies behind all of this.[73] One of the most persistent critics has been Qu Hailiang, who asks us to consider that this very Aborigine participation in baseball originated in the exploitative policies of the Japanese colonialist regime that coveted the valuable lands occupied by Taiwan's first peoples. Since then, the decades-old glib promises of baseball as "a road out" of the poverty that most of Taiwan's Aborigines still face have provided little relief, except for a handful of the finest and luckiest players.[74]

In much the same way that Chinese writer Ba Jin wrote movingly in 1986 on the need for China to construct a Cultural Revolution Museum that could allow Chinese people to truly understand the violence and crimes of that decade, Qu suggests that Taiwan construct an Aborigine Sports Hall of Fame. Such an effort could commemorate their many accomplishments while reminding Taiwanese people that, indeed, their national game would not be possible without the Aborigines who "died for the cause more than any other."[75] Former Brother Elephant infielder Wu Junda, himself an Amis Aborigine, has similarly but more broadly campaigned for a "World Aborigine Baseball Championship" that could draw First Peoples from Japan, the Philippines, Guam, Hawai'i, Thailand, Mongolia, the United States, and Canada—all places where colonialist rule has in different ways produced strong baseball traditions among these societies' most vulnerable populations.[76] Such a vision indicates once more how baseball has become Taiwan's most important medium of the "glocal," the tensions between imperialist or globalizing forces and the demands of a local population.

But it is not a condescending truism to reflect on the role of baseball in Taiwan's Aborigine culture today. Standout baseball players continue to be among the most visible representatives, as with the Little League teams four decades ago, of the Aborigine population in Taiwan and of Taiwan as a whole. The two first Taiwanese players in the American major leagues, Chin-feng Chen and Chin-hui Tsao, for example, were both Aborigines, as were eleven of twenty-five players on the 2008 Olympic baseball team roster. But closer to home, the once Japanese game of baseball has become a truly integral aspect of Taiwan Aborigines' most meaningful cultural rituals. Xie Shiyuan has written on the Amis people's yearly harvest ceremony that includes ritualized mimicking of the activities that mark a true Amis brave before the watchful eyes of their proud ancestors—dancing, archery, fishing, wrestling, and, now, baseball.[77]

For better and worse, baseball has returned young Aborigine men to the place in the Japanese-centered East Asian cultural order that they took some eight decades ago, when (as discussed in chapter 1) the finest players from the great "savage Team Nōkō" were attracted to play and study in the colonial metropole of Japan. Japanese professional teams have rediscovered a way of using their colonial ties to Taiwan to circumvent the strict limit placed on the number of foreign players they can feature on their roster. These teams now regularly scout the baseball highlands of eastern Taiwan, and easily convince standout teenage players there to move to Japan for a high school education. Once in Japan, these young men—blessed and cursed with this unique historical heritage—can relive the rewarding but alienating steps of their forefathers, apply for Japanese citizenship, be eligible to play in the Japanese professional leagues as proud and authentic Japanese citizens, and bring much glory to the still oddly named Republic of China on Taiwan. A century after young bankers and railroad workers brought their exclusive ballgame to the island, it is, in many ways, the Japanese game of baseball that provides the real stuff of Taiwanese, Chinese, and Aborigine culture and identity in contemporary Taiwan.

Appendix

Taiwanese Professional Baseball Teams and
National Origin of Foreign Players

Taiwanese Professional Baseball Teams, CPBL and TML, 1990–2010

Team	Tenure	Home City	Status
Chinese Professional Baseball League (1990–2010)			
Brother Elephants	1990–2010	Taipei City and County	Still active
First Financial Holdings Agan (2003), La new Bears (2004–2010)	2003–2010	Gaoxiong County	Still active
Jungo Bears (1993–1995), Sinon Bulls (1996–2010)	1993–2010	Taizhong City	Still active
Uni-President Lions (1990–2007), Uni-President 7-Eleven Lions (2008–2010)	1990–2010	Tainan City	Still active
Mercuries Tigers	1990–1999	Taipei City	Folded: Financial losses
Weichuan Dragons	1990–1999	Taipei City	Folded: Gambling
China Times Eagles	1993–1997	Taipei City	Disqualified: Gambling
China Trust Whales	1997–2008	Jiayi City	Folded: Gambling
Macoto Gida (2003), Macoto Cobras (2004–2007), d-Media T-Rex (2008)	2003–2008	Taipei County	Disqualified: Gambling
Taiwan Major League (1997–2002)			
Taipei Gida (Suns)	1997–2002	Taipei City	Absorbed into CPBL First Financial Holdings Agan
Kaoping Fala (Thunder Gods)	1997–2002	Gaoxiong County and Pingdong City	Absorbed into CPBL First Financial Holdings Agan
Taichung Agan (Robots)	1997–2002	Taizhong City	Absorbed into CPBL Macoto Gida
Chianan Luka (Braves)	1997–2002	Jiayi City and Tainan City	Absorbed into CPBL Macoto Gida

National Origin of Foreign Players in CPBL and TML, 1990–2009

	CPBL, 1990–2009	As Percentage	TML, 1997–2002	As Percentage	Taiwan Pro Total, 1990–2009	As Percentage
U.S.A.	332	46.8	93	59.6	409	49.7
Dominican Rep.	204	28.8	21	13.5	207	25.2
Japan	56	7.9	14	9.0	69	8.4
Venezuela	44	6.2	1	0.6	44	5.3
Mexico	20	2.8	0	0.0	20	2.4
Puerto Rico	12	1.7	5	3.2	17	2.1
Australia	8	1.1	8	5.1	14	1.7
Korea	13	1.8	1	0.6	13	1.6
Panama	7	1.0	4	2.6	9	1.1
Canada	4	0.6	4	2.6	8	1.0
Cuba	1	0.1	4	2.6	4	0.5
Netherlands	3	0.4	0	0.0	3	0.4
Brazil	2	0.3	0	0.0	2	0.2
Colombia	2	0.3	0	0.0	2	0.2
Nicaragua	1	0.1	0	0.0	1	0.1
South Africa	0	0.0	1	0.6	1	0.1
TOTAL	709	100	156	100	823	100

NOTE: Forty-two foreign players appeared in both the CPBL and TML and are counted in each of those columns, so the two columns do not add up to the total column at right.

INTRODUCTION

1. "Gov't vows to overhaul baseball," *The China Post,* 9 March 2009, www.chinapost
.com.tw/sports/baseball/2009/03/09/199277/Govt-vows.htm, accessed 9 March 2009; Chen
Yaoqi, "Tong, Jingdiansai shu dalu, Zhonghua zao taotai" (Grief: Lose to mainland in WBC,
ROC meets elimination), *Taishi xinwen* (TTV news), 7 March 2009, www.ttv.com.tw/098/
03/0980307/09803074502004L.htm, accessed 8 March 2009; Shelley Shan, "Baseball fans vent
frustrations on Internet," *Taipei Times,* 9 March 2009, www.taipeitimes.com/News/taiwan/
archives/2009/03/09/2003437978, accessed 9 March 2009; "Taiwan de bangqiu zunyan dao
na qu le" (Where has Taiwan baseball's dignity gone?), *Zhongshi dianzibao* (ChinaTimes
.com), 7 March 2009, http://blog.chinatimes.com/chou23/archive/2009/03/07/382583.html,
accessed 8 March 2009; Xin Wenbu, "Kao Liu kui, bangqiu jiu mei jiu le?" (With Premier
Liu in charge, can baseball be saved?), NOWnews.com, 10 March 2009, www.nownews.com
/2009/03/10/91–2420152.htm, accessed 30 March 2009; Robin Kwong, "Taiwan baseball defeat triggers crisis of faith," FT.com, 20 March 2009, www.ft.com/cms/s/0/44ccde80–1545–
11de-b9a9–0000779fd2ac.html?nclick_check=1, accessed 30 March 2009.

2. "Chen appears at baseball opening," *Taipei Times,* 26 March 2000, www.taipeitimes
.com/News/local/archives/2000/03/26/29457, accessed 14 August 2008; Zhang Guoqin,
"Taiwan dalianmeng kaimuzhan, A-bian zongtong de di yi ci gei le zhibang" (Taiwan Major
League opening game, President A-bian lets pro baseball have his first time), *Huaxun xinwenwang (Taiwan Today News Network),* 26 March 2000.

3. Jerry W. Leach, dir., *Trobriand Cricket: An Ingenious Response to Colonialism* (Office
of Information, Government of Papua New Guinea, 1975 film).

4. Exceptions to this universal adherence could only really come in ideological attacks on
modern sport, or on modern capitalist society altogether. In 1952, the Russian magazine *Smena*
published a piece on American baseball, calling it a "beastly battle, a bloody fight with may-

hem and murder," a harsh capitalist venture that discarded players "with ruined health and also often crippled . . . [to] increase the army of the American unemployed." The game, according to *Smena*, was merely a typically awful American perversion of the Russian game *lapta*, which had been "played in Russian villages when the United States was not even marked on the maps." "Russians Say U.S. Stole 'Beizbol,' Made It a Game of Bloody Murder," *New York Times*, 16 September 1952; "The Kremlin on Beizbol," *New York Times*, 17 September 1952.

5. Bernard S. Cohn, *Colonialism and Its Forms of Knowledge: The British in India* (Princeton, NJ: Princeton University Press, 1996), 5.

6. Leo T. S. Ching, *Becoming "Japanese": Colonial Taiwan and the Politics of Identity Formation* (Berkeley: University of California Press, 2001), 103.

7. Homi K. Bhabha, *The Location of Culture* (New York: Routledge, 1994), 86. Emphasis in the original.

8. C. L. R. James, *Cricket*, ed. Anna Grimshaw (New York: Allison and Busby, 1986), 118–124.

9. Patrick F. McDevitt, *"May the Best Man Win": Sport, Masculinity, and Nationalism in Great Britain and the Empire, 1880–1935* (New York: Palgrave Macmillan, 2004).

10. Hans Ulrich Gumbrecht, *In 1926: Living At the Edge of Time* (Cambridge, MA: Harvard University Press, 1997), 121–122.

11. Steven E. Phillips, *Between Assimilation and Independence: The Taiwanese Encounter Nationalist China, 1945–1950* (Stanford, CA: Stanford University Press, 2003).

12. Junwei Yu, *Playing In Isolation: A History of Baseball in Taiwan* (Lincoln: University of Nebraska Press, 2007). Yu also has contributed several cowritten pieces to *Identities*, *NINE: A Journal of Baseball History and Culture*, and the *International Journal of the History of Sport*.

13. Roland Robertson, "Comments on the 'Global Triad' and 'Glocalization,'" in *Globalization and Indigenous Culture*, ed. Inoue Nobutaka (Tokyo: Institute for Japanese Culture and Classics, Kokugakuin University, 1996), 221.

14. Brian Moeran, "Commodities, Culture and Japan's Corollanization of Asia," in *Japanese Influences and Presences in Asia*, ed. Marie Söderberg and Ian Reader (Richmond, UK: Curzon, 2000), 28.

1. BASEBALL IN JAPANESE TAIWAN, 1895–1920s

Epigraphs: Inazo Nitobé, *The Japanese Nation; Its Land, Its People, and Its Life, with Special Consideration to Its Relations with the United States* (New York: G. P. Putnam's Sons, 1912), 232; Takemura Toyotoshi, *Taiwan taiiku shi* (The history of sports in Taiwan) (Taihoku: Taiwan taiiku kyōkai, 1933), foreleaf.

1. Formerly Jiayi Agriculture and Forestry Institute, and presently National Jiayi University. Chen Jianren, "Jianong caochang pao yi quan, Shiba Ryōtarō haoyou lüxing yueding" (Running a lap around the Jiayi Institute of Technology field, Shiba Ryōtarō's good friend makes good on his promise), *Minshengbao*, 7 January 1999, 7.

2. See, for example, his chapter on the story of the Puyuma Aborigine shortstop Uematsu Kōichi (later known in Chinese as Chen Gengyuan) in Shiba Ryōtarō, *Taiwan kikō: Kaidō oyuku yonjū* (Journal of travels in Taiwan: On the highway goes, part 40) (Tokyo: Asahi Shimbun sha, 1994).

3. See Michael Taussig's work on contact as "an intercultural nexus . . . for discovering strangeness and confirming sameness." *Mimesis and Alterity: A Particular History of the Senses* (New York: Routledge, 1993), 195.

4. The term *yakyū* was, in part, supposed to differentiate baseball from the also-popular but spatially enclosed game of *tenisu*. Xie Shiyuan and Xie Jiafen, *Taiwan bangqiu yibainian (One Hundred Years of Baseball in Taiwan)* (Taipei: Guoshi chubanshe, 2003), 17; Ariyama Teruo, *Kōshien yakyū to Nihonjin: Media no tsukutta ibento* (Kōshien baseball and the Japanese: Media-created events) (Tokyo: Yoshikawa Kobunkan, 1997), 16–17.

5. Robert Whiting, *You Gotta Have Wa* (New York: Vintage Books, 1989), 32–33; Donald Roden, "Baseball and the Quest for National Dignity in Meiji Japan," *American Historical Review* 85, no. 3 (June 1980): 519–528.

6. John Noyes, *Colonial Space: Spatiality in the Discourse of German South West Africa, 1884–1915* (Philadelphia: Harwood Academic Publishers, 1992), 6.

7. See Robert Whiting's popular books *You Gotta Have Wa* and *The Chrysanthemum and the Bat: Baseball Samurai Style* (New York: Dodd, Mead, 1977).

8. Thomas Nolden, "On Colonial Spaces and Bodies: Hans Grimm's *Geschichten aus Südwestafrika*," in *The Imperialist Imagination: German Colonialism and Its Legacy*, ed. Sara Friedrichsmeyer, Sara Lennox, and Susanne Zantop (Ann Arbor: University of Michigan Press, 1998), 129.

9. "Chokurei dai hyaku rokujūnana gō: Hyōjunji ni kan suru ken" (Imperial Ordinance No. 167, On Standard Time), 27 December 1895, National Archives of Japan Document no. A03020211600, www.jacar.go.jp/index.html, accessed 1 August 2009.

10. Nitobé, *The Japanese Nation*, 254; "Japan as a Colonizing Power," *Spectator* (23 March 1907), 448. In 1914, travel writer T. Philip Terry also praised the government's anti-"headhunter" war of "extermination [that was] being conducted with characteristic Japanese vigor." T. Philip Terry, *Terry's Japanese Empire: Including Korea and Formosa, with Chapters on Manchuria, the Trans-Siberian Railway, and the Chief Ocean Routes to Japan: A Guidebook for Travelers* (Boston: Houghton Mifflin, 1914), 769.

11. Nitobé, *The Japanese Nation*, 257.

12. Andrew Morris, *Marrow of the Nation: A History of Sport and Physical Culture in Republican China* (Berkeley: University of California Press, 2004).

13. Yu Chien-ming, "Rizhi shiqi Taiwan xuexiao nüzi tiyu de fazhan" (The development of female physical education in Taiwan during the Japanese colonial period), *Zhongyang yanjiuyuan jindaishi yanjiusuo jikan (Bulletin of the Institute of Modern History, Academia Sinica)* 33 (June 2000): 6.

14. Xie Shiyuan, "Rizhi chuqi (1895–1916) Taiwan gongxuexiao de nüzi tiyu yu fangzu yundong" (Taiwan public school physical education for girls and the antifootbinding movement in the early Japanese occupation, 1895–1916), *Taiwan wenxian* (Taiwan documents) 55, no. 2 (June 2004): 207.

15. Cai Zongxin, "Riju shidai Taiwan bangqiu yundong fazhan guocheng zhi yanjiu— yi 1895 (Mingzhi 28) nian zhi 1926 (Dazheng 15) nian wei zhongxin" (Research into the development of Taiwanese baseball during the Japanese occupation) (Master's thesis, Guoli Taiwan shifan daxue tiyu yanjiusuo, 1992), 15.

16. Takemura, *Taiwan taiiku shi*, 5.

17. J. Jonathan Gabay, "Let's integrate baby," www.gabaynet.com/above_the_line.htm, 6 February 2004, accessed 3 February 2005.

18. "Glocalization," www.wordspy.com/words/glocalization.asp, 27 May 2003, accessed 3 February 2005.

19. Aviad E. Raz, *Riding the Black Ship: Japan and Tokyo Disneyland* (Cambridge, MA: Harvard University Asia Center, 1999), 6, 14–15.

20. Cai, "Riju shidai Taiwan bangqiu," 15. Baseball was never played in Taiwan under Qing rule, although Chinese studying in the United States were playing baseball as early as 1873.

21. Eika Tai, "Kokugo and Colonial Education in Taiwan," *positions* 7, no. 2 (Fall 1999): 504.

22. Cheng-Siang Chen, *The Sugar Industry of Taiwan* (Taipei: Fu-Min Institute of Agricultural Geography, 1955), 4–5.

23. While "Han" is a problematic term that elides the subethnic differences between the different ethnic Chinese populations of Taiwan, I use the term "Han Taiwanese" throughout here to distinguish between Chinese inhabitants of Taiwan and the Austronesian Aborigine populations.

24. Xie Shiyuan, "Diyu bangqiu feng: Houshan chuanqi, nanguo rongguang" (Local baseball culture: Mountaintop legends, southern glory), *Dadi dili zazhi (The Earth Geographic Monthly)* 197 (August 2004): 29–31.

25. Yukawa Mitsuo, *Taiwan yakyū shi* (The history of baseball in Taiwan) (Taihoku: Taiwan nichinichi shimpō sha, 1932), 1, 12–13 and 1–2 of the chronology at the end of the book.

26. *Taiwan shashinchō, daiishū* (Taiwan photograph album, volume 1), (n.p.: Taiwan shashinkai, 1915), unnumbered pages.

27. Cai, "Riju shidai Taiwan bangqiu," 80–84.

28. Takemura, *Taiwan taiiku shi,* 166.

29. Yukawa, *Taiwan yakyū shi,* 1 and 1–2 of the chronology at the end of the book; Cai, "Riju shidai Taiwan bangqiu," 79–84.

30. William W. Kelly, "The Spirit and Spectacle of School Baseball: Mass Media, State-making, and 'Edu-tainment' in Japan, 1905–1935," in *Japanese Civilization in the Modern World XIV: Information and Communication,* ed. Umesao Tadao, William W. Kelly, and Kubo Masatoshi (Osaka: National Museum of Ethnology, 2000), 107–110.

31. Alexis Dudden, *Japan's Colonization of Korea: Discourse and Power* (Honolulu: University of Hawai'i Press, 2005), 138–139.

32. Brian Stoddart, "West Indies," in *The imperial game: Cricket, culture and society,* ed. Brian Stoddart and Keith A. P. Sandiford (New York: Manchester University Press, 1998), 80; Richard Cashman, "The Subcontinent," in *The imperial game,* 118.

33. Ashis Nandy, *The Tao of Cricket: On Games of Destiny and Destiny of Games* (New Delhi: Oxford University Press, 2000), viii.

34. Yamaguchi Nobuo, *Yakyū nenkan* (Baseball yearbook) (n.p.: Asahi Shimbun sha, 1918), 120, 178–184.

35. *Undō to shumi* (Sport and interest) 3, no. 1 (January 1918).

36. Takemura, *Taiwan taiiku shi,* 179.

37. "Muzan na shiai, Kodomo to otona no sumō, tama wa ya to teppō no sa" (Merciless

game: [Like] a sumo match between a child and an adult, Like the difference between an arrow and a cannon), *Taiwan Nichinichi Shimpō,* 9 January 1921, 7.

38. See, for example, "Beikan chiimu ki o haku, sakujitsu Taihoku Shin kōen no kangei shiai" (American warship team shows their pride, Welcoming game yesterday at Taihoku's New Park), *Taiwan Nichinichi Shimpō,* 13 October 1921, 7; Takemura, *Taiwan taiiku shi,* 179; Yukawa, *Taiwan yakyū shi,* 556–559.

39. Reproduced in Cai, "Riju shidai Taiwan bangqiu," 49.

40. *Undō to shumi* 3, no. 8 (October 1918), cited in Cai, "Riju shidai Taiwan bangqiu," 94.

41. Yukawa, *Taiwan yakyū shi,* 2 of the chronology at the end of the book; Zeng Wencheng, "Taiwan bangqiu shi (san)" (History of Taiwanese baseball, part 3) (11 August 2003), http://sports.yam.com/show.php?id=0000014290.

42. Gao Zhengyuan, *Dong sheng de xuri: Zhonghua bangqiu fazhan shi* (Rising sun in the East: The history of the development of Chinese baseball) (Taipei: Minshengbao she, 1994), 41.

43. Kelly Olds, "The Biological Standard of Living in Taiwan under Japanese Occupation," *Economics and Human Biology* 1 (2003): 187, 193.

44. Ming-cheng M. Lo, *Doctors within Borders: Profession, Ethnicity, and Modernity in Colonial Taiwan* (Berkeley: University of California Press, 2002), 43, 96.

45. *Taiwan undō kai* 1, no. 2 (November 1915): 14; Lin Dingguo, "Rizhi shiqi Taiwan zhongdeng xuexiao Bangqiu yundong de fazhan: Yi 'Jiayi Nonglin' wei zhongxin de tantao (1928–1942)" (The development of Japanese-era Taiwanese middle school baseball: A study centered on the Jiayi Agriculture and Forestry Institute, 1928–1942), paper presented at the Fifth Cross-Straits Historical Conference, Nanjing University, 8 September 2004, 3.

46. Wu Zhuoliu, *Orphan of Asia,* trans. Ioannis Mentzas (Columbia University Press, 2006), 23–24.

47. George Orwell, "Shooting an Elephant" (1936), www.k-1.com/Orwell/index.cgi/work/essays/elephant.html.

48. Zeng Wencheng, "Cong 1931 nian Jianong bangqiu dui kan Riju shidai Taiwan bangqiu fazhan (san)" (The development of Japanese-occupied Taiwanese baseball seen from the perspective of the Kanō baseball team, post-1931, part 3), 21 May 2003, http://sports.yam.com/show.php?id=0000010419, accessed 13 September 2006.

49. "Taiwan taiikukai no gaikyō" (The present state of Taiwan's physical culture community), *Undō to shumi* 1, no. 1 (1916), cited in Cai, "Riju shidai Taiwan bangqiu," 16.

50. Furōsei, "Taihoku yakyū senshi (ichi)" (The history of Taihoku baseball, part 1), *Undō to shumi* 1, no. 1 (November 1916): 2. In 1932, Yukawa Mitsuo plagiarized this passage to describe this golden age. Yukawa, *Taiwan yakyū shi,* 8.

51. Takemura, *Taiwan taiiku shi,* 5.

52. For example, see Arthur Braddan Coole, *A Troubleshooter For God in China* (Mission, KS: Inter-Collegiate Press, 1976), 28–29; Koen De Ceuster, "Wholesome education and sound leisure: The YMCA sports programme in colonial Korea," *European Journal of East Asian Studies* 2, no. 1 (2003): 60.

53. Roden, "Baseball and the Quest for National Dignity," 523–524.

54. Ramachandra Guha, "Cricket and Politics in Colonial India," *Past and Present* 161 (November 1998): 159.

55. Julean H. Arnold, *Education in Formosa* (Washington, DC: Government Printing Office, 1908), 40, 43.

56. Zeng Wencheng and Yu Junwei, *Taiwan bangqiu wang (Baseball King of Taiwan)* (Taipei: Woshi chubanshe, 2004), 112–113.

57. Gao, *Dong sheng de xuri*, 140.

58. E. Patricia Tsurumi, "Mental Captivity and Resistance Lessons from Taiwanese Anti-Colonialism," *Bulletin of Concerned Asian Scholars* 12, no. 2 (April–June 1980): 2.

59. Frederick R. Dickinson, *War and National Reinvention: Japan in the Great War, 1914–1919* (Cambridge, MA: Harvard University Asia Center and Harvard University Press, 1999), 35. Section epigraphs: Baron Shimpei Gotō, "The Administration of Formosa (Taiwan)," in *Fifty Years of New Japan (Kaikoku gojūnen shi)*, vol. 2, 2nd ed. comp. Shigenobu Okuma, ed. Marcus B. Huish (London: Smith, Elder, 1910), 551; Jackie Chen, "How We Feel About the Japanese—An Aborigine Speaks," trans. David Mayer, *Guanghua zazhi (Sinorama)* 24, no. 3 (March 1999): 91.

60. This "self-determination" would be defined *not* by Taiwanese independence, but by the right for Taiwanese imperial subjects to vote for their own representatives to Japan's National Diet, and by the abolition of the hated "Law No. 63," which institutionalized discrimination in Taiwan. George H. Kerr, *Formosa: Licensed Revolution and the Home Rule Movement, 1895–1945* (Honolulu: University of Hawai'i Press, 1974), 119–125.

61. An example of the latter was the Taiwanese Communist Party, founded in 1928 and dedicated to overthrowing Japanese imperialism altogether and establishing an independent Taiwan Republic. Hsiau A-chin, *Contemporary Taiwanese Cultural Nationalism* (New York: Routledge, 2000), 30–34; Frank S. T. Hsiao and Lawrence R. Sullivan, "A Political History of the Taiwanese Communist Party, 1928–1931," *Journal of Asian Studies* 42, no. 2 (February 1983): 269–289.

It is also important to note that this reformist understanding was coeval with Japan's post–March 1 turn to a more conciliatory "cultural policy" *(bunka seiji)* in early 1920s Korea. Michael Edson Robinson, *Cultural Nationalism in Colonial Korea, 1920–1925* (Seattle: University of Washington Press, 1988), 44–77.

62. Wu Wenxing, "Riju shiqi Taiwan zongdufu tuiguang Riyu yundong chutan" (An investigation into the Taiwan colonial administration's Japanese language promotion campaigns during the Japanese occupation), *Taiwan fengwu* (Taiwan Folkways) 37, no. 1 (March 1987): 8. An overview of education during these first two decades can be found in E. Patricia Tsurumi, *Japanese Colonial Education in Taiwan, 1895–1945* (Cambridge, MA: Harvard University Press, 1977), 13–78.

63. Nitobé, *The Japanese Nation*, 255.

64. Yanaihara Tadao, *Teikokushugi ka no Taiwan* (Taiwan under imperialism) (Tokyo: Iwanami shoten, 1929; repr. Taipei: Nantian shuju, 1997), 199.

65. Ching, *Becoming "Japanese,"* 103.

66. Wu Zhuoliu, *The Fig Tree: Memoirs of a Taiwanese Patriot, 1900–1947*, trans. Duncan B. Hunter (Bloomington, IN: 1stBooks, 2002), 57.

67. Takemura, *Taiwan taiiku shi*, 8.

68. Lin Dingguo, "Rizhi shiqi Taiwan," 5.

69. De Ceuster, "Wholesome education and sound leisure," 61.

70. Paul R. Katz, *When Valleys Turned Blood Red: The Ta-pa-ni Incident in Colonial Taiwan* (Honolulu: University of Hawai'i Press, 2005), 212.

71. Komagome Takeshi and J. A. Mangan, "Japanese colonial education in Taiwan, 1895–1922: Precepts and practices of control," *History of Education* 26, no. 3 (1997): 319.

72. Cai Zhenxiong, *Riju shidai Taiwan shifan xuexiao tiyu fazhanshi* (The history of the development of normal school physical education in Japanese-occupied Taiwan) (Taipei: Shida shuyuan, 1998), 92.

73. "Undō kyōgi o hontōjin ni oyoba se" (Competitive sports and native islanders' participation), *Undō to shumi* 4, no. 8 (1919), cited in Cai, "Riju shidai Taiwan bangqiu," 93.

74. C. L. R. James, *Beyond a Boundary* (Durham: Duke University Press, 1993), 68–81, 93–97.

75. Gao Zhengyuan, "Yuanzhumin yu Taiwan bangyun (shang)" (Aborigines and Taiwan's baseball movement, part 1), *Shanhai wenhua (Taiwan Indigenous Voice Bimonthly)* 9 (March 1995): 33.

76. Aka Tami, "Higashi Taiwan he, Karenkō chō ka no bu" (Eastern Taiwan: Karenkō Prefecture section), in *Higashi Taiwan kenkyū sōsho, dai ichi hen* (Eastern Taiwan Research Series, volume 1) (Taihoku: Higashi Taiwan kenkyūkai, 1925; repr. Taipei: Chengwen chubanshe, 1985), 10–11.

77. Yanaihara Tadao, *Teikokushugi ka no Taiwan*, 185.

78. John Thomson, *Thomson's China: Travels and Adventures of a Nineteenth-century Photographer* (Hong Kong: Oxford University Press, 1993), 94; Katz, *When Valleys Turned Blood Red*, 144.

79. Cohn, *Colonialism and Its Forms of Knowledge*, 5.

80. Paul D. Barclay, " 'Gaining Confidence and Friendship' in Aborigine Country: Diplomacy, Drinking, and Debauchery on Japan's Southern Frontier," *Social Science Japan Journal* 6, no. 1 (2003): 79.

81. Wu Mi-cha, "Inō Kanori, Japanese Ethnography and the Idea of the 'Tribe,'" in *In Search of the Hunters and Their Tribes: Studies in the History and Culture of the Taiwan Indigenous People*, ed. David Faure (Taipei: Shung Ye Museum of Formosan Aborigines Publishing, 2001), 41–47.

82. Kiyasu Yukio, *Riben tongzhi Taiwan mishi: Wushe shijian zhi kang Ri quanmao* (Secret histories of Japanese rule in Taiwan: The overall view from the Wushe Incident to anti-Japanese resistance) (Taipei: Wuling chuban youxian gongsi, 1995), 184–187; Fujii Shizue, *Riju shiqi Taiwan zongdufu de lifan zhengce* (*The Aborigines Policy of Taiwan Government-General in the Period of the Japanese Dominance [1895–1915]*) (Taipei: Guoli Taiwan shifan daxue lishi yanjiusuo, 1989), 197.

83. Leo Ching, "Savage Construction and Civility Making: The Musha Incident and Aboriginal Representations in Colonial Taiwan," *positions* 8, no. 3 (Winter 2000): 795–796.

84. Katz, *When Valleys Turned Blood Red*, 144.

85. Kerr, *Formosa*, 104.

86. Mark R. Peattie, "Japanese Attitudes Toward Colonialism, 1895–1945," in *The Japanese Colonial Empire, 1895–1945*, ed. Ramon H. Myers and Mark R. Peattie, (Princeton, NJ: Princeton University Press, 1984), 88.

87. Ronald G. Knapp and Laurence M. Hauptman, " 'Civilization over Savagery': The

Japanese, the Formosan Frontier, and United States Indian Policy, 1895–1915," *Pacific Historical Review* 49, no. 4 (1980): 647–652.

88. Terry, *Terry's Japanese Empire*, 791.

89. Yabu Syat, Xu Shikai, and Shi Zhengfeng, *Wushe shijian: Taiwanren de jiti jiyi* (The Wushe Incident: Taiwanese collective memory) (Taipei: Qianwei, 2001), 225; Chen Wei-chi, "From Raw to Cooked: The Identity of the Kavalan People in the Nineteenth Century," in *In Search of the Hunters*, 28–33.

90. Jackie Chen, "Voices from a Buried History—The Takasago Volunteers," trans. Christopher MacDonald, *Guanghua zazhi (Sinorama)* 24, no. 3 (March 1999): 79–81. Prasenjit Duara has discussed a similar process in Manchuria, where early Japanese colonist-social scientists celebrated ancient racial ties between the Tungusic and Japanese peoples. Prasenjit Duara, *Sovereignty and Authenticity: Manchukuo and the East Asian Modern* (Rowman and Littlefield, 2003), 183.

A similarly meaningless term is employed in today's PRC to describe Taiwan's Aborigines as members of a single "high-mountain nationality" " *(gaoshan minzu).* A confusing *People's Daily* "Country Profile" of "Taiwan Province" testifies that "there are Han 98% and gaoshan 0.3 million in taiwan *[sic]*." "Country Profile: Taiwan Province," *People's Daily Online*, http://english.peopledaily.com.cn/data/province/taiwan.html, accessed 26 September 2006.

91. Yukawa, *Taiwan yakyū shi*, 1.

92. Xie Shiyuan, "Diyu bangqiu feng," 31.

93. Gao, *Dong sheng de xuri*, 47, 49; Jian Yongchang, *Zhonghua bangqiu shiji* (Historical records of ROC baseball) (Taipei: self-published, 1993), 13.

94. Yanaihara Tadao, *Teikokushugi ka no Taiwan*, 179–180; Shiyung Liu, "Building a Strong and Healthy Empire: The Critical Period of Building Colonial Medicine in Taiwan," *Japanese Studies* 23, no. 4 (December 2004): 309.

95. Syat, Xu, and Shi, *Wushe shijian*, 227.

96. Aka, "Higashi Taiwan he," 10.

97. Ibid.

98. Thomas Babington Macauley, "Minute on Indian Education," in *Selected Writings*, ed. John Clive and Thomas Pinney (Chicago: University of Chicago Press, 1972), 249.

99. Aka, "Higashi Taiwan he," 11–13.

100. Duara has examined a similar Japanese use of the trope of "dependence" in dealing with the "primitive" Oroqen people of northern Manchuria (*Sovereignty and Authenticity*, 186). The construction of a standard athletic masculinity by which to judge Taiwan's Aborigines and the work of their modern Japanese teachers also fits perfectly the British Empire's model of sportsmanship and masculinity (Patrick F. McDevitt, *"May the Best Man Win": Sport, Masculinity, and Nationalism in Great Britain and the Empire, 1880–1935* [New York: Palgrave Macmillan, 2004], 9).

101. Komagome and Mangan, "Japanese colonial education in Taiwan," 320.

102. Ching, *Becoming "Japanese*," 159–160.

103. Yukawa, *Taiwan yakyū shi*, 581.

104. Ibid., 251, 254–262.

105. "Chinkyaku Nōkōdan o mukahe te Maruyama kyūjō ni netsukyū tobu" (Welcom-

ing rare visitors Team Nōkō; The fastballs will be flying at Maruyama Field), *Taiwan Nichinichi Shimpō*, 22 September 1924, 3.

106. "Taishō purodan tai Nōkō no shiai ni hachi ten katte yorokobu" (Taishō Professional Team happy to defeat Nōkō by eight runs), *Taiwan Nichinichi Shimpō*, 24 September 1924, 3.

107. "Banjin chiimu Nōkōdan no ensei" (Savage Team Nōkō's road campaign), *Taiwan Nichinichi Shimpō*, 28 September 1924, 5.

108. Suzuki Akira, *Takasago zoku ni sasageru* (Dedicated to the Takasago people) (Tokyo: Chūō Kōronsha, 1976), 186; Takemura, *Taiwan taiiku shi*, 178.

109. Cai, "Riju shidai Taiwan bangqiu," 114–115.

110. "Banjin chiimu Nōkōdan no ensei," 5.

111. "Nōkōdan no naichi ensei, Taiwan senden ni wa motte koi" (Team Nōkō's home islands road trip, Perfect Taiwan propaganda), *Taiwan Nichinichi Shimpō*, 23 June 1925, 2.

112. "Banjin kōenkai, Nōkōdan ensei yoshū" (Savage Lecture Address, Team Nōkō prepares for their road trip), *Taiwan Nichinichi Shimpō*, 24 June 1925, 2.

113. "Zaikyō Nōkōdan no nittei" (Team Nōkō's Tokyo schedule), *Taiwan Nichinichi Shimpō*, 10 July 1925, 5.

114. "Shimofuri no gakuseifuku na no de, Naichijin no gan ni ha tsukanai" (Their gray student uniforms make the home islanders' eyes come out of their heads), *Taiwan Nichinichi Shimpō*, 10 July 1925, 5.

115. Ching, "Savage Construction and Civility Making," 795–796.

116. Sakamoto Shigeru and Katsura Chōhei, "Nōkō yakyūdan to banjin gakusei no seikatsu" (The Nōkō baseball team and the life of the savage students), Yakyūkai (*The Yakyukai*) 15, no. 12 (September 1925): 46.

117. Zeng and Yu, *Taiwan bangqiu wang*, 38.

118. "Nōkō yakyūdan kaeru" (The Nōkō baseball team returns), *Taiwan Nichinichi Shimpō*, 31 July 1925, 3.

119. Suzuki, *Takasago zoku ni sasageru*, 188. Officially their record was three wins, four losses, and one tie; the victory in their first game did not count since the game ended after just four innings.

120. Bert Scruggs, "Identity and Free Will in Colonial Taiwan Fiction: Wu Zhuoliu's 'The Doctor's Mother' and Wang Changxiong's 'Torrent,'" *Modern Chinese Literature and Culture* 16, no. 2 (2004): 168.

121. Hans Ulrich Gumbrecht, *In 1926: Living At the Edge of Time* (Cambridge, MA: Harvard University Press, 1997), 121–122.

122. "Kinoshita Naimu kyokuchō, Nōkōdan o negirau" (Home Affairs Minister Kinoshita's commendations to Team Nōkō), *Taiwan Nichinichi Shimpō*, 14 July 1925, 5.

123. "Uruwashii dōjō, Banjin hiteiron o tataka hasu" (Beautiful sympathy: Doing battle with the savage-denying theories), *Taiwan Nichinichi Shimpō*, 17 July 1925, 2.

124. Zeng and Yu, *Taiwan bangqiuwang*, 42. In later Chinese-language records, these men are called by the names A-xian, Luo Daohou, Luo Shawei, and Ji-sa.

125. There were only nine "Savage" students enrolled in Japanese primary schools in Taiwan in 1925. Mosei Lin, "Public Education in Formosa Under the Japanese Administration:

A Historical and Analytical Study of the Development and the Cultural Problems" (PhD diss., Columbia University, 1929), tables 1 and 37, unnumbered back matter.

126. Syat, Xu, and Shi, *Wushe shijian*, 14–16.

127. Chang Li-ke, "Taiwan bangqiu yu rentong: Yi ge yundong shehuixue de fenxi" (Taiwan baseball and identities: An analysis of sociology of sport) (Master's thesis, Guoli Qinghua daxue shehuixue yanjiusuo, 2000), 66–69.

128. Raz, *Riding the Black Ship*, 6.

129. Harry A. Franck, *Glimpses of Japan and Formosa* (New York: Century Co., 1924), 163.

130. Meanwhile, Aborigine children attended "savage public elementary schools" *(bandō kōgakkō)*. Lin, "Public Education in Formosa," table 3, unnumbered back matter.

131. "Shōnen yakyūsen honjitsu kaikai suru" (Youth baseball tournament to begin today), *Tainan shimpō* (Tainan New Times), 26 May 1923, 7. Unfortunately, however, this same newspaper engaged in this very sort of ethnic distinction just two days later, when it attributed the all-Taiwanese Tainan No. 1 Public School's victory over the Japanese Hanazono Elementary School to the fact that the Taiwanese students were older and thus enjoyed a physical advantage. "Tainan shōnen yakyūsen, Ichiko to Chūgaku yūshō su" (Tainan youth baseball tournament, No. 1 Public and Middle School win), *Tainan shimpō*, 28 May 1923, 7.

132. Lo, *Doctors within Borders*, 83.

133. Edward W. Said, *Culture and Imperialism* (New York: Alfred A. Knopf, 1993), 262.

134. There were more explicitly political analogues of this process in colonial Taiwan, like the Home Rule Movement, where Taiwanese students educated in Tokyo, citing the official rhetoric of authoritarian "imperial benevolence," sought a colonial assembly for Taiwan in the early 1920s. Kerr, *Formosa*, 113–129.

135. James, *Cricket*, 118–124.

136. "Gongming zhengda de jingzheng (Fair Play)" (Open and upright competition [Fair Play]), *Taiwan minbao* (Taiwan people's newspaper), 19 July 1925, 1.

137. Chang then cites the familiar interpretations of other sports historians like Allen Guttman ("beating them at their own game") and Joseph Arbena (sport in Latin America as "the agent of anti-colonialism and anti-imperialism"). Chang Li-ke, "Taiwan bangqiu yu rentong," 39–47.

138. Paul Dimeo, "Football and Politics in Bengal: Colonialism, Nationalism, Communalism," in *Soccer in South Asia: Empire, Nation, Diaspora,* ed. Paul Dimeo and James Mills (Portland, OR: Frank Cass Publishers, 2001), 69.

139. Stuart Hall, "When Was 'The Post-Colonial'? Thinking at the Limit," in *The Postcolonial Question: Common Skies, Divided Horizons,* ed. Iain Chambers and Lidia Curti (New York: Routledge, 1996), 247.

140. Jian Yongchang, *Ren de yisheng: Taiwanren de xiao gushi (si)* (A life: Tale of a Taiwanese, part 4) (Taipei: self-published, 2002), 77; Jian Yongchang, *Hito no isshō: Taiwanjin no monogatari (roku)* (A life: Tale of a Taiwanese, part 6) (Taipei: self-published, 2003).

141. Interview with Jian Yongchang, Taipei, Taiwan, 11 August 2004.

142. Fong Shiaw-Chian, "Hegemony and Identity in the Colonial Experience of Taiwan, 1895–1945," in *Taiwan under Japanese Colonial Rule, 1895–1945: History, Culture, Memory,* ed. Ping-hui Liao and David Der-Wei Wang (New York: Columbia University Press, 2006), 170. Mark Harrison also makes the important point that this "bridge" position was actually

first formulated by liberal politician Itagaki Taisuke in 1914. Mark Harrison, *Legitimacy, Meaning, and Knowledge in the Making of Taiwanese Identity* (New York: Palgrave Macmillan, 2006), 75.

143. Wu, *Orphan of Asia*, 59.

144. Barry Shiaw-Chian Fong, "Civilization and Individual Identities: Ye Shengji's Quest for Colonial Self in Two Cultures," *Issues & Studies* 34, no. 10 (October 1998): 99, 111.

145. Martha C. Nussbaum, "The Prohibition Era," *The New Republic* 4757–4758 (20–27 March 2006): 25.

146. Jian Yongchang, *Zhonghua bangqiu shiji*, 190.

147. Interview with Jian Yongchang, Taipei, Taiwan, 11 August 2004.

148. Jian Yongchang, *Hito no isshō*, 63–69.

149. Zeng Wencheng, ed., "Gungun bangqiu changliu Xiao Changgun" (Roll on, baseball, live on, Xiao Changgun), *Zhiye bangqiu* 225 (10 December 2000): 44.

150. "Gongxuexiao tuan duode jinbiao" (Public elementary school team wins championship), *Taiwan minbao*, 11 August 1929, 3. Xie Shiyuan has written an entire article on this controversial tournament: "1929 nian Gaoxiong di yi gongxuexiao yu di yi hui quandao shaonian yeqiu dahui" (Takao No. 1 Public School and the first islandwide youth baseball tournament, 1929), *Gaoshi wenxian (Takao Historiography)* 17, no. 3 (September 2004): 110–120.

151. "Gongxuexiao tuan duode jinbiao," 3.

152. "Tichang jiangli tiyu" (Promote and encourage physical culture), *Taiwan minbao*, 26 May 1929, 2.

2. MAKING RACIAL HARMONY IN TAIWAN BASEBALL, 1931–1945

Epigraph: Eiji Oguma, *A Genealogy of "Japanese" Self-Images*, trans. David Askew (Melbourne: Trans Pacific Press, 2002), 137.

1. Scholar Ō Ikutoku (Ong Iok-tek), cited in E. Patricia Tsurumi, *Japanese Colonial Education in Taiwan, 1895–1945* (Cambridge, MA: Harvard University Press, 1977), 177.

2. The Government-General of Taiwan, *Taiwan (Formosa): Its System of Communications and Transportation, Submitted by the Japanese Delegate for Taiwan to the Ninth Conference of the International Postal Union, Held at London, May, 1929* (Taipei: The Government-General of Taiwan, 1929), 2.

3. Nishiwaki Yoshitomo, *Taiwan chūtō gakkō yakyū shi* (History of high school baseball in Taiwan) (Kakogawa City, Hyogo Prefecture: self-published, 1996), 113–116.

4. In 1962, Taiwanese historian Shi Ming published (in Japanese) a comprehensive history titled *The Four Hundred Years of the Taiwanese People's History*, which implies a slightly different chronology as to when real "history" began in Taiwan—the arrival of larger numbers of Han mainland immigrants who began to "develop and build" Taiwan. Shi Ming, *Taiwanren sibainian shi (Hanwen ban)* (San Jose, CA: Paradise Culture Associates, 1980), iii.

5. John E. Wills Jr., "The Seventeenth-Century Transformation: Taiwan under the Dutch and the Cheng Regime," in *Taiwan: A New History*, ed. Murray A. Rubinstein (Armonk, NY: M. E. Sharpe, 1999), 87–88; Laurence M. Hauptman and Ronald G. Knapp, "Dutch-Aboriginal Interaction in New Netherland and Formosa: An Historical Geography of Empire," *Proceedings of the American Philosophical Society* 121, no. 2 (April 1977): 175.

6. Leo Ching, "Savage Construction and Civility Making: The Musha Incident and Aboriginal Representations in Colonial Taiwan," *positions* 8, no. 3 (Winter 2000): 799, 810–811. In a complex ideological move—especially for a government usually concerned about expressing the depth of Japanese influence on Taiwanese culture—Taiwan's central bank issued a NT$20 coin in 2001 bearing the likeness of Mona Rudao, the leader of this massacre who committed suicide after the event. "Aboriginal hero honored on new coin," *China Post*, 12 April 2001, www.taiwanheadlines.gov.tw/20010412/20010412b2.html, accessed 22 April 2005.

7. Section epigraph: Hans Ulrich Gumbrecht, *In 1926: Living at the Edge of Time* (Cambridge, MA: Harvard University Press, 1997), 433.

8. Zeng Wencheng, "Taiwan bangqiu shi" (History of Taiwanese Baseball) (6 September 2003), www.tzengs.com/TWN_Baseball/History_Taiwanese_Baseball.htm, accessed 22 June 2005; Tobe Yoshinari, *Bangqiu dongyouji* (Baseball journey to the east), trans. Li Shufang (Taipei: Zhonghua zhibang shiye gufen youxian gongsi, 1994), 123.

9. By the end of the 1920s, Kanō was one of three five-year agriculture and forestry vocational schools, and of six vocational schools total, in Taiwan. Mosei Lin, "Public Education in Formosa under the Japanese Administration: A Historical and Analytical Study of the Development and the Cultural Problems" (PhD diss., Columbia University, 1929), 141.

10. Mosei Lin, "Public Education in Formosa," table 3, unnumbered back matter.

11. The Government-General of Taiwan, *Taiwan (Formosa)*, 13.

12. In all, there were 14,992 applicants to secondary schools in 1929, and just twenty-one of these were Aborigines, or "Savages," in Lin's words. Mosei Lin, "Public Education in Formosa," table 35, unnumbered back matter.

13. Zheng Sanlang, ed., *Jianong koushu lishi* (Oral histories of the Jiayi Agriculture and Forestry Institute) (Jiayi: Guoli Jiayi nongye zhuanke xuexiao xiaoyouhui, 1993), 135–136.

14. Cai Wuzhang, Lin Huawei, and Lin Mei-Chun, *Diancang Taiwan bangqiushi: Jianong bangqiu, 1928–2005* (The treasured history of Taiwan baseball: Kanō baseball, 1928–2005) (Taipei: Xingzhengyuan tiyu weiyuanhui, 2005), 167.

15. Zheng Sanlang, *Jianong koushu lishi*, 100–101.

16. Xie Shiyuan, "Kua shidai de chuancheng yu guangrong—Taiwan 'Beibi Lusi' Hong Taishan (er)" (Tradition and glory across the centuries—Taiwan's 'Babe Ruth,' Hong Taishan, part 2), *Taiwan bangqiu weijiguan* ([Taiwan] Wiki Baseball), 17 January 2007, http://twbsball.dils.tku.edu.tw/wiki/index.php, accessed 14 September 2007.

17. Lin Dingguo, "Rizhi shiqi Taiwan zhongdeng xuexiao Bangqiu yundong de fazhan: Yi 'Jiayi Nonglin' wei zhongxin de tantao (1928–1942)" (The development of Japanese-era Taiwanese middle school baseball: A study centered on the Jiayi Agriculture and Forestry Institute, 1928–1942), paper presented at the Fifth Cross-Straits Historical Conference, Nanjing University, 8 September 2004, 4–6; Su Zhengsheng, "Tianxia zhi Jianong" (Kanō, champions of all under heaven), *Jianongren* (People of the Jiayi Agriculture and Forestry Institute) 1 (November 1997): 12; Zheng Sanlang, *Jianong koushu lishi*, 78, 88–89, 223.

18. Lin Dingguo, "Zhimin tongzhi xia de yundong fazhan: Yi Taiwan Tiyu Xiehui wei zhongxin de tantao" (The development of sports under colonial rule: A study focusing on the Taiwan Sports Association), *Taiwan lishi xuehui huixun* (*Newsletter of the Taiwan Historical Association*) 18 (2004): 56.

19. Takemura Toyotoshi, *Taiwan taiiku shi* (The history of sports in Taiwan) (Taihoku: Taiwan taiiku kyōkai, 1933), 14.

20. "Taiwan bangqiu shi—fazhan qiji yu gushi" (The history of Taiwan baseball—miracles and stories of its development), from Xingzhengyuan tiyu weiyuanhui (National Council on Physical Fitness and Sports), "Shuwei bowuguan: bangqiu" (Digital Museum: Baseball), 10 March 2001, www.ncpfs.gov.tw/museum/museum-1-1.aspx?No=66, accessed 1 May 2007.

21. Cai, Lin, and Lin, *Diancang Taiwan bangqiushi*, 4.

22. Chen Shouyong, "Zoufang 94 gaoling de Jianong yuanlao Tuo Hongshan" (A visit with the ninety-four-year-old Kanō elder Tuo Hongshan), *Guomin tiyu jikan* 131 (December 2001), 103–104, 108.

23. Allen Chun, "The Coming Crisis of Multiculturalism in 'Transnational' Taiwan," *Social Analysis* 46, no. 2 (Summer 2002): 103–104.

24. Edward Vickers, "Re-writing museums in Taiwan," in *Re-Writing Culture in Taiwan*, ed. Fang-long Shih, Stuart Thompson, and Paul Tremlett (New York: Routledge, 2008), 87–97.

25. Nishiwaki, *Taiwan chūtō gakkō yakyū shi*, 528.

26. "Taiwan bangqiu shi—fazhan qiji yu gushi"; Su Zhengsheng, "Tianxia zhi Jianong," 15; Zeng Wencheng, "Cong 1931 nian Jianong bangqiu dui kan Riju shidai Taiwan bangqiu fazhan (si)" (The development of Japanese-occupied Taiwanese baseball seen from the perspective of the Kanō baseball team, post-1931, part 4), 21 May 2003, http://sports.yam.com/show.php?id=0000010420, accessed 23 May 2007.

27. This formulation is often used to describe sports coaches with unusually intense but ultimately successful methods. Nishiwaki, *Taiwan chūtō gakkō yakyū shi*, 529.

28. Xie Shiyuan, "Kua shidai de chuancheng yu guangrong," part 3.

29. Su Zhengsheng, "Tianxia zhi Jianong," 16–17, 26.

30. Ibid., 18.

31. Nishiwaki, *Taiwan chūtō gakkō yakyū shi*, 211–212.

32. Ibid, passim.

33. Lin Dingguo, "Rizhi shiqi Taiwan," 8.

34. Hui-yu Caroline Ts'ai, "Administration, Assimilation, and Ambivalence: 'Improved Treatment' *(shogū kaizen)* in Wartime Taiwan, 1944," in *Minzu rentong yu wenhua jiaorong* (Ethnic identity and cultural assimilation), ed. Young-tsu Wong and Guanqun Lin (Jiayi Xian: Zhongzheng daxue Taiwan renwen yanjiu zhongxin, 2006), 373–427.

35. This collective anxiety is also borne out by the fact that it was during this same year of 1931 that Principal Mitsuya Sei of Kagi High School—in the same town as Kanō—wrote the script for *The Story of Go Hō (Go Hō den)*. The next year, this tale of one Qing dynasty official's taming of atavistic Aboriginal violence—a timely topic, if one marked by wishful thinking—was made into the film *The Righteous Go Hō (Gijin Go Hō)*. Go's mythical accomplishment—not quite as easy as teaching Aborigines how to play baseball, since it required his own dramatic self-sacrifice to shame the headhunters—was an important marker of how the colonial regime imagined civilization's crucial triumph over savagery in this post-Musha era. Ye Longyan, *Rizhi shiqi Taiwan dianying shi (The History of Taiwanese Movies*

during the Japanese Colonization) (Taipei: Yushan she, 1998), 233–236. Leo Ching also describes the colonial uses of the Go Hō myth, but in an ahistorical way. Ching, "Savage Construction and Civility Making," 804–807.

36. Ching, "Savage Construction and Civility Making," 803; Kiyasu, *Riben tongzhi Taiwan mishi,* 241.

37. "Athletic Sports: Amazing Development and World Recognition," *Present-Day Nippon, 1934: Annual English Supplement of the Asahi, Osaka and Tokyo* (Tokyo, 1934), 46.

38. Su Zhengsheng, "Tianxia zhi Jianong," 19.

39. Suzuki Akira, *Takasago zoku ni sasageru* (Dedicated to the Takasago people) (Tokyo: Chūō Kōronsha, 1976), 174.

40. Takemura, *Taiwan taiiku shi,* 156.

41. Two articles were on *Taiwan Nichinichi Shimpō,* 21 August 1931, 1, and three articles were on *Tōkyō Asahi Shimbun,* 21 August 1931, 1.

42. Tobita Suishū, "Osoru beki Kagi no mōki" (The terrifying ferocity of Kagi), and "Mōyū Kagi Nōrin, Chūkyō to sōha, kefu (niji) kesshōsen" (Fiercely vigorous and brave Kagi Agriculture and Forestry, battling with Chūkyō for the championship at 2:00), both in *Tōkyō Asahi Shimbun,* 21 August 1931, 3.

43. Gumbrecht, *In 1926,* 67.

44. Zeng Wencheng, "Taiwan bangqiu shi (qi)" (History of Taiwan baseball, part 7), 8 September 2003, http://sports.yam.com/show.php?id=0000015732, accessed 23 May 2007.

45. *Yakyūkai (The Yakyukai)* 21, no. 15 (October 1931): frontispiece.

46. "Kōshien 'meitōshu,' 'meisenshu' hyakusen" (One hundred top Kōshien pitchers and players), 6 June 2006, www.fanxfan.jp/bb/player/3.html, accessed 23 May 2007. Yoshida was elected to the Japanese Baseball Hall of Fame in 1992.

47. Suzuki, *Takasago zoku ni sasageru,* 174.

48. Tobita Suishū, *Tobita Suishū senshū, dai 3 kan: Yakyū kisha jidai* (Anthology of Tobita Suishū's works, volume 3: The baseball reporter era) (Tokyo: Besuborumagajin Sha, 1986), 169–247, 319–359.

49. Kikuchi Kan, "Namida gumashii . . . san minzoku no kyōchō" (So moving . . . the harmony of the three races), *Tōkyō Asahi Shimbun,* 22 August 1931, 3.

50. Chen Shouyong, "Zoufang 94 gaoling de Jianong yuanlao Tuo Hongshan," 104.

51. Nihon yakyū renmei and *Mainichi Shimbun* sha, eds., *Toshi taikō yakyū taikai rokujunen shi* (Sixty years' history of the Intercity Baseball Tournament) (Tokyo: Mainichi Shimbun sha, 1990), 22–24.

52. Bert Scruggs, "Identity and Free Will in Colonial Taiwan Fiction: Wu Zhuoliu's 'The Doctor's Mother' and Wang Changxiong's 'Torrent,'" *Modern Chinese Literature and Culture* 16, no. 2 (2004): 168.

53. Patrick F. McDevitt, *"May the Best Man Win": Sport, Masculinity, and Nationalism in Great Britain and the Empire, 1880–1935* (New York: Palgrave Macmillan, 2004), 129–134.

54. Leo T. S. Ching, *Becoming "Japanese": Colonial Taiwan and the Politics of Identity Formation* (Berkeley: University of California Press, 2001), 113, 132.

55. This is especially true when one considers that 1931 was the year when many radical and liberal Taiwanese political organizations, like the New Taiwan Cultural Association *(Shin Taiwan bunka kyōkai),* Taiwan People's Party *(Taiwan minshūtō),* Taiwan Workers'

League *(Taiwan kōyū sōrenmei)*, Taiwan Communist Party *(Taiwan kyōsantō)*, and Taiwan Farmers' Combine *(Taiwan nōmin kumiai)* were shut down by the colonial government.

56. Of these five appearances at Kōshien, four (1931, 1933, 1935, and 1936) were at the fall tournament and one (1935) was at the less-storied spring version. Zeng Wencheng and Yu Junwei, *Taiwan bangqiu wang (Baseball King of Taiwan)* (Taipei: Woshi chubanshe, 2004), 58; Suzuki, *Takasago zoku ni sasageru*, 180; Kang Tiancai, "Guaiwan jinlai ke hao?" (How is the Fantastic Arm now?), *Changchun yuekan* (Evergreen monthly) 6 (November 1983): 90.

57. In their first game, Kanō beat another team with important connections to Taiwan and its Aborigine population—Heian High School, the Kyoto school that had recruited so many Amis members of the "Savage Team Nōkō" in the 1920s. Their quarterfinal game, coincidentally enough, was against the eventual 1935 national champions Matsuyama Commercial School, where Kanō's "devil-manager" Kondō had once coached on the island of Shikoku.

58. Zeng Wencheng, "Taiwan bangqiu shi"; "Guaiwan—Lan Deming" (Fantastic Arm—Lan Deming), *Changchun yuekan* (Evergreen monthly) 6 (November 1983): 84–85.

59. Suzuki, *Takasago zoku ni sasageru*, 179–180.

60. Gao Zhengyuan, *Dong sheng de xuri: Zhonghua bangqiu fazhan shi* (Rising sun in the East: The history of the development of Chinese baseball) (Taipei: Minshengbao she, 1994), 85–86; Zeng and Yu, *Taiwan bangqiu wang*, 58.

61. Suzuki, *Takasago zoku ni sasageru*, 182, 178, 192.

62. Gumbrecht, *In 1926*, 353.

63. Kobayashi Yoshinori, *Taiwanlun: Xin aogu jingshen* (On Taiwan: A new spirit of pride), trans. Lai Qingsong and Xiao Zhiqiang (Tokyo: Shogakukan, 2000; Taipei: Qianwei chubanshe, 2001); John Nathan, *Japan Unbound: A Volatile Nation's Quest for Pride and Purpose* (Boston: Houghton Mifflin, 2004), 119–137.

64. Cai Wuzhang, "Jianong bangqiu shi" (A history of Kanō baseball), *Jianongren* 1 (November 1997): 34–35.

65. Cai, Lin, and Lin, *Diancang Taiwan bangqiushi*, 107. A number of visits to Kanō by Japanese television stations, corporations and admiring fans are described in Cai Qinghui, "Nanwang de 'Jiayi Nonglin' qingjie" (The unforgettable "Kagi Agriculture and Forestry" complex), *Jianongren* 6 (November 2002): 58–69.

66. *Chuanqi yu guangrong* (Legend and glory), disk two of the ten-disk set *Taiwan shiji tiyu mingren zhuan* (Biographies of famous Taiwanese athletes of the [20th] century) (Taipei: Xingzhengyuan tiyu weiyuanhui, 2002); Cai, Lin, and Lin, *Diancang Taiwan bangqiushi*, 160.

67. Ts'ai, "Administration, Assimilation, and Ambivalence," 374.

68. Xie Shiyuan, "Diyu bangqiu feng: Houshan chuanqi, nanguo rongguang" (Local baseball culture: Mountaintop legends, southern glory), *Dadi dili zazhi (The Earth Geographic Monthly)* 197 (August 2004): 31.

69. There is a large body of work on the GAA, including Mike Cronin, *Sport and Nationalism in Ireland: Gaelic Games, Soccer and Irish Identity Since 1884* (Portland, OR: Four Courts Press, 1999), and W. F. Mandle, *The Gaelic Athletic Association & Irish nationalist politics, 1884–1924* (London: Christopher Helm, 1987).

70. McDevitt, *"May the Best Man Win,"* 16–17.

71. Andrew Morris, *Marrow of the Nation: A History of Sport and Physical Culture in Republican China* (Berkeley: University of California Press, 2004), 204–227.

72. E. Patricia Tsurumi, "Mental Captivity and Resistance Lessons from Taiwanese Anti-Colonialism," *Bulletin of Concerned Asian Scholars* 12, no. 2 (April–June 1980): 5; Frantz Fanon, *The Wretched of the Earth* (New York: Grove Press, 1968), 59.

73. Thanks to Mark Harrison for his explanation of a similar idea.

74. Tay-sheng Wang, *Legal Reform in Taiwan under Japanese Colonial Rule, 1895–1945: The Reception of Western Law* (Seattle: University of Washington Press, 2000), 47, 54, 56, 115, 196–197.

75. Peng Ming-min, *A Taste of Freedom: Memoirs of a Formosan Independence Leader* (New York: Holt, Rinehart and Winston, 1972), 16–17.

76. Interview with Peng Ming-min, 20 July 1999.

77. Li Shufang, "Riben Dushi Duikangsai lishi pian" (A historical study of the Japanese Intercity Baseball Tournament) *Bangqiu shijie (Baseball World)* 4 (October 1999): 57–58.

78. Takemura, *Taiwan taiiku shi*, 235–240.

79. Cheng Jiahui, *Taiwan shi shang di yi da bolanhui: 1935 nian meili Taiwan SHOW* (Taiwan's first exposition: The enchanting Taiwan show of 1935) (Taipei: Yuanliu, 2004), 70–157; "Taibaku kenbutsu no banjin, rokusen yonhyaku goju yo mei" (The 6,450 savages who are attractions at the Taiwan Exposition) *Taiwan Nichinichi Shimpō*, 8 October 1935, 7.

80. Cheng Jiahui, *Taiwan shi shang di yi da bolanhui*, 181; "Nissen nisshō shite, Man-shūdan ga yūshō su" (With two victories in two games the Manchurian team wins), *Taiwan Nichinichi Shimpō*, 21 October 1935, 7.

81. For another example, see the story of Li Shiming, a Chinese star athlete who grew up playing baseball in Japanese Dairen and was later stigmatized in the ROC sporting community for this "collaboration." Morris, *Marrow of the Nation*, 53, 172–174.

82. "Raisei no Dairen chiimu, Tōkyō Kyōjingun to tatakafu" (The Dairen team to travel here does battle with the Tokyo Giants), *Taiwan Nichinichi Shimpō*, 6 October 1935, 7; "Dairen yakyūdan no ichigyō ra, nigiyaka ni rai Tai" (The Dairen baseball squad busy on their trip to Taiwan), *Taiwan Nichinichi Shimpō*, 8 October 1935, 7.

83. Takemura, *Taiwan taiiku shi*, 184–185. In December 1932, the Hōsei University team returned to Taiwan for another tour, this of eleven games, and again on the invitation of the publishers. This time the team's twenty-four players included three Han Taiwanese members. Tanaka Kazuji, ed., *Taiwan nenkan: Kōki ni go kyū shi nen Shōwa kyuu nen* (Taiwan yearbook: Imperial Year 2594, Shōwa Year 9) (Taihoku: Taiwan tsūshinsha, 1934), 101–102.

84. Richard Arthur Brabazon Ponsonby-Fane, *The Vicissitudes of Shinto* (Kyoto: Ponsonby Memorial Society, 1963), 344; "Kenkō jinja" (Kenkō Shrine), from page "Taiwan lao zhaopian shuwei bowuguan" (Digital Museum of Old Photos of Taiwan), www.sinica.edu.tw/photo/subject/2_temple/intro-03.html, accessed 19 April 2007.

85. Li Yicai, "Taiwan ganlanqiu yundong de huiyi" (Reminiscences of the Taiwan rugby movement), 25 June 2002, www.rugby.com.tw/rugby/show.asp?repno=20&page=8, accessed 19 April 2007.

86. Chia-Mou Chen, "Guangfu chuqi Taibei shi guomin xuexiao bangqiu fazhan yan-qiu" ("The Research of Primary School Baseball Development in Taipei City in the Initial Period of Restoration"), *Tiyu xuebao (Bulletin of Physical Education)* 30 (March 2001): 94; George H. Kerr, *Formosa: Licensed Revolution and the Home Rule Movement, 1895–1945*

(Honolulu: University of Hawai'i Press, 1974), 76; George H. Kerr, *Formosa Betrayed* (Boston: Houghton Mifflin, 1965), 16–17.

87. Nishiwaki, *Taiwan chūtō gakkō yakyū shi*, 552; Tanaka, *Taiwan nenkan*, 104.

88. Personal communication with Wu Micha, 20 March 1996. Section epigraph: Nishiwaki, *Taiwan chūtō gakkō yakyū shi*, 242.

89. Wu Wenxing, "Riju shiqi Taiwan zongdufu tuiguang Riyu yundong chutan" (An Investigation into the Taiwan Colonial Administration's Japanese Language Promotion Campaigns during the Japanese Occupation), *Taiwan fengwu* (Taiwan Folkways) 37, no. 4 (December 1987): 69; Chou Wen-yao, "Taiwanren di yi ci de 'guoyu' jingyan—xilun Rizhi moqi de Riyu yundong jiqi wenti" (The Taiwanese People's First Experience With a "National Language"—An Analysis of the Japanese Language Movement during Late Japanese Rule), *Xin shixue* (New Historiography) 6, no. 2 (June 1995): 126, 134.

90. Harry J. Lamley, "Taiwan Under Japanese Rule, 1895–1945: The Vicissitudes of Colonialism," in *Taiwan: A New History*, ed. Murray A. Rubinstein (Armonk, NY: M. E. Sharpe, 1999), 241–242.

91. Ching, *Becoming "Japanese,"* 96–97.

92. Eiji Oguma, *Genealogy of "Japanese" Self-Images*, xxvii.

93. Gao, *Dong sheng de xuri*, 94–95.

94. Shōriki Tōru et al., eds., *Tōkyō Yomiuri Kyōjingun gojunen shi* (Fifty years' history of the Tokyo Yomiuri Giants) (Tokyo: Tōkyō Yomiuri Kyōjingun 50 nen shi henshū iinshitsu, 1985), 214–217.

95. Interview with Cai Wuzhang, Taipei, Taiwan, 17 August 2007.

96. It is possible that Go left the Giants as part of the reordering of personnel in the league after two teams folded after the 1943 season, but it is odd that the Giants would let the league MVP go—unless his Taiwanese ethnicity had become a factor during the crisis of the late wartime period. Bēsubōru Magajinsha, ed., *Nihon puro yakyū rokujūnenshi* (Sixty years' history of Japanese professional baseball) (Tokyo: Bēsubōru Magajinsha, 1994), 107–108.

97. Go also pitched a no-hitter in 1946. He retired with a .272 batting average over twenty seasons and one thousand and seven hundred games. One baseball expert has ranked Go the forty-fifth best player ever to play professional baseball in Japan. Jim Albright, "Japan's Top Players," 2004, http://baseballguru.com/jalbright/analysisjalbright01.html#Shosei_Go, accessed 20 September 2007.

98. Azumada Itsusaku, *Puro yakyū tanjō zenya: Kyūshi no kūhaku o umeru* (The eve of the birth of pro baseball: Filling a gap in baseball history) (Tokyo: Tōkai daigaku shuppansha, 1989), 165, 167, 180. In 1944, Go was league coleader (with Go Shōsei) in stolen bases with nineteen.

99. Hui-yu Caroline Ts'ai, "Total War, Labor Drafts, and Colonial Administration: Wartime Mobilization in Taiwan, 1936–45," in *Asian Labor in the Wartime Japanese Empire: Unknown Histories*, ed. Paul H. Kratoska (Armonk, NY: M. E. Sharpe, 2005), 124.

100. This would include sumo workshops run by the police, and an Islandwide Takasago [Aborigine] Sumo Assembly. Masashi Watanabe, "Identity Seen in the Acculturation of Sumo Done by Indigenous Peoples of Taiwan, Chihpen Puyuma," *International Journal of Sport and Health Science* 4 (2006): 119–120.

101. Zeng Wencheng, ed., "Gungun bangqiu changliu Xiao Changgun," 46.

102. Xie Shiyuan, "Kua shidai de chuancheng yu guangrong," part 4.

103. Nishiwaki, *Taiwan chūtō gakkō yakyū shi,* 552.

104. Ibid., 482–485.

105. See, for example, "Kōgun imon yakyū taikai" (Baseball competition to provide condolences to Imperial Army), *Taiwan Nichinichi Shimpō,* 8 January 1943, 2; "Shōbyō shōshi imon taikō yakyū taikai" (Baseball competition to provide condolences to injured soldiers), *Taiwan Nichinichi Shimpō,* 4 September 1943, 3.

106. Xie Shiyuan, "Kua shidai de chuancheng yu guangrong," part 4.

107. Zeng Wencheng, "Chen Runbo koushu bangqiushi (xia)" (Chen Runbo's oral history of baseball, part 3), 15 May 2003, http://sports.yam.com/show.php?id=0000010154, accessed 8 October 2007.

108. "Yakyūjō imo hata ni tenshin" (Baseball field turned into rice field), *Taiwan Nichinichi Shimpō,* 22 March 1944, 4.

109. Wu Zhuoliu, *Orphan of Asia,* trans. Ioannis Mentzas (Columbia University Press, 2006), 246.

110. Ching, *Becoming "Japanese,"* 209.

111. Edward W. Said, *Culture and Imperialism* (New York: Alfred A. Knopf, 1993), 269.

112. This was not a uniquely Taiwanese strategy by any means; elsewhere in the Japanese Empire, the Korean nationalist martyr Yō Un-hyŏng sponsored athletics in the 1930s as a similarly indirect mode of anticolonial resistance. Hugh Deane, *The Korean War, 1945–1953* (San Francisco: China Books and Periodicals, 1999), 48.

113. Cao Heng, "Kuiwei 60 nian, Tai Ri qiuyou salei chongfeng" (After sixty years' separation, Taiwanese and Japanese baseball pals' tearful reunion), *Ziyou dianzibao* (LibertyTimes.com), 25 April 2006, www.libertytimes.com.tw/2006/new/apr/25/today-life10.htm#, accessed 27 July 2007.

3. EARLY NATIONALIST RULE, 1945–1967

Epigraphs: Huang Chih-Huei, "The Transformation of Taiwanese Attitudes toward Japan in the Postcolonial Period," in *Imperial Japan and National Identities in Asia, 1895–1945,* ed. Narangoa Li and Robert Cribb (New York: RoutledgeCurzon, 2003), 302–303; Emma Wu, "Baseball Fever," *Free China Review* 42, no. 8 (August 1992): 31.

1. This official Nationalist designation for their 1945 acquisition of Taiwan and several outlying islands is based on the idea of this territory having been "returned" to an ahistorical "China" that ceded it. Of course, the fact that Taiwan was ceded not by the ROC regime but by the Manchu Qing dynasty makes this matter quite complex. Further complicating matters are the details surrounding the authorization given by General Douglas MacArthur, Supreme Commander of the Allied Command in the Pacific, to the ROC government to take the surrender of Taiwan as a trustee on behalf of the Allied Powers. This surrender itself implied nothing about whether the ROC was the rightful "owner" of Taiwan. At the same time, Vietnam was also surrendered to Chiang as a trustee on behalf of the Allied Powers, Manchuria and northern Korea to Joseph Stalin as another such trustee, southern Korea to U.S. general John Hodge as another, and so on. Chen Lung-chu and W. M. Reisman, "Who

Owns Taiwan: A Search for International Title," *Yale Law Journal* 81, no. 4 (March 1972): 611; "Surrender Order of the Imperial General Headquarters of Japan, 2 September 1945," www.taiwandocuments.org/ghq.htm, accessed 7 February 2008. See also Chen and Reisman, "Who Owns Taiwan," and Peng Mingmin and Huang Zhaotang, *Taiwan zai guojifa shang de diwei* (The status of Taiwan in international law), trans. Cai Qiuxiong from the Japanese (Taipei: Yushan she, 1995).

2. Jian Yongchang, *Hito no isshō: Taiwanjin no monogatari (roku)* (A life: Tale of a Taiwanese, part 6) (Taipei: self-published, 2003), 76.

3. Hsu Chung Mao, *Riben qingjie: cong Jiang Jieshi dao Li Denghui (The Japan Complex— From President Chiang Kai-Shek to President Lee Teng-Hui)* (Taipei: Tianxia wenhua, 1997), 87.

4. Chang Mau-Kuei, "Middle Class and Social and Political Movements in Taiwan: Questions and Some Preliminary Observations," in *Discovery of the Middle Classes in East Asia*, ed. Hsin-Huang Michael Hsiao (Taipei: Academia Sinica Institute of Ethnology, 1993), 142–145.

5. Su Jinzhang, *Jiayi bangqiu shihua* (Items from the history of Jiayi baseball) (Taipei: Lianjing chuban shiye gongsi, 1996), 27.

6. George H. Kerr, *Formosa Betrayed* (Boston: Houghton Mifflin, 1965), 75.

7. Steven E. Phillips, *Between Assimilation and Independence: The Taiwanese Encounter Nationalist China, 1945–1950* (Stanford, CA: Stanford University Press, 2003), 56.

8. Tong Xiangzhao, "Cong Taiwan xuanshou tan qi" (Speaking about the Taiwan athletes), *Zhengyanbao quanyun tekan* (The Truth Report, National Games Special Publication), 11 May 1948, 4.

9. Hsiau A-chin, *Contemporary Taiwanese Cultural Nationalism* (New York: Routledge, 2000), 53.

10. Huang, "The Transformation of Taiwanese Attitudes," 308; Huang Ying-Che, "Were Taiwanese Being 'Enslaved'? The Entanglement of Sinicization, Japanization, and Westernization," in *Taiwan Under Japanese Colonial Rule, 1895–1945: History, Culture, Memory*, ed. Ping-hui Liao and David Der-Wei Wang (New York: Columbia University Press, 2006), 317; Phillips, *Between Assimilation and Independence*, 60.

11. Pamela Crossley, in her groundbreaking work on Manchu Qing dynasty imperial ideology, offers a critique of our historical willingness to accept explanations of Chinese culture's unique abilities to "assimilate" or "Sinicize" other Asian peoples: " 'Sinicization' has no purpose other than as a vessel for a set of ideological impositions describing assimilation and acculturation as having causes and meanings with relation to China that are somehow special." Pamela Kyle Crossley, *A Translucent Mirror: History and Identity in Qing Imperial Ideology* (Berkeley: University of California Press, 1999), 13.

12. Martin Sökefeld, "From Colonialism to Postcolonial Colonialism: Changing Modes of Domination in the Northern Areas of Pakistan," *Journal of Asian Studies* 64, no. 4 (November 2005): 939.

13. "Supotsu no shinkō he, seidai na taiiku saiten" (Promoting sports—A great sports festival), *Taiwan xinshengbao* (Taiwan New Life Times), 19 April 1946, 4.

14. Hsu Hsueh-chi, "Taiwan Guangfu chuqi de yuwen wenti" (Language questions from early Retrocession period in Taiwan), *Si yu yan (Thought and Words)* 29, no. 4 (December 1991): 170–171.

15. Hsiau, *Contemporary Taiwanese Cultural Nationalism,* 54, 57–58.

16. Andrew Morris, *Marrow of the Nation: A History of Sport and Physical Culture in Republican China* (Berkeley: University of California Press, 2004), 100–237.

17. "Juxing quanxian yundong dahui, Tainan jian'er daxian shenshou" (All-country athletic meet underway, Healthy Tainan youth show their talents to the full), *Minbao,* 1 October 1946, 4; "Gangshan qu juxing tiyu dahui" (Gangshan area athletic meet under way), *Minbao,* 2 October 1946, 4.

18. Su Zhengsheng, "Tianxia zhi Jianong" (Kanō, champions of all under heaven), *Jianongren* (People of the Jiayi Agriculture and Forestry Institute) 1 (November 1997): 23.

19. Provincial Chief Administrator Chen Yi served as Meet Chairman. Taiwan sheng di yi jie quansheng yundong dahui xuanchuan zu (First Taiwan Provincial Games Information Section), eds., *Taiwan sheng di yi jie quansheng yundong dahui* (The First Taiwan Provincial Games) (n.p.: Taiwan sheng di yi jie quansheng yundong dahui xuanchuan zu, 1946), 7, 15–52, 82–84; Su Jinzhang, *Jiayi bangqiu shihua,* p. 27.

20. I have defined this term elsewhere; see Morris, *Marrow of the Nation,* 102.

21. "Quansheng yundong dahui, Taiwan jian'er zhan shenshou" (Provincial Games: Taiwan youth show their skills), *Minbao,* 3 October 1946, 3.

22. Taiwan sheng jiaoyuting (Taiwan Provincial Education Department), ed., *Taiwan jiaoyu fazhan shiliao huibian, tiyu jiaoyu pian* (Historical materials from the development of Taiwan education, Physical education volume) (Taipei: Taiwan sheng jiaoyuting, 1988), 968.

23. Ke Yuanfen, "Ji Taiwan sheng shoujie yundonghui shimo" (A record of Taiwan's first Provincial Games), *Zhuanji wenxue* 35 (October 1979): 98.

24. "Shoujie shengyunhui zuo kaimu, Jiang zhuxi qinlin xunci, dui qingnian Taibao xumian youjia" (First Provincial Games begin, Chairman Chiang speaks in person and exhorts the Taiwanese youth), *Minbao,* 26 October 1946, 3.

25. "Zhengda de yundong jingshen" (The great spirit of sportsmanship), *Minbao,* 1 November 1946, 1.

26. Zeng Wencheng, "Taiwan bangqiu shi (ba)" (History of Taiwan baseball, part 8), 22 September 2003, http://sports.yam.com/show.php?i =0000016320, accessed 1 June 2007.

27. Lai Tse-han, Ramon H. Myers, and Wei Wou, *A Tragic Beginning: The Taiwan Uprising of February 28, 1947* (Stanford, CA: Stanford University Press, 1991), 105–107, 121–134. Note the use, by these pro-Nationalist authors, of the word "tragic"—again, as Gumbrecht predicts, expressing "an elementary unwillingness to discuss guilt or responsibility."

28. Nishiwaki, *Taiwan chūtō gakkō yakyū shi* (History of high school baseball in Taiwan) (Kakogawa City, Hyogo Prefecture: self-published, 1996), 545–546. In a similarly daring move, the Gaoxiong baseball team that won the 1952 Provincial Games baseball title wore jerseys that read "TAKAO," this being the Japanese name for their home city! Zhonghua minguo bangqiu xiehui (Chinese Taipei Baseball Association), eds., *Taiwan bangqiu bainian shi (History of Baseball In Taiwan, 1906–2006)* (Taipei: Zhonghua minguo bangqiu xiehui, 2006), 71.

29. Gao Zhengyuan, *Dong sheng de xuri: Zhonghua bangqiu fazhan shi* (Rising sun in the East: The history of the development of Chinese baseball) (Taipei: Minshengbao she, 1994), 47–50.

30. Ibid., 31.

31. Zeng Wencheng and Yu Junwei, *Taiwan bangqiu wang (Baseball King of Taiwan)* (Taipei: Woshi chubanshe, 2004), 104.

32. Interview with Jian Yongchang, Taipei, 11 August 2004.

33. Zhan Deji, "Woguo bangqiu yundong de fawei yu zhanwang" (The development of and perspectives on our nation's baseball movement), *Jiaoyu ziliao jikan* (Educational Information Quarterly) 10 (June 1985): 436.

34. J. Bruce Jacobs, "Taiwanese and the Chinese Nationalists, 1937–1945: The Origins of Taiwan's 'Half-Mountain People' (Banshan ren)," *Modern China* 16, no. 1 (January 1990): 100–104.

35. Su Shichang, "Zhuixun yu huiyi; Zhang Wojun jiqi zuopin yanjiu" (Searching and memories; Research into Zhang Wojun and his work) (Master's thesis, Zhongxing daxue Zhongguo wenxue yanjiusuo, 1998), http://ws.twl.ncku.edu.tw/hak-chia/s/sou-se-chhiong/sek-su/ch-01.htm, accessed 22 April 2005; Yang Qing, "Zhang Wojun zai Zhongguo" (Zhang Wojun in China), in *Rizhi shiqi Taiwan zhishifenzi zai Zhongguo* (Japanese-era Taiwan intellectuals in China), ed. Lin Qingzhang (Taipei: Taibei shi wenxian weiyuanhui, 2004), 87–118.

36. Phillips, *Between Assimilation and Independence,* 72.

37. *Di qi jie quanguo yundonghui huikan* (Official publication of the Seventh National Games) (Shanghai: Shenbaoguan, 1948), 30.

38. Even their efforts to attach an orthodox Chinese history to the game had to carry an appropriate "Taiwanese" flavor; in the 1960s the government sponsored a series of Koxinga Baseball Cups commemorating Zheng Chenggong, the (half-Japanese) Ming dynasty loyalist and military leader who defeated the Dutch to capture Taiwan in 1662.

39. It should be noted, though, that this term for 1940s Chinese immigrants to Taiwan does fit with Nationalist ideology in naturalizing Taiwan as one among many Chinese "provinces."

40. Gao, *Dong sheng de xuri,* 13–16; Zeng and Yu, *Taiwan bangqiu wang,* 106.

41. Zeng Wencheng, "Huang Renhui koushu Taiwan bangqiushi (zhong)" (Huang Renhui's oral history of Taiwan baseball, part 2), 14 July 2003, http://sports.yam.com/show.php?id=0000012924, accessed8 October 2007; "Taibangdui zuori fu Fei" (Taiwan baseball team to Philippines yesterday), *Lianhebao (United Daily News),* 20 April 1953, 3; "Taiwan zheng Fei bangqiudui" (Taiwan baseball team that went to Philippines), *Lianhebao,* 16 May 1953, 3.

42. "Zhonghua bangqiudui, zuo di Han fangwen" (Chinese Baseball Team to Korea yesterday), *Lianhebao,* 1 July 1955, 3.

43. Zeng and Yu, *Taiwan bangqiu wang,* 107.

44. "Ren di shengshu yingxiang xia, wo fang Han bangqiudui, shou zhan zaoyu cuozhe" (In an unfamiliar place, our baseball team visiting Korea encounters setback in first game), *Lianhebao,* 4 July 1955, 3.

45. Morris, *Marrow of the Nation,* 120; Chia-Mou Chen, "Guangfu chuqi Taibei shi yinhang gonghui bangqiudui fazhan yanjiu (1948–1968)" ("Early Post-Recovery Period Taipei Bankers Association Baseball League Development Research [1948–1968]"), *Tiyu xuebao (Bulletin of Physical Education)* 32 (March 2002): 255.

46. Chen Wenfa, "Taiwan shaonian de guangrong, Taiwanren de shengli" (Glory of Tai-

wanese youth, Victory of the Taiwanese people), *Taiwan qingnian* (Taiwan youth) 106 (5 September 1969): 3.

47. Zeng Wencheng, "Huang Renhui koushu Taiwan bangqiushi (zhong)."

48. Zeng Wencheng, "Huang Renhui koushu Taiwan bangqiushi (xia)" (Huang Renhui's oral history of Taiwan baseball, part 3), 21 July 2003, http://sports.yam.com/show.php?id=0000013253, accessed 8 October 2007.

49. Zeng Wencheng, "Chen Runbo koushu bangqiushi (xia)" (Chen Runbo's oral history of baseball, part 3), 15 May 2003, http://sports.yam.com/show.php?id=0000010154, accessed 8 October 2007; Chia-Mou Chen, "Guangfu chuqi Taibei shi guomin xuexiao bangqiu fazhan yanqiu" (The research of primary school baseball development in Taipei City in the initial period of restoration), *Tiyu xuebao (Bulletin of Physical Education)* 30 (March 2001): 94.

50. John W. Garver, *The Sino-American Alliance: Nationalist China and American Cold War Strategy in Asia* (Armonk, NY: M. E. Sharpe, 1997), 16–31.

51. "Quanshengxing liang xiang jinbiaosai" (Two provincial tournaments), *Lianhebao*, 26 September 1952, 3.

52. "Zhong-Mei hezuo jinian bangsai, jinri kaiqiu" (Baseball tournament to commemorate Sino-American cooperation begins today), *Lianhebao*, 16 May 1953, 3.

53. "Jinxiangjiang bangqiu da bisai" (Big Golden Statue Baseball Tournament), "Zhonghua minguo xinwen" (ROC News[reel]) 142, no. 3 (1955–56).

54. Zeng Wencheng, "Huang Renhui koushu Taiwan bangqiushi (zhong)."

55. Interview with Lin Huawei, Taizhong, 30 July 2004.

56. Xie Shiyuan and Xie Jiafen, *Taiwan bangqiu yibainian (One Hundred Years of Baseball in Taiwan)* (Taipei: Guoshi chubanshe, 2003), 91–92.

57. For an example of this particular American fantasy, see Major Roger B. Doulens, "Chinese Grabbing Chance to Learn Game," *Sporting News*, 14 March 1946, 13.

58. Jiang Canlin, "Bangqiu shihua" (Stories from baseball history), *Lianhebao*, 7 November 1953, 4.

59. Al Campanis, *Zenyang da bangqiu (The Dodgers' Way to Play Baseball)*, trans. Jian Yongchang (Taipei: Taiguang chubanshe, 1960).

60. Interview with Jian Yongchang, Taipei, 11 August 2004.

61. Ze Zhijiang, dir., *Shaonian, bangqiu, guanjun (Barefoot Little Leaguers)* (Taipei: Guanghua yingpian ziliao gongyingshe, 1979).

This ideological project was continued in another way as well, by scholars who (into the 1980s and 1990s) explained Taiwan's baseball programs as a continuation of the tiny baseball movement in the Qing dynasty and early ROC eras. For example, see Zhan Deji, "Woguo bangqiu yundong de fawei yu zhanwang," 433–436; Gao, *Dong sheng de xuri*, 19–29.

62. Morris, *Marrow of the Nation*, 266n73.

63. Liu Junqing and Wang Xinliang, *Shiguang suidao: Taiwan lanyun liushi nian* (The tunnel of time: Sixty years of Taiwan basketball) (Taipei: Minshengbao she, 1999). See also Chang Chi-hsiung and Pan Kwang-che, interviewers, Wang Ching-ling, recorder, *Tang Mingxin xiansheng fangwen jilu (The Reminiscences of Mr. Tang Ming-hsin)* (Taipei: Zhongyanyuan jindaishi yanjiusuo, 2005). This work describes Tang's official work in the international basketball and Olympic communities after he left Shanghai for Taiwan in 1948.

64. Chia-Mou Chen, "Guangfu chuqi Taibei shi guomin xuexiao," 92.

65. Chen Yingzhen, "Di yi jian chaishi" (First assignment), in *Di yi jian chaishi* (First assignment), Chen Yingzhen (Taipei: Yuanjing, 1975), 138–140.

66. Ku Ling, "Xiang wo juancun de dixiongmen" (Thinking of my brothers in the military projects), *Lianhebao,* 7 April 1985, 8, and 8 April 1985, 8.

67. Bruce Jacobs, "Taiwan's Colonial History and Post-Colonial Nationalism," paper presented at the conference on Taiwan Studies in International Perspectives, University of California, Santa Barbara, 27 October 2007, 8.

68. Xie Shiyuan, "Baodao xiezhen: Shancheng na yi duan bangqiu suiyue" (Treasure island portrait: That moment of baseball history from the Mountain City), Arts.ChinaTimes.com, 29 November 2005, www.wretch.cc/blog/htycy&article_id=2480292, accessed 3 December 2007; Personal communication with Xie Shiyuan, 30 December 2005; Huang Xuanhan, "Baise kongbu shouhaizhe, Chen Yanchuan yu shen xuan lingdaoren" (White terror victim Chen Yanchuan urges caution in selecting a leader), *Lianhebao,* 9 March 2000.

69. Section epigraph: Gao, *Dong sheng de xuri,* 127.

70. "Zaoda bangqiudui di Tai, Ming shou zhan Beishi liandui" (Waseda University baseball team arrives in Taiwan, First game tomorrow versus All-Taipei team), *Lianhebao,* 18 December 1953, 3.

71. "Zaoda bangqiudui, Jin fangwen Xinzhu" (Waseda University baseball team visits Xinzhu today), *Lianhebao,* 25 December 1953, 3.

72. "'Heibaiji': Youdian kanbuguan" (In black and white: Frowning upon something a bit), *Lianhebao,* 19 December 1953, 3.

73. "Zhong-Ri bangsai di qi huihe, Tailian chuchuan jiebao" (Seventh game of the Sino-Japanese baseball tourney, the first report of victory from the All-Taiwan team), *Lianhebao,* 30 December 1953, 3. Waseda also played the Navy, Bankers Association, and All-Taipei teams during this tour.

74. "Ri Zaoda bangqiudui, jiesu fang Tai saicheng" (Japan's Waseda University baseball team completes their Taiwan schedule), *Lianhebao,* 7 January 1954, 3.

75. "Zaoda bangqiudui, zuo li Tai fan Ri" (Waseda University baseball team leaves Taiwan yesterday to return to Japan), *Lianhebao,* 9 January 1954, 3.

76. Nishiwaki, *Taiwan chūtō gakkō yakyū shi,* 545; Jian Yongchang, *Zhonghua bangqiu shiji,* 56.

77. The six banks sponsoring baseball teams were: Taiwan Cooperative Bank, Hua Nan Bank, Land Bank (Tudi yinhang), First Bank (Di yi yinhang), Bank of Taiwan (Taiwan yinhang), and Chang Hwa Bank (Zhanghua yinhang).

78. Yu Junwei, *Playing In Isolation: A History of Baseball in Taiwan* (Lincoln: University of Nebraska Press, 2007), 25.

79. Zeng and Yu, *Taiwan bangqiu wang,* 64.

80. Hall, "When Was 'The Post-Colonial'?" 247–248.

81. Su Jiaxiang, "Bainian Aoyun yu Zhongguo: Zhang Xingxian canjia Aoyun Taiwan di yi ren" (The Olympics and China, one hundred years: Zhang Xingxian the first Taiwanese to take part in the Olympics), *Minshengbao,* 7 May 1996, 2.

82. Hsu Hsueh-chi, "Tamen weishenme 'pangguan': Tan *Pangguan Zazhi* de shidai yiyi" (Why were they 'spectators'? On the historical significance of *The Spectacle Miscellanea*),

Quanguo xinshu zixun yuekan (New Books: Recent Publications in Taiwan, ROC) (September 2007): 61.

83. Zhang Ming, "Heku bangqiu wushi nian" ("Cooperative Bank Baseball Club Since 1948"), *Bangqiu shijie (Baseball World)* 1 (July 1999): 46, 49.

84. Zhang, "Heku bangqiu," 47.

85. Chia-Mou Chen, "Guangfu chuqi Taibei shi yinhang gonghui," 255.

86. Zhang Ming, "Chuancheng bangqiu, jue bu duandian—Taidian bangqiu wushisan nian shi" (Propagating baseball with nary a blackout—Taiwan Electric's fifty-three-year baseball history), *Bangqiu shijie (Baseball World)* 3 (September 1999): 55.

87. Interview with Jian Yongchang, Taipei, 11 August 2004; Zhang, "Heku bangqiu," 48; Zeng and Yu, *Taiwan bangqiu wang*, 68.

88. William W. Kelly, comments at workshop "Public Culture in Contemporary East Asia: Global Flows, Cultural Intimacy, and the Nation-State," Fairbank Center for East Asian Research, Harvard University, 22 April 2006.

89. Jeremy Taylor, "Colonial Takao: The making of a southern metropolis," *Urban History* 31, no. 1 (May 2004): 48–71.

90. Interview with Jian Yongchang, Taipei, Taiwan, 11 August 2004; Li Guoyan, "Bangqiu shenshi Fang Shuiquan (shang)" (Baseball gentleman Fang Shuiquan, part 1), *Bangqiu shijie (Baseball World)* 5 (November 1999): 46–47.

91. Xie Shiyuan, "Kua shidai de chuancheng yu guangrong—Taiwan 'Beibi Lusi' Hong Taishan (si)" (Tradition and glory across the centuries—Taiwan's 'Babe Ruth,' Hong Taishan, part 4), *Taiwan bangqiu weijiguan* ([Taiwan] Wiki Baseball), 17 January 2007, http://twbsball.dils.tku.edu.tw/wiki/index.php, accessed 14 September 2007.

92. This team also starred Xue Yongshun, a very rare non-Taiwanese Chinese baseball player—Xue was born in Fujian and grew up in Yokohama—who had played previously as Sei Kiyoshi for the professional Nagoya Golden Dolphins from 1936 to 1940. Zeng and Yu, *Taiwan bangqiu wang*, 64.

93. Li Guoyan, "Zeng Ji'en de shi ge gushi (shang)" (Ten stories about Zeng Ji'en, part 1), *Bangqiu shijie (Baseball World)* 3 (September 1999): 62; Lai Shuming, *Taiwan bangqiu Zeng Ji'en: Bangtan shengya 50 nian* (Taiwan baseball's Zeng Ji'en: Fifty years in the baseball world) (Taipei: Zhidao chuban youxian gongsi, 1991), 32.

94. Gao, *Dong sheng de xuri*, 147.

95. Ts'ai, "Total War, Labor Drafts, and Colonial Administration," 107, 126.

96. Lai Shuming, *Taiwan bangqiu Zeng Ji'en*, 47, 52, 59, 344.

97. Zeng Wencheng, "Hong Taishan koushu Taiwan bangqiushi (si)" (Hong Taishan's oral history of Taiwan baseball, part 4), 25 June 2003, http://sports.yam.com/show.php?id=0000011984, accessed 5 November 2007.

98. Zeng Wencheng, "Huang Renhui koushu Taiwan bangqiushi (xia)."

99. Wu Xiangmu, *Jue bu qingyan fangqi! Bangqiu de meihao niandai* (Never give up easily! Baseball's beautiful age) (Taipei: Yuanshen, 1996), 21.

100. Zeng and Yu, *Taiwan bangqiu wang*, 58.

101. Suzuki, *Takasago zoku ni sasageru*, 184, 192.

102. "Zhong-Ri-Han bangqiudui, yuandan zai Tai bisai" (Chinese, Japanese, Korean baseball teams to compete on New Year's Day in Taiwan), *Lianhebao*, 8 December 1955, 3.

103. "Zhong-Ri bangqiusai di er zhang, Mingda qingqu Heku" (Second battle of the Sino-Japanese Baseball Tourney: Meiji U. easily takes Cooperative Bank), *Lianhebao*, 3 January 1956, 3; "Zhong-Ri bangsai chuan wo fangshui, Tailiandui zuo canbai" (We fail in the Sino-Japanese Baseball Tourney, All-Taiwan team loses badly), *Lianhebao*, 5 January 1956, 3.

104. "Ri Mingzhi daxue xiaozhang Xiaodao Xian di Tai, tuichong wo wenhua" (Japan's Meiji University president Kojima Akira arrives in Taiwan, promotes our culture), *Lianhebao*, 11 January 1956, 3.

105. "Mingzhi bangqiudui, zi Tai fan Ri" (Meiji baseball team leaves Taiwan for Japan), *Lianhebao*, 21 January 1956, 3.

106. "Ri Mingda bangqiudui, zai Jia xiaosheng Tailian" (Japan's Meiji University baseball team narrowly defeats All-Taiwan at Jiayi), *Lianhebao*, 8 January 1956, 3.

107. "Mingda bangdui tiqian fan Ri, saicheng biangeng" (Meiji University baseball team to return early to Japan, schedule changes), *Lianhebao*, 6 January 1956, 3.

108. Chia-Mou Chen, "Guangfu chuqi Taibei shi yinhang gonghui," 256.

109. "Ri Qingda ticaodui, jin xu biaoyan liang chang" (Japanese Keio University gymnastics team to continue with two demonstrations today), *Lianhebao*, 23 December 1962, 2; "Bangqiu ji, zai xingchengzhong" (Baseball season taking shape), *Lianhebao*, 19 December 1964, 11.

110. "Ri liang daxue bangdui jin duichen, zai Tai xiaoyou jiang ge wei muxiao zhuwei" (Two Japanese university baseball teams to face off today, Taiwan alumni to help their alma maters show their strength), *Lianhebao*, 1 January 1963, 2.

111. "Zao Qing bangdui yidi jiaosui, Qingda zuo lingxian" (Waseda and Keio baseball teams retreat to a new battlefield, Keio goes ahead yesterday), *Lianhebao*, 4 January 1963, 2; "Guoying nülei zheng Gang shou chuan jie" (Guoying women's softball team reaches Hong Kong, send word of victory in first contest), *Lianhebao*, 6 January 1963, 2.

112. "Wo haijun bangdui yangwei, zuo jibao Ri Xionggu dui" (Our Navy team displays their power, beats Japanese Kumagaya team yesterday), *Lianhebao*, 28 September 1962, 2.

113. "Zhong-Ri bangsai kedui shuang chuan jie, wofang liang qiudui zuo jun shili" (The visiting teams take two victories in Sino-Japanese baseball games, both of our teams lose), *Lianhebao*, 13 January 1963, 2; "Guoying nülei zheng Gang dajie, sa san bi ling mengji Ganglian" (Guoying women's softball team earns big victory in Hong Kong, brutally beating All-Hong Kong 33–0), *Lianhebao*, 14 January 1963, 2.

114. "Han landui jinwan yingzhan liandui, Qingda bangdui zai sheng Zaodaotian" (Korean basketball team to battle All-Taiwan team tonight, Keio U. baseball team beats Waseda again), *Lianhebao*, 6 January 1963, 2.

115. "Huanan jinxiangjiang bangsai, ding mingri kaimu" (Hua Nan Big Golden Statue Baseball Tournament to begin tomorrow), *Lianhebao*, 3 May 1957, 3.

116. "Ri nü bangqiudui, zuo di Tai fangwen" (Japanese women's baseball team arrived in Taiwan yesterday for visit), *Lianhebao*, 10 May 1958, 3.

117. Susan K. Cahn, *Coming on Strong: Gender and Sexuality in Twentieth-Century Women's Sport* (New York: Maxwell Macmillan International, 1994), 209.

118. "Guoguang landui kaixuan, gansai yanchu jingcai" (Guoguang basketball team returns triumphantly, Rugby game played outstandingly), *Lianhebao*, 28 March 1959, 3.

119. Cahn, *Coming on Strong*, 214.

120. "Bangqiu yinyuan, Riben nüzi bangqiu duizhang xupei bensheng Chen Chaoyi jun" (Baseball marriage destiny: Captain of Japanese women's baseball team betrothed to Taiwanese Mr. Chen Chaoyi), *Lianhebao*, 23 April 1959, 2.

121. He Fan, "Boli dian shang, dian shang shi ling" (Collected trivialities from atop my desk), *Lianhebao fukan* (*United Daily News* Supplement), 15 May 1958, 6.

122. Section epigraph: Ano Kōji, *Renjian Wang Zhenzhi* (Oh Sadaharu the Man), trans. Zhang Beilei (Taipei: Maitian chuban gufen youxian gongsi, 1998), back cover.

123. Or even that he was born in Taiwan; see John Saar, "Oh's Fans Get Ready to Celebrate His 756th as World Homer Mark," *Washington Post*, 14 August 1977.

124. Sima Sangdun, "Fengmi Riben de bangqiu xuanshou Wang Zhenzhi" (Baseball player Oh Sadaharu, fashionable in Japan), *Lianhebao*, 25 April 1964, 2.

125. "Lü Ri Huaqiao bangqiu mingxing, Wang Zhenzhi po Riben jilu" (Overseas Chinese baseball star, having traveled to Japan [sic], sets Japanese record), *Lianhebao*, 8 September 1964, 2.

126. "Wang Zhenzhi, jin fanguo" (Oh Sadaharu returning to the country today [sic]), *Lianhebao*, 1 April 1965, 2.

127. "Qiuwang zhi zongtongfu, qianming zhijing" (Baseball king to the Presidential Palace, autographs and greetings), *Lianhebao*, 7 December 1965, 3; and "Bangqiu wang Wang Zhenzhi zai zuguo" (Baseball king Oh Sadaharu in the motherland), "Zhonghua minguo xinwen" (ROC News[reel]) 623 (1965).

128. "Chicheng qiuchang fengbamian, gaoji jubang ba yi tian" (Galloping to the stadium and inspiring awe all around, Holding the giant bat high and ruling the day), *Lianhebao*, 4 December 1965, 3; "Jianju fu dalu, yi xin hui zuguo" (Resolutely refusing to travel to the mainland, returning [sic] to the motherland wholeheartedly), *Lianhebao*, 5 December 1965, 3.

129. "Bangqiu wang Wang Zhenzhi zai zuguo"; "Qiuwang zhi zongtongfu, qianming zhijing."

130. "Huiguo xinqing qingsong, bushi lai zhao nüyou" (Returning to his country [sic] in a relaxed frame of mind, not looking for a girlfriend), *Lianhebao*, 5 December 1965, 3.

131. Sima Sangdun, "Wang Zhenzhi si ri fanguo, wang jinye zongtong zhijing" (Oh Sadaharu returning to the country on the fourth to pay formal visit to the President), *Lianhebao*, 1 December 1965, 3.

132. "Bangqiu wang Wang Zhenzhi zai zuguo"; Jian, "Wang Zhenzhi de 'xuanfeng'" (The Oh Sadaharu "whirlwind"), *Lianhebao*, 13 December 1965, 2.

133. "Yazhou bangqiusai, jin zai Min jiemu" (Asian Baseball Championships open today in Southeast Asia), *Lianhebao*, 4 December 1965, 2.

134. "Yazhou bangqiusai, wo jibai Riben, zixingchedui jinwan fan Tai" (Asian Baseball Championships: We beat Japan; Cycling team returns to Taiwan tonight), *Lianhebao*, 8 December 1965, 2; Zhao Musong, "Wenqi Gongzi, ban ru mi" (When asking [Oh] about Kyoko, he becomes enigmatic), *Lianhebao*, 6 December 1965, 3.

135. "Zongtong gao Ri jingjijie fangwentuan" (President speaks to Japanese economic delegation), *Lianhebao*, 11 December 1965, 2.

136. Zeng and Yu, *Taiwan bangqiu wang*, p. 136.

137. "Riben xiaojie, Zhongguo taitai" (Japanese young lady, Chinese wife), *Lianhebao*, 2 December 1966, 3; "Bangqiu zhi wang liying pianpian, miyue huache xian dao Taiwan" (King

of baseball and spouse make a graceful couple, honeymoon coach to Taiwan first), *Lianhebao,* 4 December 1966, 3.

138. "Wang Zhenzhi jin fanguo, xie xinniang du miyue" (Oh Sadaharu returning to the country today, accompanying his wife for honeymoon), *Lianhebao,* 3 December 1966, 3; "Hanbilou ye zongtong" (Paying a visit to the president at the Blue Jade Mansion), *Lianhebao,* 5 December 1966, 2.

139. "Nanwang zuguo renqing wennuan" (The unforgettable warmth of the people of the motherland *[sic]*), *Lianhebao,* 8 December 1966, 3.

140. Zeng and Yu, *Taiwan bangqiu wang,* 139.

141. "Tizhuan liu ming xuesheng, canjia Juren lianqiu" (Six PE College students join Giants' Training), *Lianhebao,* 12 February 1968, 6.

142. Xie Shiyuan, "Baodao xiezhen."

143. He Ping, dir., *Gan'en suiyue (Honor Thy Father)* (Taipei: Zhongyang dianying, 1989).

144. "Sadaharu Oh named ambassador-at-large for sports," Central News Agency, 13 November 2001.

145. "Taipei mayor opens Japanese baseball game," Central News Agency, 15 August 2001.

146. "Baseball strikes out politics," *Taipei Times,* 14 November 2003, www.taipeitimes.com/News/taiwan/archives/2003/11/14/2003075755, accessed 6 February 2008.

147. "Jinian guofu danchen, gedi fenbie jihui, chanyang guofu yijiao" (Commemorating the birth of the father of the country, Assemblies all over praise and explain the father of the country's last will and testament), *Lianhebao,* 13 November 1953, 4.

148. "Han zongtong Li Chengwan, kuan wo bangqiudui" (Korean president Syngman Rhee hosts our baseball team), *Lianhebao,* 3 July 1955, 3.

149. Edward W. Said, *Culture and Imperialism* (New York: Alfred A. Knopf, 1993), 210.

150. Joseph R. Allen, "Taipei Park: Signs of Occupation," *Journal of Asian Studies* 66, no. 1 (February 2007): 192–193.

151. "Quan Mei zhiye bangqiu mengzhu, Yangke dui jiang fang Tai" (Lords of American pro baseball, the Yankees will visit Taiwan), *Lianhebao,* 20 February 1962, 2.

152. "Taibei dazhuan bangsai jin kailuo" (Opening gong to ring tonight on Taipei college baseball tournament), *Lianhebao,* 8 April 1962, 2.

153. "Guanghua jin zhan quan Gang lianjun" (Guanghua to battle all-Hong Kong tonight), *Lianhebao,* 15 May 1962, 2.

154. "Yayun paiqiudui xuanbasai" (Asian Games volleyball team selection tournament), *Lianhebao,* 24 May 1962, 2.

155. It is noteworthy that DPP presidential candidate Frank Chang-ting Hsieh, during the campaign for the 2008 election, declared that if elected president, he would invite the New York Yankees to Taiwan to play some friendly baseball games with their Taiwanese counterparts. "Hsieh pans 'cross-strait common market' policy," *Taipei Times,* 23 July 2007, www.taipeitimes.com/News/taiwan/archives/2007/07/23/2003370882, accessed 26 July 2007.

4. TEAM OF TAIWAN, LONG LIVE THE REPUBLIC OF CHINA, 1968–1969

Epigraphs: "Aboriginal Milestones, 1951 A.D.–1998 A.D." (1998), www.tacp.gov.tw/english/intro/great/great10.htm (accessed 12 February 2008); "Taiwan shaonian bangqiudui wei Taiwanren zhengguang" (The Taiwan Little League baseball team wins glory for the Taiwanese people), *Taiwan qingnian* (Taiwan Youth) 106 (5 September 1969), 7, 9.

1. *Sports Illustrated,* 23 December 1963, front cover. Just before the 1964 Olympics, President Chiang Kai-shek informed Yang that he *had* to win a gold medal for the sake of the pride of the Republic of China. However, PRC intelligence agents enticed two of Yang's Olympic teammates to drug him before the decathlon. Ma Qingshan and Chen Jue earned the right to defect back to the mainland by spiking Yang's orange juice just days before the competition, preventing Yang from embarrassing the Communist regime with a sure gold-medal effort. Yang finished a disappointing fifth place, a finish that puzzled the sporting world; he only learned of this plot in 1978 from an ROC intelligence agent. "Sports legend alleges foul play," *China Post,* 5 April 1997; Rafer Johnson with Philip Goldberg, *The Best That I Can Be: An Autobiography* (New York: Doubleday, 1998), 172.

2. Gong Shusen, *Tieren Yang Chuanguang* (Iron Man C. K. Yang) (Taipei: Zhongwai tushu chubanshe, 1977), 74.

3. Yang also played for the Taidong baseball team in the Fifth Taiwan Provincial Games held in 1950. Cai Zongxin, "Taiwan dongbu yuanzhumin bangqiu yundong zhi fazhan" (The development of baseball among Taiwan's eastern Aborigines), *Shanhai wenhua (Taiwan Indigenous Voice Bimonthly)* 9 (March 1995): 41.

4. Darryl Sterk, "Romancing the Formosan Pocahontas: Romantic National Allegories in Modern Taiwanese Fiction," presented at the conference on Taiwan Studies in International Perspectives, University of California, Santa Barbara, 27 October 2007.

5. Cho-Yee To, "Education of the Aborigines in Taiwan: An Illustration of How Certain Traditional Beliefs of a Majority People Determine the Education of a Disadvantaged Minority," *The Journal of Negro Education* 41, no. 3, (Summer 1972): 184–187.

6. Cited in To, "Education of the Aborigines," 193.

7. "Canjia Shiyun xiaozu jueding, xuanba shanbao yundong rencai" (Olympic committee decides to select the best of mountain compatriot athletic talent), *Lianhebao,* 17 August 1967, 5; Shi Kemin, "Fajue tiyu xin rencai, juban shandi yundonghui" (Excavating new athletic talent, holding a Mountain Areas Athletic Meet), *Lianhebao,* 31 August 1967, 5; "Shoujie shandi yundong dahui, shiyi yue zai Pingdong juxing" (First Mountain Areas Athletic Meet to be held in Pingdong in November), *Lianhebao,* 31 August 1967, 5; Shi Kemin, "Shandi yundonghui de zhijie" (Mountain Areas Athletic Meet issues), *Lianhebao,* 4 September 1967, 8.

8. One 1,250-word piece used this phrase five times. Shi Kemin, "Shandi yundonghui de zhijie," 8.

9. Shi Kemin, "Shandi yundonghui de zhijie," 8.

10. "Tixie chou bu chu jingfei, Shandi yundonghui tingban" (CNAAF does not provide funds, Mountain Areas Athletic Meet cancelled), *Lianhebao,* 24 November 1967, 6.

11. Li Yanquan, "Yingxiong wuta xiangshan dicun luo, Pingdong shandi yundonghui jiemu" (Heroes dance and step, resounding through the mountain village, Mountain Areas Athletic Meet opens in Pingdong), *Minshengbao,* 7 May 1988, 2.

12. Section epigraphs: Cheng Sheng, "Yongyuan de Hongye" (Maple Leaf forever), *Shiyou yuekan (The Educator Monthly)* 339 (September 1995): 67; Philip Roth, *The Great American Novel* (New York: Vintage International, 1995), 115–116.

13. "Bangqiu de haizi: Zonglun" (The children of baseball: Introduction), tape one of a ten-part series (Taipei: Gonggong dianshi wenhua shiye jijinhui, 2000).

14. Despite the power of this ideology of Maple Leaf poverty, it seems that the team did have some elementary equipment. Qiu Jiawen, "Hongye zhong xiaojiang qiancheng ru jing" (Maple Leaf little generals' future prospects are smooth), *Xinwen tiandi (Newsdom)* 24, no. 35 (31 August 1968): 22; Chen Chia-Mou, "Taiwan guomin xuexiao bangqiu yundong fazhan zhi yanjiu (1945–1968)" (Research into the development of elementary school baseball in Taiwan, 1945–1968), *Taidong shiyuan xuebao* (Taidong Normal University Bulletin) 13, no. 1 (2002): 158.

15. "Bangqiu de haizi: zonglun."

16. "Tongxin bang, xiaoxiao de ji'e, dada de wenqing" (Sympathy at bat: Small, small hunger, big, big warmth and friendship), *Lianhebao,* 27 April 1965, 3.

17. "Nian jie Xuetong bangsai, Hongye que lüfei, jing wufa canjia" (Twentieth Students' Baseball Tournament: Maple Leaf out of funds and likely unable to appear), *Lianhebao,* 5 April 1968, 6.

18. Ruan Aihui, "Xie Zhiwei qiangsheng pilu Hongye youlai" (Xie Zhiwei boldly reveals the roots of Maple Leaf), *Taiwan shibao (Taiwan Times),* 16 July 2004, 15; Mixielu, "Yige zhengzhifan de 'Wangzi' meng" (A political prisoner's "princely" dream), *Zhongguo shibao (China Times),* 29 August 2004, E3.

19. Mixielu, "Wangzi yu Hongye" (Prince and Maple Leaf), *Zhongguo shibao (China Times),* 29 August 2004, E3.

20. Cheng Yuan-ching, "Hongye de gushi" (Red leaves of baseball past), *Guanghua zazhi (Sinorama)* 18, no. 1 (January 1993): 45; Cheng Sheng, "Yongyuan de Hongye," 64.

21. Ai-bo-er, "Hongye shaobangdui 'zisheng' ji" (Record of the Maple Leaf youth baseball team's quest to survive), *Xinwen tiandi (Newsdom)* 24, no. 36 (7 September 1968): 17; Mixielu, "Wangzi yu Hongye," E3.

22. "Hongye bu fu zhongwang, guoxiao bangsai chengwang" (Maple Leaf does not let down the crowd's hope, crowned kings of national [elementary] school baseball tourney), *Lianhebao,* 22 May 1968, 6.

23. Sun Jianzheng, "Ri shaonian bangdui, shili poushi" (Japanese Little League team's strengths dissected), *Lianhebao,* 21 August 1968, 6.

24. "Zhong-Ri shaonian bangqiu duikang, saicheng quanbu paiding" (Sino-Japanese Little League Baseball confrontation: Schedule all set), *Lianhebao,* 21 August 1968, 6.

25. Sun Jianzheng, "Chuiyang jiechu sui bai you rong" (Chuiyang excellent, still glorious in defeat), *Lianhebao,* 25 August 1968, 3.

26. "Zuori Xinzhu bangsai, guanzhong renshan renhai" (Yesterday's baseball game at Xinzhu: Multitudes in attendance), *Lianhebao,* 29 August 1968, 3; Zeng Wencheng and Yu Junwei, *Taiwan bangqiu wang (Baseball King of Taiwan)* (Taipei: Woshi chubanshe, 2004), 145.

27. Wang Huimin, *Hongye de gushi* (The Story of Maple Leaf) (Taipei: Minshengbao she, 1994), 66–74.

28. Zhao Musong, "Liuxing bang, zhui yun tui, Hongye fanfei" (Bats like comets, running to chase the clouds, Maple Leaf darts and flies), *Lianhebao,* 26 August 1968, 3.

29. "Bangqiu de haizi: zonglun."

30. "Jiang Jingguo jiejian Hongyedui duiyuan" (Chiang Ching-kuo greets Maple Leaf team members), *Lianhebao,* 27 August 1968, 3.

31. "Yan buzhang jiamian Hongye duiyuan, jianku fendou biaoxian youyi" (Minister Yan gives esteemed exhortations to the Maple Leaf team members and their exceptional spirit of struggling through difficulty), *Lianhebao,* 28 August 1968, 3.

32. "A5 bi yi, hao chengji" (5–1, a great result), *Lianhebao,* 28 August 1968, 3.

33. "Zuori Xinzhu bangsai, guanzhong renshan renhai," 3.

34. Murray A. Rubinstein, "Taiwan's Socioeconomic Modernization, 1971–1996," in *Taiwan: A New History,* ed. Murray A. Rubinstein (New York: M. E. Sharpe, 1999), 369–371.

35. Yuan-li Wu, "Income Distribution in the Process of Economic Growth in Taiwan," in *The Taiwan Experience, 1950–1980: Contemporary Republic of China,* ed. James C. Hsiung (New York: Praeger, 1981), 163–164.

36. He Fan, "Boli dian shang, Hongye zhansheng yihou" (From atop my desk: After the Maple Leaf victory), *Lianhebao,* 26 August 1968, 9.

37. "'Heibaiji': Hao 'bang' a!" (In black and white: What a 'hit'!), *Lianhebao,* 26 August 1968, 3.

38. See, for example, Cheng Yuan-ching, "Hongye de gushi," 42; Cheng Sheng, "Yongyuan de Hongye," 63.

39. Neil H. Jacoby, *U.S. Aid to Taiwan: A Study of Foreign Aid, Self-Help, and Development* (New York: Frederick A. Praeger, 1966), 38, 118.

40. *Xinwen tiandi (Newsdom)* 24, no. 36 (7 September 1968): front cover.

41. Stratosphere salon, "Lao shengyin de soucang zaji (san)—Cong katong dianying 'Hongye guxiang' yinfa de lishi suixiang" (Notes on the collection of old voices, part 3—Historical thoughts on the cartoon "Maple Leaf Hometown") (14 August 2006), http://blog.yam.com/stratosphere_salon/article/6334253, accessed 22 February 2008.

42. Zhang Zhichao, dir., *Hongye xiaojuren* (Little Giants of Maple Leaf) (Taipei: Xuepu youxian gongsi, 1988 film).

43. Ibid.

44. "Bangqiu de haizi: zonglun."

45. Advertisement in Changrong kongzhong shangdian *(EVA Sky Shop)* (Taoyuan: Changrong guoji gufen youxian gongsi, 2000), 85.

46. Qiu Jiawen, "Hongye zhong xiaojiang qiancheng ru jing," 22; Ai-bo-er, "Hongye shaobangdui 'zisheng' ji," 17.

47. "Hongye cun" (Maple Leaf Village), *Zhonghua minguo xinwen* (ROC News[reel]) 781 (1968).

48. "Hongye bangqiudui" (Maple Leaf baseball team), *Zhonghua minguo xinwen* (ROC News[reel]) 797 (1968).

49. "Hongye guoxiao quanti xuetong, jiang ke huo gong yingyang wucan" (Maple Leaf Elementary student body to have access to supplied nutritious lunches), *Lianhebao,* 29 August 1968, 6.

This also happened to be a riff on an existing tune in Nationalist rhetoric, an equally pornographic fascination with the famines produced by the Communists that had their mainland cousins subsisting on tree bark and grass.

50. "Hongye bangdui gushi, Zhongying ban shang yinmu" (Central Pictures to take Maple Leaf baseball team story to silver screen), *Lianhebao,* 1 September 1968, 5; "Zhongying zhipian fangzhen, gai wei jiankang zongyi luxian" (Central Pictures production direction shifts to the line of healthy art), *Lianhebao,* 11 September 1968, 5.

51. "Hongye duiyuan shengao tizhong, buxun Ri Mei tongling xuetong" (Maple Leaf players' height and weight not inferior to Japanese and American children's of the same age), *Lianhebao,* 4 September 1968, 6.

52. Qiu Zhenrong, "Jietan xiangyi, wei le canjia Xuetong bangqiu bisai, bangqiu duiyuan jiti liuji" (The word on the street: Baseball team members stay back in school together for the purpose of playing in the Students' Cup), *Lianhebao,* 21 August 1968, 4.

What is strange about this episode is that the *United Daily News* even treated this like an open secret, referring explicitly to star catcher Jiang Honghui as a thirteen-year-old in one piece about the August games. Another article published before the Japanese team's arrival stated clearly that this round of games would not follow official Little League rules and therefore boys who had graduated from elementary school that year would be eligible to play. "A5 bi yi, hao chengji," 3; "Zhong-Ri shaonian bangqiu duikang, saicheng quanbu paiding," 6.

53. "Hongye bangqiudui wen Taizhong" (Maple Leaf baseball team visits Taizhong), *Zhonghua minguo xinwen* (ROC News[reel]) 777 (1968).

54. "Bangqiu de haizi: zonglun."

55. "Hongye bangqiudui, wu duiyuan gaiming" (Five Maple Leaf baseball players change their names), *Lianhebao,* 9 October 1968, 6; Wang, *Hongye de gushi,* 5–6.

56. He Zhenfen, "Hongye piaoling qiqing kemin, facao xunqiu jiuji tujing" (Maple Leaf drifting-age situation regretful, Legal community searches for emergency way out), *Lianhebao,* 10 September 1969, 3; Wang, *Hongye de gushi,* 79.

Yu Junwei has also written on the Maple Leaf victories of 1968; since his book is largely meant to be a muckraking exposé of Taiwanese Little League Baseball, he devotes more time to the particulars of the Maple Leaf efforts to cheat and subsequent legal consequences. Thus, his work to address the "myth of Hongye" and the "Hongye legend" is quite literal and does not address the social and political "myths" of this team or their implications. Yu Junwei, *Playing In Isolation: A History of Baseball in Taiwan* (Lincoln: University of Nebraska Press, 2007), 37–47; Yu Junwei, "The Hongye Legend in Taiwanese Baseball: Separating Myth from Reality," *The International Journal of the History of Sport* 24, no. 10 (October 2007): 1264–1277.

57. "Bangqiu de haizi: zonglun."

58. Chen Shui-bian, "Bridging the New Century: New Year's Eve Address" (31 December 2000), www.gio.gov.tw/taiwan-website/4-oa/chen/press891231.htm, accessed 5 March 2006.

59. Michael Herzfeld, *Cultural Intimacy: Social Poetics in the Nation-State,* 2nd edition (New York: Routledge, 2004), 4, 29.

60. Ibid., 3.

61. Ernest Renan, "What Is a Nation?" in *Becoming National: A Reader,* ed. Geoff Eley and Ronald Grigor Suny (New York: Oxford University Press, 1996), 45, 53. Thanks to Darryl Sterk for reminding me of this element from Renan.

62. "Shao bao nianling, Hongye piaoling" (The Maple Leaves wither over the under-reported ages), *Lianhebao,* 9 September 1969, 3.

It should also be noted that the Maple Leaf offenders were all given nighttime court hearings so as to minimize the harm done to the nation's reputation. Jiao Tong, *Taiwan wenxue de jietou yundong: 1977—shijimo* (Street movements in Taiwan literature: 1977–present) (Taipei: Shibao wenhua chuban qiye gufen youxian gongsi, 1998), 40.

63. Herzfeld, *Cultural Intimacy,* 29.

64. "Shaobang tuixing zhi dao" (The way to promote Little League baseball), *Guomin tiyu jikan (Physical Education Quarterly)* 2, no. 3 (June 1971): 1–2.

65. Xu Xiulin, "Shitan qiuchang fei zhanchang" (Discussing why the ballfield is not a battlefield), *Guomin tiyu jikan (Physical Education Quarterly)* 2, no. 4 (September 1971): 18.

66. Zeng and Yu, *Taiwan bangqiu wang,* 166.

67. "Shaobang tuixing zhi dao," 1.

68. "Bangqiu de haizi: zonglun."

69. Herzfeld, *Cultural Intimacy,* 3.

70. "Bangqiu de haizi: zonglun."

71. Li Tong, *Longmenxia de Hongye* (Maple Leaf of Dragon Gate Gorge) (Taipei: Yuanshen chubanshe, 1999), 29.

72. Zhang Qijiang, "Hu Wuhan yu wo" (Hu Wuhan and I), in *Taiwan bangqiu xiaoshuo fazhan xiaoshi,* ed. Xu Jincheng (A short history of the development of Taiwan baseball fiction) (Taipei: Jiuge, 2005), 149.

73. Nancy Guy, "Farewell to Rational Actors: Music, Emotion and Social Movement in Taiwan," presented at the conference on Taiwan Studies in International Perspectives, University of California, Santa Barbara, 26 October 2007, 6–9, 11, 14, 16.

74. Jeremy Taylor, "Pop music as postcolonial nostalgia in Taiwan," in *Refashioning Pop Music in Asia: Cosmopolitan Flows, Political Tempos and Aesthetic Industries,* ed. Allen Chun, Ned Rossiter, and Brian Shoesmith, (New York: Routledge, 2004), 178–181.

75. Thanks to Tak Fujitani for this insight.

76. Foreign teams were not allowed to compete at Williamsport in 1975, so the Taiwanese boys won ten titles in twelve years of competition.

77. Jinri Zhonghua minguo: Qingzhu Zongtong Jiang gong ba zhi huadan teji *(Republic of China Today: Special Issue in Celebration of President Chiang Kai-shek's Eightieth Birthday)* (Taipei: Qiaowu weiyuanhui, 1966), no page numbers.

78. Jinri Zhonghua minguo *(Republic of China Today)* (Taipei: Qiaowu weiyuanhui, 1968).

79. Lin Qiwen, "Yundong yu zhengquan weiji: Jiedu zhanhou Taiwan bangqiu fazhan shi" (Sports and the preservation of political power: A reading of the postwar development of Taiwan baseball) (master's thesis, Guoli Taiwan daxue shehuixue yanjiusuo, 1995), 51–52.

80. Taifeng, "Jiang ducai zhengquan xisheng xia de Taiwanren tiyu" (The Taiwanese people's sports sacrificed by the Chiang dictatorial regime), *Duli Taiwan (Viva Formosa)* 14 (August 1969): 22.

81. Ibid., 24, 28.

82. Zhonghua ribao congshu weiyuanhui, eds., *Wudi Jinlong: Zhonghua shaonian bang-*

qiudui yongduo shijie guanjun jishi (The unrivalled Golden Dragons: The true record of the ROC youth baseball team's brave capture of the world championship) (Taipei: Zhonghua ribao she, 1969), 5–6.

83. "Bangqiu de haizi: Jinlong de gushi" (The children of baseball: The Golden Dragons' story), tape two of the ten-part series (Taipei: Gonggong dianshi wenhua shiye jijinhui, 2000); Zhonghua ribao congshu weiyuanhui, *Wudi Jinlong,* 7; "Zhonghua shaonian bangqiu daibiaodui, juexuansai ding mingri kaishi" (ROC national youth baseball team selections to start tomorrow), *Lianhebao,* 4 June 1969, 6

84. Zhonghua shaonian bangqiudui fendou shi bianyi weiyuanhui, eds., *Zhonghua shaonian bangqiudui fendou shi (The endeavouring history of The Youth Baseball Team of the Republic of China)* (Taipei: Zhonghua minguo lishi wenhua chubanshe, 1972), 314.

85. Zhonghua ribao congshu weiyuanhui, eds., *Wudi Jinlong,* 3.

86. Ibid., 7; "Bangqiu de haizi: Jinlong de gushi."

87. Jian Yongchang, *Bangqiu yu wo* (Baseball and me) (Taipei: self-published, 1977), 22.

88. Zhonghua ribao congshu weiyuanhui, eds., *Wudi Jinlong,* 1–2.

89. Fox Butterfield, "Taiwan Little Leaguers Stun Japan," *New York Times,* 3 August 1969.

90. "Bangqiu de haizi: Jinlong de gushi"; Jian Yongchang, *Bangqiu yu wo,* 42.

91. Jian Yongchang, *Bangqiu yu wo,* 26; Butterfield, "Taiwan Little Leaguers Stun Japan," S4.

92. "Bangqiu de haizi: Jinlong de gushi"; Xu Boxiong, *Zhonghua shaobang duokui ji* (A record of the ROC youth baseball seizing [the title]) (Taipei: Dongfang yu xifang chubanshe, 1969), 19–23.

93. Guo Yuanzhi, *Reqiu* (Fireball) (Taipei: Xin zhongyuan chubanshe, 1998), 45.

94. "Bangqiu de haizi: Jinlong de gushi."

95. Jian Yongchang, *Bangqiu yu wo,* 23.

96. "Bangqiu de haizi: Jinlong de gushi."

97. Ray Keyes, "Taiwan team springs upset . . . tops Santa Clara in L. L. final," *The Sporting News,* 6 September 1969, page unavailable.

98. Xu Boxiong, *Zhonghua shaobang duokui ji,* 12.

99. Jian Yongchang, *Bangqiu yu wo,* 19.

100. "Wei wo shaonian bangdui zhuwei" (Helping our youth baseball team express strength), *Lianhebao,* 17 August 1969, 5.

101. Xu Boxiong, *Zhonghua shaobang duokui ji,* 5.

102. Herzfeld, *Cultural Intimacy,* 25–26.

103. Lance Van Auken and Robin Van Auken, *Play Ball! The Story of Little League® Baseball* (University Park: Pennsylvania State University Press, 2001), 167.

104. "Taiwan shaonian bangqiudui wei Taiwanren zhengguang," 7, 9; "Bangqiu de haizi: Jinlong de gushi."

105. Chen Wenfa, "Taiwan shaonian de guangrong," 6.

106. *Taiwan duli jianguo lianmeng de gushi (WUFI: A History of World United Formosans for Independence)* (Taipei: Qianwei, 2000), 58.

107. "Chinese-Speaking Factions Clash at Williamsport Game," *New York Times,* 24 August 1969.

108. "Xiang Zhonghua shaobangdui huanhu" (Acclaim for the ROC youth baseball team), *Xinwen tiandi (Newsdom)* 25, no. 35 (30 August 1969): 3.

109. Zhonghua ribao congshu weiyuanhui, *Wudi Jinlong*, 1.

110. Laura Li, "Empowering the People: Fifty Years of Struggle," trans. Brent Heinrich, *Guanghua zazhi (Sinorama)* 24, no. 10 (October 1999): 101.

111. Peng Ge, "Haizimen dailai de" (What the children gave us), *Lianhebao*, 29 August 1969, 9.

112. Wang Fudan, "Cong Jinlong shaonian bangqiudui chenggong shuoqi: Tan Zhongguo quanmin tiyu de zhiben zhi dao" (On the topic of the Golden Dragons youth baseball team's success: Discussing the issues at the heart of Chinese sports for the people), *Guomin tiyu jikan (Physical Education Quarterly)* 1, no. 3 (December 1969): 3–5.

113. Xu Boxiong, *Zhonghua shaobang duokui ji*, 13–18.

114. "Xiang Zhonghua shaobangdui huanhu," 3.

115. "'Heibaiji': Haizimen de shengli" (In black and white: The children's victory), *Lianhebao*, 2 August 1971, 3; Yao Liye, *Zhonghua qing-shaobang fazhan shishi* (The history of the development of ROC youth baseball) (Taipei: Huanqiu zazhi she, 1977), ii; Ze Zhijiang, dir., *Shaonian, bangqiu, guanjun (Barefoot Little Leaguers)* (Taipei: Guanghua yingpian ziliao gongyingshe, 1979).

116. Michael Szonyi, *Cold War Island: Quemoy on the Front Line* (New York: Cambridge University Press, 2008), 41, 257.

117. Sun Jianzheng, "Cong qiuchang fei dao zhanchang, guangrong yu jiangshi fenxiang" (Flying from the ballfield to the battlefield, sharing glory with the officers and soldiers), *Lianhebao*, 19 September 1969, 3; Sun Jianzheng, "Jinlong bangdui qiuju, zengsong Jincheng xiaoxue" (Golden Dragons give baseball equipment to Golden City Elementary School), *Lianhebao*, 19 September 1969, 3; "Jinmen shizai weida, Mashan qianxiao hanhua" (Jinmen is truly great, Forward sentries broadcast from Horse Mountain), *Lianhebao*, 19 September 1969, 3.

118. Sun Jianzheng, "Gelia hao" (Both brothers fine), *Lianhebao*, 19 September 1969, 3; "Xiongdi liang yingxiong" (Two brother heroes), *Jingji ribao (Economic Daily News)*, 19 September 1969, 8.

119. This text combines two mostly overlapping accounts in "Jinmen shizai weida," 3; Wang Fudan, "Cong Jinlong shaonian bangqiudui chenggong shuoqi," 3.

120. Beiping ("Northern Peace") was the official ROC name for the city of Beijing (literally "Northern Capital"), since they maintained that the capital of China was still in Nanjing ("Southern Capital"). Wang Fudan, "Cong Jinlong shaonian bangqiudui chenggong shuoqi," 4.

121. Guo Yuanzhi, *Reqiu*, 48.

122. Chen Wenfa, "Taiwan shaonian de guangrong," 5–6.

123. "Taiwan shaonian bangqiudui wei Taiwanren zhengguang," 8–9.

124. "Jiang zongtong ji furen zhaojian tianjing nüjie Ji Zheng yu Zhonghua shaonian bangqiudui xuanshou" (President Chiang and the First Lady grant visit to women's track hero Ji Zheng and ROC youth baseball team), *Xinwen tiandi (Newsdom)* 25, no. 38 (20 September 1969): front cover.

125. Interview with Jian Yongchang, Taipei, 11 August 2004.

126. Xu Boxiong, *Zhonghua shaobang duokui ji*, 23–28.

127. Herzfeld, *Cultural Intimacy*, 56.

5. "CHINESE" BASEBALL AND ITS DISCONTENTS, 1970s–1980s

Epigraphs: James Wei, *China Yearbook 1971–72* (Taipei: China Publishing, 1972), 330; Leonard Pratt, "East Meets West in Taiwan," *Lima News* (Lima, Ohio), 4 June 1972.

1. Yu Junwei, *Playing In Isolation: A History of Baseball in Taiwan* (Lincoln: University of Nebraska Press, 2007), 170–171.

2. Ibid., 47–73.

3. Scott A. Sandage, *Born Losers: A History of Failure in America* (Cambridge, MA: Harvard University Press, 2005), 2, 9, 88.

4. Michael Herzfeld, *Cultural Intimacy: Social Poetics in the Nation-State,* 2nd ed. (New York: Routledge, 2004), 3.

5. Gao Zhengyuan, *Dong sheng de xuri: Zhonghua bangqiu fazhan shi* (Rising sun in the East: The history of the development of Chinese baseball) (Taipei: Minshengbao she, 1994), 170.

6. Taiwan sheng jiaoyuting (Taiwan Provincial Education Department), ed., *Taiwan jiaoyu fazhan shiliao huibian, tiyu jiaoyu pian* (Historical materials from the development of Taiwan education, Physical education volume) (Taipei: Taiwan sheng jiaoyuting, 1988), 806.

7. Yao Liye, *Zhonghua qing-shaobang fazhan shishi,* (The history of the development of ROC youth baseball) (Taipei: Huanqiu zazhi she, 1977), i; Yao Liye, *Zhonghua qing-shaobang shijie yangming ji* (A record of ROC youth baseball fame and triumph) (Taipei: Jianxing, 1978), i.

8. "Bangqiu de haizi: Juren de gushi" (The children of baseball: The Giants' story), tape four of a ten-part series (Taipei: Gonggong dianshi wenhua shiye jijinhui, 2000).

9. Sheldon L. Appleton, "Taiwan: The Year It Finally Happened," *Asian Survey* 12, no. 1 (1972): 37; Lin Qiwen, "Yundong yu zhengquan weiji: Jiedu zhanhou Taiwan bangqiu fazhan shi" (Sports and the preservation of political power: A reading of the postwar development of Taiwan baseball) (Master's thesis, Guoli Taiwan daxue shehuixue yanjiusuo, 1995), 47.

10. Peng Ge, "Shengli de qishi" (Revelation: Victory), *Lianhe fukan* (*United Daily News* supplement), 3 September 1971, 12.

11. Chen Bijia, "Tan shaobang yundong yu minzu zixinxin de huifu" (On the Little League Baseball movement and the recovery of racial self-confidence), *Daxue zazhi (The Intellectual)* 69 (October 1973): 24–26.

12. Ji Wei, "Huaxing yu Juren" (Huaxing [Middle School] and the Giants), *Zhongyang yuekan* (Central monthly) 5, no. 12 (October 1973): 40–42.

13. Robert Darnton, *The Great Cat Massacre and Other Episodes In French Cultural History* (New York: Basic Books, 1984), 89–90.

14. Jonathan Rutherford, *Forever England: Reflections on race, masculinity and Empire* (London: Lawrence & Wishart, 1997), 19, 26.

15. Paul Hoch, *White hero, Black beast: Racism, sexism, and the mask of masculinity* (London: Pluto Press, 1979), 134, 137.

16. Yang Naifan, "Bangyun guoyun" (The baseball movement, the national movement), *Zhongyang yuekan* (Central monthly) 5, no. 12 (October 1973): 43.

17. Chang, Kao-wu, "Giants of boys' baseball," *Free China Review* 21, no. 9 (September 1971): 27.

18. Jiao Tong, *Taiwan wenxue de jietou yundong: 1977—shijimo* (Street movements in Taiwan literature: 1977–present) (Taipei: Shibao wenhua chuban qiye gufen youxian gongsi, 1998), 41; also cited in Junwei Yu and Alan Bairner, "Proud to be Chinese: Little League Baseball and National Identities in Taiwan during the 1970s," *Identities: Global Studies in Culture and Power 15, no. 2* (April 2008): 235.

19. *Taiwan duli jianguo lianmeng de gushi (WUFI: A History of World United Formosans for Independence)* (Taipei: Qianwei, 2000), 58; Taipingshan, "Wei-lian-si-bao guan qiu ji" (A record of watching the game at Williamsport), *Duli Taiwan (Viva Formosa)* 38 (October 1971): 54–55.

A very similar tactic was used in 2006 at the World Baseball Classic, when anti-Castro forces flew a Cessna trailing a banner reading "Abajo Fidel" over Team Cuba's game in Puerto Rico. Kevin Baxter, "Protests, refusal to meet media mar Cuba's WBC showing," *Miami Herald,* 14 March 2006, www.miami.com/mld/miamiherald/sports/baseball/14092956.htm, accessed 6 April 2006).

20. Lance Van Auken and Robin Van Auken, *Play Ball! The Story of Little League® Baseball* (University Park: Pennsylvania State University Press, 2001), 164.

21. Jin Feng, "You yi ci dui Jiang douzheng de shengli: Yijiuqisi nian qingshaobangsai ceji" (Another victory in the anti-Chiang struggle: One record of the 1974 Senior League tournament), *Taidu yuekan (Independent Taiwan)* 32 (28 October 1974): 6.

22. The KMT also kept on payroll "professional students" who spied on and infiltrated pro-Taiwanese organizations including baseball and softball teams. Winston T. Dang, ed., *Taiwangate: Documents on the blacklist policy and human rights of Taiwan* (Washington, DC: Center for Taiwan International Relations, 1991), 163.

23. *Taiwan duli jianguo lianmeng de gushi,* 58; Taipingshan, "Wei-lian-si-bao guan qiu ji," 54; Van Auken and Van Auken, *Play Ball!,* 167.

The New York Times reported, "A brief fistfight broke put among the spectators during the game . . . between two factions of Chinese fans, one group composed of people born on Taiwan and another of those born in mainland China." "Taiwan Wins Little League Final, 12 to 3," *New York Times,* 29 August 1971.

24. *Taiwan duli jianguo lianmeng de gushi,* 58.

25. Yi wei Taiwanren, "Binzhou qiusai changbian wuda xiaoji" (A short record of the fighting outside the ballpark in Pennsylvania), *Duli Taiwan (Viva Formosa)* 50 (November 1972): 45–46; Van Auken and Van Auken, *Play Ball!,* 164.

26. Herzfeld, *Cultural Intimacy,* 26.

27. Bill Buford, *Among the Thugs: The Experience, and the Seduction, of Crowd Violence* (New York: W. W. Norton, 1991), 193.

28. Herzfeld, *Cultural Intimacy,* 36.

29. Taipingshan, "Wei-lian-si-bao guan qiu ji," 54; "Xiang Zhonghua shaobangdui huanhu" (Acclaim for the ROC youth baseball team), *Xinwen tiandi (Newsdom)* 25, no. 35 (30 August 1969): 3.

30. *Taiwan duli jianguo lianmeng de gushi,* 59.

31. Herzfeld, *Cultural Intimacy,* 2.

32. Guo Yuanzhi, *Reqiu* (Fireball) (Taipei: Xin zhongyuan chubanshe, 1998), 26; Susan

Kendzulak, "Celebrating our differences," *Taipei Times*, 28 May 2000, 18, www.taipeitimes .com/news/2000/05/28/story/0000037873, accessed 2 April 2008.

33. Zhonghua shaonian bangqiudui fendou shi bianyi weiyuanhui, eds., *Zhonghua shaonian bangqiudui fendou shi (The endeavouring history of The Youth Baseball Team of the Republic of China)* (Taipei: Zhonghua minguo lishi wenhua chubanshe, 1972), 19; "Dongjing qiaobao, huansong Juren" (Tokyo overseas compatriots joyously send off Giants), *Lianhebao*, 12 September 1971, 3.

34. Zhonghua shaonian bangqiudui fendou shi bianyi weiyuanhui, eds., *Zhonghua shaonian bangqiudui*, ii.

35. Chang, "Giants of boys' baseball," 27

36. Herzfeld, *Cultural Intimacy*, 29.

37. Cui Jian, "Yi kuai hong bu" (A piece of red cloth), *Jiejue* (Resolution) (Beijing: Zhong-guo wencai shengxiang chuban gongsi, 1991).

38. Chen Shui-bian, "Qianjin Yadian, Taiwan jiayou" (Onward to Athens, go Taiwan), *A-bian zongtong dianzibao* (President A-bian's electronic bulletin) 137 (22 July 2004), www.president.gov.tw/1_epaper/93/930722.html, accessed 2 April 2008.

39. Wei, *China Yearbook 1971–72*, 1.

40. Shoujuzi, "Ranshao, shaobang!" (Burn on, Little League baseball!), *Zhongguo shibao (China Times)*, 26 July 1993, 27.

41. Chang Li-ke, "Taiwan bangqiu yu renting," 58.

42. "Maigaowen jin li Hua" (McGovern leaving ROC today), *Lianhebao*, 4 June 1970, 3.

43. Luo Kaiming, "You Qihu shaobangdui de shengli fenxi yundong jingsai de xinli yinsu" (An analysis of the psychological factors of competitive sport using the Seven Tiger youth baseball team's victory), *Guomin tiyu jikan (Physical Education Quarterly)* 1, no. 6 (September 1970): 5–6.

44. "Bangqiu de haizi: Qihu de gushi" (The Children of baseball: The Seven Tigers' story), tape three of a ten-part series (Taipei: Gonggong dianshi wenhua shiye jijinhui, 2000).

45. Xu Zongmao, *Sanguanwang zhi meng (Dreams Come True)* (Taipei: Dadi chuban-she, 2004), 111.

46. "'Heibaiji': Dui bu qi" (In black and white: Sorry), *Lianhebao*, 27 August 1970, 3.

47. "Bangqiu de haizi: Qihu de gushi."

48. Shoujuzi, "Ranshao, shaobang!" 27; Yao Liye, *Zhonghua qing-shaobang fazhan shi-shi*, 27.

49. Yao Liye, *Zhonghua qing-shaobang fazhan shishi*, 28; "Jiang fuyuanzhang qinying xiaoguoshou, Songshan jichang reqing dajiaoliu" (Vice Premier Chiang meets the national team, a warm exchange at the Songshan airport), *Lianhebao* 7 September 1970, 3.

50. Weng Jiaming, "Bangqiu de meili yu aichou" (The beauty and sorrow of baseball), *Zhongguo luntan (China Tribune)* 384 (September 1992), 29–30.

51. There are fifty-three pictures in all. Xingzhengyuan tiyu weiyuanhui (National Coun-cil on Physical Fitness and Sports), "Shuwei bowuguan: bangqiu" (Digital Museum: Base-ball) (November 2005), www.ncpfs.gov.tw/museum/museum-1.aspx?No=9, accessed 2 April 2008.

52. "Zongtong zuo mianli Qihu duiyuan, cong shibai jingyan yingqu shengli" (President

gives encouragement to Seven Tigers players yesterday, speaks on using the experience of defeat to achieve victory), *Lianhebao,* 10 September 1970, 2.

53. See Cohen's insightful account of the official ROC rendering of the story of Goujian, king of the defeated Yue state in the fifth century B.C.E. Goujian's decision to redeem himself and his kingdom through ritual humiliation ("sleeping on brushwood and tasting gall") was a powerful historical metaphor for a modern defeat and retreat that Chiang Kai-shek saw as similarly shameful. Paul A. Cohen, *Speaking to History: The Story of King Goujian in Twentieth-Century China* (Berkeley: University of California Press, 2009), 87–135.

Chiang's wife Song Meiling was less forgiving of defeat. Huaxing Middle School, which enjoyed her generous support—to the tune of NT$3 billion [US$75 million]—was founded for the education of the children of revolutionary martyrs. In 1969, in special recognition of the Taizhong Golden Dragons' world championship, those players too were awarded enrollment. The Seven Tigers players received no such invitation and instead enrolled en masse in Meihe Middle School in southern Pingdong, creating an instant baseball rivalry which captivated the island during the 1970s. Interview with Lin Huawei, Taizhong, Taiwan, 30 July 2004.

54. This was the same magazine that provided important material support for the Maple Leaf youth team in 1968.

55. "Bangqiu xiao yinghao" (Little baseball hero [part 1]), *Wangzi* (Prince magazine) 82 (1 July 1970): 153–167; "Bangqiu xiao yinghao 2" (Little baseball hero, part 2), *Wangzi* 83 (15 July 1970): 21–35; "Bangqiu xiao yinghao" (Little baseball hero [part 3]), *Wangzi* 84 (1 August 1970); 59–73.

56. "Bangqiu xiao yinghao" (Little baseball hero [part 3]): 62–66.

57. Hsiao Yeh, "Forced Out," in *Winter Plum: Contemporary Chinese Fiction,* ed. Nancy Ing (Taipei: Chinese Materials Center, 1982), 139–151; Xiaoye, "Fengsha" (Forced out), in *Fengsha* (Taipei: Wenhao chubanshe, 1979), 72–87.

58. Xiaoye, "Fengsha" (Forced out), in *Taiwan bangqiu xiaoshuo fazhan xiaoshi* (A short history of the development of Taiwan baseball fiction), ed. Xu Jincheng (Taipei: Jiuge, 2005), 32.

59. Liao Hsien-hao, "Ruqinzhe" (The invader), in *Taiwan bangqiu xiaoshuo fazhan xiaoshi,* ed. Xu Jincheng (Taipei: Jiuge, 2005), 48–77.

60. Milan Kundera, *The Book of Laughter and Forgetting* (New York: Penguin, 1981), 121–122.

61. Yan Shannong, "Xin rentong de peifang" (A new formulation for identity), *Zhongguo luntan (China Tribune)* 384 (September 1992): 32–35.

62. Edward Yang, dir., *Qingmei zhuma (Taipei Story)* (Taipei: Wannianqing dianying gongsi, 1985 film); see also Tonglin Lu, *Confronting Modernity in the Cinemas of Taiwan and Mainland China* (Cambridge: Cambridge University Press, 2002), 120–132.

63. Liu Yidong, dir., *Fendou* (Struggle) (Taipei: Taiwan dianying zhipianchang, 1988 film).

64. Section epigraphs: "Great Moments in Little League World Series History," *The Onion,* 17 August 2006, www.theonion.com/content/node/51806, accessed 5 April 2008.

65. For more on this issue, see Yu, *Playing in Isolation,* 69–71.

66. Interview with anonymous former Little League player, Taiwan, summer 2007.

67. Su Jinzhang, *Jiayi bangqiu shihua,* 55, 71.

68. Paul Li, "Baseball Tries to Make a Comeback," *Taipei Journal* 17, no. 45 (10 November 2000): 8.

69. "Bangqiu xiaojiang yangwei haiwai de yiyi yu qishi" (The significance and revelation of the young baseball generals showing their strength abroad), *Lianhebao*, 18 August 1975, 2.

70. Keyes, "Taiwan team springs upset." The good (if short-lived) American sportsmanship mentioned earlier also drew comment in Taiwan. "Ying Qihu yuanzheng guiguo, lun quanmin tiyu zhenggui" (Welcome the Seven Tigers home from their journey abroad, discuss the correct road for a physical culture for the people), *Lianhebao*, 6 September 1970, 2.

71. Joseph Timothy Sundeen, "A 'Kid's Game'? Little League Baseball and National Identity in Taiwan," *Journal of Sport & Social Issues* 25, no. 3 (August 2001): 257.

72. Van Auken and Van Auken, *Play Ball!,* 169.

73. Ibid., 176.

74. For good measure, the Giants' utter domination can be seen in the following statistics: They had a team batting average of .417. Their pitchers faced only fifty-six batters in the three games (the minimum would be fifty-four), striking out forty-six and walking two. One of these runners attempted to steal against the Giants, and was cut down at second base. Their opponents committed thirteen errors, ten wild pitches and fifteen passed balls; Taiwan had only one error overall. Peter Carry, "Going to Bat for Taiwan," *Sports Illustrated,* 19 August 1974, 66–67.

75. "Taiwan, on 3d No-Hitter, Wins Little League Title," *New York Times*, 26 August 1973; "Taiwan Little Leaguers Too Good," *Press-Citizen* (Iowa City), 27 August 1973; "Little League Plans Investigation," *New York Times*, 28 August 1973.

76. Fang Junling, "Zhidao Juren shaobangdui de jingguo ji ganxiang" (Thoughts on the experience of coaching the Giants youth baseball team), *Guo jiao zhi you* (Friend of the nation's teachers) 373 (December 1971): 39–40. For more factual information on brutal training of young teams in the 1970s and '80s, see Yu, *Playing in Isolation,* 84–90.

77. Paul Conrad cartoon, *Los Angeles Times*, 28 August 1973, .

78. "Little League Clears Taiwan," *New York Times*, 28 October 1973.

79. Bill Lyon, "Taiwan Plays Ball like It's Tong War," *Philadelphia Inquirer,* 25 August 1974.

80. J. Anthony Lukas, "The Nationalist Pastime," *Rolling Stone* 175 (5 December 1974), 58, 63.

81. Ibid.

82. Sundeen, "A 'Kid's Game'?" 257.

83. "Little League Bars Foreigners," *New York Times*, 12 November 1974.

84. Herzfeld, *Cultural Intimacy,* 3.

85. Chunwei Yu, "I have a lot to say on the part of Taiwan," Amazon.com review of Joseph Reaves, *Taking in a Game: A History of Baseball in Asia,* 18 December 2002, www.amazon.com/gp/product/0803239432/qid=1042137211/sr=1-2/ref=sr_1_2/103-0487842-4844607?s=books&v=glance&n=283155, accessed 11 March 2006.

86. Allen Chun, "Democracy as Hegemony, Globalization as Indigenization, or the 'Culture' in Taiwanese National Politics," *Journal of Asian and African Studies* 35, no. 1 (February 2000): 10.

87. This became more and more onerous as the authorities wanted to guarantee a world champion. In 1981, the Taiping team had to play fourteen games in the Taiwan tournament before proceeding to the Far East and world tourneys. Zhang Jingguo, *Zhonghua minguo shaonian, qingshaonian, qingnian bangqiu fazhan shishi* (Historical facts of the develop-

ment of ROC Little League, Senior League and Big League Baseball) (Taipei: self-published, 1983), 16.

88. "Bangqiu de haizi: Puzi Ronggong de gushi" (The Children of Baseball: The Puzi and Ronggong Stories), tape ten of a ten-part series (Taipei: Gonggong dianshi wenhua shiye ji-jinhui, 2000).

6. HOMU-RAN BATTA, 1990–PRESENT

Epigraphs: "ROC Establishes Professional Baseball League," Central News Agency (Taiwan), 23 October 1989. Mark Whicker, "Mets want some Mora: The Valentine favorite, who once played in Taiwan, helps keep them alive," *Orange County Register*, 17 October 1999.

1. Gao Zhengyuan, *Dong sheng de xuri: Zhonghua bangqiu fazhan shi* (Rising sun in the East: The history of the development of Chinese baseball) (Taipei: Minshengbao she, 1994), 167.

2. "Ri Shizi bangqiudui, tu luozhi Chen Xiuxiong" (Japanese Lions baseball club plotting to catch and deliver Chen Xiuxiong), *Lianhebao*, 27 December 1972, 6.

3. Zhang Zhaoxiong, "Shizi zhiye bangdui, zuori kaishi caobing, waichuan Chen Xiuxiong canjia xunlian yi shuo bu que" (Lions professional baseball team begins training troops yesterday, rumors that Chen Xiuxiong is joining in are false), *Lianhebao*, 17 February 1973, 6.

4. Howard Boorman, ed., *Biographical Dictionary of Republican China*, vol. 4 (New York: Columbia University Press, 1971), 7–9; "Yang Sen zuotian biaoshi, fandui qiuyuan wailiu" (Yang Sen yesterday expresses his opposition to players going abroad), *Lianhebao*, 26 November 1972, 6.

5. Zhang Zhaoxiong, "Qing Chen Xiuxiong, shenzhong kaolü" (Asking Chen Xiuxiong to think carefully), *Lianhebao*, 29 December 1972, 6.

6. "Chen Xiuxiong fu Taizhong, xiang Shizidui taojiao, waichuan canjia jixun bu que" (Chen Xiuxiong to Taizhong, seeks instruction from Lions, rumors that he is joining in training are false), *Lianhebao*, 19 February 1973, 6.

7. Gao, *Dong sheng de xuri*, 167.

8. "Yeqiuren de tiankong—qu ta de minzu qinggan" (Yakyū man's world: To hell with his racial-nationalist sentiments) (9 October 2005), http://mypaper.pchome.com.tw/news/ehano955/3/1260359514/20051029110321/, accessed 7 May 2008.

9. Sun Jianzheng, "Gao Yingjie Li Laifa, fu Mei wei qi fei yuan" (Eng-jey Kao and Lai-hua Lee to leave for America soon), *Lianhebao*, 4 December 1974, 8.

10. "People in Sports: Braves Trade Reed For Sadecki, Sosa," *New York Times*, 29 May 1975; "Cincinnati Signs 2 Taiwan Players," *Mansfield News Journal*, 25 May 1975.

11. Bob Cooper, "Reds still hope to sign Taiwan baseball stars," *Post Crescent* (Appleton, Wisconsin), 25 April 1976; "Contract Problems," *Mansfield News Journal* (Mansfield, Ohio), 5 August 1976.

The Los Angeles Dodgers and Pittsburgh Pirates also pursued Kao and Lee. Sun Jianzheng, "Gao Yingjie Li Laifa jiameng Hongrendui, jinnianchu yi qianle 'yuyue'" (Eng-jey Kao and Lai-hua Lee joining the Reds, have signed preliminary contract at the beginning of the year), *Lianhebao*, 30 May 1975, 3.

12. By this time, there was already one Taiwanese player in the American minor leagues.

Hsin-Min Tan, who eventually was signed by the Seibu Lions after they failed to acquire Chen Xiuxiong in 1973, was sent to play for the San Francisco Giants' Single A farm team in Fresno as part of an exchange relationship between the Giants and Lions. Yang Wuxun, "Tan Xin-min ding ri nei fu Mei, kaishi yinian kulian shengya" (Hsin-Min Tan to America soon, to begin year of bitter training), *Lianhebao,* 27 February 1974, 8.

13. "Gao Yingjie Li Laifa, yuedi jiang fu Riben, jiameng Nanhai Ying dui" (Eng-jey Kao and Lai-hua Lee to go to Japan at the end of the month to join Nankai Hawks), *Lianhebao,* 23 November 1979, 5.

14. Yao Jiasui, "Riben Banshen bangdui shentan, lai Tai wuse gaoshou jiameng" (Scout from Japanese Hanshin baseball club to Taiwan, from the looks of things trying to get best players to join [his team]), *Lianhebao,* 21 September 1980, 5.

15. Guo Yuanzhi, *Reqiu* (Fireball) (Taipei: Xin zhongyuan chubanshe, 1998), 76.

16. Ibid., 26, 28.

17. Ibid., 76; Yao Jiasui, "Guo Yuanzhi ding qi yue fu Ri" (Guo Yuanzhi to Japan in July), *Lianhebao,* 28 March 1981, 5.

18. *Nihon puro yakyū gaikokujin senshu (1936–1994)* (Japanese professional baseball's foreign players [1936–1994]), *Beisubōru magajin (Baseball Magazine)* 18, no. 3 (Summer 1994); 74.

Other Taiwanese players took on Japanese citizenship, largely because they would no longer count as "foreign players" against the league limit of two per team. For example, Li Zongyuan pitched as Miyake Sōgen for the Lotte Orions and Yomiuri Giants from 1979 to 1985. Needless to say, this option was not available to Western players, who could never be as easily assimilated as Taiwanese players, whose own parents had once been Japanese subjects.

19. Gao Zhengyuan, *Shanyao yibai sheng: Guo Taiyuan* (One hundred shining victories: Guo Taiyuan) (Taipei: Minshengbao she, 1994), 7, 41.

20. Gao Zhengyuan, *Lü Mingci chuanqi: Mai xiang juren zhi lu* (The legend of Lü Mingci: His road to the Giants) (Taipei: Minshengbao she, 1988), 175, 183.

21. For example, see Gao Zhengyuan, *Lü Mingci chuanqi,* 141.

22. Robert K. Fitts, *Remembering Japanese Baseball: An Oral History of the Game* (Carbondale: Southern Illinois University Press, 2005), 205.

23. Qu Hailiang, "Taiwan yuanzhumin de bangqiu chuanqi" (Taiwan Aborigines' baseball miracle), *Shanhai wenhua (Taiwan Indigenous Voice Bimonthly)* 9 (March 1995): 28.

24. Xiao Meijun, "Wo qi ming bangqiuyuan zai Ri, zhi you liang ren shoudao zhongyong" (Of our seven baseball players in Japan, only two are used properly), *Lianhebao,* 3 June 1982, 5.

25. Yang Wuxun and Gao Zhengyuan, *Aoyun bangqiu guoshou dianjianglu* (List of national players appointed to Olympic baseball team) (Taipei: Minshengbao she, 1984), 73.

26. Interview with Lin Huawei, Taizhong, Taiwan, 30 July 2004.

27. *Chu cai Jin yong,* meaning "talent of the Chu kingdom being employed by the Jin." Guo Cheng, "Fazhan ziji de zhiye bangqiudui" (Develop our own professional baseball teams), *Ziyou qinginian* (Free youth) 73, no. 1 (January 1985): 33.

28. Shi Zhongchuan, "Taiwan bangqiu haoshou zouhong Riben" (Taiwanese baseball players popular in Japan), *Riben wenzhai (Japan Digest)* 39 (April 1989): 110.

29. Gao Zhengyuan, "Taiwan zhibang, nian nian xifu ao cheng po . . ." (Taiwanese pro baseball—After twenty years the daughter-in-law has proudly become a mother-in-law . . .), *Zhonghua bangqiu zazhi (R.O.C. Baseball Quarterly)* 21 (December 1988); 4.

30. Yu Zhongzhou, "Chengli zhibang, buyi cao zhi guoji" (In establishing pro baseball it's inappropriate to act with too much haste), *Zhonghua bangqiu zazhi (R.O.C. Baseball Quarterly)* 18 (March 1988): 38–39.

31. Guo Jianyi, "Zhibang, buneng zai tuo yi tian" (Pro baseball—can't delay another day), *Zhonghua bangqiu zazhi (R.O.C. Baseball Quarterly)* 19 (June 1988); 50–51.

32. "ROC Promotes World Harmony through Baseball," Central News Agency (Taiwan), 11 August 1987.

33. Zeng Wencheng, "Zhibang caochuang bilu lanlü" (The early years of professional baseball, the hard life of pioneers), *Zhiye bangqiu (Professional Baseball)* 167–168 (January–February 1997): 22.

34. The league was officially founded in October 1989, with Tang as the first league commissioner *(huizhang)*. "ROC Establishes Professional Baseball League," Central News Agency (Taiwan), 23 October 1989.

35. "ROC Pro Ball in 1990," *Free China Journal*, 8 September 1988, 2.

36. Andrew Morris, "Taiwan: Baseball, Colonialism, and Nationalism," in *Baseball Without Borders: The International Pastime*, ed. George Gmelch (Lincoln: University of Nebraska Press, 2006), 65–88; Andrew Morris, "Baseball, History, the Local and the Global in Taiwan," in *The Minor Arts of Daily Life: Popular Culture in Taiwan*, ed. David K. Jordan, Andrew Morris, and Marc L. Moskowitz (Honolulu: University of Hawai'i Press, 2004), 175–203. This chapter includes material from these earlier pieces.

37. "Table of Important Chinese Terms and their English Translations Used by the President in His Speeches and Important Messages," published by the Government Information Office, Republic of China, 23 July 2004, www.gio.gov.tw/taiwan-website/4-oa/politics/trans/, accessed 16 April 2004.

38. A. Cvetkovich and D. Kellner, "The Intersection of the Local and the Global," in *Globalization: The Reader*, ed. John Beynon and David Dunkerley (New York: Routledge, 2001), 134.

39. Arturo J. Marcano Guevara and David P. Fidler, *Stealing Lives: The Globalization of Baseball and the Tragic Story of Alexis Quiroz* (Bloomington: Indiana University Press, 2002), 28–30, 33.

40. Craig Stroupe, "Glocalization," www.d.umn.edu/~cstroupe/ideas/glocalization.html, accessed 24 February 2005.

41. Wayne Gabardi, *Negotiating Postmodernism* (Minneapolis: University of Minnesota Press, 2001), 33.

42. The Mercuries players came largely from the Cooperative Bank and Veterans Hospital semipro teams. Zeng Wencheng, "Taiwan zhibang shi (er)" (History of Taiwan professional baseball, part 2), 13 February 2006, http://sports.yam.com/show.php?id=0000065456, accessed 30 November 2006; Zeng Wencheng, "Taiwan zhibang shi (san)" (History of Taiwan professional baseball, part 3), 19 February 2006, http://sports.yam.com/show.php?id=0000065922, accessed 30 November 2006.

43. Shih Chih-pin, "A Study of the Relationship Between Media Coverage, Audience Behavior, and Sporting Events: An Analysis of Taiwan Professional Baseball Booster Club Members" (PhD diss., University of Northern Colorado, 1998), 37–39, 80.

44. Zhou Dayou, "Qiumi dian xi, yao kan Sanshang Xiongdi zhi zhan" (Fans select the

performance, insist on watching Tigers play Elephants), *Lianhebao*, 29 May 1990, 16; Zeng Wencheng, "Taiwan zhibang shi (si)" (History of Taiwan professional baseball, part 4), 27 February 2006, http://sports.yam.com/show.php?id=0000066495, accessed 30 November 2006.

45. Zhou Dayou, "Qiusai da bu da, dangchang fu gongjue? Qiudui quyue guanzhong zuo fengdai shangque" (Should a public referendum decide whether a game is to be played? Teams trying to please crowds and even asking for suggestions), *Lianhebao*, 8 June 1990, 5; Zhou Dayou, "Xiongdi pei guanzhong, da chang youyisai" (Elephants accompany fans in friendly game), *Lianhebao*, 8 June 1990, 5.

46. Of the nineteen foreigners who played during the CPBL's first season, only two had major league experience: Tiger infielder Jose Moreno (.206 average in eighty-two games for the 1980 NY Mets, 1981 San Diego Padres, and 1982 California Angels) and Elephant pitcher Jose Roman (1–8, 8.12 ERA in fourteen games for the 1984 through 1986 Cleveland Indians).

47. Interview with Tony Metoyer (Jungo Bears pitcher), 31 August 1993.

48. The Chunichi minor leaguers were joined by the big-league Dragons' two Taiwanese stars, Guo Yuanzhi and Chen Dafeng.

49. William W. Kelly, "Blood and Guts in Japanese Professional Baseball," in *The Culture of Japan as Seen through Its Leisure,* ed. Sepp Linhart and Sabine Frühstück (Albany: SUNY Press, 1998), 105–107.

50. Jackie Chen, "Major League Controversies—Professional Baseball Enters a New Era," trans. Phil Newell, *Guanghua zazhi (Sinorama)* 21, no. 3 (March 1996): 80.

51. Jeffrey P. Wilson, "Taiwan Enters the Big Leagues: A Look at Disputes Involving Foreign Professional Baseball Players," *For The Record* 4, no. 5 (October–November 1993): 3.

52. Appendix 2 lists the national origins of these foreign players. Roughly half of these foreign players came to Taiwan with experience in the American or Japanese major leagues.

53. Personal communication, 6 August 2009.

54. Lin Xinhui, "Qiumi yao Bing-shan" (The fans want Goldberg), *Lianhebao*, 25 February 1998, 28. A more contemporary example of this kind of affection can be seen in the YouTube video (complete with Richard Marx lyrics) posted in honor of Canadian third baseman Todd Betts by La new Bears fans upon his release from the team in 2006. "Todd Betts MV," 28 July 2006, http://youtube.com/watch?v=GpUXHO7j4jU, accessed 26 June 2008.

55. The current limit in the CPBL is three. Japanese and Korean pro teams are today allowed to carry four and two foreigners on their rosters, respectively.

56. "Diary of a Comeback Kid" (15–16 May 1995), www.net-endeavors.com/diary/, accessed 12 February 2002.

57. Lin Yijun, "Xiong, kangzheng de yangjiang, dasheng" (Bears and resistant foreign players win big), *Lianhebao*, 15 September 1995, 24.

58. Gu Hong, *Zhibang yangjiang xing chouwen: Jiefa nüqiumi yu yangjiang de taose jiaoyi* (Foreign pro baseball players' sex scandals: Exposing the illicit relations between female baseball fans and foreign players) (Taipei: Rizhen chubanshe, 1997).

59. Marc L. Moskowitz, "Multiple Virginity and Other Contested Realities in Taipei's Foreign Club Culture," *Sexualities* 11, no. 3 (June 2008): 333, 337–343.

60. Zhou Dayou, "Yangjiang nan guanli, bu qing hai bu xing" (Foreign players hard to supervise, but we cannot not hire them), *Lianhebao*, 17 October 1993, 17; Yan Shannong, "Ai-bo zhi si ling ren zhenjing, yangjiang zai Tai shenghuo, ying you ren guanli" (Harper's

death shocking, foreign players need to have someone supervise their personal lives in Taiwan), *Lianhebao,* 21 October 1993, 11; Wang Jingwen, "Ai-bo cu si, qiaoxiang yangjiang guanli jingzhong" (Harper's premature death sounds alarm to supervise foreign players), *Lianhe wanbao (United Daily Evening News),* 17 October 1993, 15; Lin Youying, "Zhibang yangjiang guanli wenti zhongzhong" (Many problems with supervision of foreign pro baseball players), *Minshengbao,* 18 October 1993, 4.

Sadly, the 2005 death of the Macoto Cobras' Dominican outfielder Mario Encarcion revived this cruel discourse of the hard-to-manage and wild-living dead foreign player who was harming Taiwanese baseball with his presence—despite the fact that Encarcion was later found to have died of a congenital medical condition. For example, see Zhu Kaixiang and Yang Shangren, "Zhibang 16 nian yangjiang shang qian ren, wenhua gehe da nan guanli" (The number of [Taiwanese] pro baseball's foreign players in sixteen years passes one thousand *[sic],* cultural gap very difficult to manage), ETtoday.com, 3 October 2005, www.ettoday.com/2005/10/03/341-1852194.htm, accessed 4 October 2005.

61. Chen Xiaoyu, "Ai-bo yiti yan chu andu fanying" (Amphetamines detected in Harper's corpse), *Minshengbao,* 8 November 1993, 5.

62. Lin Youying, "Zhibang yangjiang guanli wenti zhongzhong," 4; Yan Shannong, "Ai-bo zhi si ling ren zhenjing," 11.

63. After thirty-eight CPBL games that year, foreign pitchers had won thirty-five decisions and thrown 81 percent of the innings. Wu Qingzheng, "Zhonghua zhibang toushouqiu lun wei waiguo zujie" (Calling the CPBL pitching mound a foreign concession), *Ziyou shibao (Liberty Times),* 25 March 1998, C8.

64. Of the second-place Sinon Bulls' eleven pitchers, nine were foreign. Their foreign pitchers' combined record was 57–45–2 that year, and their two Taiwanese pitchers were 1–0–0.

65. Not only were a great percentage of the players foreign, but many teams preferred to hire foreign managers, who were thought to have a more worldly grasp of strategy than native Taiwanese managers. The success of Elephant Manager Yamane Toshihide, who led his team to three straight championships from 1992 to 1994, made quite an impression. By 1995, five of six CPBL teams were managed by Japanese helmsmen.

66. Chen Dashun, "Zhaochu wenti, jiejue wenti" (Locate the problem, solve the problem), *Zhiye bangqiu (Professional Baseball)* 219 (12 June 2000): 19.

67. Chen Yiping, *Baimao pindao (Channel White)* (Taizhong: Shuiyong chubanshe, 1997), 93–94.

68. Ao Youxiang, *Zhibang kuangxiangqu* (Pro baseball rhapsody) (Taipei: Zhonghua zhibang shiye gufen youxian gongsi, 1994), 28; Morris, "Baseball, History, the Local and the Global in Taiwan," 193.

69. Ao, *Zhibang kuangxiangqu,* 42.

70. An indication of foreign dominance of the CPBL in 1997 can be seen in the season's statistical leaders. The following indicates the number of foreign players in the top ten for each category: batting average, eight; home runs, eight; runs batted in, seven; wins, seven; earned run average, six. Only one major category (victories) was led by a Taiwanese player—the Lions' Wu Junliang, who in the eyes of one reporter, "was the only [player] to save a bit of face for the 'Chinese.'" Wang Yingming, "Na yi guo de zhibang banjiang dianli?" (Which country's awards ceremony [was this]?), *Ziyou shibao (Liberty Times),* 8 October 1997, 30.

71. "Na-po-li, kewang zhousi shangchang" (Al Osuna to pitch Thursday), *Ziyou shibao (Liberty Times)*, 27 May 1998, 33.

72. Xie Daiying, "Li-ba-shan, An-shou-duo tongtong shi nongyao" (Alvin Brown, Ron Maurer all [have names that] are pesticides), *Ziyou shibao*, 11 March 1998, C6; Chang Li-ke, "Taiwan bangqiu yu rentong: Yi ge yundong shehuixue de fenxi" (Taiwan Baseball and identities: An analysis of sociology of sport) (Master's thesis, Guoli Qinghua daxue shehuixue yanjiusuo, 2000), 83.

73. Chen Ying, "Rao fu chuangyi de Xingnong Niudui yangjiang mingming" (Creativity to spare—The Sinon Bulls foreign players' assigned names) (30 July 2007), http://blog .pixnet.net/ottocat/post/6884586, accessed 29 May 2008; "Taiwan nongchanpin anquan zhuisu zixunwang" ("Taiwan Agriculture and Food Traceability System"), http://taft.coa.gov .tw/index.asp?a=mp&mp=11, accessed 2 June 2008. These Sinon pesticides were both originally named for Shaolin martial arts forms.

One writer has recently compiled a history of the often strange Chinese names assigned to foreign baseball players in Taiwan. Jackson Broder, " 'Amorous Feelings': Weird Chinese Names of Former CPBL Players," 26 July 2009, http://eastwindupchronicle.com/ amorous-feelings-weird-chinese-names-of-former-cpbl-players/#comments, accessed 13 August 2009.

74. Lin Yijun, "Liangnian nei, Dao-qi yao zhu Niu fengwang" (Dodgers to help Bulls win championship within two years), *Lianhebao*, 18 December 1996, 24.

75. Deng Zhengdun, "Xingnong Dao-qi lianshou, nichuang zhibang xuexiao" (Sinon and Dodgers join hands, plan professional baseball school), *Taiwan ribao (Taiwan Daily)*, 17 February 1997, 9; Li Guoyan, "Xingnong ni fu dalu shexiao" (Sinon plans to establish school in mainland), *Lianhebao*, 17 February 1997, 24.

76. Lin Yijun, "Liang lianmeng kaimuzhan, shiwu ding shengfu" (Both leagues' opening games decided by errors), *Lianhebao*, 1 March 1997, 24; *Taiwan ribao*, 24 February 1997, 9.

77. Xu Liyu, "Chen Jinfeng zhengshi jiameng Dao-qi" (Chen Chin-feng officially joins Dodgers), *Taiwan ribao*, 6 January 1999, 22; Deng Zhengdun, "Dao-qi sahuang, Naluwan yangyan duibu gongtang" (Dodgers lie, TML threatens legal action), *Taiwan ribao*, 7 January 1999, 22.

This case was likely the impetus for the later agreements signed between MLB and the Japanese and Korean pro leagues, "preventing the Asian teams from simply becoming 'farm teams' for the major leagues . . . protecting the Asian leagues from 'American baseball imperialism.' " Guevara and Fidler, *Stealing Lives*, 28–30.

78. Gao Lisan, "Yong mengxiang ji xinxin, dazao di er ge wangguo" (Using dreams and faith to build a second kingdom), *Naluwan zhoubao (Naluwan Weekly)* 5 (4 January 1997): 2.

79. Xu Liyu, "Xiongdi jiang chonghui Heshi fengge" (Brother to bring back the Japanese way), *Taiwan ribao*, 14 August 1998, 20; Deng Zhengdun, "Dubian Jiuxin zhuanzhan Naluwan" (Watanabe Hisanobu moves to the TML), *Taiwan ribao*, 29 December 1998, 22.

80. "Ri qiuyuan haoyong, Naluwan zhidao" (TML knows the usefulness of Japanese players), *Huaxun xinwenwang (Taiwan Today News Network)*, 13 June 2000.

81. Leo Ching, "Globalizing the Regional, Regionalizing the Global: Mass Culture and Asianism in the Age of Late Capital," *Public Culture* 12, no. 1 (2000); 236.

82. "Qiuyuan quan chong mote'er: Zhanpao shanliang xianshen" (Ballplayers moon-

lighting as models, battle gear unveiled in its glory), *Naluwan zhoubao (Naluwan Weekly)* 7 (1 February 1997): 3.

83. Deng Zhengdun, "Taiyang bingquan huigui bentu" (Suns' leadership returns to local control), *Taiwan ribao,* 3 December 1998, 23.

84. This concept was most likely based on the Japanese professional soccer J-League's official "Mission" of community sport. Richard Light and Wataru Yasaki, "Breaking the Mould: J League Soccer, Community and Education in Japan," *Football Studies* 6, no. 1 (April 2003); 41–42.

This is not to say that some in the CPBL did not attempt to appeal to the local sentiment that is such an important part of Taiwanese baseball culture. The old Jungo Bears, owned by construction magnate Chen Yiping, were the first team to explicitly campaign for the loyalties of a specific city—Taizhong, the home of Chen's construction dynasty. Bears hats (designed to look like the green and gold caps worn by the then dominant Oakland Athletics) featured a "TC" (for "Taichung"), and Bears uniforms sported the Chinese characters for their home city.

85. "Jin'gang chuan qing, xiangqin xian'ai" (Robots profess their devotion, local folk present their love), *Naluwan zhoubao* 7 (1 February 1997), 6.

86. Lin Yijun, "Jin'gang, jue changqi touru zaiqu Fujian" (Robots commit to long-term reconstruction of disaster area), *Lianhebao,* 5 October 1999, 29.

87. Liu Changxin, "Yongshidui, duobiao husheng gao" (Braves' desire to compete loud and clear), *Taiwan ribao,* 12 February 1997, 9.

88. Xu Zhengyang, "Zhengzhi + bangqiu = Naluwan" (Politics + baseball = Taiwan Major League), *Ziyou shibao,* 8 November 1997, C8.

89. Gao, "Yong mengxiang ji xinxin," 2.

90. Jia Yizhen, "Li zongtong jiejian Riben Dongya daxue bangqiudui: Zhong-Ri bangqiu jiaoliu yao zai jiaqiang" (President Lee receives Japan's Asia University baseball team: Hopes to strengthen Sino-Japanese baseball ties), *Lianhebao,* 2 December 1994, 24.

91. "Zhonghua zhibang kaiqiu zhao A-bian" (CPBL asks A-bian to throw out first pitch), *Huaxun xinwenwang (Taiwan Today News Network),* 21 January 1998.

92. Xu, "Zhengzhi + bangqiu," C8.

93. Ibid.

94. Xu Zhengyang, "Zhengzhi xiu, you lai cou renao" (A political show to build excitement), *Ziyou shibao,* 28 October 1997, C8.

Magistrate Chen even included in his successful 1997 election platform the goal of rebuilding the once-proud Maple Leaf Elementary School baseball dynasty that brought glory to Taidong County thirty years earlier. Other successful candidates, like Gaoxiong County Magistrate Yu Zhengxian (known as "The Baseball Magistrate"), also made great political hay in 1997 of their efforts to build new professional baseball parks in their home districts. " 'Bangqiu xianzhang anquan shanglei,' Bangyun zhanshang defen weizhi" ("The Baseball Magistrate safely reaches base," Baseball movement moves into scoring position), *Huaxun Xinwenwang (Taiwan Today News Network),* 1 December 1997; Xu, "Zhengzhi + bangqiu," C8.

95. Jia Yizhen, "Zhenggang yingxiong de linglei 228, Taiwan dalianmeng jinwan kaida" (A heroic and alternative 28 February, TML to begin season tonight), *Lianhebao,* 28 February 1997, 24.

96. Lin Xinhui, "Yiwan siqian ren, dao Jiashi kanqiu" (Fourteen thousand to Jiayi to watch game), *Lianhebao*, 23 September 1998, 29; CPBL box scores, *Lianhebao*, 23 September 1998, 29.

97. The official recording of the anthem, performed by seven Aboriginal singers, was made into a baseball music video, and also sold in stores on an official Taiwan Major League CD. " 'Zhenggang de yingxiong' qianggong xuanchuan tantou" ("True Heroes" attacking the publicity beachheads), *Naluwan zhoubao (Naluwan Weekly)* 5 (4 January 1997); 5.

98. The first four lines of the anthem were in Mandarin, the fifth in Taiwanese, the sixth in English and Taiwanese, the seventh in Japanese and Taiwanese, the eighth in "Aborigine" and Taiwanese. Huang Jianming, "Naluwan—zhenggang de yingxiong (Naluwan zhibang lianmeng zhuti gequ)" (Naluwan—True Heroes [Taiwan Major League Theme Song]), *Naluwan zhoubao (Naluwan Weekly)* 5 (4 January 1997); 5.

99. Chen Donghao, "Yingdui qiuyuan dou shou qian, Fangshui daijia mei chang 750 wan" (Eagles players all on the take, price to throw a game is NT\$7.5 million), *Taiwan ribao*, 2 February 1997, 1. Dubbed the "Black Eagles" (*Heiying*, the team was suspended from the league in late 1997, and formally disbanded in 1998. Lin Yijun, "Jiesan! Shibao Ying fei jin lishi" (Disbanded! China Times Eagles fly into history), *Lianhebao*, 16 September 1998, 29.

100. They were Zhuo Kunyuan, Cai Minghong, and Zhang Zhengxian. Cai and Zhang were also members of the Puzi Tornadoes team that won the 1979 Little League World Series.

101. Guo Sheng'en, "Zhonghua zhibang dubo'an 'Xiaojia ban' shexian chongdang zutou" (CPBL gambling case: Xiao family suspected of being organizers), *Lianhebao*, 2 February 1997, 3; *Lianhebao*, 14 February 1997, 3.

102. After being banned from Taiwan professional baseball, Jiang got a second chance five years later in mainland China as coach of the Tianjin Lions of the new China Baseball League and manager of the PRC national team. The Tianjin team also hired fallen Taiwan stars Guo Jiancheng and Zheng Baisheng, both banned in 1997 for throwing CPBL games, as coaches. Jeffrey Wilson, "Baseball player at center of betting scandal resurfaces," *Taipei Times*, 9 May 2002, 14, www.taipeitimes.com/News/sport/archives/2002/05/09/135326, accessed 6 June 2006.

103. Gao Nianyi, "Zhibang dubo, zhishao san jituan caokong qianzhu" (Pro baseball gambling controlled by at least three groups), *Lianhebao*, 14 February 1997, 3.

104. Wu Mingliang, "Yi jiang Wu Linlian liewei shizong renkou" (Wu Linlian added to missing persons list), *Lianhebao*, 15 February 1997, 7.

105. Fu Zhihou, "Zhiyao 'fang' diao yi chang qiu, tamen gei wo erqianwan" (Just for 'throwing' one game, they gave me NT\$20 million [US\$700,000]), *Shangye zhoukan (Business Weekly)* 484 (3 March 1997); 74.

106. Cai Zhengyan, "Sanshang Hu qi qiuyuan zao heidao xiechi ouru" (Seven Mercuries Tigers players abducted, beaten, and humiliated by mob), *Lianhebao*, 7 August 1997, 1.

107. Xu Shengming, *Cuilian* (Temper and train) (Taipei: Kaite wenhua, 2007), 187.

108. Xu Zhengyang, "Dubo shanghai tiaokuan, xian na yangjiang kaidao" (Gambling harm clause operates on foreigners first), *Ziyou shibao*, 21 November 1997, C8.

109. One player who attempted to make the jump but was also found to have thrown games in the CPBL was Lion pitcher Guo Jinxing, the finest pitcher in Taiwan during the mid-1990s. He was banned from playing in either league, but soon made headlines anyway

when he was arrested in 1999 for using a knife to rob a mahjong partner of her ATM card. Lan Kaicheng, "Zhibang Tongyi Shi qian dangjia toushou Guo Jinxing she xiechi duke taoze" (Former Uni-President Lions ace Pitcher Guo Jinxing involved in abducting a gambler in order to settle debt), *Lianhebao,* 29 June 1999, 9.

110. Li Guoyan, "Zhibang shi nian saicheng qiaoding" (Schedule hammered out for pro baseball's tenth season), *Lianhebao,* 6 February 1999, 29; *Taiwan ribao,* 6 February 1999, B8.

111. Li Guoyan, "Kaiwen Kousina, yu Xiang gongwu" (Kevin Costner dances with Elephants), *Lianhebao,* 20 January 1998, 28; Li Guoyan, "Zhonghua zhibang jiu nian jiang rang Lian Zhan kaiqiu" (CPBL to let Lien Chan throw out first pitch for their ninth season), *Lianhebao,* 17 February 1998, 28.

112. Li Guoyan, "Niu Long fu dalu bisai, kewang chengxing" (Bulls-Dragons game on mainland hopefully to come about), *Lianhebao,* 31 July 1998, 29.

113. CPBL box scores, *Shijie ribao (World Journal),* 8 October 1999, B6.

114. If nothing else, downsizing to four CPBL teams solved the problem of foreign players' dominance of the league. Where there were too few good Taiwanese players to fill seven CPBL team rosters, prompting the need for so many *yangjiang,* there were enough to fill four. As of the 2000 season, CPBL teams only carried two foreign players at a time, later raising this number back to three.

115. Chris Foster, "Quite a Retro-Fit: Reliever Weber May Live in the Past a Bit, but He Has Been a Valued Addition to the Angel Bullpen," *Los Angeles Times,* 19 June 2001.

116. Matthew Tresaugue, "Weber thrives on pressure," *Press-Enterprise* (Riverside, CA), 13 September 2002; Stephanie Storm, "Ben Weber's . . . Anonymous Odyssey," *Fresno Bee,* 6 July 1999.

117. Foster, "Quite a Retro-Fit."

118. Storm, "Ben Weber's . . . Anonymous Odyssey"; Walter Hammerwold, "Weber Effective With Funky Form: Angels Reliever Getting Notice," *Daily News of Los Angeles,* 16 August 2002. Taiwanese pro baseball's shame only grew when radio announcer Vin Scully, filling time during an April 2000 appearance by Weber for the San Francisco Giants, passed these sordid stories on to millions of listeners all over Southern California.

Two-time American League all-star Melvin Mora, then playing for the New York Mets, told similarly dramatic stories about gambling in Taiwanese pro baseball to the *New York Times.* George Vecsey, "Confident Mora Still Stands," *New York Times,* July 24, 2000.

119. Ling Zhaoxiong, "Taiwan de bangqiu yundong he qu he cong" (Taiwanese baseball: Where to go from here?), *Bangqiu shijie* 1 (July 1999), 88.

120. Steve Bornfeld, "Tai Game," *Las Vegas Weekly,* 28 July 2005, www.lasvegasweekly .com/2005/07/28/feature2.html, accessed 1 August 2005.

121. Bornfeld, "Tai Game."

122. At Chen's debut at Dodger Stadium, a celebratory message from Taiwan President Chen Shui-bian was shown on the big-screen scoreboard before the game. Nike also planned for December 2002 the release of Chen's own signature baseball cleats, "Air Zoom Respect SP." Jules Quartly, "Taiwan's Chen 'dares to dream' of playoffs," *Taipei Times,* 13 September 2002, www.taipeitimes.com/news/2002/09/13/story/0000167947, accessed 6 June 2008.

123. Chen became the career leader in home runs for the Dodgers' AAA team, the Las Vegas 51s, but hit only .091 in nineteen games in the major leagues. As one columnist put

it, "As surely as the sun rises in the east, when the Los Angeles Dodgers break spring train-ing and head west, Chin-Feng Chen gets dropped off in Las Vegas." Matt Youmans, "Chen won't complain about starting year with 51s," *Las Vegas Review-Journal,* 7 April 2005, www.re-viewjournal.com/lvrj_home/2005/Apr-07-Thu-2005/sports/26239946.html, accessed 8 April 2005.

124. Lin Junfan, "Shei yao Guo Hongzhi?" (Who wants Hong-chih Kuo?), *Bangqiu shi-jie* 2 (August 1999), 62–64.

125. Lin Yijun and Li Guoyan, "'Toudu' youzhi qiuyuan . . . li suo dangran, guowai chibukai . . . huiguo zhaoyang qiangshou" (Excellent players 'steal away,' of course, but when they cannot make it abroad they come home and act like stars), *Lianhebao,* 13 July 1999, 29.

126. Troy E. Renck, "Hampton returns," ColoradoRockies.com, 4 May 2001, http://rockies.mlb.com, accessed 21 August 2001.

127. John Sickels, "Rockies right-hander Chin-hui Tsao," ESPN.com, 8 October 2003, http://sports.espn.go.com/mlb/columns/story?id=1633579, accessed 21 September 2004.

128. Lan Peiyu, "Guo Hongzhi shijian—bangqiu, rang wozai ai yi ci" (On the Hong-chih Kuo incident: Baseball, please make me love you again), *Lianhebao,* 18 July 1999, 15.

129. "Pop star gives baseball league the F word," *The China Post,* 1 April 2001, www.chi-napost.com.tw/archive/detail.asp?ID=9363&GRP=1&onNews, accessed 6 June 2008.

CONCLUSION

1. Chen Shui-bian, "Bridging the New Century: New Year's Eve Address" (31 December 2000), www.gio.gov.tw/taiwan-website/4-oa/chen/press891231.htm, accessed 5 March 2006); Chen Shui-bian, "Zongtong fabiao kua shiji tanhua" (The president's century-bridging ad-dress), the Office of the President of the Republic of China, 31 December 2000, www.president.gov.tw/1_news/index.html, accessed 30 June 2001.

2. Section epigraph: Jay Zhou (Zhou Jielun), "Jiandan ai" (Simple Love), from the album *Fantexi* (Fantasy), (Taipei: Sony BMG Taiwan, 2001).

3. Cai Wuzhang, Lin Huawei and Lin Mei-Chun, *Diancang Taiwan bangqiushi: Jianong bangqiu, 1928–2005* (The precious history of Taiwan baseball: Kanō baseball, 1928–2005) (Taipei: Xingzhengyuan tiyu weiyuanhui, 2005), 150.

4. The Braves' Australian infielders Paul Gonzalez and James Buckley were even able to participate, playing the role of the "enemy" Santa Clara team defeated by the 1969 Golden Dragons. Zeng Wenqi, "Yongshi men bu fu A-bian suo tuo" (Braves do not betray A-bian's trust), *Huaxun Xinwenwang (Taiwan Today News Network),* 21 May 2000.

5. Lisa Liang, "Fixing Taiwan baseball," *Taiwan Journal* 24, no. 2 (12 January 2007), http://taiwanjournal.nat.gov.tw/ct.asp?CtNode=122&xItem=23699, accessed 1 August 2008.

6. The Brother Elephants long led the league in this regard; in 2004 their uniforms, hats, and helmets featured more than one dozen advertisements, not including the "Salonpas" ad on the catcher's chest protector. In 2010, the Sinon Bulls' uniforms featured seventeen cor-porate logos.

7. "Chen Jinfeng—wanshi daka, youqing wujia" (Chin-feng Chen: The card to achieve anything, friendship is priceless) (11 March 2008), http://sg.sevenload.com/item/yt/oAR4 nwSvtoY, accessed 13 August 2009.

8. *Bangqiu shijie (Baseball World)* 4 (October 1999) and 5 (November 1999).

9. Deng Zhengdun, "2002 Taiwan da lianmeng qiuji kouhao 'It's My War!'" (TML league slogan for 2002: 'It's My War!'), Naluwan.com, 12 March 2002, www.naluwan.com.tw/news.php?news_id=818, accessed 16 March 2002.

10. "Zhibang shijiu nian zhutiqu! Fei wo mo shu, zhuchang: Lin Zongxing & Gao Ruiqin" (Pro baseball theme song! Nobody but me! Sung by Lin Zongxing and Gao Ruiqin), 11 March 2008, www.youtube.com/watch?v=leh2jiJKMGA, viewed 1 August 2008.

11. "Qianjin dalianmeng: Quanmin da bangqiu 2" (Advance to the major leagues: Everybody play baseball 2), 1 August 2008, www.bbonline.com.tw/cover/080801_MLB/index.html, accessed 1 August 2008.

12. "Wo shi nage wangpai? Xinli ceyan rang ni zhi" (Which ace am I? A psychological test to let you know), www.wasabii.com.tw/BBonline/event/MLBeventTest/index.html, accessed 7 August 2009.

13. Zhang Guoqin, "Qiuyuan da fangshuiqiu? Baolong qiutuan hanyuan" (Players throwing games? T-Rex owner cries out), *Zhongguo shibao (China Times)*, 24 July 2008, http://sports.chinatimes.com/2007Cti/2007Cti-News/Inc/2007cti-news-Sport-inc/Sport-Content/0,4752,11051202+112008072400414,00.html, accessed 28 July 2008.

14. "Hope for Little Leaguers: Taiwan Drops Out," *Buffalo News*, 17 April 1997.

15. "Taiwan Pulls Out of Little League," *San Jose Mercury News*, 17 April 1997.

16. Jia Yizhen, "Lixing shaobang, jinjun shijiesai" (Diligence LLB team qualifies for world championships), *Lianhebao*, 15 July 2007, D8.

17. Zhang Guoqin, "Zhonghua shaobang, ling dao Wei-lian-po-te menpiao" (ROC LLB gets ticket to Williamsport), *Zhongguo shibao (China Times)*, 15 July 2007, D8.

18. Fan Wenbin and Yuan Huixin, "Rang Guishan shaobangdui yuan Wei-lian-po-te meng" (Let the Turtle Mountain LLB team realize their Williamsport dream), NOWnews, 30 July 2009, www.nownews.com/2009/07/30/11461-2485271.htm, accessed 3 August 2009.

19. *Dahua xinwen* (Big talk news), SETV, 18 August 2004. Section epigraph: "New York Yankees Taiwanese pitcher [Chien-ming Wang]," 25 March 2007, www.youtube.com/watch?v=geeREH9pkYQ, accessed 1 August 2008.

20. Lan Zongbiao, "Tiantian you yangji, kuai bian Zhonghuadui le" (Yankees on everyday, have almost become the ROC national team), *Upaper*, 18 July 2007, 24.

21. "57 Jinqian bao: Yangji xie'e diguo da yinmou" (57 Money Explosion: The Yankee Evil Empire's great conspiracy?), 15 December 2009, www.youtube.com/user/TaiwanTalks#p/f/125/BGkTsMmWXPI, accessed 14 January 2010.

22. "Man clubbed to death for stolen baseball supplement," *China Post*, 1 October 2007, www.chinapost.com.tw/taiwan/2007/10/01/124769/Man%2Dclubbed.htm, accessed 10 October 2007.

23. For instance, in the 2006 World Baseball Classic, ace Pan Wei-lun (37–24, 2.45 ERA as a professional in Taiwan) was reserved to defeat China in Taiwan's third game, the day after an overmatched Hsu Chu-chien (22–24, 4.77 ERA) was destroyed by eventual WBC champions Japan, 14–3.

24. "Liang'an zhan: Zhonghua gaohan bang" (Cross-Straits war: ROC shouts superiority), *Shijie ribao (World Journal)*, 8 August 2008, F2.

25. There were conspiracy theories present even before the game began. Taiwan's team

had to play the morning of the fifteenth just hours after completing their game against Japan the night before; they were the only team in the whole tournament to face such a disadvantage. Huang Zhongrong and Peng Xianjun, "Zhuchang youshi? Jing Ao bangqiu saicheng anzheng Taiwan" (Zhuchang youshi? Beijing Olympic baseball schedule obscurely sets fix against Taiwan), *Ziyou shibao dianzibao (The Liberty Times)*, 11 August 2008, www.libertytimes.com.tw/2008/new/aug/11/today-t1.htm#, accessed 31 August 2008.

26. "Xuduo youxing, wuxing de shiwu, zaocheng Zhonghua shu Zhongguo" (Many visible and invisible errors make ROC lose to China), NOWnews.com, 15 August 2008, www.nownews.com/2008/08/15/91–2320806.htm, accessed 15 August 2008.

27. Hong Zhenyuan, "Yanchang 12 ju Zhonghua 7:8 zao Zhongguo nizhuan, tun xia zui beiru de yi bai" (ROC loses to China 7–8 in twelve innings, swallows the most sorrowful and insulting defeat), *Li Tai yundong bao (LT Sports)*, 15 August 2008, www.ltsports.com.tw/main/news.asp?no=60910&N_Class=2, accessed 15 August 2008.

28. Xiao Baoyang, "Shi shang zui nankan yi zhan, Taiwan sho ci shu Zhongguo" (The most embarrassing battle in history, Taiwan's first loss to China), *Yam News*, 15 August 2008, http://news.yam.com/tsna/sports/200808/20080815157685.html, accessed 15 August 2008.

29. "815 guochiri, wangyou huyu Taiwan jiangbanqi zhi'ai" (15 August a day of national humiliation, bloggers call for Taiwan to lower flag to half-mast to express grief), NOWnews .com, 15 August 2008, www.nownews.com/2008/08/15/341–2320715.htm, accessed 15 August 2008.

30. Hong Jinghong, "Aoyun zhenghou qun, qiusai nizhuan ta cu si" (An Olympic-sick people, one dies after tide turns in ballgame), *Lianhebao*, 20 August 2008, http://udn.com/NEWS/HEALTH/HEA1/4480679.shtml, accessed 28 August 2008.

31. "815 guochiri, wangyou huyu Taiwan jiangbanqi zhi'ai."

32. Zhang Yahui, "Beifuyin: 1/3 yuncai wanjia saiqian kanshuai Zhonghua dui dalu" (Taipei's Fubon Bank: one-third of sports lottery participants picked the ROC to lose against the mainland before the ballgame), *Zhongguang xinwenwang (Sina.com)*, 28 August 2008, http://news.sina.com.tw/article/20080828/764774.html, accessed 5 September 2008; "Aoyun da jiaqiu yiyun, Hong Yizhong fanwen meiti: Nimen bulei ma?" (Haze of doubts and suspicions about Olympic game-throwing, Hong Yizhong asks media: Aren't you tired?), *NOWnews*, 30 August 2008, www.nownews.com/2008/08/30/341–2327576.htm, accessed 5 September 2008; "Taiwan defeat at Beijing Olympics in focus: Reports say several members of the gambling syndicate traveled to China at the time," *Taiwan News*, 12 February 2010, www.etaiwannews.com/etn/news_content.php?id=1179291&lang=eng_news&cate_img=14 5.jpg&cate_rss=news_Sports, accessed 16 February 2010.

33. "Taiwan's baseball team Dmedia involved in foul play," *Taiwan News*, 9 October 2008, www.etaiwannews.com/etn/news_content.php?id=759107, accessed 12 October 2008; He Ruiling, et al., "Heibang hezi, zhibang Midiya laoban she da jiaqiu" (Joint venture with gangsters, pro baseball d-Media boss involved in game-fixing), *Ziyou shibao (Liberty Times)*, 9 October 2008, www.libertytimes.com.tw/2008/new/oct/9/today-t1.htm#, accessed 8 October 2008.

34. Michael Herzfeld, *Cultural Intimacy: Social Poetics in the Nation-State* (New York: Routledge, 2004), 56.

35. Lin Shuling, "Jingdiansai, A-bian: Taiwan guanjun xiang" (World Baseball Classic:

A-bian: Taiwan looks like a champion), *Zhongguo shibao (China Times)*, 23 December 2005, http://news.chinatimes.com/Chinatimes/newslist/newslist-content/0,3546,110512+112005122300306,00.html, accessed March 2006.

36. Ko Shu-ling, "Activists want Taiwan name change," *Taipei Times*, 10 December 2001, www.taipeitimes.com/News/local/archives/2001/12/10/115153, accessed 5 August 2008; "Baseball event positive lesson for Taiwan," *Liberty Times*, 7 November 2001, www.taiwan-headlines.gov.tw/20011107/2001110702.html, accessed November 2001.

37. Lin Chieh-yu, "Chen uses baseball tournament to attack KMT," *Taipei Times*, 8 November 2001, www.taipeitimes.com/news/2001/11/08/story/0000110600, accessed November 2001.

38. "Baseball event positive lesson for Taiwan."

39. Lin Yijun and Li Guoyan, "Biao haibao, bi kouhao, you qing Zheng Chenggong zuo zhen" (A whirlwind of banners, slogans abound, even asking Koxinga to suppress [the Dutch]), *Lianhebao*, 17 November 2001, 3.

40. "Gambling becomes a big pull for punters at baseball matches," *Taipei Times*, 15 November 2001, www.taipeitimes.com/news/2001/11/15/story/0000111691, accessed 5 August 2008; "Baseball as a metaphor for life," *Taipei Times*, 20 November 2001, www.taipeitimes.com/news/2001/11/20/story/0000112334, accessed 5 August 2008.

41. "'Women gan': Taiwan zai Shibangsai zhong nadao de dajiangbei" (The great prize won by Taiwan in the Baseball World Cup), *Lianhebao*, 18 November 2001, 2.

42. Zeng Wenqi, "Bangqiu feng yin bao" (Baseball insanity ignites), *Zhongguo shibao (China Times)*, 7 November 2001, 30.

43. Jeffrey Wilson, "Baseball in Chiayi a dud as volunteers outnumber the fans," *Taipei Times*, 8 November 2001, www.taipeitimes.com/news/2001/11/08/story/0000110676, accessed 5 August 2008.

44. "Baseball as a metaphor for life."

45. Ko Shu-ling, "Games bring back baseball buzz," *Taipei Times*, 18 November 2001, www.taipeitimes.com/news/2001/11/18/story/0000112039, accessed 5 August 2008.

46. Chang Chiung-fang, "Baseball Fever: Taiwan Catches It (Again) from Baseball World Cup," trans. Phil Newell, *Guanghua zazhi (Sinorama)* 26, no. 12 (December 2001): 65–66.

47. Jules Quartly, "Morning has broken for local baseball," *Taipei Times*, 14 January 2003, www.taipeitimes.com/News/sport/archives/2003/01/14/191019, accessed 5 August 2008; Jason Pan, "President heralds new era for local professional baseball," *Taiwan News*, 14 January 2003, www.etaiwannews.com/Taiwan/2003/01/14/1042505365.htm, accessed 16 January 2003.

48. Yu Junwei and Dan Gordon, "Nationalism and National Identity in Taiwanese Baseball," *NINE: A Journal of Baseball History and Culture* 14, no. 2 (Spring 2006): 36.

49. Yu Junwei, *Playing In Isolation: A History of Baseball in Taiwan* (Lincoln: University of Nebraska Press, 2007), 144–155.

50. Jason Pan, "CPBL pleads for fan backing amid corruption allegations: Acting commissioner announces tough rules including lifetime ban for guilty players," *Taiwan News*, 28 July 2005, www.etaiwannews.com/Sports/2005/07/28/1122517899.htm, accessed 30 July 2005.

51. Jason Pan, "Match-rigging claim hits Taiwan baseball," *Taiwan News*, 8 July 2005, www.etaiwannews.com/Sports/2005/07/08/1120787389.htm, accessed 10 July 2005.

52. Habibul Haque Khondker, "Glocalization as Globalization: Evolution of a Sociological Concept," *Bangladesh e-Journal of Sociology* 1, no. 2 (July 2004): 4.

53. Herzfeld, *Cultural Intimacy*, 43.

54. Ibid.

55. Lin Shuling, "Jingdiansai, A-bian."

56. Cai Surong, "Zongtong pan Taiwandui qianjin Bangqiu jingdiansai 2008 Aoyun duojin" (President looks forward to the Taiwan team advancing in the World Baseball Classic and winning gold in the 2008 Olympics), *Duowei News*, 3 March 2006, www5.chinesenewsnet .com/MainNews/SinoNews/Taiwan/cna_2006_03_03_04_00_08_088.html, accessed March 2006.

57. "Mass Rally for Embattled Taiwanese President," Agence France-Presse, 30 September 2006, http://theseoultimes.com/ST/?url=/ST/db/read.php?idx=4114, accessed 13 August 2008.

58. Herzfeld, *Cultural Intimacy*, 44.

59. Zhuang Jinguo, "Renquan, zunyan, xin Taiwan, Renquan xuanyan zai maibu" (Human rights, dignity, new Taiwan, Declaration of Human Rights marches forward again), *Xin Taiwan xinwen zhoukan (New Taiwan)* 595 (17 August 2007): 59, 60.

60. Li Ni, "Guomindang panbian fenghuo siqi" (KMT traitors fire from all directions), *Yihao renwu (Mr. Winner)* 66 (July 2007): 46–47.

61. "Ma Yingjiu, Xiao Wanchang guanfang wangzhan: Rang women yiqi chongfan bangqiuchang!!!" (Ma Ying-jeou and Vincent Siew official website: Let's get back to the baseball park!!!), http://baseball.ma19.net (now defunct).

62. Zhu Zhengting, "Tuiyi guoshou, yuanhan ru cuohang" (Former national team players cry out in grief over wrong career choice), *Xingbao* (Star news), 18 July 2004, C3; Zhong Lianfang, "Xujiu da linggong, Hongye shaobang yingxiong beige" (Heavy drinking and piece work, the tragic song of the Maple Leaf baseball heroes), *Minshengbao*, 18 July 2004, A2.

Section epigraphs: Nanfang Shuo cited in Chang Li-ke, "Taiwan bangqiu yu rentong: Yi ge yundong shehuixue de fenxi" (Taiwan baseball and identities: An analysis of sociology of sport), Master's thesis, Guoli Qinghua daxue shehuixue yanjiusuo," 66; Debby Wu, "Chen praises star baseball player for pitching excellence," *Taipei Times*, 1 August 2003, www.taipei times.com/News/taiwan/archives/2003/08/01/2003061811, accessed 12 August 2008; "Taitung Tourism," 27 December 2002, http://tour.taitung.gov.tw/english/tourinfo/districtfeature3 .asp, accessed 13 August 2008.

63. Lei Guanghan, "Hongye diaoling, banshu mei huoguo 50 sui" (Maple Leaves languish and drift, half don't live to age fifty), *Lianhebao*, 22 August 2005, A6.

64. Cheng Yuan-ching, "Hongye de gushi," 42.

65. Chen Shumei, "Beinan shaobangying de yi tian" ("A Day in the Life of the Pei Nan Baseball Camp"), *Guanghua zazhi (Sinorama)* 17, no. 9 (September 1992): 42.

66. Lin Sanfeng, "Shenyong yuanzhumin Lin Zhisheng" (The miraculously brave Aborigine Lin Zhisheng), *Zhiye bangqiu (Professional Baseball)* 297 (10 December 2006), www.cpbl.com.tw/magzine/Mag_content.asp?Pnum=297&Qnum=1, accessed 13 August 2008.

67. Lin Sanfeng, "Wang Guojin sia^n-mih long m-kia^n" (Wang Guojin fears nothing), *Zhiye bangqiu (Professional Baseball)* 268 (10 July 2004):56, 59.

68. "Tongyi qiuxing Pingdong Changle xian ai xin" (Uni-President [Lions] baseball stars bring their love to Pingdong's Changle [School]), CPBL.com, 1 May 2007, www.cpbl.com .tw/news/Newsread1.asp?Nid=4589, accessed 12 August 2008.

69. "Zhibang hao xin qing qian shi ming, yuanzhumin qiuyuan zhan qi ming" (Good news in pro baseball salaries, Seven Aborigines out of ten highest [paid]), CPBL.com, 19 March 2007, www.cpbl.com.tw/news/Newsread1.asp?Nid=4434, accessed 13 August 2008.

70. Lin Xinhui, "Chen Yixin shishen, Yongshi shuqiu" (Chen Yixin loses his spirit, Braves lose the ballgame), *Lianhebao*, 31 October 1997, 28.

71. Lin Xinhui, "Fanzai shijian" (The savage incident), *Lianhebao*, 1 November 1997, 28.

72. Lai Degang, "Shao xiao lijia yuan xiang yuan" (Leaving home young, the village gets farther away), *Zhibang mi (HIT!)* 20 (January 2005): 34.

73. Chang Li-ke, "Taiwan bangqiu yu rentong," 67.

74. Qu Hailiang, "Taiwan yuanzhumin de bangqiu chuanqi" (Taiwan Aborigines' base-ball miracle), *Shanhai wenhua (Taiwan Indigenous Voice Bimonthly)* 9 (March 1995): 27, 29.

75. Ibid., 31.

76. "Wu Junda tiyuan jing xiwang yuban yuanzhumin shijiebei" (Wu Junda submits his bright hope for an Aborigine World Cup), *Huaxun Xinwenwang (Taiwan Today News Network)*, 6 December 2003.

77. Xie Shiyuan, "Diyu bangqiu feng: Houshan chuanqi, nanguo rongguang" (Local base-ball culture: Mountaintop legends, southern glory), *Dadi dili zazhi (The Earth Geographic Monthly)* 197 (August 2004): 26.

GLOSSARY OF CHINESE, JAPANESE,
AND TAIWANESE TERMS AND NAMES

In this volume I transliterate Chinese, Japanese, and Taiwanese terms using the Hanyu Pinyin, revised Hepburn, and Taiwanese romanization forms. There are two types of exceptions: those terms that are widely known by other spellings (e.g., Taipei, Tokyo, Chiang Kai-shek, Oh Sadaharu, KMT, *Asahi Shimbun*) and the personal names of those individuals who have a documented preference for other romanizations.

A-cai　阿財

A-de　阿德

Ah Q　阿Q

Aikuai　愛快

Andō Shinya　安藤信哉

Ao Youxiang　敖幼祥

Arakawa Hiroshi　荒川博

Aramaki Ichitada　荒卷市尹

Awashima Chikage　淡島千景

A-xian　阿仙

Ba Jin　巴金

baise kongbu　白色恐怖

Baiwei　百威

banchi　蕃地

bandō　蕃童

bandō kōgakkō　蕃童公學校

Bang bangqiu　棒棒球

bangqiu　棒球

Bangqiu meiyou guoyu　棒球沒有國語

Bangqiu xiao yinghao　棒球小英豪

banjin chiimu Nōkōdan　蕃人チーム
能高團

banjin senden　蕃人宣傳

banshanren　半山人

banzoku sankōkan　蕃族參考館

baochang　包場

benleida　本壘打

bentu　本土

Brother Elephants (Xiongdi Xiang)
兄弟象

bu fen guoji, bu fen zuqun　不分國籍,
不分族群

Bu powang　補破網

225

bu shou jushu, ziyou zizai   不受拘束,
　自由自在

bu zhong bu xi   不中不西

Bunka sanbyaku nen kinen zentō chūtō
　gakkō yakyū taikai   文化三百年紀念
　全島中等學校野球大會

bunka seiji   文化政治

bushidō   武士道

Cai Huanglang   蔡惶郎

Cai Kunlin   蔡焜霖

Cai Minghong   蔡明宏

Cai Songchuan   蔡松川

Cai Songhui   蔡松輝

Cai Wuzhang   蔡武璋

Cai Zhizhong   蔡志忠

Cai Zhongnan   蔡仲南

chaiqiu   柴球

Chang Chen-yue (Zhang Zhenyue)
　張震嶽

Chen Chaoyi   陳超鎰

Chen Cheng   陳誠

Chen, Chin-feng (Chen Jinfeng)
　陳金鋒

Chen Dafeng   陳大豐

Chen Dashun   陳大順

Chen Gengyuan   陳耕元

Chen Hongpi   陳弘丕

Chen Jiannian   陳健年

Chen Jue   陳覺

Chen Qingxing   陳慶星

Chen Runbo   陳潤波

Chen Shengtian   陳盛沺

Chen Shui-bian (Chen Shuibian)   陳水扁

Chen Xiuxiong   陳秀雄

Chen Yanchuan   陳嚴川

Chen Yi   陳儀

Chen Yiping   陳一平

Chen Yixin   陳義信

Chen Zhixin   陳執信

Chen Zhiyuan   陳智源

chiah-pa khoaⁿ ia-kiu   食飽看野球

Chiang Ching-kuo (Jiang Jingguo)
　蔣經國

Chiang Kai-shek (Jiang Jieshi)   蔣介石

chihō jichi   地方自治

China Times Eagles (Shibao Ying)
　時報鷹

China Trust Whales (Hexin Jing)   和信鯨

Chiu Chuang-chin (Qiu Chuangjin)
　邱創進

Chou, Justin (Zhou Shoushun)   周守訓

Chu cai Jin yong   楚材晉用

Chu Tien-wen (Zhu Tianwen)   朱天文

Chūma Kanoe   中馬庚

Cui Jian   崔健

d-Media T-Rex (Midiya Baolong)   米迪亞
　暴龍

Dahua xinwen   大話新聞

Daimai   大每

daisharin   大車輪

Di yi yinhang   第一銀行

Dibo   帝波

dikang   抵抗

dochakuka   土着化

dōka   同化

dong Ya bingfu   東亞病夫

Dongfang tekuaiche   東方特快車

dongyang feng   東洋風

Eguchi Ryōzaburō   江口良三郎

fajue   發掘

fan zuguo   返祖國

Fang Junling   方俊靈

fangtong　仿同

fei wo mo shu　非我莫屬

First Financial Holdings Agan (Diyi Jinkong Jingang)　第一金控金剛

fulingdui　副領隊

Gao Guoqing　高國慶

gaoshan minzu　高山民族

Gaoxiong-Pingdong Thunder Gods/Fala (Gao-Ping Leigong)　高屏雷公

Genji　源治

Gijin Go Hō　義人吳鳳

Go Hō den　吳鳳伝

Go Shōsei　吳昌征

Gokoku jinja hōnō chūtō gakkō yakyū taikai　護國神社奉納中等學校野球大會

gongming zhengda de jingzheng　公明正大的競爭

Gotō Shimpei　後藤新平

Gu Jincai　古進財

Guangfu　光復

Guo Jiancheng　郭建成

Guo Jinxing　郭進興

Guo Taiyuan (Kaku Taigen)　郭泰源

Guo Yuanzhi (Kaku Genji)　郭源治

guochou　國臭

guomin youxi　國民遊戲

Guomindang　國民黨

guoqiu　國球

guoyu tuixing yundong　國語推行運動

Hagiwara Hiroshi　荻原寬

hakui no yūshi　白衣の勇士

Hamaguchi Mitsuya　濱口光也

Hao Gengsheng　郝更生

He Fan　何凡

He Xianfan　何獻凡

Heiying　黑鷹

heshi fengge　和式風格

Hezuo jinku　合作金庫

hibunmei　非文明

Higashi Kazuichi　東和一

Higashi Kumon　東公文

Higuchi Takashi　樋口孝

Hisamitsu seiyaku kabushiki kaisha　久光製薬株式会社

Hito no isshō: Taiwanjin no monogatari　人の一生: 台灣人の物語

ho ia lang　好野人

hoan-a　番仔

Hong Taishan　洪太山

Hong Tengsheng　洪騰勝

Hongye　紅葉

Hongye guxiang　紅葉故鄉

Hōraimaru　蓬萊丸

Hou Dezheng　侯德正

Hou Hsiao-hsien (Hou Xiaoxian)　侯孝賢

houyuanhui　後援會

Hsiao Bi-khim (Xiao Meiqin)　蕭美琴

Hsieh, Chang-ting (Xie Changting)　謝長廷

Hsu Chu-chien (Xu Zhujian)　許竹見

Hu Mingcheng　胡明澄

Hu Taiming　胡太明

Hu Xueli　胡學禮

Hu Yonghui　胡勇輝

huaiqiu　壞球

Huanan yinhang　華南銀行

Huang Jie　黃杰

Huang Pingyang　黃平洋

Huang Qingjing　黃清境

Huang Renhui　黃仁惠

Huang Yongxiang　黃永祥

Huang Zhengyi　黃正一

Huang Zhixiong   黃志雄

Huang Zhongyi   黃忠義

huizhang   會長

hun kou fanchi   混口飯吃

ia-kiu   野球

Imakurusu Sunao   今久留主淳

imon yakyū taikai   慰問野球大會

Inada Teruo   稻田照夫

Inoue Kaoru   井上馨

Iseda Gō   伊勢田剛

Ishii Masayuki   石井昌征

isshi dōjin   一視同仁

Itagaki Taisuke   板垣退助

Itō Jirō   伊藤次郎

Itō Masao   伊藤正雄

Japan Rising Sun Company (Nippon Asahikumi)   日本旭組

Jian Mingjing   簡明景

Jian Yongchang   簡永昌

Jiang Honghui   江紅輝

Jiang Taiquan   江泰權

Jiang Wanxing   江萬行

Jiang Weishui   蔣渭水

Jiang Zemin   江泽民

Jiangquandang   蔣犬黨

Jiayi-Tainan Braves/Luka (Jia-Nan Yongshi)   嘉南勇士

Jiayou Taiwan dui   加油台灣隊

Jin'gang   金剛

Jingbei silingbu   警備司令部

Ji-sa   紀薩

jiti jiyi   集體記憶

jiyūjin   自由人

juancun   眷村

juku   熟

Jungo Bears (Junguo Xiong)   俊國熊

ka   化

Kaiwan   怪腕

Kaku   佳久

Kangyō ginkō   勸業銀行

Kanō   嘉農

Kao, Eng-jey (Gao Yingjie)   高英傑

Keihatsukai   啟發會

Kenkō jinja   建功神社

khiukhiu   糗糗

Kigen nisen roppyaku nen hōshuku zentō chūtō gakkō yakyū taikai   紀元2600年奉祝全島中等學校野球大會

Kikuchi Kan   菊池寬

Kim Yong Woon   金容雲

Kinoshita Makoto   木下信

Kitashirakawa Yoshihisa   北白川宮能久

Kobayashi Yoshinori   小林善紀

Kodama Gen   兒玉玄

kōenkai   後援会

kōgakkō   公學校

Kojima Akira   小島憲

kōkaidō   公會堂

kokugi   国技

Kokugo   國語

kōmin rensei   皇民練成

kōminka   皇民化

kōminka undō   皇民化運動

Kondō Hyōtarō   近藤兵太郎

konjō   根性

Kōshien   甲子園

Koyae Kyoko   小八重恭子

Ku Ling   苦苓

kubetsu   區別

Kuo, Hong-Chih (Guo Hongzhi)   郭泓志

La new Bears (La new Xiong) La new 熊

Lai, Leon (Li Ming)   黎明

Lan Dehe   藍德和

Lan Deming   藍德明

laowai   老外

Lee, Lai-hua (Li Laifa)   李來發

Lee Teng-hui (Li Denghui)   李登輝

Leigong   雷公

Li Juming   李居明

Li Kunzhe   李坤哲

Li Shiji   李詩計

Li Shiming   李世明

Li Tong   李潼

Li Wei   李偉

Li Yajing   李雅景

Li Yuan   李遠

Li Zhijun   李志俊

Li Zongyuan   李宗源

Li Zongzhou   李宗洲

Liao, Hsien-hao (Liao Xianhao)   廖咸浩

Lien Chan   連戰

lihai   厲害

Lin Guixing   林桂興

Lin Huawei   林華韋

Lin Huazhou   林華洲

Lin Zhisheng   林智勝

Lin Zhupeng   林珠鵬

li-tuo-si   力脫死

Liu Canglin   劉蒼麟

Liu Jinyao   劉金約

Liu Qiunong   劉秋農

Liu Tianlu   劉天祿

Lixing   力行

Lü Mingci   呂明賜

Lu Ruitu   盧瑞圖

Lu Xun   魯迅

luanxiang   亂象

Luo Daohou   羅道厚

Luo Shawei   羅沙威

Ma Qingshan   馬晴山

Ma Ying-jeou (Ma Yingjiu)   馬英九

Macoto Cobras (Chengtai Cobras)   誠泰 Cobras

Macoto Gida (Chengtai Taiyang)   誠泰太陽

maiguozei   賣國賊

Maruyama Field (Maruyama kyūjō)   圓山球場

Mayama Uichi   真山卯一

Meile   美樂

Meilehei   美樂黑

Mercuries Tigers (Sanshang Hu)   三商虎

miaohui   廟會

minzu   民族

minzu gonghe   民族共合

minzu zhuyi   民族主義

Mishima Yukibumi   美島行武美

Mitsuya Sei   三屋靜

Miyake Sōgen   三宅宗源

mōyū Kagi Nōrin   猛雄嘉義農林

Muramatsu Ichizō   邨松一造

Musha Incident (Musha jiken)   霧社事件

mushidō   無私道

Nagashima Shigeo   長嶋茂雄

Nagayama Yoshitaka   永山義高

naichi enchō   內地延長

naichijin   內地人

Naluwan   那魯灣

Naluwan—chia^n-kang e eng-hiong   那魯灣—正港的英雄

Nanbu Chuhei   南部忠平

Nanfang Shuo   南方朔

nansei　南征

Napoli　拿坡里

neidiren　內地人

Ni, Fu-te (Ni Fude)　倪福德

ningen kikansha　人間機関車

Nishimura Kazō　西村嘉造

Nishiwaki Yoshitomo　西脇良朋

Nitobe Inazō　新渡戸稲造

nng-khi-a　兩齒仔

Nōkō　能高

nüzi laladui　女子啦啦隊

Oh Sadaharu (Ō Sadaharu)　王貞治

Okamura Toshiaki　岡村俊昭

Ōkoshi Kanji　大越貫司

Okuda Hajime　奧田元

oni kantoku　鬼監督

Ong Iok-tek (Wang Yude)　王育德

Ōshika　大鹿

osoru beki Kagi no mōki　恐るべき嘉義の
　猛氣

Ōta Masahiro　太田政弘

Pan Wei-lun (Pan Weilun)　潘威倫

Peng Mengqi　彭孟緝

Peng Ming-min (Peng Mingmin)　彭明敏

Peng Zhengmin　彭政閔

Ping Lu　平路

qiangli bangqiu　強力棒球

qiangshou　槍手

Qiaofu　巧福

Qingbang　青棒

Qingmei zhuma　青梅竹馬

Qingshaobang　青少棒

Qinmindang　親民黨

Qiu Chunguang　邱春光

Qiu Fusheng　邱復生

Qu Hailiang　瞿海良

qu zhiminhua　去殖民化

Quanjiafu　全家福

quanleida　全壘打

quanmin da bangqiu　全民打棒球

Ren de yisheng: Taiwanren de xiao gushi
　人的一生: 台灣人的小故事

renao　熱鬧

rencai baoku　人才寶庫

Rhee, Syngman　李承晚

riban jigyō　理蕃事業

Rihan seisaku taikō　理蕃政策大綱

rōshū　陋習

Sakuma Samata　佐久間左馬太

san fan dao　三番刀

san minzoku no kyōchō　三民族の
　協調

Sankyō seiyaku gaisha　三共製薬会社

sanzu gonghe　三族共和

Sasada Toshio　佐佐田利雄

sei　生

Sei Kiyoshi　瀨井清

seiban　生蕃

seibu hyōjunji　西部標準時

sententeki　先天的

shanbao　山胞

Shandi jianshe xiehui　山地建設協會

shandi pingdihua　山地平地化

Shaobang　少棒

Shaolin　少林

Shaonian bangqiu　少年棒球

Shaonian moqiu　少年魔球

Shasi Hanjian　殺死漢奸

Shen geng Taiwan, buju quanqiu　深耕
　台灣, 佈局全球

Sheng Zhuru   盛竹如

shengchan yundongyuan   盛產運動員

Shengmaige   聖麥格

shenshe   神社

Shiba Ryōtarō   司馬遼太郎

Shih Jian-hsin (Shi Jianxin)   施建新

Shimauchi Tsuneaki   島內庸明

Shimomura Hiroshi   下村宏

Shin Taiwan bunka kyōkai   新台灣文化協會

Shina   支那

Shinminkai   新民會

Shisei yonju shunen kinen Taiwan haku-rankai   始政四十周年記念臺灣博覽會

shōgakkō   小學校

Shokusan kyoku   殖產局

shudi zhuyi   屬地主義

Sinon Bulls (Xingnong Niu)   興農牛

sōbetsu shiai   送別試合

Sōkeisen   早慶戰

Song Meiling   宋美齡

Sonobe Hisashi   園部久

Soong, James (Song Chuyu)   宋楚瑜

Su Zhengsheng   蘇正生

Sun Lingfeng   孫岭峰

Sun Liren   孫立人

Sun Ta-chuan (Sun Dachuan)   孫大川

Suzuki Akira   鈴木明

Suzuki Ichirō   鈴木一朗

Tai   台

Taibei shi yinhang gonghui   台北市銀行公會

Taidu wansui   台独万岁

Tainan Giants (Tainan Juren)   台南巨人

Tainan shūritsu Kagi nōrin gakkō   台南州立嘉義農林學校

Taipei Suns/Gida (Taibei Taiyang)   台北太陽

Taisheng   台生

Taiwan bunka kyōkai   台灣文化協會

Taiwan dalianmeng   台灣大聯盟

Taiwan dianli gongsi   台灣電力公司

Taiwan duli wansui   台湾独立万岁

Taiwan jidu changlao jiaohui   台灣基督長老教會

Taiwan jinja   台湾神宮

Taiwan kōyū sōrenmei   台灣工友總聯盟

Taiwan kyōsantō   台灣共產黨

Taiwan minshūtō   台灣民眾黨

Taiwan Nichinichi Shimpō   臺灣日日新報

Taiwan nōmin kumiai   台灣農民組合

Taiwan seinen   台灣青年

Taiwan sheng bangqiu xiehui   台灣省棒球協會

Taiwan shengli Jiayi nongye zhiye xuexiao   臺灣省立嘉義農業職業學校

Taiwan shitan   台灣石炭

Taiwan shōnenkō   台灣少年工

Taiwan taiikukai no gaikyō   台灣體育界の概況

Taiwan xinshengbao   台灣新生報

Taiwan yinhang   台灣銀行

Taiwan youxian, bentu di yi   台灣優先, 本土第一

Taiwan youxian, quanqiu buju   台灣優先, 全球佈局

Taiwan zhi guang   台灣之光

Taiyang   太陽

Taizhong Jinlong   台中金龍

Taizhong Robots/Agan (Taizhong Jin'gang)   臺中金剛

Takasago   高砂

tamashii no yakyū   魂の野球

Tan, Hsin-Min (Tan Xinmin)　譚信民

Tang, Harvey (Chen Hedong)　陳河東

Tang, P. P. (Tang Panpan)　唐盼盼

tangtang zhengzheng de Zhongguoren
堂堂正正的中國人

Tazawa Sanae　田澤早苗

tianjing yundong rencai de baozang　田徑
運動人才的寶藏

tianxia Jianong　天下嘉農

tianxing　天性

Tiebushan　鐵布衫

Tieshazhang　鐵砂掌

Tobita Suishū　飛田穗州

Tonooka Mojūrō　外岡茂十郎

tōseiteki no mono　統制的のもの

Toshi taikō yakyū taikai　都市对抗野球
大会

Tōzumi Tomi　当住登美

Tsai Chin　蔡琴

Tsao, Chin-hui (Cao Jinhui)　曹錦輝

Tudi yinhang　土地銀行

Tuo Hongshan　拓弘山

Uematsu Kōichi　上松耕一

Umeno Seitarō　梅野清太郎

Undō kyōgi o hontōjin ni oyoba se
運動競技を本島人に及ばせ

Uni-President Lions (Tongyi Shi)　統一獅

waiguo zujie　外國租界

waishengren　外省人

Wang, Chen-chu (Wang Zhenzhi)　王貞治

Wang, Chien-ming (Wang Jianmin)
王建民

Wang Gongzi　王恭子

Wang Guojin　王國進

Wang Jinping　王金平

Wang Junlang　王俊郎

Wang Shifu　王仕福

Wang Yuanxuan　王元選

Wang Yuren　王裕仁

Wangzi　王子

Wei Xinwu　韋新武

Weichuan Dragons (Weichuan Long)
味全龍

Wo yao dang wangpai!　我要當王牌

women gan　我們感

Wu Bo　吳波

Wu Dunyi　吳敦義

Wu Junda　吳俊達

Wu Junliang　吳俊良

Wu Linlian　吳林煉

Wu Micha　吳密察

Wu Mingjie　吳明捷

Wu Mintian　吳敏添

Wu Nien-jen (Wu Nianzhen)　吳念真

Wu Xiangmu　吳祥木

Wu Xinheng　吳新享

Wu Zhuoliu　吳濁流

wumei jialian　物美價廉

Xia Chengying　夏承楹

Xiao Changgun　蕭長滾

Xiaoye　小野

Xie Changheng　謝長亨

Xie Dongmin　謝東閔

Xie Guocheng　謝國城

Xie Shiyuan　謝仕淵

Xie Yufa　謝欲發

Xu Jinmu　許金木

Xu Shengming　徐生明

Xu Xinliang　許信良

Xue Yongshun　薛永順

xuezhangzhi　學長制

yakyū　野球

Yakyū sokuhō　野球速報

Yamane Toshihide　山根俊英

Yamato　大和

Yan Zhenxing　閻振興

Yang, C. K. (Yang Chuanguang)　楊傳廣

Yang, Edward (Yang Dechang)　楊德昌

Yang Sen　楊森

Yang Yuanxiong　楊元雄

yangjiang　洋將

Yano　矢野

Yasuaki Taihoh (Yasuaki Taihō)　大豐泰昭

Ye Tiansong　葉天送

Ye Zhixian　葉志仙

Yingxia　鷹俠

Yō Un-hyōng　呂運亨

Yongshi　勇士

Yoshida Masao　吉田正男

Yu Hongkai　余宏開

Yu, Junwei　盂峻瑋

yu sheng ju lai　與生俱來

Yu Zhengxian　余政憲

Yuye hua　雨夜花

zaoshi　造勢

Zeng Ji'en　曾紀恩

Zeng Zhizhen　曾智偵

Zhang Guanlu　張灌錄

Zhang Meiyao　張美瑤

Zhang Taishan　張泰山

Zhang Wojun　張我軍

Zhang Xingxian　張星賢

Zhang Zhengxian　張正憲

Zhanghua yinhang　彰化銀行

Zhao Shiqiang　趙士強

Zheng Baisheng　鄭百勝

Zheng Chenggong　鄭成功

Zheng Zhaohang　鄭兆行

Zhongguo qingnian fangong jiuguotuan　中國青年反共救國團

Zhongguo shiyou　中國石油

Zhonghua minguo　中華民國

Zhonghua quanguo tiyu xiejinhui　中華全國體育協進會

Zhonghua zhiye bangqiu da lianmeng　中華職業棒球大聯盟

Zhonghua zhiye bangqiu lianmeng　中華職業棒球聯盟

Zhong-Ri qinshan youyi bangqiu bisai　中日親善友誼棒球比賽

Zhongshantang　中山堂

Zhou, Jay (Zhou Jielun)　周杰倫

Zhuang Kaiping　莊凱評

Zhuo Kunyuan　卓琨原

Ziyou Zhongguo Taiwan bangqiudui　自由中國台灣棒球隊

Ziyou Zhongguo Zhonghua bangqiudui　自由中國中華棒球隊

zuo jiayishang　作嫁衣裳

SELECTED BIBLIOGRAPHY

A note regarding citations of Chinese or Japanese publications with English subtitles: the English titles that accompany many of these publications often give insight to how an author or publisher understood a certain work, and are thus too valuable to discard or replace with my own translations. Therefore, Chinese or Japanese publications that carry English subtitles are cited to include them in parentheses and italics, as follows: *"Duli Taiwan (Viva Formosa)."* This is opposed to publications for which I provide translations, which appear with English translations in roman typeface, for example: *"Taiwan yakyū shi* (The history of baseball in Taiwan)." Also, commas have been inserted in Chinese- and Japanese-language news article titles to indicate the places where new headline lines began.

In the interests of space, I have created an extended bibliography that consists of 344 newspaper articles, newsreels, websites, and online articles cited in the notes of this volume but not included here. It is available at http://taiwanbbmorris.weebly.com/.

A-bian zongtong dianzibao 阿扁總統電子報 (President A-bian's electronic bulletin).

Ai-bo-er 艾波爾. "Hongye shaobangdui 'zisheng' ji" 紅葉少棒隊'自生'記 (Record of the Maple Leaf youth baseball team's quest to survive). *Xinwen tiandi* 新聞天地 *(Newsdom)* 24, no. 36 (7 September 1968): 17.

Aka Tami 緋蒼生. "Higashi Taiwan he, Karenkō chō ka no bu" 東臺灣へ, 花蓮港廳下の部 (Eastern Taiwan: Karenkō Prefecture section). In *Higashi Taiwan kenkyū sōsho, dai ichi hen* 東臺灣研究叢書, 第一編 (Eastern Taiwan Research Series, volume 1), pp. 5–74. Taihoku: Higashi Taiwan kenkyūkai 東臺灣研究會, 1925; reprint, Taipei: Chengwen chubanshe 成文出版社, 1985.

Allen, Joseph R. "Taipei Park: Signs of Occupation." *Journal of Asian Studies* 66, no. 1 (February 2007): 159–199.

Ano Kōji 阿野鉱二. *Renjian Wang Zhenzhi* 人間王貞治 (Oh Sadaharu the Man). Translated by Zhang Beilei 章蓓蕾. Taipei: Maitian chuban gufen youxian gongsi 麥田出版股份有限公司, 1998.

Ao Youxiang 敖幼祥. *Zhibang kuangxiangqu* 職棒狂想曲 (Pro baseball rhapsody). Taipei: Zhonghua zhibang shiye gufen youxian gongsi 中華職棒事業股份有限公司, 1994.

Appleton, Sheldon L. "Taiwan: The Year it Finally Happened." *Asian Survey* 12, no. 1 (1972): 32–37.

Ariyama Teruo 有山輝雄. *Kōshien yakyū to Nihonjin: Media no tsukutta ibento* 甲子園野球と日本人：メディアのつくったイベント (Kōshien baseball and the Japanese: Media-created events). Tokyo: Yoshikawa kobunkan 吉川弘文館, 1997.

Arnold, Julean H. *Education in Formosa.* Washington, DC: Government Printing Office, 1908.

"Athletic Sports: Amazing Development and World Recognition." *Present-Day Nippon, 1934: Annual English Supplement of the Asahi, Osaka and Tokyo.* Tokyo, 1934.

Azumada Itsusaku 東田一朔. *Puro yakyū tanjō zenya: Kyūshi no kūhaku o umeru* プロ野球誕生前夜：球史の空白をうめる (The eve of the birth of pro baseball: Filling a gap in baseball history). Tokyo: Tōkai daigaku shuppansha 東海大學出版社, 1989.

"Bangqiu de haizi: Jinlong de gushi" 棒球的孩子: 金龍的故事 (The children of baseball: The Golden Dragons' story). Tape two of a ten-part series. Taipei: Gonggong dianshi wenhua shiye jijinhui 公共電視文化事業基金會, 2000.

"Bangqiu de haizi: Juren de gushi" 棒球的孩子: 巨人的故事 (The children of baseball: The Giants' story). Tape four of a ten-part series. Taipei: Gonggong dianshi wenhua shiye jijinhui 公共電視文化事業基金會, 2000.

"Bangqiu de haizi: Puzi Ronggong de gushi" 棒球的孩子: 朴子榮工的故事 (The children of baseball: The Puzi and Ronggong stories). Tape ten of a ten-part series. Taipei: Gonggong dianshi wenhua shiye jijinhui 公共電視文化事業基金會, 2000.

"Bangqiu de haizi: Qihu de gushi" 棒球的孩子: 七虎的故事 (The children of baseball: The Seven Tigers' story). Tape three of a ten-part series. Taipei: Gonggong dianshi wenhua shiye jijinhui 公共電視文化事業基金會, 2000.

"Bangqiu de haizi: Zonglun" 棒球的孩子: 總論 (The children of baseball: Introduction). Tape one of a ten-part series. Taipei: Gonggong dianshi wenhua shiye jijinhui 公共電視文化事業基金會, 2000.

"Bangqiu xiao yinghao" 棒球小英豪 (Little baseball hero [part 1]). *Wangzi* 王子 (Prince magazine) 82 (1 July 1970): 153–167.

"Bangqiu xiao yinghao 2." 棒球小英豪 2 (Little baseball hero, part 2). *Wangzi* 83 (15 July 1970): 21–35.

"Bangqiu xiao yinghao" 棒球小英豪 (Little baseball hero [part 3]). *Wangzi* 84 (1 August 1970): 59–73.

Barclay, Paul D. "'Gaining Confidence and Friendship' in Aborigine Country: Diplomacy, Drinking, and Debauchery on Japan's Southern Frontier." *Social Science Japan Journal* 6, no. 1 (2003): 77–96.

Bēsubōru Magajinsha ベ-スボ-ルマガジン社, ed. *Nihon puro yakyū rokujūnenshi* 日本プロ野球六十年史 (Sixty years' history of Japanese professional baseball). Tokyo: Bēsubōru Magajinsha, 1994.

Bhabha, Homi K. *The Location of Culture.* New York: Routledge, 1994.

Boorman, Howard, ed. *Biographical Dictionary of Republican China,* volume 4. New York: Columbia University Press, 1971.

Buford, Bill. *Among the Thugs: The Experience, and the Seduction, of Crowd Violence.* New York: W. W. Norton, 1991.

Cahn, Susan K. *Coming on Strong: Gender and Sexuality in Twentieth-Century Women's Sport.* New York: Maxwell Macmillan, 1994.

Cai Qinghui 蔡清輝. "Nanwang de 'Jiayi Nonglin' qingjie" 難忘的'嘉義農林'情結 (The unforgettable 'Kagi Agriculture and Forestry' complex). *Jianongren* 嘉農人 6 (November 2002): 58–69.

Cai Wuzhang 蔡武璋. "Jianong bangqiu shi" 嘉農棒球史 (A history of Kanō baseball). *Jianongren* 嘉農人 1 (November 1997): 28–36.

Cai Wuzhang 蔡武璋, Lin Huawei 林華韋, and Lin Mei-Chun 林玫君 (Lin Meijun). *Diancang Taiwan bangqiushi: Jianong bangqiu, 1928–2005* 典藏台灣棒球史: 嘉農棒球 1928–2005 (The precious history of Taiwan baseball: Kanō baseball, 1928–2005). Taipei: Xingzhengyuan tiyu weiyuanhui 行政院體育委員會, 2005.

Cai Zhenxiong 蔡禎雄. *Riju shidai Taiwan shifan xuexiao tiyu fazhanshi* 日據時代臺灣師範學校體育發展史 (The history of the development of normal school physical education in Japanese-occupied Taiwan). Taipei: Shida shuyuan 師大書苑, 1998.

Cai Zongxin 蔡宗信. "Riju shidai Taiwan bangqiu yundong fazhan guocheng zhi yanjiu—yi 1895 (Mingzhi 28) nian zhi 1926 (Dazheng 15) nian wei zhongxin" 日據時代台灣棒球運動發展過程之研究—以 1895 (明治28) 年至1926 (大正15) 年為中心 ("Research into the Development of Taiwanese Baseball during the Japanese Occupation"). Master's thesis, Guoli Taiwan shifan daxue tiyu yanjiusuo 國立臺灣師範大學體育研究所, 1992.

———. "Taiwan dongbu yuanzhumin bangqiu yundong zhi fazhan" 台灣東部原住民棒球運動之發展 (The development of baseball among Taiwan's eastern Aborigines). *Shanhai wenhua* 山海文化 *(Taiwan Indigenous Voice Bimonthly)* 9 (March 1995): 37–43.

Campanis, Al. *The Dodgers' Way to Play Baseball.* New York: E. P. Dutton, 1954.

Carry, Peter. "Going To Bat For Taiwan." *Sports Illustrated,* 19 August 1974: 64–74.

Cashman, Richard. "The Subcontinent." In *The imperial game: Cricket, culture and society,* edited by Brian Stoddart and Keith A. P. Sandiford, pp. 116–134. New York: Manchester University Press, 1998.

Chang Chi-hsiung 張啟雄 (Zhang Qixiong) and Pan Kwang-che 潘光哲 (Pan Guangzhe), interviewers. Wang Ching-ling 王景玲 (Wang Jingling), recorder. *Tang Mingxin xiansheng fangwen jilu* 湯銘新先生訪問紀錄 *(The Reminiscences of Mr. Tang Ming-hsin).* Taipei: Zhongyanyuan jindaishi yanjiusuo 中研院近代史研究所, 2005.

Chang Chiung-fang. "Baseball Fever: Taiwan Catches It (Again) from Baseball World Cup." Translated by Phil Newell. *Guanghua zazhi* 光華雜誌 *(Sinorama)* 26, no. 12 (December 2001): 65–66.

Chang, Kao-wu. "Giants of boys' baseball." *Free China Review* 21, no. 9 (September 1971): 27–31.

Chang Li-ke 張力可 (Zhang Like). "Taiwan bangqiu yu rentong: Yi ge yundong shehuixue de fenxi" 台灣棒球與認同: 一個運動社會學的分析 ("Taiwan Baseball and Identities: An Analysis of Sociology of Sport"). Master's thesis, Guoli Qinghua daxue shehuixue yanjiusuo 國立清華大學社會學研究所, 2000.

Chang, Mau-Kuei. "Middle Class and Social and Political Movements in Taiwan: Questions and Some Preliminary Observations." In *Discovery of the Middle Classes in East Asia*, edited by Hsin-Huang Michael Hsiao, pp. 121–176. Taipei: Academia Sinica Institute of Ethnology, 1993.

Changrong kongzhong shangdian 長榮空中商店 *(EVA Sky Shop)*. Taoyuan: Changrong guoji gufen youxian gongsi 長榮國際股份有限公司 2000.

Chen Bijia 陳必佳. "Tan shaobang yundong yu minzu zixinxin de huifu" 談少棒運動與民族自信心的恢復 (On the Little League Baseball movement and the recovery of racial self-confidence). *Daxue zazhi* 大學雜誌 *(The Intellectual)* 69 (October 1973): 23–26.

Chen, Cheng-Siang. *The Sugar Industry of Taiwan.* Taipei: Fu-Min Institute of Agricultural Geography, 1955.

Chen, Chia-Mou 陳嘉謀 (Chen Jiamou). "Guangfu chuqi Taibei shi guomin xuexiao bangqiu fazhan yanqiu" 光復初期台北市國民學校棒球發展研究 ("The Research of Primary School Baseball Development in Taipei City in the Initial Period of Restoration"). *Tiyu xuebao* 體育學報 *(Bulletin of Physical Education)* 30 (March 2001): 91–100.

———. "Guangfu chuqi Taibei shi yinhang gonghui bangqiudui fazhan yanjiu (1948–1968)" 光復初期台北市銀行公會棒球隊發展研究 (1948–1968) ("Early Post-Recovery Period Taipei Bankers Association Baseball League Development Research [1948–1968]"). *Tiyu xuebao* 體育學報 *(Bulletin of Physical Education)* 32 (March 2002): 253–264.

———. "Taiwan guomin xuexiao bangqiu yundong fazhan zhi yanjiu (1945–1968)" 台灣國民學校棒球運動發展之研究 (1945–1968) (Research into the development of elementary school baseball in Taiwan, 1945–1968). *Taidong shiyuan xuebao* 台東師院學報 (Taidong Normal University Bulletin) 13, no. 1 (2002): 137–170.

Chen Dashun 陳大順. "Zhaochu wenti, jiejue wenti" 找出問題, 解決問題 (Locate the problem, solve the problem). *Zhiye bangqiu* 職業棒球 *(Professional Baseball)* 219 (12 June 2000): 19–21.

Chen, Jackie. "How We Feel About the Japanese—An Aborigine Speaks." Translated by David Mayer. *Guanghua zazhi* 光華雜誌 *(Sinorama)* 24, no. 3 (March 1999): 91, 93.

———. "Major League Controversies—Professional Baseball Enters a New Era." Translated by Phil Newell. *Guanghua zazhi* 光華雜誌 *(Sinorama)* 21, no. 3 (March 1996): 76–87.

———. "Voices from a Buried History—The Takasago Volunteers." Translated by Christopher MacDonald. *Guanghua zazhi* 光華雜誌 *(Sinorama)* 24, no. 3 (March 1999): 78–91.

Chen, Lung-chu, and W. M. Reisman. "Who Owns Taiwan: A Search for International Title." *The Yale Law Journal* 81, no. 4 (March 1972): 599–671.

Chen Shouyong 陳守庸. "Zoufang 94 gaoling de Jianong yuanlao Tuo Hongshan" 走訪94高齡的嘉農元老拓弘山 (A visit with the ninety-four-year-old Kanō elder Tuo Hongshan). *Guomin tiyu jikan* 國民體育季刊 131 (December 2001): 103–110.

Chen Shui-bian 陳水扁. "Bridging the New Century: New Year's Eve Address" (31 December 2000). www.gio.gov.tw/taiwan-website/4-oa/chen/press891231.htm (accessed 5 March 2006).

———. "Zongtong fabiao kua shiji tanhua" 總統發表跨世紀談話 (The president's century-bridging address). The Office of the President of the Republic of China, 31 December 2000. www.president.gov.tw/1_news/index.html (accessed 30 June 2001).

Chen Shumei 陳淑美. "Beinan shaobangying de yi tian" 卑南少棒營的一天 ("A Day in the

Life of the Pei Nan Baseball Camp"). *Guanghua zazhi* 光華雜誌 *(Sinorama)* 17, no. 9 (September 1992): 40–44.

Chen, Wei-chi. "From Raw to Cooked: The Identity of the Kavalan People in the Nineteenth Century." In *In Search of the Hunters and Their Tribes: Studies in the History and Culture of the Taiwan Indigenous People,* edited by David Faure, 28–38. Taibei: Shung Ye Museum of Formosan Aborigines Publishing 順益台灣原住民博物館, 2001.

Chen Wenfa 陳文發. "Taiwan shaonian de guangrong, Taiwanren de shengli" 台灣少年的光榮, 台灣人的勝利 (Glory of Taiwanese youth, victory of the Taiwanese people). *Taiwan qingnian* 台灣青年 (Taiwan youth) 106 (5 September 1969): 3.

Chen Yingzhen 陳映真. "Di yi jian chaishi" 第一件差事 (First assignment). In *Di yi jian chaishi* 第一件差事 (First assignment). Taipei: Yuanjing 遠景, 1975.

Chen Yiping 陳一平. *Baimao pindao* 白毛頻道 *(Channel White).* Taizhong: Shuiyong chubanshe 水永出版社, 1997.

Cheng Jiahui 程佳惠. *Taiwan shi shang di yi da bolanhui: 1935 nian meili Taiwan SHOW* 台灣史上第一大博覽會: 1935年魅力台灣SHOW (Taiwan's first exposition: The enchanting Taiwan show of 1935). Taipei: Yuanliu 遠流, 2004.

Cheng Sheng 程笙. "Yongyuan de Hongye" 永遠的紅葉 (Maple Leaf forever). *Shiyou yuekan* 師友月刊 *(The Educator Monthly)* 339 (September 1995): 62–67.

Cheng Yuan-ching 鄭元慶. "Hongye de gushi" 紅葉的故事 ("Red Leaves of Baseball Past"). *Guanghua zazhi* 光華雜誌 *(Sinorama)* 18, no. 1 (January 1993): 42–45.

Ching, Leo T. S. *Becoming "Japanese": Colonial Taiwan and the Politics of Identity Formation.* Berkeley: University of California Press, 2001.

———. "Globalizing the Regional, Regionalizing the Global: Mass Culture and Asianism in the Age of Late Capital." *Public Culture* 12, no. 1 (2000): 233–257.

———. "Savage Construction and Civility Making: The Musha Incident and Aboriginal Representations in Colonial Taiwan." *positions* 8, no. 3 (Winter 2000): 795–818.

"Chokurei dai hyaku rokujūnana gō: Hyōjunji ni kan suru ken" 勅令第百六十七号・標準時ニ関スル件 (Imperial Ordinance No. 167: On Standard Time). 27 December 1895. National Archives of Japan Document No. A03020211600, www.jacar.go.jp/index.html (accessed 1 August 2009).

Chou Wen-yao 周婉窈 (Zhou Wanyao). "Taiwanren di yi ci de 'guoyu' jingyan—xilun Rizhi moqi de Riyu yundong jiqi wenti" 台灣人第一次的「國語」經驗—析論日治末期的日語運動及其問題 (The Taiwanese people's first experience with a "national language"—An analysis of the Japanese language movement during late Japanese rule). *Xin shixue* 新史學 (New Historiography) 6, no. 2 (June 1995): 113–159.

Chuanqi yu guangrong 傳奇與榮耀 (Legend and glory). Disk no. 2 of the ten-disk set *Taiwan shiji tiyu mingren zhuan* 臺灣世紀體育名人傳 (Biographies of famous Taiwanese athletes of the [20th] century). Taipei: Xingzhengyuan tiyu weiyuanhui 行政院體育委員會, 2002.

Chun, Allen. "The Coming Crisis of Multiculturalism in 'Transnational' Taiwan." *Social Analysis* 46, no. 2 (Summer 2002): 102–122.

———. "Democracy as Hegemony, Globalization as Indigenization, or the 'Culture' in Taiwanese National Politics." *Journal of Asian and African Studies* 35, no. 1 (February 2000): 7–27.

Cohen, Paul A. *Speaking to History: The Story of King Goujian in Twentieth-Century China.* Berkeley: University of California Press, 2009.

Cohn, Bernard S. *Colonialism and Its Forms of Knowledge: The British in India.* Princeton, NJ: Princeton University Press, 1996.

Coole, Arthur Braddan. *A Troubleshooter For God in China.* Mission, KS: Inter-Collegiate Press, 1976.

Cronin, Mike. *Sport and Nationalism in Ireland: Gaelic Games, Soccer and Irish Identity Since 1884.* Portland, OR: Four Courts Press, 1999.

Crossley, Pamela Kyle. *A Translucent Mirror: History and Identity in Qing Imperial Ideology.* Berkeley: University of California Press, 1999.

Cui Jian 崔健. "Yi kuai hong bu" 一塊紅布 (A piece of red cloth). *Jiejue* 解決 (Resolution). Beijing: Zhongguo wencai shengxiang chuban gongsi 中国文采声像出版公司, 1991.

Cvetkovich, A., and D. Kellner. "The Intersection of the Local and the Global." In *Globalization: The Reader,* edited by John Beynon and David Dunkerley, 134–135. New York: Routledge, 2001.

Dang, Winston T., ed., *Taiwangate: Documents on the blacklist policy and human rights of Taiwan.* Washington, DC: Center for Taiwan International Relations, 1991.

Darnton, Robert. *The Great Cat Massacre and Other Episodes In French Cultural History.* New York: Basic Books, 1984.

De Ceuster, Koen. "Wholesome education and sound leisure: The YMCA sports programme in colonial Korea." *European Journal of East Asian Studies* 2, no. 1 (2003): 53–88.

Deane, Hugh. *The Korean War, 1945–1953.* San Francisco: China Books and Periodicals, 1999.

Di qi jie quanguo yundonghui huikan 第七屆全國運動會會刊 (Official publication of the Seventh National Games). Shanghai: Shenbaoguan 申報館, 1948.

Dickinson, Frederick R. *War and National Reinvention: Japan in the Great War, 1914–1919.* Cambridge, MA: Harvard University Asia Center and Harvard University Press, 1999.

Dimeo, Paul. "Football and Politics in Bengal: Colonialism, Nationalism, Communalism." In *Soccer in South Asia: Empire, Nation, Diaspora,* edited by Paul Dimeo and James Mills, 57–74. Portland, OR: Frank Cass Publishers, 2001.

Duara, Prasenjit. *Sovereignty and Authenticity: Manchukuo and the East Asian Modern.* Rowman and Littlefield, 2003.

Dudden, Alexis. *Japan's Colonization of Korea: Discourse and Power.* Honolulu: University of Hawai'i Press, 2005.

Eiji Oguma. *A Genealogy of 'Japanese' Self-Images.* Translated by David Askew. Melbourne: Trans Pacific Press, 2002.

Fang Junling 方俊靈. "Zhidao Juren shaobangdui de jingguo ji ganxiang" 指導巨人少棒隊的經過及感想 (Thoughts on the experience of coaching the Giants youth baseball team). *Guo jiao zhi you* 國教之友 (Friend of the nation's teachers) 373 (December 1971): 34–40.

Fanon, Frantz. *The Wretched of the Earth.* 1963. Reprint, New York: Grove, 1968.

Fine, Gary Alan. *With the Boys: Little League Baseball and Preadolescent Culture.* Chicago: University of Chicago Press, 1987.

Fitts, Robert K. *Remembering Japanese Baseball: An Oral History of the Game.* Carbondale: Southern Illinois University Press, 2005.

Fong, Barry Shiaw-Chian. "Civilization and Individual Identities: Ye Shengji's Quest for Colonial Self in Two Cultures." *Issues & Studies* 34, no. 10 (October 1998): 93–124.

Fong Shiaw-Chian. "Hegemony and Identity in the Colonial Experience of Taiwan, 1895–1945." In *Taiwan Under Japanese Colonial Rule, 1895–1945: History, Culture, Memory,* edited by Ping-hui Liao and David Der-Wei Wang, 160–183. New York: Columbia University Press, 2006.

Franck, Harry A. *Glimpses of Japan and Formosa.* New York: Century Co., 1924.

Fu Zhihou 傅之後. "Zhiyao 'fang' diao yi chang qiu, tamen gei wo erqianwan"只要 '放' 掉一場球, 他們給我二千萬 (Just for 'throwing' one game, they gave me NT$20 million [US$700,000]). *Shangye zhoukan* 商業週刊 *(Business Weekly)* 484 (3 March 1997): 72–76.

Fujii Shizue 藤井志津枝. *Riju shiqi Taiwan zongdufu de lifan zhengce* 日據時期臺灣總督府的理蕃政策 (*The Aborigines Policy of Taiwan Government-General in the Period of the Japanese Dominance [1895–1915]*). Taipei: Guoli Taiwan shifan daxue lishi yanjiusuo 國立臺灣師範大學歷史研究所, 1989.

Furōsei 不老生. "Taihoku yakyū senshi (ichi)" 臺北野球戰史(一) (The history of Taihoku baseball, part 1). *Undō to shumi* 1, no. 1 (November 1916): 2–5.

Gabardi, Wayne. *Negotiating Postmodernism.* Minneapolis: University of Minnesota Press, 2001.

Gabay, J. Jonathan. "Let's integrate baby." www.gabaynet.com/above_the_line.htm, 6 February 2004 (accessed 3 February 2005).

Gao Lisan 高立三. "Yong mengxiang ji xinxin, dazao di er ge wangguo" 用夢想及信心, 打造第二個王國 (Using dreams and faith to build a second kingdom). *Naluwan zhoubao* 那魯灣週報 *(Naluwan Weekly)* 5 (4 January 1997): 2.

Gao Zhengyuan 高正源. *Dong sheng de xuri: Zhonghua bangqiu fazhan shi* 東昇的旭日:中華棒球發展史 (Rising sun in the east: The history of the development of Chinese baseball). Taipei: Minshengbao she 民生報社, 1994.

———. *Lü Mingci chuanqi: mai xiang juren zhi lu* 呂明賜傳奇: 邁向巨人之路 (The legend of Lü Mingci: His road to the Giants). Taipei: Minshengbao she 民生報社, 1988.

———. *Shanyao yibai sheng: Guo Taiyuan* 閃耀一百勝: 郭泰源 (One hundred shining victories: Guo Taiyuan). Taipei: Minshengbao she 民生報社, 1994.

———. "Taiwan zhibang, nian nian xifu ao cheng po . . . " 台灣職棒, 廿年媳婦熬成婆 . . . (Taiwanese pro baseball—After twenty years the daughter-in-law has proudly become a mother-in-law . . .). *Zhonghua bangqiu zazhi* 中華棒球雜誌 *(R.O.C. Baseball Quarterly)* 21 (December 1988): 4–8.

———. "Yuanzhumin yu Taiwan bangyun (shang)" 原住民與台灣棒運(上) (Aborigines and Taiwan's baseball movement, part 1). *Shanhai wenhua* 山海文化 *(Taiwan Indigenous Voice Bimonthly)* 9 (March 1995): 32–36.

Garver, John W. *The Sino-American Alliance: Nationalist China and American Cold War Strategy in Asia.* Armonk, NY: M. E. Sharpe, 1997.

Gong Shusen 龔樹森. *Tieren Yang Chuanguang* 鐵人楊傳廣 (Iron Man C.K. Yang). Taipei: Zhongwai tushu chubanshe 中外圖書出版社, 1977.

Gotō, Baron Shimpei. "The Administration of Formosa (Taiwan)." In *Fifty Years of New Japan (Kaikoku gojūnen shi),* compiled by Shigenobu Okuma, edited by Marcus B. Huish, 530–553. 2nd ed. Vol. 2. London: Smith, Elder, & Co., 1910.

The Government-General of Taiwan. *Taiwan (Formosa): Its System of Communications and*

Transportation, Submitted by the Japanese Delegate for Taiwan to the Ninth Conference of the International Postal Union, Held at London, May, 1929. Taihoku: The Government-General of Taiwan, 1929.

Grasmuck, Sherri. *Protecting Home: Class, Race, and Masculinity in Boys' Baseball.* New Brunswick, NJ: Rutgers University Press, 2005.

Gu Hong 孤紅. *Zhibang yangjiang xing chouwen: Jiefa nüqiumi yu yangjiang de taose jiaoyi* 職棒洋將性醜聞: 揭發女球迷與洋將的桃色交易 (Foreign pro baseball players' sex scandals: Exposing the illicit relations between female baseball fans and foreign players). Taipei: Rizhen chubanshe 日臻出版社, 1997.

"Guaiwan—Lan Deming" 怪腕—藍德明 (Fantastic Arm—Lan Deming). *Changchun yuekan* 常春月刊 (Evergreen monthly) 6 (November 1983): 84–85.

Guevara, Arturo J. Marcano, and David P. Fidler. *Stealing Lives: The Globalization of Baseball and the Tragic Story of Alexis Quiroz.* Bloomington: Indiana University Press, 2002.

Guha, Ramachandra. "Cricket and Politics in Colonial India." *Past and Present* 161 (November 1998): 155–190.

Gumbrecht, Hans Ulrich. *In 1926: Living At the Edge of Time.* Cambridge, MA: Harvard University Press, 1997.

Guo Cheng 郭成. "Fazhan ziji de zhiye bangqiudui" 發展自己的職業棒球隊 (Develop our own professional baseball teams). *Ziyou qinginian* 自由青年 (Free youth) 73, no. 1 (January 1985): 32–34.

Guo Jianyi 郭健一. "Zhibang, buneng zai tuo yi tian" 職棒, 不能再拖一天 (Pro baseball—can't delay another day). *Zhonghua bangqiu zazhi* 中華棒球雜誌 *(R.O.C. Baseball Quarterly)* 19 (June 1988): 50–51.

Guo Yuanzhi 郭源治. *Reqiu* 熱球 (Fireball). Taipei: Xin zhongyuan chubanshe 新中原出版社, 1998.

Guy, Nancy. "Farewell to Rational Actors: Music, Emotion, and Social Movement in Taiwan." Presented at the conference on Taiwan Studies in International Perspectives, University of California, Santa Barbara, 26 October 2007.

Hall, Stuart. "When Was 'The Post-Colonial'? Thinking at the Limit." In *The Postcolonial Question: Common Skies, Divided Horizons,* edited by Iain Chambers and Lidia Curti, 242–260. New York: Routledge, 1996.

Harrison, Mark. *Legitimacy, Meaning, and Knowledge in the Making of Taiwanese Identity.* New York: Palgrave Macmillan, 2006.

Hauptman, Laurence M., and Ronald G. Knapp. "Dutch-Aboriginal Interaction in New Netherland and Formosa: An Historical Geography of Empire." *Proceedings of the American Philosophical Society* 121, no. 2 (April 1977): 166–182.

He Ping 何平, dir. *Ganen suiyue* 感恩月歲 *(Honor Thy Father).* Taipei: Zhongyang dianying 中央電影, 1989 film.

Herzfeld, Michael. *Cultural Intimacy: Social Poetics in the Nation-State.* 2nd edition. New York: Routledge, 2004.

Hoch, Paul. *White hero, Black beast: Racism, sexism, and the mask of masculinity.* London: Pluto Press, 1979.

Hsiao, Frank S. T., and Lawrence R. Sullivan. "A Political History of the Taiwanese Communist Party, 1928–1931." *Journal of Asian Studies* 42, no. 2 (February 1983): 269–289.

Hsiao Yeh (Xiaoye 小野). "Forced Out." In *Winter Plum: Contemporary Chinese Fiction,* edited by Nancy Ing, 137–151. Taipei: Chinese Materials Center, 1982.

Hsiau A-chin. *Contemporary Taiwanese Cultural Nationalism.* New York: Routledge, 2000.

Hsu Chung Mao 徐宗懋 (Xu Zongmao). *Riben qingjie: cong Jiang Jieshi dao Li Denghui* 日本情結:從蔣介石到李登輝 *(The Japan Complex—From President Chiang Kai-Shek to President Lee Teng-Hui).* Taipei: Tianxia wenhua 天下文化, 1997.

Hsu Hsueh-chi 許雪姬 (Xu Xueji). "Taiwan Guangfu chuqi de yuwen wenti" 台灣光復初期的語文問題 (Language questions from early retrocession period in Taiwan). *Si yu yan* 思與言 *(Thought and Words)* 29, no. 4 (December 1991): 155–184.

———. "Tamen weishenme 'pangguan': Tan *Pangguan Zazhi* de shidai yiyi" 他們為什麼「旁觀」: 談《旁觀雜誌》的時代意義 (Why were they 'spectators'? On the historical significance of *The Spectacle Miscellanea*). *Quanguo xinshu zixun yuekan* 全國新書資訊月刊 *(New Books: Recent Publications in Taiwan, ROC)* no. 105 (September 2007): 57–66.

Huang Chih-Huei. "The Transformation of Taiwanese Attitudes toward Japan in the Postcolonial Period." In *Imperial Japan and National Identities in Asia, 1895–1945,* edited by Narangoa Li and Robert Cribb, 296–314. New York: RoutledgeCurzon, 2003.

Huang Jianming 黃建銘. "Naluwan—zhenggang de yingxiong (Naluwan zhibang lianmeng zhuti gequ)" 那魯灣—正港的英雄 (那魯灣職棒聯盟主體歌曲) (Naluwan—True Heroes [Taiwan Major League Theme Song]). *Naluwan zhoubao* 那魯灣週報 *(Naluwan Weekly)* 5 (4 January 1997): 5.

Huang Ying-Che. "Were Taiwanese Being 'Enslaved'? The Entanglement of Sinicization, Japanization, and Westernization." In *Taiwan under Japanese Colonial Rule, 1895–1945: History, Culture, Memory,* edited by Ping-hui Liao and David Der-Wei Wang, 312–326. New York: Columbia University Press, 2006.

Jacobs, J. Bruce. "Taiwanese and the Chinese Nationalists, 1937–1945: The Origins of Taiwan's 'Half-Mountain People' (Banshan ren)." *Modern China* 16, no. 1 (January 1990): 84–118.

———. "Taiwan's Colonial History and Post-Colonial Nationalism." Presented at the conference on Taiwan Studies in International Perspectives, University of California, Santa Barbara, 27 October 2007.

Jacoby, Neil H. *U.S. Aid to Taiwan: A Study of Foreign Aid, Self-Help, and Development.* New York: Frederick A. Praeger, 1966.

James, C. L. R. *Beyond a Boundary.* Durham, NC: Duke University Press, 1993.

———. *Cricket.* Edited by Anna Grimshaw. New York: Allison and Busby, 1986.

"Japan as a Colonizing Power." *Spectator* (23 March 1907): 447–448.

Ji Wei 季薇. "Huaxing yu Juren" 華興與巨人 (Huaxing [Middle School] and the Giants). *Zhongyang yuekan* 中央月刊 (Central monthly) 5, no. 12 (October 1973): 40–42.

Jian Yongchang 簡永昌. *Bangqiu yu wo* 棒球與我 (Baseball and me). Taipei: self-published, 1977.

———. *Hito no isshō: Taiwanjin no monogatari (roku)* 人の一生: 台灣人の物語 [六] (A life: Tale of a Taiwanese, part 6). Taipei: self-published, 2003.

———. *Ren de yisheng: Taiwanren de xiao gushi (si)* 人的一生: 台灣人的小故事 [四] (A life: Tale of a Taiwanese, part 4). Taipei: self-published, 2002.

———. *Zenyang da bangqiu* 怎樣打棒球 (*The Dodgers' Way to Play Baseball*). Translated by Al Campanis. Taipei: Taiguang chubanshe 台光出版社, 1960.

———. *Zhonghua bangqiu shiji* 中華棒球史記 (Historical records of ROC baseball). Taipei: self-published, 1993.

"Jiang zongtong ji furen zhaojian tianjing nüjie Ji Zheng yu Zhonghua shaonian bangqiu-dui xuanshou" 蔣總統暨夫人召見田徑女傑紀政與中華少年棒球隊選手 (President Chiang and First Lady grant visit to women's track hero Ji Zheng and ROC youth baseball team). *Xinwen tiandi* 新聞天地 (*Newsdom*) 25, no. 38 (20 September 1969): front cover.

Jiao Tong 焦桐. *Taiwan wenxue de jietou yundong: 1977—shijimo* 台灣文學的街頭運動: 一九七七—世紀末 (Street movements in Taiwan literature: 1977–present). Taipei: Shibao wenhua chuban qiye gufen youxian gongsi 時報文化出版企業股份有限公司, 1998.

Jin Feng 錦楓. "You yi ci dui Jiang douzheng de shengli: Yijiuqisi nian qingshaobangsai ceji" 又一次對蔣鬥爭的勝利: 一九七四年青少棒賽側記 (Another victory in the anti-Chiang struggle: One record of the 1974 Senior League tournament). *Taidu yuekan* 台獨月刊 (*Independent Taiwan*) 32 (28 October 1974): 6.

"Jin'gang chuan qing, xiangqin xian'ai" 金剛傳情, 相親獻愛 (Robots profess their devotion, local folk present their love). *Naluwan zhoubao* 那魯灣週報 7 (1 February 1997): 6.

Jinri Zhonghua minguo 今日中華民國 (*Republic of China Today*). Taipei: Qiaowu weiyuan-hui 僑務委員會, 1968.

Jinri Zhonghua minguo: Qingzhu Zongtong Jiang gong ba zhi huadan teji 今日中華民國: 慶祝總統蔣公八秩華誕特輯(*Republic of China Today: Special Issue in Celebration of President Chiang Kai-shek's Eightieth Birthday*). Taipei: Qiaowu weiyuanhui 僑務委員會, 1966.

Johnson, Rafer, with Philip Goldberg. *The Best That I Can Be: An Autobiography*. New York: Doubleday, 1998.

Johnston, William. *Geisha, Harlot, Strangler, Star: A Woman, Sex, and Morality in Modern Japan*. Columbia University Press, 2005.

Jordan, David K., Andrew Morris, and Marc L. Moskowitz, eds. *The Minor Arts of Daily Life: Popular Culture in Taiwan*. Honolulu: University of Hawai'i Press, 2004.

Kang Tiancai 康添財. "Guaiwan jinlai ke hao?" 怪腕近來可好 (How is the Fantastic Arm now?). *Changchun yuekan* (Evergreen monthly) 6 (November 1983): 88–90.

Katz, Paul R. *When Valleys Turned Blood Red: The Ta-pa-ni Incident in Colonial Taiwan*. Honolulu: University of Hawai'i Press, 2005.

Ke Yuanfen 柯遠芬. "Ji Taiwan sheng shoujie yundonghui shimo" 記臺灣省首屆運動會始末 (A record of Taiwan's first provincial games). *Zhuanji wenxue* 傳記文學 (Biographical literature) 35 (October 1979): 97–98.

Kelly, William W. "Blood and Guts in Japanese Professional Baseball." In *The Culture of Japan as Seen Through its Leisure*, edited by Sepp Linhart and Sabine Frühstück, 95–111. Albany: SUNY Press, 1998.

———. "The Spirit and Spectacle of School Baseball: Mass Media, Statemaking, and 'Edutainment' in Japan, 1905–1935." In *Japanese Civilization in the Modern World XIV: Information and Communication*, edited by Umesao Tadao, William W. Kelly, and Kubo Masatoshi, 105–115. Osaka: National Museum of Ethnology, 2000.

Kerr, George H. *Formosa: Licensed Revolution and the Home Rule Movement, 1895–1945*. Honolulu: University of Hawai'i Press, 1974.

———. *Formosa Betrayed.* Boston: Houghton Mifflin, 1965.

Kiyasu Yukio 喜安幸夫. *Riben tongzhi Taiwan mishi: Wushe shijian zhi kang Ri quanmao* 日本統治台灣秘史: 霧社事件至抗日全貌 (Secret histories of Japanese rule in Taiwan: The overall view from the Wushe Incident to anti-Japanese resistance). Taipei: Wuling chuban youxian gongsi 武陵出版有限公司, 1995.

Klein, Alan M. *Sugarball: The American Game, The Dominican Dream.* New Haven, CT: Yale University Press, 1991.

Knapp, Ronald G., and Laurence M. Hauptman. "'Civilization over Savagery': The Japanese, the Formosan Frontier, and United States Indian Policy, 1895–1915." *Pacific Historical Review* 49, no. 4 (1980): 647–652.

Kobayashi Yoshinori 小林善紀. *Taiwanlun: xin aogu jingshen* 台灣論: 新傲骨精神 (On Taiwan: A new spirit of pride). Translated by Lai Qingsong 賴青松 and Xiao Zhiqiang 蕭志強. Tokyo: Shogakukan, 2000; Taipei: Qianwei chubanshe 前衛出版社, 2001.

Komagome Takeshi and J. A. Mangan. "Japanese colonial education in Taiwan, 1895–1922: Precepts and practices of control." *History of Education* 26, no. 3 (1997): 307–322.

Kondō Masami 近藤正己. *Soryokusen to Taiwan: Nihon shokuminchi hokai no kenkyu* 總力戰と台灣: 日本殖民地崩壊の研究 (Total war and Taiwan: Research into the collapse of Japanese colonialism). Tokyo: Tosui shobo 刀水書房, 1996.

Ku Ling 苦苓. "Xiang wo juancun de dixiongmen" 想我眷村的弟兄們 (Thinking of my brothers in the military projects). *Lianhebao,* 7 April 1985, 8; 8 April 1985, 8.

Kundera, Milan. *The Book of Laughter and Forgetting.* New York: Penguin, 1981.

Lai Degang 賴德剛. "Shao xiao lijia yuan xiang yuan" 少小離家原鄉遠 (Leaving home young, the village gets farther away). *Zhibang mi* 職棒迷 *(HIT!)* 20 (January 2005): 33–34.

Lai Shuming 賴樹明. *Taiwan bangqiu Zeng Ji'en: Bangtan shengya 50 nian* 台灣棒球曾紀恩: 棒壇生涯50年 (Taiwan baseball's Zeng Ji'en: Fifty years in the baseball world). Taipei: Zhidao chuban youxian gongsi 知道出版有限公司, 1991.

Lamley, Harry J. "Taiwan Under Japanese Rule, 1895–1945: The Vicissitudes of Colonialism." In *Taiwan: A New History,* edited by Murray A. Rubinstein, 201–260. Armonk, NY: M. E. Sharpe, 1999.

Leach, Jerry W., dir. *Trobriand Cricket: An Ingenious Response to Colonialism.* Office of Information, Government of Papua New Guinea, 1975 film.

Li Guoyan 李國彥. "Bangqiu shenshi Fang Shuiquan (shang)" 棒球紳士方水泉(上) (Baseball gentleman Fang Shuiquan, part 1). *Bangqiu shijie* 棒球世界 *(Baseball World)* 5 (November 1999): 46–52.

———. "Zeng Ji'en de shi ge gushi (shang)" 曾紀恩的十個故事(上) (Ten stories about Zeng Ji'en, part 1). *Bangqiu shijie* 棒球世界 *(Baseball World)* 3 (September 1999): 60–64.

Li, Laura. "Empowering the People: 50 Years of Struggle." Translated by Brent Heinrich. *Guanghua zazhi* 光華雜誌 *(Sinorama)* 24, no. 10 (October 1999): 100–107.

Li Ni 李泥. "Guomindang panbian fenghuo siqi" 國民黨叛變烽火四起 (KMT traitors fire from all directions). *Yihao renwu* 一號人物 *(Mr. Winner)* 66 (July 2007): 46–47.

Li, Paul. "Baseball Tries to Make a Comeback." *Taipei Journal* 17, no. 45 (10 November 2000): 8.

Li Shufang 李淑芳. "Riben Dushi Duikangsai lishi pian" 日本都市對抗賽歷史篇 (A historical study of the Japanese Intercity Baseball Tournament). *Bangqiu shijie* 棒球世界 *(Baseball World)* 4 (October 1999): 57–61.

Li Tong 李潼. *Longmenxia de Hongye* 龍門峽的紅葉 (Maple Leaf of Dragon Gate Gorge). Taipei: Yuanshen chubanshe 圓神出版社, 1999.

Liang, Lisa. "Fixing Taiwan baseball." *Taiwan Journal* 24, no. 2 (12 January 2007). http://taiwanjournal.nat.gov.tw/ct.asp?CtNode=122&xItem=23699 (accessed 1 August 2008).

Liang Shuling 梁淑玲. "Shehui fazhan, quanli yu yundong wenhua de xinggou: Taiwan bangqiu de shehui, lishi, wenhua fenxi (1895–1990)" 社會發展, 權力與運動文化的形構: 臺灣棒球的社會, 歷史, 文化分析(1895–1990) (The development of the structure of society, power and sport culture: A sociological, historical and cultural analysis of Taiwan baseball, 1895–1990). Master's thesis, Guoli Zhengzhi daxue shehuixue xi 國立政治大學社會學系, 1993.

Liao Hsien-hao 廖咸浩 (Liao Xianhao). "Ruqinzhe" 入侵者 (The invader). In *Taiwan bang qiu xiaoshuo fazhan xiaoshi* 台灣棒球小說發展小史 (A short history of the development of Taiwan baseball fiction), edited by Xu Jincheng 徐錦成, 46–77. Taipei: Jiuge 九歌, 2005.

Liao, Ping-hui, and David Der-Wei Wang, eds. *Taiwan Under Japanese Colonial Rule, 1895–1945: History, Culture, Memory.* New York: Columbia University Press, 2006.

Light, Richard, and Wataru Yasaki. "Breaking the Mould: J League Soccer, Community and Education in Japan." *Football Studies* 6, no. 1 (April 2003): 37–50.

Lin Dingguo 林丁國. "Rizhi shiqi Taiwan zhongdeng xuexiao bangqiu yundong de fazhan: Yi 'Jaiyi Nonglin' wei zhongxin de tantao (1928–1942)" 日治時期台灣中等學校棒球運動的發展: 以「嘉義農林」為中心的探討(1928–1942) (The development of Japanese-era Taiwanese middle school baseball: A study centered on the Jiayi Agriculture and Forestry Institute, 1928–1942). Paper presented at the Fifth Cross-Straits Historical Conference, Nanjing University, 8 September 2004.

———. "Zhimin tongzhi xia de yundong fazhan: Yi Taiwan Tiyu Xiehui wei zhongxin de tantao" 殖民統治下的運動發展: 以台灣體育協會為中心的探討 (The development of sports under colonial rule: A study focusing on the Taiwan Sports Association). *Taiwan lishi xuehui huixun* 台灣歷史學會會訊 (*Newsletter of the Taiwan Historical Association*) 18 (2004): 50–66.

Lin Jiwen 林繼文. *Riben ju Tai moqi (1930–1945) zhanzheng dongyuan tixi zhi yanjiu* 日本據台末期 (1930–1945) 戰爭動員之研究 (Research into the Wartime Mobilization Structure of the Late Japanese Colonial Period, 1930–1945). Banqiao: Daoxiang chubanshe 稻鄉出版社, 1996.

Lin Junfan 林俊帆. "Shei yao Guo Hongzhi?" 誰要郭泓志? (Who wants Hong-chih Kuo?). *Bangqiu shijie* 棒球世界 (*Baseball World*) 2 (August 1999): 60–64.

Lin Maosheng 林茂生 (Mosei Lin). *Riben tongzhi xia Taiwan de xuexiao jiaoyu: qi fazhan ji youguan wenhua zhi lishi fenxi yu tantao* 日本統治下臺灣的學校教育: 其發展及有關文化之歷史分析與探討 (Translation of PhD dissertation, Columbia University, 1929: "Public Education in Formosa Under the Japanese Administration: A Historical and Analytical Study of the Development and the Cultural Problems"). Taipei: Xin ziran zhuyi gufen youxian gongsi 新自然主義股份有限公司, 2000.

Lin, Mosei 林茂生 (Lin Maosheng). "Public Education in Formosa Under the Japanese Administration: A Historical and Analytical Study of the Development and the Cultural Problems." PhD dissertation, Columbia University, 1929.

Lin Qiwen 林琪雯. "Yundong yu zhengquan weiji: Jiedu zhanhou Taiwan bangqiu fazhan shi"

運動與政權維繫: 解讀戰後台灣棒球發展史 (Sports and the preservation of political power: A reading of the postwar development of Taiwan baseball). Master's thesis, Guoli Taiwan daxue shehuixue yanjiusuo 國立臺灣大學社會學研究所, 1995.

Lin Sanfeng 林三豐. "Shenyong yuanzhumin Lin Zhisheng" 神勇原住民林智勝 (The miraculously brave Aborigine Lin Zhisheng). *Zhiye bangqiu* 職業棒球 *(Professional Baseball)* 297 (10 December 2006). www.cpbl.com.tw/magzine/Mag_content.asp?Pnum=297& Qnum=1 (accessed 13 August 2008).

———. "Wang Guojin sia^n-mih long m-kia^{n}" 王國進啥米攏嘸驚 (Wang Guojin fears nothing). *Zhiye bangqiu* 職業棒球 *(Professional Baseball)* 268 (10 July 2004): 56–59.

Ling Zhaoxiong 凌照雄. "Taiwan de bangqiu yundong he qu he cong" 台灣的棒球運動何去何從 (Taiwanese baseball: Where to go from here?). *Bangqiu shijie* 棒球世界 *(Baseball World)* 1 (July 1999): 88–89.

Liu Junqing 劉俊卿 and Wang Xinliang 王信良. *Shiguang suidao: Taiwan lanyun liushi nian* 時光隧道: 台灣籃運六十年 (The tunnel of time: Sixty years of Taiwan basketball). Taipei: Minshengbao she 民生報社, 1999.

Liu, Shiyung. "Building a Strong and Healthy Empire: The Critical Period of Building Colonial Medicine in Taiwan." *Japanese Studies* 23, no. 4 (December 2004): 301–314.

Liu Yidong 劉益東, dir. *Fendou* 奮鬥 (Struggle). Taipei: Taiwan dianying zhipianchang 灣電影製片廠, 1988 film.

Lo, Ming-cheng M. *Doctors within Borders: Profession, Ethnicity, and Modernity in Colonial Taiwan.* Berkeley: University of California Press, 2002.

Lu, Tonglin. *Confronting Modernity in the Cinemas of Taiwan and Mainland China.* New York: Cambridge University Press, 2002.

Lukas, J. Anthony. "The Nationalist Pastime." *Rolling Stone* 175 (5 December 1974): 58–63.

Luo Kaiming 羅開明. "You Qihu shaobangdui de shengli fenxi yundong jingsai de xinli yinsu" 由七虎少棒隊的勝利分析運動競賽的心理因素 (An analysis of the psychological factors of competitive sport using the Seven Tiger youth baseball team's victory). *Guomin tiyu jikan* 國民體育季刊 *(Physical Education Quarterly)* 1, no. 6 (September 1970): 5–6.

Macauley, Thomas Babington. "Minute on Indian Education." In *Selected Writings,* edited and with an introduction by John Clive and Thomas Pinney, 237–251. Chicago: University of Chicago Press, 1972.

Mandle, W. F. *The Gaelic Athletic Association & Irish nationalist politics, 1884–1924.* London: Christopher Helm, 1987.

McDevitt, Patrick F. *"May the Best Man Win": Sport, Masculinity, and Nationalism in Great Britain and the Empire, 1880–1935.* New York: Palgrave Macmillan, 2004.

Moeran, Brian. "Commodities, Culture and Japan's Corollanization of Asia." In *Japanese Influences and Presences in Asia,* edited by Marie Söderberg and Ian Reader, 25–50. Richmond, UK: Curzon, 2000.

Morris, Andrew. "Baseball, History, the Local and the Global in Taiwan." In *The Minor Arts of Daily Life: Popular Culture in Taiwan,* edited by David K. Jordan, Andrew Morris, and Marc L. Moskowitz, 175–203. Honolulu: University of Hawai'i Press, 2004.

———. *Marrow of the Nation: A History of Sport and Physical Culture in Republican China.* Berkeley: University of California Press, 2004.

———. "Taiwan: Baseball, Colonialism and Nationalism." In *Baseball Without Borders: The*

International Pastime, ed. George Gmelch, 65–88. Lincoln: University of Nebraska Press, 2006.

Moskowitz, Marc L. "Multiple Virginity and Other Contested Realities in Taipei's Foreign Club Culture." *Sexualities* 11, no. 3 (June 2008): 327–351.

Nandy, Ashis. *The Tao of Cricket: On Games of Destiny and Destiny of Games.* New Delhi: Oxford University Press, 2000.

Nathan, John. *Japan Unbound: A Volatile Nation's Quest for Pride and Purpose.* Boston: Houghton Mifflin, 2004.

Nihon puro yakyū gaikokujin senshu (1936–1994) 日本プロ野球外國人選手 (1936–1994) (Japanese professional baseball's foreign players [1936–1994]). Special issue of *Beisubōru magajin* ベースボール・マガジン *(Baseball Magazine)* 18, no. 3 (Summer 1994).

Nihon yakyū renmei 日本野球連盟 and Mainichi Shimbun sha 每日新聞社, eds. *Toshi taikō yakyū taikai rokujunen shi* 都市対抗野球大會60年史 (Sixty years' history of the Intercity Baseball Tournament). Tokyo: Mainichi Shimbun sha 每日新聞社, 1990.

Nishiwaki Yoshitomo 西脇良朋. *Taiwan chūtō gakkō yakyū shi* 臺灣中等學校野球史 (History of high school baseball in Taiwan). Kakogawa City, Hyogo Prefecture 兵庫縣加古川市: self-published, 1996.

Nitobé, Inazo. *The Japanese Nation; Its Land, Its People, and Its Life, with Special Consideration to Its Relations with the United States.* New York: G. P. Putnam's Sons, 1912.

Nolden, Thomas. "On Colonial Spaces and Bodies: Hans Grimm's *Geschichten aus Südwestafrika.*" In *The Imperialist Imagination: German Colonialism and Its Legacy,* edited by Sara Friedrichsmeyer, Sara Lennox, and Susanne Zantop, 125–138. Ann Arbor: University of Michigan Press, 1998.

Noyes, John. *Colonial Space: Spatiality in the Discourse of German South West Africa, 1884–1915.* Philadelphia: Harwood Academic Publishers, 1992.

Nussbaum, Martha C. "The Prohibition Era." *The New Republic* 4757–4758 (20–27 March 2006): 21–28.

Olds, Kelly. "The Biological Standard of Living in Taiwan under Japanese Occupation." *Economics and Human Biology* 1 (2003): 187–206.

Peattie, Mark R. "Japanese Attitudes Toward Colonialism, 1895–1945." In *The Japanese Colonial Empire, 1895–1945,* edited by Ramon H. Myers and Mark R. Peattie, 80–127. Princeton: Princeton University Press, 1984.

Peng, Ming-min. *A Taste of Freedom: Memoirs of a Formosan Independence Leader.* New York: Holt, Rinehart and Winston, 1972.

Peng Mingmin 彭明敏 and Huang Zhaotang 黃昭堂. *Taiwan zai guojifa shang de diwei* 臺灣在國際法上的地位 (The status of Taiwan in international law). Translated by Cai Qiuxiong 蔡秋雄 from the Japanese. Taipei: Yushan she 玉山社, 1995.

Phillips, Steven E. *Between Assimilation and Independence: The Taiwanese Encounter Nationalist China, 1945–1950.* Stanford University Press, 2003.

Ponsonby-Fane, Richard Arthur Brabazon. *The Vicissitudes of Shinto.* London: Royal Anthropological Institute of Great Britain and Ireland, 1931. Reprint, Kyoto: Ponsonby Memorial Society, 1963.

Qiu Jiawen 裴嘉聞. "Hongye zhong xiaojiang qiancheng ru jing" 紅葉眾小將前程如鏡 (Maple

Leaf little generals' future prospects are smooth). *Xinwen tiandi* 新聞天地 *(Newsdom)* 24, no. 35 (31 August 1968): 22.

"Qiuyuan quan chong mote'er: Zhanpao shanliang xianshen" 球員權充模特兒, 戰袍閃亮現身 (Ballplayers moonlighting as models: Battle gear unveiled in its glory). *Naluwan zhoubao* 那魯灣週報 *(Naluwan Weekly)* 7 (1 February 1997): 3.

Qu Hailiang 瞿海良. "Taiwan yuanzhumin de bangqiu chuanqi" 台灣原住民的棒球傳奇 (Taiwan Aborigines' baseball miracle). *Shanhai wenhua* 山海文化 *(Taiwan Indigenous Voice Bimonthly)* 9 (March 1995): 25–31.

Raz, Aviad E. *Riding the Black Ship: Japan and Tokyo Disneyland.* Cambridge, MA: Harvard University Asia Center, 1999.

Renan, Ernest. "What Is a Nation?" In *Becoming National: A Reader,* edited by Geoff Eley and Ronald Grigor Suny, 42–55. New York: Oxford University Press, 1996.

Robertson, Roland. "Comments on the 'Global Triad' and 'Glocalization.'" In *Globalization and Indigenous Culture,* edited by Inoue Nobutaka, 217–225. Tokyo: Institute for Japanese Culture and Classics, Kokugakuin University, 1996.

Robinson, Michael Edson. *Cultural Nationalism in Colonial Korea, 1920–1925.* Seattle: University of Washington Press, 1988.

"ROC Pro Ball In 1990." *Free China Journal,* 8 September 1988: 2.

Roden, Donald. "Baseball and the Quest for National Dignity in Meiji Japan." *American Historical Review* 85, no. 3 (June 1980): 511–534.

Roth, Philip. *The Great American Novel.* New York: Vintage International, 1995.

Rubinstein, Murray A. "Taiwan's Socioeconomic Modernization, 1971–1996." In *Taiwan: A New History,* edited by Murray A. Rubinstein, 366–402. Armonk, NY: M. E. Sharpe, 1999.

Rutherford, Jonathan. *Forever England: Reflections on race, masculinity and Empire.* London: Lawrence & Wishart, 1997.

Said, Edward W. *Culture and Imperialism.* New York: Alfred A. Knopf, 1993.

Sakamoto Shigeru 坂本茂 and Katsura Chōhei 桂長平. "Nōkō yakyūdan to banjin gakusei no seikatsu" 能高野球團と蕃人學生の生活 (The Nōkō Baseball Team and the life of the savage students). Yakyūkai 野球界 *(The Yakyukai)* 15, no. 12 (September 1925): 46–48.

Sandage, Scott A. *Born Losers: A History of Failure in America.* Cambridge, MA: Harvard University Press, 2005.

Scruggs, Bert. "Identity and Free Will in Colonial Taiwan Fiction: Wu Zhuoliu's 'The Doctor's Mother' and Wang Changxiong's 'Torrent.'" *Modern Chinese Literature and Culture* 16, no. 2 (2004): 160–183.

"Shaobang tuixing zhi dao" 少棒推行之道 (The way to promote Little League baseball). *Guomin tiyu jikan* 國民體育季刊 *(Physical Education Quarterly)* 2, no. 3 (June 1971): 1–2.

Shi Ming 史明. *Taiwanren sibainian shi (Hanwen ban)* 台灣人四百年史 (漢文版) (The four hundred years of the Taiwanese people's history [Chinese edition]). San Jose, CA: Pengdao wenhua gongsi 蓬島文化公司 Paradise Culture Associates, 1980.

Shi Zhongchuan 施中川. "Taiwan bangqiu haoshou zouhong Riben" 台灣棒球好手走紅日本 (Taiwanese baseball players popular in Japan). *Riben wenzhai* 日本文摘 *(Japan Digest)* 39 (April 1989): 110–112.

Shiba Ryōtarō 司馬遼太郎. *Taiwan kikō: Kaidō oyuku yonjū* 台灣紀行: 街道をゆく四十 (Journal of travels in Taiwan: On the highway goes, part 40). Tokyo: Asahi Shimbun sha 朝日新聞社, 1994.

Shih, Chih-pin. "A Study of the Relationship Between Media Coverage, Audience Behavior, and Sporting Events: An Analysis of Taiwan Professional Baseball Booster Club Members." PhD dissertation, University of Northern Colorado, 1998.

Shōriki Tōru 正力亨 et al., eds. *Tōkyō Yomiuri Kyōjingun gojunen shi* 東京読売巨人軍五十年史 (Fifty years' history of the Tokyo Yomiuri Giants). Tokyo: Tōkyō Yomiuri Kyōjingun 50 nen shi henshū iinshitsu 東京読売巨人軍50年史編集委員室 1985.

Sökefeld, Martin. "From Colonialism to Postcolonial Colonialism: Changing Modes of Domination in the Northern Areas of Pakistan." *Journal of Asian Studies* 64, no. 4 (November 2005): 939–973.

Sterk, Darryl. "Romancing the Formosan Pocahontas: Romantic National Allegories in Modern Taiwanese Fiction." Presented at the conference on Taiwan Studies in International Perspectives, University of California, Santa Barbara, 27 October 2007.

Stoddart, Brian. "West Indies." In *The imperial game: Cricket, culture and society,* edited by Brian Stoddart and Keith A. P. Sandiford, 79–92. New York: Manchester University Press, 1998.

Stroupe, Craig. "Glocalization." www.d.umn.edu/~cstroupe/ideas/glocalization.html (accessed 24 February 2005).

Su Jinzhang 蘇錦章. *Jiayi bangqiu shihua* 嘉義棒球史話 (Items from the history of Jiayi baseball). Taipei: Lianjing chuban shiye gongsi 聯經出版事業公司, 1996.

Su Shichang 蘇世昌. "Zhuixun yu huiyi; Zhang Wojun jiqi zuopin yanjiu" 追尋與回憶; 張我軍及其作品研究 (Searching and memories; Research into Zhang Wojun and his work). Master's thesis, Zhongxing daxue Zhongguo wenxue yanjiusuo 中興大學中國文學研究所, 1998. http://ws.twl.ncku.edu.tw/hak-chia/s/sou-se-chhiong/sek-su/ch-01.htm, accessed 22 April 2005.

Su Zhengsheng 蘇正生. "Tianxia zhi Jianong" 天下之嘉農 (Kanō, champions of all under heaven). *Jianongren* 嘉農人 (People of the Jiayi Agriculture and Forestry Institute) 1 (November 1997): 11–27.

Sundeen, Joseph Timothy. "A 'Kid's Game'? Little League Baseball and National Identity in Taiwan." *Journal of Sport & Social Issues* 25, no. 3 (August 2001): 251–265.

Suzuki Akira 鈴木明. *Takasago zoku ni sasageru* 高砂族に捧げる (Dedicated to the Takasago people). Tokyo: Chūō Kōronsha 中央公論社, 1976.

Szonyi, Michael. *Cold War Island: Quemoy on the Front Line.* New York: Cambridge University Press, 2008.

"Table of Important Chinese Terms and their English Translations Used by the President in His Speeches and Important Messages 有關總統重要講詞與談話專門用語英譯對照表 (核定版)." Government Information Office, Republic of China, 23 July 2004. www.gio.gov.tw/taiwan-website/4-oa/politics/trans/ (accessed 16 April 2004).

Tai, Eika. "Kokugo and Colonial Education in Taiwan." *positions* 7, no. 2 (Fall 1999): 503–540.

Taifeng 台風. "Jiang ducai zhengquan xisheng xia de Taiwanren tiyu" 蔣獨裁政權犧牲下的台灣人體育 (The Taiwanese people's sports sacrificed by the Chiang dictatorial regime). *Duli Taiwan* 独立台湾 *(Viva Formosa)* 14 (August 1969): 22–29.

Taipingshan 太平山. "Wei-lian-si-bao guan qiu ji" 威廉斯堡觀球記 (A record of watching the game at Williamsport). *Duli Taiwan* 獨立台灣 *(Viva Formosa)* 38 (October 1971): 54–55.

Taiwan duli jianguo lianmeng de gushi 台灣獨立建國聯盟的故事 *(WUFI: A History of World United Formosans for Independence)*. Taipei: Qianwei 前衛, 2000.

"Taiwan shaonian bangqiudui wei Taiwanren zhengguang" 台灣少年棒球隊為台灣人爭光 (The Taiwan Little League baseball team wins glory for the Taiwanese people). *Taiwan qingnian* 台灣青年 (Taiwan Youth) 106 (5 September 1969): 7–9

Taiwan shashinchō, daiishū 臺灣寫真帖, 第壹集 (Taiwan photograph album, volume 1). N.p.: Taiwan shashinkai 臺灣寫真會, 1915.

Taiwan sheng di yi jie quansheng yundong dahui xuanchuan zu 臺灣省第一屆全省運動大會宣傳組 (First Taiwan Provincial Games information section), eds. *Taiwan sheng di yi jie quansheng yundong dahui* 臺灣省第一屆全省運動大會 (The First Taiwan Provincial Games). N.p.: Taiwan sheng di yi jie quansheng yundong dahui xuanchuan zu 臺灣省第一屆全省運動大會宣傳組, 1946.

Taiwan sheng jiaoyuting 臺灣省教育廳 (Taiwan Provincial Education Department), ed. *Taiwan jiaoyu fazhan shiliao huibian, tiyu jiaoyu pian* 臺灣教育發展史料彙編, 體育教育篇 (Historical materials from the development of Taiwan education, Physical education volume). Taipei: Taiwan sheng jiaoyuting 臺灣省教育廳, 1988.

Taiwan undō kai 台灣運動界 1, no. 2 (November 1915): 14.

Takemura Toyotoshi 竹村豐俊. *Taiwan taiiku shi* 台灣體育史 (The history of sports in Taiwan). Taipei: Taiwan taiiku kyōkai 台灣體育協會, 1933.

Tanaka Kazuji 田中一二, ed. *Taiwan nenkan: Kōki ni go kyū shi nen Shōwa kyuu nen* 臺灣年鑑: 皇紀二五九四年昭和九年 (Taiwan yearbook: Imperial Year 2594, Shōwa Year 9). Taipei Taiwan tsūshinsha 臺灣通信社, 1934.

Taussig, Michael. *Mimesis and Alterity: A Particular History of the Senses.* (New York: Routledge, 1993.

Taylor, Jeremy. "Colonial Takao: The making of a southern metropolis." *Urban History* 31, no. 1 (May 2004): 48–71.

———. "Pop music as postcolonial nostalgia in Taiwan." In *Refashioning Pop Music in Asia: Cosmopolitan Flows, Political Tempos and Aesthetic Industries,* edited by Allen Chun, Ned Rossiter, and Brian Shoesmith, 173–182. New York: Routledge, 2004.

Terry, T. Philip. *Terry's Japanese Empire: Including Korea and Formosa, with Chapters on Manchuria, the Trans-Siberian Railway, and the Chief Ocean Routes to Japan: A Guidebook for Travelers.* Boston: Houghton Mifflin, 1914.

Thomson, John. *Thomson's China: Travels and Adventures of a Nineteenth-century Photographer.* Hong Kong: Oxford University Press, 1993.

To, Cho-Yee. "Education of the Aborigines in Taiwan: An Illustration of How Certain Traditional Beliefs of a Majority People Determine the Education of a Disadvantaged Minority." Special issue, *The Journal of Negro Education* 41, no. 3, (Summer 1972): 183–194.

Tobe Yoshinari 戶部良也. *Bangqiu dongyouji* 棒球東遊記 (Baseball journey to the east). Translated by Li Shufang 李淑芳. Taipei: Zhonghua zhibang shiye gufen youxian gongsi 中華職棒事業股份有限公司, 1994.

Tobita Suishū 飛田穗州. *Tobita Suishū senshū, dai 3 kan: Yakyū kisha jidai* 飛田穗洲選集,

第3巻: 野球記者時代 (Anthology of Tobita Suishū's works, volume 3: The baseball reporter era). Tokyo: Besuborumagajin sha, 1986.

Tong Xiangzhao 童祥昭. "Cong Taiwan xuanshou tan qi" 從台灣選手談起 (Speaking about the Taiwan athletes). *Zhengyanbao quanyun tekan* 正言報全運特刊 (The Truth Report, National Games Special Publication), 11 May 1948, 4.

Ts'ai, Hui-yu Caroline. "Administration, Assimilation, and Ambivalence: 'Improved Treatment' (*shogū kaizen* 處遇改善) in Wartime Taiwan, 1944," In *Minzu rentong yu wenhua jiaorong* 民族認同與文化交融 (Ethnic identity and cultural assimilation), edited by Youngtsu Wong 汪榮祖 and Guanqun Lin 林冠群, 373–427. Jiayi Xian: Zhongzheng daxue Taiwan renwen yanjiu zhongxin 中正大學臺灣人文研究中心, 2006.

———. "Total War, Labor Drafts, and Colonial Administration: Wartime Mobilization in Taiwan, 1936–45." In *Asian Labor in the Wartime Japanese Empire: Unknown Histories,* edited by Paul H. Kratoska, 101–126. Armonk, NY: M. E. Sharpe, 2005.

Tsurumi, E. Patricia. *Japanese Colonial Education in Taiwan, 1895–1945.* Cambridge, MA: Harvard University Press, 1977.

———. "Mental Captivity and Resistance Lessons from Taiwanese Anti-Colonialism." *Bulletin of Concerned Asian Scholars* 12, no. 2 (April–June 1980): 2–13.

Undō to shumi 運動と趣味 (Sport and interest) 3, no. 1 (January 1918).

Van Auken, Lance, and Robin Van Auken. *Play Ball! The Story of Little League® Baseball.* University Park: Pennsylvania State University Press, 2001.

Vickers, Edward. "Re-writing museums in Taiwan." In *Re-Writing Culture in Taiwan,* edited by Fang-long Shih, Stuart Thompson, and Paul Tremlett, 69–101. New York: Routledge, 2008.

Wang Fudan 王復旦. "Cong Jinlong shaonian bangqiudui chenggong shuoqi: Tan Zhongguo quanmin tiyu de zhiben zhi dao" 從金龍少年棒球隊成功說起: 談中國全民體育的治本之道 (On the topic of the Golden Dragons youth baseball team's success: Discussing the issues at the heart of Chinese sports for the people). *Guomin tiyu jikan* 國民體育季刊 (*Physical Education Quarterly)* 1, no. 3 (December 1969): 3–5.

Wang Huimin 王惠民. *Hongye de gushi* 紅葉的故事 (The story of Maple Leaf). Taipei: Minshengbao she 民生報社, 1994.

Wang, Tay-sheng. *Legal Reform in Taiwan under Japanese Colonial Rule, 1895–1945: The Reception of Western Law.* Seattle: University of Washington Press, 2000.

Watanabe, Masashi. "Identity Seen in the Acculturation of Sumo Done by Indigenous Peoples of Taiwan, Chihpen Puyuma." *International Journal of Sport and Health Science* 4 (2006): 110–124.

Wei, James (Wei Jingmeng 魏景蒙). *China Yearbook 1971–72.* Taibei: China Publishing, 1972.

Weng Jiaming 翁嘉銘. "Bangqiu de meili yu aichou" 棒球的美麗與哀愁 (The beauty and sorrow of baseball). *Zhongguo luntan* 中國論壇 (*China Tribune)* 384 (September 1992): 27–31.

Whiting, Robert. *The Chrysanthemum and the Bat: Baseball Samurai Style.* New York: Dodd, Mead, 1977.

———. *You Gotta Have Wa.* New York: Vintage Books, 1989.

Wills, John E., Jr. "The Seventeenth-Century Transformation: Taiwan Under the Dutch and the Cheng Regime." In *Taiwan: A New History,* edited by Murray A. Rubinstein, 84–106. Armonk, NY: M. E. Sharpe, 1999.

Wilson, Jeffrey P. "Taiwan Enters the Big Leagues: A Look at Disputes Involving Foreign Professional Baseball Players." *For The Record* 4, no. 5 (October–November 1993): 3–4.

Wu, Emma. "Baseball Fever." *Free China Review* 42, no. 8 (August 1992): 30–39.

Wu Mi-cha 吳密察. "Inō Kanori, Japanese Ethnography and the Idea of the 'Tribe.'" In *In Search of the Hunters and Their Tribes: Studies in the History and Culture of the Taiwan Indigenous People,* edited by David Faure, 39–49. Taibei: Shung Ye Museum of Formosan Aborigines Publishing 順益台灣原住民博物館, 2001.

Wu Wenxing 吳文星. "Riju shiqi Taiwan zongdufu tuiguang Riyu yundong chutan" 日據時期臺灣總督府推廣日語運動初探 (An Investigation into the Taiwan Colonial Administration's Japanese Language Promotion Campaigns during the Japanese Occupation). *Taiwan fengwu* 臺灣風物 (Taiwan Folkways) 37, no. 1 (March 1987): 1–31; 37, no. 4 (December 1987): 53–86.

Wu Xiangmu 吳祥木. *Jue bu qingyan fangqi! Bangqiu de meihao niandai* 絕不輕言放棄! 棒球的美好年代 (Never give up easily! Baseball's beautiful age). Taipei: Yuanshen 圓神, 1996.

Wu, Yuan-li. "Income Distribution in the Process of Economic Growth in Taiwan." In *The Taiwan Experience, 1950–1980: Contemporary Republic of China,* edited by James C. Hsiung, 162–173. New York: Praeger, 1981.

Wu Zhuoliu. *The Fig Tree: Memoirs of a Taiwanese Patriot, 1900–1947.* Translated by Duncan B. Hunter. Bloomington, IN: 1stBooks, 2002.

———. *Orphan of Asia.* Translated by Ioannis Mentzas. New York: Columbia University Press, 2006.

"Xiang Zhonghua shaobangdui huanhu" 向中華少棒隊歡呼 (Acclaim for the ROC youth baseball team). *Xinwen tiandi* 新聞天地 *Newsdom* 25, no. 35 (30 August 1969): 3.

Xiaoye 小野. "Fengsha" 封殺 (Forced out). In *Fengsha* 封殺, 72–87. Taipei: Wenhao chubanshe 文豪出版社, 1979.

———. "Fengsha" 封殺 (Forced out). In *Taiwan bangqiu xiaoshuo fazhan xiaoshi* 台灣棒球小說發展小史 (A short history of the development of Taiwan baseball fiction), edited by Xu Jincheng 徐錦成, 14–32. Taipei: Jiuge 九歌, 2005.

Xie Shiyuan 謝仕淵. "1929 nian Gaoxiong Di yi gongxuexiao yu di yi hui quandao shaonian yeqiu dahui" 1929年高雄第一公學校與第一回全島少年野球大會 (Takao No. 1 Public School and the first islandwide youth baseball tournament, 1929). *Gaoshi wenxian* 高市文獻 *(Takao Historiography)* 17, no. 3 (September 2004): 110–120.

———. "Diyu bangqiu feng: Houshan chuanqi, nanguo rongguang" 地域棒球風: 後山傳奇, 南國榮光 (Local baseball culture: Mountaintop legends, southern glory). *Dadi dili zazhi* 大地地理雜誌 *(The Earth Geographic Monthly)* 197 (August 2004): 24–31.

———. "Rizhi chuqi (1895–1916) Taiwan gongxuexiao de nüzi tiyu yu fangzu yundong" 日治初期 (1895–1916) 臺灣公學校的女子體育與放足運動 (Taiwan public school physical education for girls and the antifootbinding movement in the early Japanese occupation, 1895–1916). *Taiwan wenxian* 臺灣文獻 (Taiwan documents) 55, no. 2 (June 2004): 206–230.

Xie Shiyuan 謝仕淵 and Xie Jiafen 謝佳芬. *Taiwan bangqiu yibainian* 台灣棒球一百年 *(One Hundred Years of Baseball in Taiwan).* Taipei: Guoshi chubanshe 果實出版社, 2003.

Xingzhengyuan tiyu weiyuanhui 行政院體育委員會 (National Council on Physical Fitness and Sports). "Shuwei bowuguan: Bangqiu" 數位博物館: 棒球 (Digital museum: Baseball).

November 2005. www.ncpfs.gov.tw/museum/museum-1.aspx?No=9 (accessed 2 April 2008).

Xinwen tiandi 新聞天地 *(Newsdom)* 24, no. 36 (7 September 1968).

Xu Boxiong 續伯雄. *Zhonghua shaobang duokui ji* 中華少棒奪魁記 (A record of the ROC youth baseball seizing [the title]). Taipei: Dongfang yu xifang chubanshe 東方與西方出版社, 1969.

Xu Shengming 徐生明. *Cuilian* 淬煉 (Temper and train). Taipei: Kaite wenhua 凱特文化, 2007.

Xu Xiulin 許秀鄰. "Shitan qiuchang fei zhanchang" 試談球場非戰場 (Discussing why the ballfield is not a battlefield). *Guomin tiyu jikan* 國民體育季刊 *(Physical Education Quarterly)* 2, no. 4 (September 1971): 18.

Xu Zongmao 徐宗懋. *Sanguanwang zhi meng* 三冠王之夢 *(Dreams Come True)*. Taipei: Dadi chubanshe 大地出版社, 2004.

Yabu Syat, Xu Shikai 許世楷, and Shi Zhengfeng 施正鋒. *Wushe shijian: Taiwanren de jiti jiyi* 霧社事件: 台灣人的集體記憶 (The Wushe Incident: Taiwanese collective memory). Taipei: Qianwei 前衛, 2001.

Yamaguchi Nobuo 山口信雄. *Yakyū nenkan* 野球年鑑 (Baseball yearbook). N.p.: Asahi Shimbun sha 朝日新聞社, 1918.

Yan Shannong 晏山農. "Xin rentong de peifang" 新認同的配方 (A new formulation for identity). *Zhongguo luntan* 中國論壇 *(China Tribune)* 384 (September 1992): 32–36.

Yanaihara Tadao 矢內原忠雄. *Teikokushugi ka no Taiwan* 帝國主義下の台灣 (Taiwan under imperialism). Tokyo: Iwanami shoten 岩波書店, 1929; Taipei: Nantian shuju 南天書局, 1997 reprint.

Yang, Edward 楊德昌 (Yang Dechang), dir. *Qingmei zhuma* 青梅竹馬 *(Taipei Story)*. Taipei: Wannianqing dianying gongsi 萬年青電影公司, 1985 film.

Yang Naifan 楊乃藩. "Bangyun guoyun" 棒運國運 (The baseball movement, the national movement). *Zhongyang yuekan* 中央月刊 (Central monthly) 5, no. 12 (October 1973): 43–44.

Yang Qing 楊菁. "Zhang Wojun zai Zhongguo" 張我軍在中國 (Zhang Wojun in China). In *Rizhi shiqi Taiwan zhishifenzi zai Zhongguo* 日治時期臺灣知識分子在中國 (Japanese-era Taiwan intellectuals in China), edited by Lin Qingzhang 林慶彰, 87–118. Taipei: Taibei shi wenxian weiyuanhui 臺北市文獻委員會, 2004.

Yang Wuxun 楊武勳 and Gao Zhengyuan 高正源. *Aoyun bangqiu guoshou dianjianglu* 奧運棒球國手點將錄 (List of national players appointed to Olympic baseball team). Taipei: Minshengbao she 民生報社, 1984.

Yao Liye 姚立業. *Zhonghua qing-shaobang fazhan shishi* 中華青少棒發展史實 (The history of the development of ROC youth baseball). Taipei: Huanqiu zazhi she 環球雜誌社, 1977.

———. *Zhonghua qing-shaobang shijie yangming ji* 中華青少棒世界揚名記 (A record of ROC youth baseball fame and triumph). Taipei: Jianxing 健行, 1978.

Ye Longyan 葉龍彥. *Rizhi shiqi Taiwan dianying shi* 日治時期台灣電影史 *(The History of Taiwanese Movies during the Japanese Colonization)*. Taipei: Yushan she 玉山社, 1998.

Yi wei Taiwanren 一位台灣人. "Binzhou qiusai changbian wuda xiaoji" 賓州球賽場邊武打小記 (A short record of the fighting outside the ballpark in Pennsylvania). *Duli Taiwan* 獨立台灣 *(Viva Formosa)* 50 (November 1972): 45–46.

Yu Chien-ming 游鑑明 (You Jianming). "Rizhi shiqi Taiwan xuexiao nüzi tiyu de fazhan"

日治時期臺灣學校女子體育的發展 ("The Development of Female Physical Education in Taiwan during the Japanese Colonial Period"). *Zhongyang yanjiuyuan jindaishi yanjiusuo jikan* 中央研究院近代史研究所集刊 (*Bulletin of the Institute of Modern History, Academia Sinica*) 33 (June 2000): 5–75.

Yu, Junwei. "The Hongye Legend in Taiwanese Baseball: Separating Myth from Reality." *The International Journal of the History of Sport* 24, no. 10 (October 2007): 1264–1280.

———. *Playing In Isolation: A History of Baseball in Taiwan.* Lincoln: University of Nebraska Press, 2007.

Yu, Junwei, and Alan Bairner. "Proud to be Chinese: Little League Baseball and National Identities in Taiwan during the 1970s." *Identities: Global Studies in Culture and Power* 15, no. 2 (April 2008): 216–239.

Yu, Junwei, and Dan Gordon. "Nationalism and National Identity in Taiwanese Baseball." *NINE: A Journal of Baseball History and Culture* 14, no. 2 (Spring 2006): 27–39.

Yu Zhongzhou 宇中宙. "Chengli zhibang, buyi cao zhi guoji" 成立職棒, 不宜操之過急 (In establishing pro baseball it's inappropriate to act with too much haste). *Zhonghua bangqiu zazhi* 中華棒球雜誌 (*R.O.C. Baseball Quarterly*) 18 (March 1988): 38–39.

Yukawa Mitsuo 湯川充雄. *Taiwan yakyū shi* 臺灣野球史 (The history of baseball in Taiwan). Taipei: Taiwan nichinichi shimpō sha 臺灣日日新報社, 1932.

Ze Zhijiang 迮芷江, dir. *Shaonian, bangqiu, guanjun* 少年, 棒球, 冠軍 (*Barefoot Little Leaguers*). Taipei: Guanghua yingpian ziliao gongyingshe 光華影片資料供應社, 1979 film.

Zeng Wencheng 曾文誠. "Chen Runbo koushu bangqiushi" 陳潤波口述棒球史 (Chen Runbo's oral history of baseball). Article posted online in three parts, 15 May 2003 (accessed 8 October 2007), http://sports.yam.com/list.php/baseball/history/3.

———. "Cong 1931 nian Jianong bangqiu dui kan Riju shidai Taiwan bangqiu fazhan" 從1931年嘉農棒球隊看日據時代台灣棒球發展 (The development of Japanese-occupied Taiwanese baseball seen from the perspective of the Kanō baseball team, post-1931). Article posted online in four parts, 21 May 2003 (accessed 13 September 2006), http://sports.yam.com/list.php/baseball/history/3.

———, ed. "Gungun bangqiu changliu Xiao Changgun" 滾滾棒球長流蕭長滾 (Roll on, baseball, live on, Xiao Changgun). *Zhiye bangqiu* 職業棒球 (*Professional Baseball*) 225 (10 December 2000): 44–47.

———. "Hong Taishan koushu Taiwan bangqiushi" 洪太山口述台灣棒球史 (Hong Taishan's oral history of Taiwan baseball). Article posted online in four parts, 25 June 2003 (accessed 5 November 2007), http://sports.yam.com/list.php/baseball/history/3.

———. "Huang Renhui koushu Taiwan bangqiushi" 黃仁惠口述台灣棒球史 (Huang Renhui's oral history of Taiwan baseball). Article posted online in three parts, 9–21 July 2003 (accessed 8 October 2007), http://sports.yam.com/list.php/baseball/history/3.

———. "Taiwan bangqiu shi" 台灣棒球史 (History of Taiwan baseball). Article posted online in sixteen parts, 29 July 2003—8 March 2004 (accessed 23 May 2007), http://sports.yam.com/list.php/baseball/history/3.

———. "Taiwan zhibang shi" 台灣職棒史 (History of Taiwan professional baseball). Article posted online in eleven parts, 8 February 2006—25 September 2006. http://sports.yam.com/list.php/baseball/history/3 (accessed 30 November 2006).

———. "Weiquan bangqiudui shi" 味全棒球隊史 (History of the Wei-Chuan baseball team).

Article posted online in sixteen parts, 15 March 2004—15 March 2005. http://sports.yam
.com/show.php?id=0000026016 (accessed 25 May 2004, 21 June 2005).

———. "Zhibang caochuang bilu lanlü" 職棒草創篳路藍縷 (The early years of professional
baseball, the hard life of pioneers). *Zhiye bangqiu* 職業棒球 *(Professional Baseball)* 167–
168 (January–February 1997): 21–24.

Zeng Wencheng 曾文誠 and Yu Junwei 盂峻瑋. *Taiwan bangqiu wang* 台灣棒球王 *(Baseball
King of Taiwan)*. Taipei: Woshi chubanshe 我識出版社, 2004.

Zhan Deji 詹德基. "Woguo bangqiu yundong de fawei yu zhanwang" 我國棒球運動的發微
與展望 (The development of and perspectives on our nation's baseball movement).
Jiaoyu ziliao jikan 教育資料季刊 (Educational Information Quarterly) 10 (June 1985):
433–483.

Zhang Jingguo 張敬果. *Zhonghua minguo shaonian, qingshaonian, qingnian bangqiu fazhan
shishi* 中華民國少年, 青少年, 青年棒球發展史實 (Historical facts of the development of
ROC Little League, Senior League, and Big League Baseball). Taipei: self-published,
1983.

Zhang Ming 張明. "Chuancheng bangqiu, jue bu duandian—Taidian bangqiu wushisan nian
shi" 傳承棒球, 絕不斷電—台電棒球五十三年史 (Propagating baseball with nary a black-
out—Taiwan Electric's fifty-three-year baseball history). *Bangqiu shijie* 棒球世界 *(Baseball World)* 3 (September 1999): 52–57.

———. "Heku bangqiu whushi nian" 合庫棒球五十年 ("Cooperative Bank Baseball Club since
1948"). *Bangqiu Shijie* 棒球世界 *(Baseball World)* 1 (July 1999): 46–51.

Zhang Qijiang 張啟疆. "Hu Wuhan yu wo" 胡武漢與我 (Hu Wuhan and I). In *Taiwan bangqiu
xiaoshuo fazhan xiaoshi* 台灣棒球小說發展小史 (A short history of the development of
Taiwan baseball fiction), edited by Xu Jincheng 徐錦成, 147–149. Taipei: Jiuge 九歌, 2005.

Zhang Zhichao 張志超, dir. *Hongye xiaojuren* 紅葉小巨人 (Little Giants of Maple Leaf). Taipei:
Xuepu youxian gongsi 學甫有限公司, 1988 film.

Zheng Sanlang 鄭三郎, ed. *Jianong koushu lishi* 嘉農口述歷史 (Oral histories of the Jiayi Agriculture and Forestry Institute). Jiayi: Guoli Jiayi nongye zhuanke xuexiao xiaoyouhui
國立嘉義農業專科學校校友會, 1993.

"'Zhenggang de yingxiong' qianggong xuanchuan tantou" 「正港的英雄」搶攻宣傳灘頭 ("True
Heroes" attacking the publicity beachheads). *Naluwan zhoubao* 那魯灣週報 *(Naluwan
Weekly)* 5 (4 January 1997): 5.

Zhonghua minguo bangqiu xiehui 中華民國棒球協會 (Chinese Taipei Baseball Association),
eds. *Taiwan bangqiu bainian shi* 台灣棒球百年史 *(History of Baseball In Taiwan, 1906–
2006)*. Taipei: Zhonghua minguo bangqiu xiehui 中華民國棒球協會, 2006.

Zhonghua ribao congshu weiyuanhui 中華日報叢書委員會, eds. *Wudi Jinlong: Zhonghua
shaonian bangqiudui yongduo shijie guanjun jishi* 無敵金龍：中華少年棒球隊勇奪世界
冠軍紀實 (The unrivalled Golden Dragons: The true record of the ROC youth baseball
team's brave capture of the world championship). Taipei: Zhonghua ribao she 中華日報社,
1969).

Zhonghua shaonian bangqiudui fendou'shi bianyi weiyuanhui 中華少年棒球隊奮鬥史編譯
委員會, eds. *Zhonghua shaonian bangqiudui fendou shi* 中華少年棒球隊奮鬥史 *(The Endeavouring History of the Youth Baseball Team of the Republic of China)*. Taipei: Zhonghua minguo lishi wenhua chubanshe 中華民國歷史文化出版社, 1972.

Zhou, Jay (Zhou Jielun 周杰倫). "Jiandan ai" 簡單愛 (Simple Love). From album *Fantexi* 范特西 (Fantasy). Taipei: Sony BMG Taiwan, 2001.

Zhuang Jinguo 莊金國. "Renquan, zunyan, xin Taiwan, Renquan xuanyan zai maibu" 人權, 尊嚴, 新台灣, 人權宣言再邁步 (Human rights, dignity, new Taiwan, Declaration of Human Rights marches forward again). *Xin Taiwan xinwen zhoukan* 新台灣新聞周刊 *(New Taiwan)* 595 (17 August 2007): 58–61.

INDEX

Aborigines. *See* Amis Aborigines; Atayal Aborigines; Austronesian Aborigines; Bunun Aborigines; Puyuma Aborigines
African-American/jazz culture, 1920s, 22–23, 38
Agnew, Spiro, 108, 111
Ah Q, 133
Aichi, 22, 40
Amaterasu the Sun Goddess, 47
American Broadcasting Company (ABC), 96, 97, 110
American imperialism, 59
American Indian policy, 18
American major leagues. *See* Major League Baseball
American military, 60, 61, 62, 94, 95; and baseball teams, 12, 61–62
American minor leagues, 12, 133, 134, 146, 147, 210n12, 218n123
American sport, 7–8, 12, 87
Amis Aborigines, 17–24, 34, 40, 42–43, 47, 50, 58, 79, 94, 127, 155, 164, 165, 185n57, *figure 7*
Andō Shinya, 32
anticommunism, 61, 63, 64, 66, 69, 74, 78, 84, 93, 100, 152
Ao Youxiang, 138, *figure 10*
Arakawa Hiroshi, 76
Aramaki Ichitada, 21
Arbena, Joseph, 180n137
Arnold, Julean, 14–15

Asahi Shimbun, 7, 11, 16, 36, 38, 39, 42
Asian Baseball Championships, 74–75, 125
Asian Baseball League, 60
Asian Games, 78
assimilation: and foreign players in Taiwan, 133; and French imperialism, 10; ideology of "assimilation" and Chinese culture, 80, 189n11; as Japanese colonial subject, 3, 6, 10, 16–17, 19–20, 24, 26, 28, 32, 34, 36, 37, 39, 41–42, 44, 47, 66
Atayal Aborigines, 31, 154
Austronesian Aborigines: and "assimilation," 6, 21–24; and baseball, 6, 17–25, 31–43, 50, 52, 58, 81–89, 110–11, 123, 127, 141, 143, 162–66, *figure 14*; and Chinese assumptions of physical gifts, 24, 80, 162, 163–64; under Dutch rule, 30; exoticized in media, 32, 38; and "headhunting," 20, 25, 173n10, 183n35; and Japanese assumptions of physical gifts, 17, 21, 24, 33, 38, 80, 127; and Japanese colonialism, 3, 4, 8, 15, 17–24, 178n100, 182n12; in Japanese stories and films, 31, 183n35; on Japanese teams, 40, 47, 50, 185n57; as metaphors and symbols, 31–33, 38, 80, 81, 84, 85, 112, 163; and Qing Dynasty, 17, 18; in ROC era, 79–92, 94, 112, 127, 128, 141, 150, 154, 162–66; and romantic/tragic histories, 39, 42–43; as "savages," 17–25, 32, 40, 46, 70, 173n10,

Austronesian Aborigines *(continued)*
    179n125, 182n12; and tours of Japan, 18,
    22; as ultraprimitive and ultramodern, 23,
    32, 38
Awashima Chikage, 73

Ba Jin, 165
Bank of Formosa, 21
Bank of Taiwan semipro team, 72, 193n77
bank-sponsored semipro teams (ROC), 58, 59,
    61, 65, 66–68, 69, 70, 71, 72, 75, 193nn73,77,
    212n42
Baseball Bulletin (Yakyū sokuhō), 36
baseball in Taiwan: and American presence, 2,
    8, 61, 78, 94, 116, 117, 121, 123, 129, 131,
    133, 136, 139–40, 156, 162, 165, 215n77;
    and assimilation as Japanese subjects, 10, 17,
    20–25, 27, 37–39, 40–42, 63, 66; as *bangqiu*,
    58, 69, 157; as *bēsubōru*, 7; and capitalist
    ideology, 83–88, 120, 152–53, 155; and colo-
    nial unity in Taiwan, 37, 41, 45–47, 151; and
    competing Taiwanese/Chinese nationalisms,
    96–98, 101–3, 105–11; and discourse of Tai-
    wan unity, 158–60; and discourses of shame,
    embarrassment, loss, and victimization, 1,
    89–92, 103, 105, 108, 112–20, 123–24, 156–
    57; and film, 63, 75, 86–88, 114–15, 118–20;
    as *ia-kiu*, 2, 58, 66, 77; and identification
    with ROC state, 2, 96–97, 108, 151, 191n38;
    and the "individual," 151–53; and Japanese
    colonialism, 1–4, 6, 7–52, 116, 127, 129; as
    Japanese game, 1–2, 3–4, 5, 7–15, 55, 58, 59,
    62, 63, 66, 67, 69, 85, 93, 98, 103, 104, 105,
    149, 152, 155, 156, 166; and *kōminka*, 47–
    51, 151; and mainlander participation, 64,
    70, 97, 118, 142, 161–62; and masculinity,
    33, 44–45, 71–72, 178n100; and Nationalist
    goal of "retaking the mainland," 6, 92, 98, 99,
    101, 102, 106, 112; and Nationalist hubris,
    88, 93, 99–101; and race, 107, 113, 114, 141,
    164–65, *figure 10*; and ROC currency, *figure
    14*; and subethnic tensions, 65, 72, 90, 97–98,
    101–2; and Taiwan politics, 76, 142–43, 154,
    155, 160, 161, 197n155, *figures 13,15*; and
    Taiwanese discourses of nostalgia, 51, 52,
    86–87, 89–92, 113, 123–24, 141, 150, 151,
    152, 156, 157; as Taiwan's "national game,"
    2, 52, 119, 146, 154–55, 156, 157, 158–60;
    as *yakyū*, 7–8, 58, 66, 69, 77, 157, 173n4
Baseball World (Yakyūkai), 22, 39
basketball, 2, 59, 60, 63–64, 71, 92, 93, 154

Beatles, 90
Bee Gees, 115
Beigang (Yunlin County), 142
Beijing/Beiping, 59, 85, 101, 156, 204n120
Beinan Township (Taidong County), 82
Bell of Sayon, 31
Betts, Todd, 213n54
Bhabha, Homi, 3, 22, 36
Big League division, LLB (*Qingbang*), 104, 107
boys, symbolic value of, 107
British colonialism, 3–4, 9, 11, 13, 14, 17, 26, 31,
    41; and sport, 3–4, 11, 13, 14, 17, 26, 41, 44,
    178n100
Broadcasting Corporation of China, 129
Brother Elephants (CPBL), 131, 132, 133, 135,
    145, 148, 152, 154, 155, 165, 168, 213n46,
    214n65, 219n6
Buckley, James, 219n4
Buddhism, 48, 134
Bunun Aborigines, 78, 81–89, 162–63
Burma, 13
bushidō, 26

Cai Huanglang, 155
Cai Kunlin, 82
Cai Minghong, 217n100
Cai Songchuan, 100
Cai Songhui, 100, 103
Cai Wuzhang, 150
Cai Zhizhong, 113
Cai Zhongnan, 153
Campanis, Al, 63
Cano, Jose, 133
capitalist ideology, 83–88, 120, 152–53, 155
Castro, Fidel, 206n19
Central Monthly (Zhongyang yuekan), 106, 107
Central Motion Pictures Company, 76, 88
Chang Chen-yue, 147–48
Chang Hwa Bank semipro team, 68, 193n77
Changle Elementary School (Pingdong), 164
Chen, Chin-feng, 140, 146–47, 152, 155, 165,
    218nn122,123
Chen Chaoyi, 72
Chen Cheng, 66, 73
Chen Dafeng (Yasuaki Taihoh), 128, 213n48
Chen Dashun, 138
Chen Gengyuan (Akawats, Uematsu Kōichi),
    40, 58, 79, 143, 172n2, *figure 2*
Chen Hongpi, 95, 96
Chen Jiannian, 142–43, 216n94
Chen Jue, 198n1

Chen Qingxing, 94
Chen Runbo, 68–69, 127
Chen Shengtian, 140
Chen Shui-bian, 2, 76, 89, 92, 130, 149, 150, 151, 157, 158, 159, 160–61, 162, 163, 218n122
Chen Xiuxiong, 125–26, 211n12
Chen Yanchuan, 64, 75
Chen Yi, 190n19
Chen Yingzhen, 64
Chen Yiping, 138, 154, 216n84
Chen Yixin, 155, 164
Chen Zhixin, 164
Chen Zhiyuan, 96, 100–101
Chengqing Lake Stadium (Gaoxiong County), 148
Chiang Ching-kuo, 74, 84, 86, 115, 129–30
Chiang Kai-shek, 27, 56–57, 61, 64, 70, 73, 75, 78, 85, 93, 99, 100, 102, 103, 105, 106, 109, 111, 113, 115, 122, 152, 158, 188n1, 198n1, 208n53, figure 14
Children of Baseball, The (2000), 87, 88, 114–15
China Art and Literature Association, 117
China Baseball League (PRC), 217n102
China National Amateur Athletic Federation (ROC), 80
China Times (Zhongguo shibao), 113, 154
China Times Eagles (CPBL), 133, 135, 136, 164
China Trust Whales (CPBL), 121, 138, 144, 145, 164
China Youth Anti-Communist National Salvation Corps, 74, 84, 90
Chinese Communist Party, 61, 73
Chinese Culture University, 127
Chinese Daily (Zhonghua ribao), 90, 94
Chinese Nationalist Party (KMT, Guomindang), 2, 4, 6, 43, 54, 55, 59, 60, 63, 67, 73, 96, 102, 109, 110, 111, 112, 124, 130, 132, 142, 150, 155, 158, 206n22; and baseball, 6, 56–59, 70, 72–78, 82–86, 93, 94–95, 96–98, 100, 126, 150–52, 161–62; and construction of "Chinese culture" in Taiwan, 6, 59, 70, 77, 124, 152; and mainland diaspora, 54, 55; and mainlander dominance, 59, 60, 65; and sport, 56–57, 93; and view of Taiwanese as "slaves," 55; and "white terror," 57–58, 59, 64, 66, 92
Chinese Petroleum Corporation semipro team, 64
Chinese Professional Baseball League (CPBL, Chinese Professional Baseball Major League), 125, 130–40, 141, 142, 143, 144–48, 152–54, figure 8; and Chinese/Taiwanese/local culture, 133, 134, 141, 216n84; and competition

with TML, 140, 142, 144, 145, 146; and connections to mob, 137, 144–46; and corporate team ownership, 131–32, 152; and electoral politics, 142, 155, 161–62; and fan clubs, 132; and fan violence, 132; and foreign players (yangjiang), 132–33, 135–39, 213nn54,55, 214nn63,64,70, 218n114; and former Little League heroes, 134; and gambling scandals, 144–46, 160, 164, 217nn102,109; and merger with TML, 147, 159; official league slogans, 146, 153; planning of league, 128–30; and popular protest, 132; and relationships with foreign leagues, 134; and television broadcast contracts, 135, 144; uniforms and corporate advertisements, 132, 152, 219n6; and video games, 153
Chinese Taipei (ROC) Amateur Baseball Association, 129, 140. See also Republic of China Baseball Association, Taiwan Province Baseball Association
"Chinese Taipei" formula, 158
Chineseness: mythologies of in Nationalist Taiwan, 55, 57, 63, 77
Ching, Leo, 3, 16, 20, 22, 31, 41, 48, 184n35
Chiu Chuang-chin, figure 15
Chou, Justin, 155
Chu Tien-wen, 119
Chuiyang Elementary School (Jiayi), 82, 83, 84, 88, 103
Chūkyō Business School (Aichi), 32, 38, 39
Chūma Kanoe, 7
Chun, Allen, 35, 124
Coca-Cola, 62
"Cocacolonization," 5, 6, 162
Cohn, Bernard, 3, 18, 19
cold war, 59, 60, 61, 62, 77, 78, 123, 151
"collaborators," 4, 59, 67, 186n81
Collins, Terry, 1
Colonial Development University (Tokyo), 11
colonialism: American, 29; and bodies, 8–9, 13, 14–15; British, 3–4, 9, 11, 13, 14, 17, 26, 31, 41, 44; French, 10; as global system, 2, 30; and mimesis, 3, 22–23, 173n3; and sport, 3, 7–9, 13, 14. See also Dutch colonialism in Taiwan; Japanese colonialism
Costner, Kevin, 146
CPBL. See Chinese Professional Baseball League
cricket, 3, 11, 14, 17, 26, 41
Cui Jian, 112
"cultural intimacy," 89–90, 96, 105, 112–13, 115–16, 120, 157

Dalian (Dairen), 16, 37, 40, 45, 46, 186n81
Daxi (Takei, Taoyuan County), 28
decolonization, 54–55, 59, 67, 76, 77
Democratic Progressive Party (DPP, *Minjin-dang*), 142, 155, 160, 161, *figures 13,15*
de-Taiwanization, 54–55, 59
Diligence Elementary School (Taizhong), 154
dissidents, Taiwan, 79, 97–98, 101–2, 108–10, 113–14, 121
d-Media T-Rex (CPBL), 157. *See also* Macoto Cobras
dōka (assimilation), 16, 21, 23–24, 25–26, 27, 29, 32, 37, 41
Dominican Republic, 133, 136, 139, 140
Dongshi (Taizhong County), 142
Douliu (Toroku, Yunlin County), 33
DPP. *See* Democratic Progressive Party
Dutch colonialism in Taiwan, 2, 30, 158, 191n38

East Asia Vocational School (Jiayi County), 126
Eastern Taiwan Research Association, 19
"economic miracle" in Taiwan, 81, 86, 105, 107–8, 112, 115, 117, 118–19, 120, 124
Eguchi Ryōzaburō, 17, 19, 20, 21
Eiji Oguma, 30
Elkinton, Joseph, 18
Encarcion, Mario, 214n60
Enlightenment Society, 15
Ensui Sugar, 12
Era Communications, 140
Evergreen Shipping Agency, 132
"extension of the homeland" (*naichi enchō*), 11, 15
extermination (of "savages"), 173n10

Fang Junling, 122
Fang Shuiquan, 68
Far Eastern Championship Games, 14, 16, 63
February 28th Massacre (1947), 57–58, 77, 79, 111, 143, 161
First Bank semipro team, 193n77
First Financial Holdings Agan (CPBL). *See* La new Bears
football hooliganism, Europe, 109–10
"Forced Out" (1977), 117–18
Ford, Gerald, 108
foreign baseball players in Taiwan (*yangjiang*), 132–33, 135–36, 140–41, 146, 169, 213nn52,55, 218n114; and Chinese names, 133, 139, 215n73; and coaching, 133; and discourses of problems they cause, 136–37, 214n60; and

game-throwing/gambling scandals, 145–46; as overrepresented on CPBL teams, 136, 137, 214nn63,64,70; and popularity, 135–36, 146, 213n54; and resentment, 136–39; and Sinicized identities, 133; and Taiwanese anti-black racism, 137, 138, 141; and tropes of colonialism, 137, 138
Foreign Pro Baseball Players' Sex Scandals (1997), 137
Formosan Christians for Self-Determination, 97
Free China Chinese Baseball Team, 60, 76
Free China Taiwan Baseball Team, 60
Freehan, Bill, 100
Fu Jen Catholic University (Xinzhuang, Taipei County), 128
Fudan University (Shanghai), 58
Fujian Province (PRC), 100–101, 160, 194n92

Gaelic games, 3, 44
game-throwing/gambling scandals, 144–46, 157, 160, 164, 217nn102,109, 218n118
Gangshan Township (Gaoxiong County), 56
Gao Guoqing, 151
Gao Zhengyuan, 15, 49, 126
Gaoxiong (Takao), 12, 19, 28–29, 44, 45, 47, 62, 67, 68, 71, 111, 114, 122, 132, 142, 143, 145, 157, 161, 190n28, 216n94
Gaoxiong-Pingdong Fala (Thunder Gods, TML), 141, 142, 148
Giles, Brian, 133
globalization, 130, 131, 136, 138, 140, 160, 162
glocalization: 5, 9, 24–25, 26, 28, 55, 97–98, 131, 132, 136, 140–41, 160
Go Ha. *See* Wu Bo
Go Shōsei. *See* Wu Bo
Goffman, Erving, 23
Goldberg, Lonnie, 136
Gonzalez, Jose, 133
Gonzalez, Paul, 219n4
Gotō Shimpei, 9, 15, 18
Goujian, king of Yue, 208n53
Graham, Katherine, 129
Great Britain, 3, 4, 10, 11, 14, 20, 26, 31, 41, 44, 107, 110
Great Leap Forward famine, 87, 99
Great Proletarian Cultural Revolution, 98, 152, 165
Greater East Asia Co-Prosperity Sphere, 151
Green Island prison, 82
Gu Jincai, 83
Gumbrecht, Hans, 22–23, 31, 43, 190n27
Guo Jiancheng, 217n102

Guo Jinxing, 145, 217n109
Guo Taiyuan (Kaku Taigen), 111, 127
Guo Yuanzhi (Kaku Genji), 94, 95, 103, 111, 119–20, 127, 128, 213n48, *figure 7*
Guomindang. See Chinese Nationalist Party
guoshu, 45
guoyu. See Mandarin language
Guttman, Allen, 180n137

Hakka ethnicity, 68
"half-mountain people" (*banshanren*), 58–59
Hall, Stuart, 26–27, 67
Hamaguchi Mitsuya (Guo Guangye), 127
"Han" ethnicity in Taiwan, 6, 10, 16, 17, 18, 19, 20, 24, 25, 31–32, 36, 37, 39, 41, 44, 64, 162, 163–64, 174n23, 178n90, 181n4, 186n83
"Hands Across Taiwan" (2004), 161, *figure 13*
Hao Gengsheng, 79
Harper, Milt, 136, 137, *figure 9*
Harrison, Mark, 180n142
He Fan (Xia Chengying), 84–85
He Xianfan, 138
Heian High School (Kyoto), 23, 185n57
Herzfeld, Michael, 89–90, 96, 103, 105, 113, 157
Higuchi Takashi, 34
Hinshaw, George, 136
Hirohito, Crown Prince, 22, 47
Hiroshima, 22, 68
Hodge, John, 188n1
Home Rule Movement, 180n134
Hong Taishan, 33, 35, 50, 52–53, 56, 60, 66, 68, 69
Hong Tengsheng, 131
Hongye Elementary School. *See* Maple Leaf (Hongye) Elementary School
Honor Thy Father (1989), 76
Hōsei University (Tokyo), 12, 23, 46–47, 186n83
Hou Dezheng, 114
Hou Hsiao-hsien, 119
Hsiao Bi-khim, 155
Hsieh, Frank Chang-ting, 197n155
Hsu Chu-chien, 220n23
Hu Mingcheng, 163
Hu Wuhan, 91. *See also* Jiang Wanxing
Hu Xueli, 82
Hu Yonghui, 89. *See also* Jiang Honghui
Hua Nan Bank, 61, 65, 71, 193n77; semipro team, 67
Hualian (Karenkō), 17, 19, 91, 155
Huang Jie, 84
Huang Pingyang, 134
Huang Qingjing, 138

Huang Renhui, 60–62, 69
Huang Yongxiang, 114
Huang Zhengyi, 103
Huang Zhixiong, 114
Huang Zhongyi, 164
Huatan Township (Zhanghua County), *figure 15*
Huaxing Middle School (Taipei), 122, 128; and Song Meiling, 208n53
Hurst, Jonathan, 135

Iglesias, Luis, 133, 135
Imakurusu Sunao, 69
Inada Teruo, 23
India, 14, 20
Inoue Kaoru, 15
Intercity Baseball Tournament (Japan), 40, 45, 50, 128
International Baseball Association, 105; and IBA World Cup, 105, 125, 158–60
"Invader, The" (1977), 118
Ireland, 3, 44–45
Iseda Gō, 11
Islandwide High School Baseball Tournament, 34, 36
isshi dōjin ("impartiality and equal favor"), 25, 35, 66, 150, 151
Itagaki Taisuke, 181n142
Itō Jirō (Luo Daohou), 23, 47, 50
Itō Masao, 23, 47

James, C. L. R., 3, 17, 26
Japan, contemporary role of, in Taiwanese baseball, 155, 162, 165–66
Japanese baseball: Japanese Baseball Hall of Fame, 49, 184n46; Little League Baseball, 78, 83, 84, 87, 88, 93, 95, 96; players and managers in Taiwan, 140–41, 214n65; postwar trips to Taiwan, 65–66, 70–72, 77; semipro teams, 21, 40, 50, 60, 71, 134; terminology, 2–3, 20, 58, 155, 217n98
Japanese Baseball League (1936–49), 42, 48, 49–50. *See also* Japanese professional baseball teams; Nippon Professional Baseball
Japanese colonialism, 15, 80, 163, 176nn60,61, 178nn90,100, 188n112; and baseball, 1–4, 6, 7–53, 116, 127, 129, 150–51, 161, 165; and education, 16–17, 23, 25, 26, 29, 32–34, 54, 55–56, 179n125, 180n131, 182nn9,12, 185n57; and nostalgia, 34–35, 43–44, 64, 70–71, 78, 152; and physical education, 8, 14–15, 17; in Southeast Asia, 12, 32, 68

Japanese Industrial Leagues, 128; Japan Oil team, 75; Kawai Musical Instruments team, 128; Kumagai Gumi Construction team, 128; Yamaha Motor Company team, 128

Japanese military, 68–69

Japanese professional baseball teams: Chunichi Dragons, 119, 127, 128, 134, 136, 147, 155, 213n48; Hanshin Tigers, 49, 128; Hiroshima Carp, 103; Mainichi/Lotte Orions 49, 211n18; Nagoya Golden Dolphins, 194n92; Nankai/ Fukuoka Hawks, 50, 76, 127; Orix Blue Wave, 140, 153; Rakuten Golden Eagles, 154; Seibu Lions, 69, 125–26, 127, 140, 147, 211n12; Tokyo Giants/Tokyo Yomiuri Giants, 42, 46, 49, 50, 72–73, 75, 103, 128, 134–35, 157, 187n96, 211n18; Tokyo Senators, 50; Yamato Baseball Club, 50. See also Japanese Baseball League; Nippon Professional Baseball

Japanese women's baseball: Salonpas women's baseball team, 71–72; Sankyō Pharmaceutical Corporation women's baseball team, 71, 72; Tokyo Women's Baseball Club, 71

Jian Mingjing, 142

Jian Yongchang, 27–28, 36, 54, 63, 67–68, 94, 102, 125–26

Jiang Honghui (alias Hu Yonghui), 83–84, 88–89, 90–91, 163, 201n52

Jiang Taiquan, 145, 217n102

Jiang Wanxing (alias Hu Wuhan), 84, 91

Jiang Weishui, 27

Jiang Zemin, 5

Jiayi (Kagi), 10, 12, 31–38, 42–44, 49, 66, 70, 79, 82, 83, 90, 94, 95, 103, 114, 118, 121, 126, 142, 143, 144–45, 183n35

Jiayi Agriculture and Forestry Institute, 172n1. See also Kanō

Jiayi Institute of Technology, 7. See also Kanō

Jiayi Municipal Stadium, 143, 144

Jiayi Seven Tigers (LLB), 113–15, 118, 120, 121, 208n53

Jiayi-Tainan Luka (Braves, TML), 141, 142, 143, 151, 155, 219n4

Jinmen (Quemoy) Island, 100–101, 106, 107, 118

J-League (Japanese professional soccer), 216n84

Johnson, Rafer, 79

juancun military housing complexes, 64, 118

Jungo Bears (CPBL), 133, 135, 136–37, 138, 139, 154, 216n84. See also Sinon Bulls

Kainan Vocational School (Taipei), 71–72

Kanō (Tainan shūritsu Kagi nōrin gakkō, Tainan District Kagi Agriculture and Forestry Institute), 31–44, 47–49, 50, 53, 56, 60, 66, 67, 68, 70, 127, 150, 172n1, 182n9, 183n56, 185n57, figures 1,2,3,4,11; and baseball and nostalgia, 33, 35, 41, 43–44, 79–80, 150; and baseball and racism, 35–36. and baseball and "tri-ethnic harmony," 4, 31–33, 35, 38–39, 41, 52, 58; and baseball and violence, 35–36; See also Jiayi Agriculture and Forestry Institute; Jiayi Institute of Technology; National Jiayi University; Taiwan Provincial Jiayi Agriculture Vocational School

Kao, Eng-jey (Gao Yingjie), 126–27, 210n11

Karenkō Agricultural Study Institute, 17, 21

Katz, Paul, 16–17

Keiō University, 12, 19, 67, 70–71

Kelly, William, 11, 68, 134

Kenkō Shintō Shrine, 47, 48

Kentucky Fried Chicken, 5

Kerr, George, 4, 47

Kikuchi Kan, 39

Kim Yong Woon, 139

Kinoshita Makoto, 23

Kisa, 21, 22

KMT (Guomindang). See Chinese Nationalist Party

Kobayashi Yoshinori, 43

Kodama Gen, figure 3

Kojima Akira, 70

kōminka ("imperial-subjectification"), 47–51, 151

Komodo, 21, 22

Konami Cup, 164

Kondō Hyōtarō, 34–36, 185n57

Konno Tadao, 52–53

Korea, 12, 16, 37, 46, 49, 176n61, 188nn112,1. See also North Korea; South Korea

Korean War, 60

Kōshien National High School Baseball Tournament, 16, 23, 31–32, 36, 37–42, 45, 185nn56,57

Koyae Kyoko (Wang Gongzi), 75

Ku Ling (Wang Yuren), 64

Kundera, Milan, 105, 118

Kuo, Hong-Chih (Guo Hongzhi), 147, 156

Kwantung Leased Territory (northeast China), 38

Kyoto, 23

La new Bears (CPBL), 147, 154, 213n54

Lai, Leon, 153

Lan Dehe (Higashi Kazuichi), 42, figure 2

Lan Deming (Higashi Kumon), 42–43, 69

Land Bank semipro team, 71, 193n77
lapta, 172n4
Lee, Lai-hua (Li Laifa), 126–27, 144, 210n11
Lee Teng-hui (Li Denghui), 125, 142, 143, 161
Li Juming, 148
Li Kunzhe, 121
Li Shiji, 67
Li Shiming, 186n81
Li Yajing, 142
Li Zhijun, 128
Li Zongyuan (Miyake Sōgen), 211n18
Li Zongzhou, 115
Liao, Hsien-hao, 118
Liberty Times (*Ziyou shibao*), 137, 142, 145, 158
Lide Elementary School (Gaoxiong), 122
Lien Chan (Lian Zhan), 146
Lin Guixing, 17, 18, 19, 58
Lin Huawei, 62, 113, 128
Lin Huazhou, 108
Lin Zhisheng, 164
Lin Zhupeng, 81–82
Liren Elementary School (Tainan), 88
litost, 116, 118
"Little Baseball Hero" (1970), 116–17, *figure 5*
Little Giants of Maple Leaf (1988), 86–87
Little League Baseball (LLB), 99–100, 114, 122;
    and American pride in spreading game to
    Taiwan, 121, 209n70; and Americans booing
    Taiwanese children, 121–23; and Far East/
    Asia-Pacific Region playoffs, 90, 93, 94,
    108, 114, 209n87; and official probes into
    Taiwanese cheating, 122
Little League Baseball in Taiwan (*Shaonian
    bangqiu, Shaobang*), 4–5, 6, 81, 89–90, 92–
    124, 149, 152, 154–55, 156, 162–63; and
    cheating, 90, 94, 114, 120–21, 123, 201n56;
    and "embarrassment" trope, 89, 113; and
    erroneous household registration, 120–21;
    and violence, 90, 98, 102, 109–10, 112, 123,
    206n23
Little League Baseball World Series (William-
    sport, Pennsylvania), 83, 92, 95–99, 100–
    102, 104, 105–6, 109–10, 113–15, 120–23,
    151, 154, 202n76, 209n87, 217n100
Liu Canglin, 128
Liu Jinyao, 33
Liu Qiunong, 128
Liu Tianlu, 73
LLB. *See* Little League Baseball
Loggins, Kenny, 119
Los Angeles Times, 122, 146

Louis, Joe, 87
Lü Mingci, 128
Lu Ruitu, 114
Lu Xun, 133
Lukas, Anthony, 122–23

Ma Qingshan, 198n1
Ma Ying-jeou (Ma Yingjiu), 76, 150, 161–62
MacArthur, Douglas, 188n1
Macaulay, Thomas, 20
Macoto Cobras (CPBL), 214n60. *See also*
    d-Media T-Rex
Macoto Gida (CPBL). *See* d-Media T-Rex;
    Macoto Cobras
Mainichi Broadcasting System, 43
"mainlanders" in Taiwan (*waishengren*), 59, 64,
    68, 72, 97, 100, 112, 118–19, 142, 161
Major League Baseball (MLB, U.S. and Canada),
    131, 135, 165, 213n52, 215n77; Atlanta Braves,
    140; Baltimore Orioles, 128; Brooklyn/Los
    Angeles Dodgers, 63, 134, 139–40, 146–
    47, 152, 156, 210n11, 218n123; California/
    Anaheim Angels, 146, 213n46; Cincinnati
    Reds, 103, 126, 139, 144; Cleveland Indians,
    137, 213n46; Colorado Rockies, 147; Detroit
    Tigers, 78, 100, 156; Houston Astros, 133,
    139; New York Mets, 96, 125, 133, 213n46;
    218n118; New York Yankees, 78, 147, 154–
    55, 156, 159, 161, 197n155, *figure 12*; Oakland
    A's, 139, 216n84; Pittsburgh Pirates, 210n11;
    San Diego Padres, 134, 136, 139, 213n46;
    San Francisco Giants, 157, 211n12, 218n118;
    Tampa Bay Devil Rays, 154; Toronto Blue
    Jays, 127
Manchuria, 12, 16, 37, 46, 49, 178nn90,100,
    188n1
Manchus, 64. *See also* Qing Dynasty
Mandarin language (*guoyu*), 3, 58, 67–68, 99,
    135, 143, 155, 217n98
Manila, 60, 74, 75
Mantle, Mickey, 78
Manzanillo, Ravelo, 133
Mao Zedong, 99, 109, 113
Maple Leaf (Hongye) Elementary School, 81–92,
    94, 95, 103, 121, 162–63, 208n54, 216n94;
    and cheating, 88–89, 94, 201nn52,56; and
    literature, 91; and 1968 defeats of Wakayama
    team, 83–88, 90–91, 93, 94; and nostalgia,
    86–87, 89–92; and players' adult lives, 89,
    90–91; and trope of poverty, 81, 84, 85, 87,
    162–63, 199n14

martial law (1948–87), 112, 123, 130, 132
Martinez, Osvaldo, 135
Marx, Richard, 213n54
masculinity, 33, 44–45
Mazu (Matsu) Island, 106
McClendon, Lloyd, 113, 120
McDonald's, 62, 148, 152, *figure 12*
McGovern, Peter J., 99, 114
McKay, Jim, 97
Meihe Middle School (Pingdong), 208n53
Meiji era, 47; and Japanese colonialism, 7–8, 9–10
Meiji Jingu Stadium, 40, 45
Meiji Shrine, 22, 34, 40
Meiji University, 67, 70, 77
Mejia, Cesar, 133
Mercuries Tigers (CPBL), 125, 131, 132, 133, 135, 139, 145, 212n42, 213n46; and folding of team, 146
Metoyer, Tony, 133, 137, *figure 9*
Miaoli, 64, 65, 75
Minbao (People's News), 56, 57
Ming Dynasty, 191n38
Mishima Yukibumi, 28
Mitsui Sugar, 10
Mitsuya Sei, 183n35
MLB. *See* Major League Baseball
modernization: and trauma, 105, 118–19
Mona Rudao, 182n6
Mora, Melvin, 125, 218n118
Moreno, Jose, 213n46
Morita, Akio, 9, 26
Moskowitz, Marc, 137
Mountain Areas Athletic Meet, 80–81
Muramatsu Ichizō, 14
Murdoch, Rupert, 135
Musha Incident (1930), 20, 31, 37, 38, 40–41, 182n6, 183n35

Nagashima Shigeo, 75
Nagayama Yoshitaka, 7
Nagoya University, 128
Naluwan Corporation, 140
"Naluwan—True Heroes" (1997), 143–44, 217nn97,98
Nanbu Chuhei, 49
Nanfang Shuo, 162, 164–65
Nanjing, 101, 204n120
Nantou County, 142
National Games (ROC, 1948), 59
National Jiayi University, 150, 172n1, *figure 11*. *See also* Kanō

National Reunification Council, 161
National Taidong Junior College, 164
National Taiwan College of Physical Education, 128
National Taiwan University, 56, 64, 118, 132
New Park (Taipei), 61, 77
New People's Society, 15
New Taiwan Cultural Association, 184n55
New York Times, 98, 121, 126, 218n118
Ni Fu-te (Ni Fude), 156
Nicaragua, 113–15
Nippon Professional Baseball (NPB, 1950–present), 125–29, 131, 134–35, 213n55, 215n77. *See also* Japanese Baseball League; Japanese professional baseball teams
Nishimura Kazō, 23
Nishiwaki Yoshitomo, 35, 36
Nitobé Inazo (Nitobe Inazō), 7, 8, 16, 18
Nixon, Richard, 97, 108, 113
Nōkō Baseball Team ("savage Team Nōkō"), 17–24, 47, 50, 58, 89, 165–66, 185n59; and 1924 Taiwan tour, 21; and 1925 Japan tour, 21–23, 179n119
North Korea, 61, 188n1. *See also* Korea
nostalgia: and baseball, 51, 52, 86–87, 89–92, 113, 123–24, 141, 150, 151, 152, 156, 157; and Japanese colonialism, 34–35, 43–44, 64, 70–71, 78, 152; and Kanō, 33, 35, 41, 43–44, 79–80, 150; and Little League Baseball, 86–87, 89–92

Oh Sadaharu (Wang Zhenzhi), 72–76, 128; and Chinese language and culture, 75; and 1989 biopic, 76; and PRC government, 73; and "return trips" to motherland, 73–75; and ROC citizenship, 73; and ROC government leaders, 73–76, 157, 161
Okamura Toshiaki (Ye Tiansong), 50
Okinawa, 8
Ōkoshi Kanji, 127
Okuda Hajime, *figure 3*
Olympic Games: of 1932 and 1936, 67; of 1960, 79; of 1964, 198n1; of 1968, 80; of 1980, 87; of 1992, 135, 144, 145; of 2004, 155; of 2008, 156–57, 165, 220n25
O'Malley, Peter, 139
Orwell, George, 13
Osaka, 31, 40, 68
Osaka Asahi Shimbun, 22
Osuna, Al, 139
Ōta Masahiro, 38

Overseas Chinese, 73, 121; in Japan, 111; in Southeast Asia, 59, 60; in U.S., 95, 96, 97, 98, 101–2, 109–10, 111, 112, 114, 174n20

Pan Wei-lun, 156, 220n23
Paris Exhibition (1900), 18
pastoral, 7–8, 150, 151
Peng Mengqi, 111–13
Peng Ming-min, 45
Peng Zhengmin, 152
Penghu Islands, 56, 106
People First Party (*Qinmindang*), 76
People's Republic of China (PRC), 2, 5, 6, 85, 87, 92, 99, 100, 101, 107, 113, 121, 130–31, 139, 149, 152, 155–57, 158, 160, 161, 162, 178n90, 198n1, 200n49, 217n102; national baseball team, 1, 146, 156–57, 217n102, 220n23
Phelps, Michael, 157
Philippines, 12, 29, 60, 69, 74, 75, 151, 165; and "Overseas Chinese" baseball team, 59
Physical Education Quarterly (Guomin tiyu jikan), 90, 99
Ping Lu, 87
Pingdong (Heitō), 51, 68, 70, 76, 80, 132, 135, 136, 164, 208n53
postcolonial, 67, 69, 78
Powell, Alonzo, 128
PRC. *See* People's Republic of China
Presbyterian Church in Taiwan, 161
Prince (Wangzi) Magazine, 82, 116, *figure 5*
Prince Kitashirakawa Yoshihisa, 47, 48
Province-wide Students' Cup, 81
Pusan, 16
Puyuma Aborigines, 40, 58, 164, 172n2, *figure 14*
Puzi (Jiayi County), 142
Puzi Elementary School Tornadoes, 121, 217n100

Qing Dynasty, 2, 7, 8, 9, 17, 18, 99, 147, 174n20, 183n35, 188n1, 189n11, 192n61
Qingbang. See Big League division, LLB
Qingshaobang. See Senior League division, LLB
Qiu Chunguang, 163
Qiu Fusheng, 140
Qu Hailiang, 165
Quinones, Luis, 139

Renan, Ernest, 89
Republic of China (ROC): Aboriginal policy, 80–81, 82; Council of Aboriginal Affairs, 15; educational system of, 60, 77, 80, 84, 88, 90, 93, 100, 101, 123, 124, 126, 163, 208n53; Government Information Office, 73, 104; Legislative Yuan, 142, 148; Ministry of Education, 84, 88, 93; and 1971 withdrawal from the United Nations, 108; and 1970s diplomatic isolation, 108, 121, 151, 160; and "Retrocession" of Taiwan, 4, 54, 56; secret police, 64; and suppression of Japanese/Taiwanese culture, 54–56, 150
Republic of China and sport: and baseball hubris, 88, 93, 99–101, 106–8, 114; and courtship of Oh Sadaharu, 72–76; and denial of Japanese history of baseball, 54, 62–63, 77–78, 98, 112, 125–26; and gifts and privileges given to LLB champions, 111, 208n53; ROC National Amateur Athletic Federation, 125; ROC Professional Baseball Preparatory Committee, 130; and sporting ideology from mainland China, 56, 93, 105, 124; and weak support of baseball, 60–61, 85, 92, 93, 105, 125, 154
Republic of China Baseball Association, 74, 77–78, 83, 93, 94, 95, 114, 115, 116. *See also* Chinese Taipei (ROC) Amateur Baseball Association; Taiwan Province Baseball Association
Republic of China military, 63, 64, 69, 74, 100–101, 106, 111, 126; Air Force baseball team, 59, 74, 126; Army baseball team, 127; Navy baseball team, 60, 69, 71, 193n73; Police baseball team, 59
Republic of China official ideology: as "Free China," 60, 63, 66, 78, 104, 109, 113, 120, 151; discourses of reunification of mainland China, 57, 92, 99, 101, 106–7, 112, 200n49; discourses of Chinese culture, 55, 57, 63, 73, 77, 106, 107, 114, 124
"resistance," 26, 27, 29
"Retrocession" (*Guangfu*, 1945), 4, 54, 56, 59, 65, 72, 77, 188n1
Rhee, Syngman, 76–77
Rice, Grantland, 39
Rickey, Branch, 34
Rivera, Elvin, 133
Robertson, Roland, 5, 9
ROC. *See* Republic of China
Rolling Stone, 122–23
Roman, Jose, 213n46
Rōsawai, 22
rugby, 47, 52, 161
Ruth, Babe, 45

Sakuma Samata, 13
Sampo Electronics, 140
Sasada Toshio, 35
Sauma, 17
"savage governance" (*riban jigyō*), 18, 19, 38, 52
"savage Team Nōkō." *See* Nōkō Baseball Team
Scruggs, Bert, 22, 36, 40
Scully, Vin, 218n118
self-Orientalism, 15
Senior League division, LLB (*Qingshaobang*), 104, 107, 109, 122
Seoul (Keijō), 37, 40, 45–46, 76
Shandong Province, 63
Shanghai, 16, 58, 59, 63, 64, 192n63
Shaobang. See Little League Baseball in Taiwan
Shaolin martial arts, 215n73
Shaonian bangqiu. See Little League Baseball in Taiwan
Shea, William, 96
Sheng Zhuru, 114
Shiba Ryōtarō, 7, 161
Shih Jian-hsin, 157
Shimauchi Tsuneaki, 37
Shimomura Hiroshi, 16
Shintō shrines: in Taiwan, 10, 33, 47–48, 50, 56, 61; in Japan, 22, 34, 40, 46, 118
Shōwa era, 35
Sichuan Province, 105, 125
"Sick Man of East Asia" cliché, 99
"Sinicization," 54–56, 150, 189n11
Sinon Agrochemical Corporation, 139, 215n73
Sinon Bulls (CPBL), 135, 139, 145, 146, 164, 214n64, 219n6. *See also* Jungo Bears
Sinorama (*Guanghua zazhi*), 159, 163–64
Slusarski, Joe, 139
soccer, 2, 13, 26, 60, 64, 92, 93, 104, 105, 109–10, 216n84
Song Chaon-seng, 97
Song Meiling, 56, 75, 102, 106, 208n53
Songshan Airport (Taipei), 65, 115
Sonobe Hisashi, *figure 3*
Soong, James, 142
South Korea, 60, 61, 69, 71, 72, 76–77, 129, 131, 151, 156, 159, 213n55, 215n77. *See also* Korea
Sport and Interest (*Undō to shumi*), 12, 14
Sporting News, The, 96, 121
Sports Illustrated, 79
Stalin, Joseph, 188n1
Stoole, Steve, 133
Story of Go Hō, The (1931), 183n35

"street movement," 132
Strong, Joe, 135
Struggle (1988), 119–20, 127
Students' Cup tournament, 82, 88
Su Zhengsheng, 15, 35, 36, 39, 40, 43–44, 56, 66
sugar corporations: and baseball teams in Taiwan, 10, 11, 12, 13, 19, 42, 58, 68, 70
sumo, 9, 12, 50, 187n100
Sun Lingfeng, 157
Sun Liren, 63
Sun Moon Lake, 5, 75
Sun Ta-chuan, 15
Sun Yat-sen, 76, 99; Baseball Stadium (Jiayi), 70; birthday, 80; halls, 55; Museum (Taipei), 73; and Three People's Principles, 28
Suzuki, Ichirō, 153
Suzuki Akira, 13–14, 39, 42–43

Taidong (Taitō), 34, 42, 66, 79, 81, 84, 88, 94, 103, 142, 162, 198n3, 216n94
Taidong Agricultural School, 79
Taihoku baseball leagues, 46
Taihoku Commercial School, 21, 36, 47
Tainan, 12, 36, 51, 56, 62, 67, 68, 69, 71, 88, 94, 114, 121, 131, 132, 135, 139
Tainan Baseball Association, 21
Tainan District Kagi Agriculture and Forestry Institute, 31. *See also* Kanō
Tainan Giants (LLB), 90, 105–6, 107, 109, 111–13, 120, 122, 157, 209n74, *figure 6*
Tainan New Times (*Tainan shimpō*), 25
Taipei (Taihoku), 10, 11, 12, 13, 16, 19, 21, 22, 28, 36, 37, 40, 45–46, 51, 53, 67, 68, 69–70, 71, 76, 81, 82, 83, 84, 86, 87, 88, 90, 95, 102, 103, 114, 115, 117, 118–19, 121, 122, 128, 132, 137, 143, 158–59, 160, 161
Taipei Bankers Association baseball league, 66–67
Taipei Braves (LLB), 109
Taipei Gida (Suns, TML), 141, 146, 148, 164
Taipei Municipal Baseball Stadium, 70, 73, 74, 83, 87, 108, 112, 132
Taipei Park (Taipei New Park, February 28 Peace Park), 61, 77
Taipei Story (1985), 118–19
Taiping LLB champions (1981), 209n87
Taishō era, 11
Taiwan Aborigines. *See* Austronesian Aborigines
Taiwan Coal semipro team, 58, 68, 69
"Taiwan consciousness/identity," 45, 85, 149–50; and professional baseball, 130, 135, 140

Taiwan Cooperative Bank semipro team, 59, 67, 68, 69, 70, 75, 193n77, 212n42

Taiwan Electric semipro team, 67, 68, 69, 131

Taiwan Exposition Commemorating Forty Years of [Japanese] Rule, 46

Taiwan Farmers' Combine, 185n55

Taiwan Independence movement, 60, 156; and publicity work at Williamsport, 97–98, 101–2, 108–10, 185n55

Taiwan Major League (TML), 136, 140–44, 145, 146, 147–48, 153, 161, 164; and "Aborigine culture," 141, 143, 217nn97,98; and competition with CPBL, 141–44, 145, 146; and connections to foreign leagues and teams, 140; and electoral politics, 142; and February 28 Opening Night, 142, 143; and gambling scandals, 146, 218n118; and merger with CPBL, 147, 159; official league slogans, 141, 153; and stated preference for Japanese players, 140–41; and "Taiwanese" branding, 140, 142–44; and "territorial philosophy," 141–42

Taiwan Minbao, 26, 28–29

Taiwan Nichinichi Shimpō, 9, 21, 22, 23, 37, 38, 46, 51, 55

Taiwan People's Party, 184n55

Taiwan Power semipro team, 58

Taiwan Province Baseball Association, 58, 65. *See also* Chinese Taipei (ROC) Amateur Baseball Association; Republic of China Baseball Association

Taiwan Provincial Assembly, 74

Taiwan Provincial Games, 56–57, 66, 190nn19,28, 198n3

Taiwan Provincial Jiayi Agriculture Vocational School, 58. *See* Kanō

Taiwan Provincial Physical Education College (Taizhong), 75

Taiwan Provincial Police Command, 56

Taiwan Shrine, 47, 61

Taiwan Sports Association, 7, 9

Taiwan Sugar, 70; semipro team, 12, 58

Taiwan Television, 83, 114, 142

Taiwan Workers' League, 184n55

Taiwan Youth (*Taiwan qingnian*), 101

Taiwan Youth (*Taiwan seinen*), 16

Taiwanese Communist Party, 176n61, 185n55

Taiwanese Cultural Association, 15

Taiwanese language, 2, 57, 58, 86, 91, 135, 143, 155, 217n98

Taiwanese players in Japan, 6, 49–50, 125–29,
134, 166, 185n57, 186n83, 211nn12,18, 213n48

Taizhong (Taichū), 34, 36, 47, 50, 69, 71, 74, 75, 88, 90, 94, 95, 132, 141, 151, 154, 157, 163, 216n84

Taizhong Agan (Robots, TML), 136, 141–42, 143

Taizhong Golden Dragons (LLB), 79, 90, 93–103, 119, 121, 208n53, 219n4; illegal composition of, 94, 121; and Japanese legacy, 103; in U.S., 95–97

Taizhong Municipal Stadium, 75

Takasago Baseball League, 19, 44

Takasago Baseball Team, 17, 18, 19. *See also* Nōkō Baseball Team

Takemura Toyotoshi, 46

Tan Hsin-Min, 211n12

Tang, Harvey (Chen Hedong), 132, 159

Tang, P. P., 129

Taoyuan, 65, 154, 156

Ta-pa-ni Incident (1915), 17

Tazawa Sanae, 72

tennis, 14, 15, 17, 34, 52, 161, 173n4

Tenth Credit Union semipro team, 74

Thomson, John, 17

Three People's Principles, 56, 57

Tianjin Lions (China Baseball League), 217n102

Tiburcio, Freddy, 133, 135

TML. *See* Taiwan Major League

Tobita Suishū, 39, 42

Tokyo, 1, 7, 16, 22–23, 34, 38, 40, 45, 68, 93, 103, 111, 112, 164

Tōkyō Asahi Shimbun, 38

Tokyo Big Six University League, 12, 46, 67

Tokyo Broadcasting System, 52–53

Tokyo Disneyland, 9

Tōkyō Nichinichi Shimpō, 40

Tokyo No. 1 High School (*Ichikō*), 7, 14

Tokyo University, 16

Tonooka Mojūrō, 65–66

Tōzumi Tomi, 73

tragedy and ideology, 42–43, 120, 163

Trobriand Cricket (1975), 3

Ts'ai, Huiyu Caroline, 37, 44, 50, 69

Tsai Chin, 118–19

Tsao, Chin-hui (Cao Jinhui), 147, 165

Tucheng (Taipei County), 147

Tuo Hongshan (Mayama Uichi), 34, 40, 43

Turtle Mountain Elementary (Guishan, Taoyuan County), 154

TV Tokyo, 43

TVIS, 135, 140, 144

two thousand and six hundredth anniversary of mythical founding of Japan, 50

Umeno Seitarō, 17, 19

Uni-President Lions (Uni-President 7–Eleven Lions, CPBL), 131–32, 133, 134, 137, 145, 151, 217n109, *figure 9*

United Daily News (*Lianhebao*), 60, 62–63, 65, 70, 71, 72, 73, 74–75, 78, 81, 82, 83, 84–85, 88, 114, 115, 117, 126, 128, 132, 143, 147, 154, 157, 158, 201n52

United Formosans in America for Independence, 79, 97

United Nations: and ROC forfeiture of seat, 87, 113

Urawa, U.S. military base at, 94

U.S. aid to ROC, 61, 86, 92

U.S. Military Assistance Advisory Group (MAAG), 61

USSR, 61, 87, 171n4

Valdez, Rafael, 133

Vasquez, Aguedo, 133

Veterans Hospital semipro team, 212n42

Viva Formosa (*Duli Taiwan*), 93, 109

waishengren. See "mainlanders" in Taiwan

Wakayama LLB team, 83, 84, 87, 88, 90

Wang, Chien-ming (Wang Jianmin), 154, 155, 156, 161, *figure 12*

Wang Gongzi. *See* Koyae Kyoko

Wang Guojin, 164

Wang Jinping, 142, 148

Wang Junlang, 139

Wang Shifu, 73

Wang Zhenzhi. *See* Oh Sadaharu

Waseda-Keiō War, 67, 70–71

Waseda University, 11–12, 34, 39, 40, 49, 65–66, 70–71, 77, 193n73

Washington Post, 129

Weber, Ben, 146, 218n118

Wei, James, 104

Weichuan Dragons (CPBL), 131, 132, 134, 135, 137–38, 145, 146; and folding of team, 146

West Indies, 3, 17, 26, 41

"white terror," 57–58, 59, 64, 66, 92

Williams, Ted, 111

Williamsport, Pennsylvania, 6, 92, 95–98, 99, 101–2, 103, 104, 108–10, 114, 120, 122–23,

154; and anti-Taiwanese racism, 121–23; and Taiwan Independence activities, 79, 97–98, 101–2, 108–10, 113–14, 121. *See also* Little League Baseball World Series

Wilson, Woodrow, 15, 32

World Aborigine Baseball Championship, 165

World Baseball Classic, 1, 157, 206n19, 220n23

World Trade Organization, 149

World War I, 15–16

World War II, 47–51, 54, 56, 62, 84, 87, 94, 150, 151

Wu Bo (Go Ha, Go Shōsei, Ishii Masayuki), 49, 187nn96,97,98

Wu Dunyi, 142

Wu Junda, 165

Wu Junliang, 214n70

Wu Linlian, 145

Wu Mingjie, 39, 40, *figure 2*

Wu Mintian, 114–15, 118

Wu Nien-jen, 119

Wu Xiangmu, 69

Wu Xinheng (Go Shintei, Hagiwara Hiroshi), 49–50, 187n98

Wu Zhuoliu, 13, 16, 27, 51, 54

Wushe. *See* Musha Incident

Xiamen, 139, 146

Xiao Changgun, 28

Xiao crime gang (Jiayi), 145

Xiaoye (Li Yuan), 117–18

Xie Changheng, *figure 9*

Xie Dongmin, 58, 70, 74

Xie Guocheng, 65, 78, 95, 115

Xie Shiyuan, 35, 62, 165

Xie Yufa, 64

Xingang (Jiayi County), 142

Xinzhu (Shinchiku), 16, 27–28, 65, 72, 83, 132, 135

Xu Jinmu, 120–21

Xu Shengming, 145

Xu Xinliang, 142

Xue Yongshun (Sei Kiyoshi), 194n92

Yamane Toshihide, 214n65

"Yamato" ideology, 44

Yan Zhenxing, 88

Yanaihara Tadao, 19

Yang, C. K. (Yang Chuanguang), 79, 198nn1,3

Yang, Edward (Yang Dechang), 118–19

Yang Sen, 125–26

Yang Yuanxiong, *figure 3*

yangjiang. See foreign baseball players in Taiwan
Yanshui (Ensui, Tainan County), 12
Yasuaki Taihoh. *See* Chen Dafeng
Yasukuni Shrine, 46
Ye Zhixian, 1
Yilan, 82, 88
Yō Un-hyŏng, 188n112
Yokohama, 58, 194n92
Yokohama College of Commerce, 40, 67
Yokohama Country Athletic Club, 14
Yomiuri Shimbun, 11
Yonamine, Wally, 134
Yoshida Masao, 39
Yu Chien-ming, 8
Yu Hongkai (Yu Hung-kai), 79, 94, 95, 103, 121
Yu Junwei, 4–5, 104, 159–60, 172n12, 201n56
Yu Zhengxian, 216n94
Yuanshan Field (Maruyama Field), 47, 51, 61

Zeng Ji'en, 68–69
Zeng Zhizhen, 134, *figure 9*
Zhang Guanlu, 86
Zhang Meiyao, 74
Zhang Taishan, 164
Zhang Wojun, 59
Zhang Xingxian (Chō Seiken), 67
Zhang Zhengxian, 217n100
Zhanghua County, *figure 15*
Zhao Shiqiang, 142
Zhejiang Province, 73, 160
Zheng Baisheng, 217n102
Zheng Chenggong (Koxinga), 158, 191n38
Zheng Zhaohang, 164
Zhongxing (Nantou County), 74
Zhou, Jay (Zhou Jielun), 150
Zhou Shukai, 96
Zhuang Kaiping, 103
Zhuo Kunyuan, 217n100

TEXT
10/12.5 Minon Pro

DISPLAY
Minion Pro

COMPOSITOR
Integrated Composition Systems

CARTOGRAPHER
Bill Nelson

PRINTER AND BINDER
Thomson-Shore, Inc.